T0229930

This collection takes the exciting step of examining natural language phenomena from the perspectives of both computational linguistics and formal semantics. Computational linguistics has until now been primarily concerned with the construction of computational models for handling the complexities of linguistic form, but has not tackled the questions of representing or computing meaning. Formal semantics, on the other hand, has attempted to account for the relations between forms and meanings, without necessarily attending to computational concerns. *Computational linguistics and formal semantics* introduces the reader to the two disciplines and considers the prospects for the more unified and comprehensive computational theory of language which might obtain from their amalgamation. Of great interest to those working in the fields of computation, logic, semantics, artificial intelligence and linguistics generally, it includes both tutorial and advanced material in order to orient the reader to both the concepts and the problems that are at issue.

Studies in Natural Language Processing

Computational linguistics and formal semantics

Studies in Natural Language Processing
Editor: Branimir K. Boguraev
Sponsored by the Association for Computational Linguistics

This series publishes monographs, texts, and edited volumes within the interdisciplinary field of computational linguistics. It represents the range of topics of concern to scholars working in this increasingly important field, whether their background is in formal linguistics, psycholinguistics, cognitive psychology or artificial intelligence.

Also in this series

Computational linguistics and formal semantics

Edited by

MICHAEL ROSNER AND RODERICK JOHNSON
Istituto Dalle Molle IDSIA, Lugano, Switzerland

CAMBRIDGE
UNIVERSITY PRESS

CAMBRIDGE UNIVERSITY PRESS
Cambridge, New York, Melbourne, Madrid, Cape Town,
Singapore, São Paulo, Delhi, Mexico City

Cambridge University Press
The Edinburgh Building, Cambridge CB2 8RU, UK

Published in the United States of America by Cambridge University Press, New York

www.cambridge.org
Information on this title: www.cambridge.org/9780521419598

First published 1992

A catalogue record for this publication is available from the British Library

Library of Congress Cataloguing in Publication Data

Computational linguistics and formal semantics / edited by Michael Rosner
and Roderick Johnson.
    p.   cm. –(Studies in natural language processing)
Includes bibliographical references and index.
ISBN 0 521 41959 X (hardback) ISBN 0 521 42988 9 (paperback)
1. Computational linguistics. 2. Semantics. I. Rosner, Michael.
II. Johnson, Roderick. III. Series.
p98.5.S45C66   1992
410'.285–dc20   92-10872 CIP

ISBN 978-0-521-41959-8 Hardback
ISBN 978-0-521-42988-7 Paperback

To Franco Boschetti

Contents

Contributors

CHRISTINE DEFRISE
Free University of Brussels

JENS ERIK FENSTAD
University of Oslo

PER-KRISTIAN HALVORSEN
Xerox PARC

RODERICK JOHNSON
IDSIA, Lugano

MARTIN KAY
Xerox PARC and Stanford University

MARGARET KING
ISSCO, Geneva

TORE LANGHOLM
University of Bergen

SERGEI NIRENBURG
Carnegie Mellon University

BARBARA H. PARTEE
University of Massachusetts

MICHAEL ROSNER
IDSIA, Lugano

C. J. RUPP
IDSIA, Lugano

RAYMOND TURNER
University of Essex

JOHAN VAN BENTHEM
University of Amsterdam

ESPEN VESTRE
University of Saarland

YORICK WILKS
New Mexico State University

Preface
Michael Rosner and Roderick Johnson

The workshop that inspired this book was the high point of a collaborative research project entitled 'Incorporation of Semantics into Computational Linguistics', supported by the EEC through the COST13 programme. The workshop was also the first official academic event to be organized by IDSIA, a newly inaugurated institute of the Dalle Molle Foundation situated in Lugano, Switzerland devoted to artificial intelligence research.

A few words about the project may help to place the contents of the book in its proper context. The underlying theme was that although human language is studied from the standpoint of many different disciplines, there is rather less *constructive interaction* between the disciplines than might be hoped for, and that for such interaction to take place, a common framework of some kind must be established. Computational linguistics (CL) and artificial intelligence (AI) were singled out as particular instances of such disciplines: each has focused on rather different aspects of the relationship between language and computation.

Thus, what we now call CL grew out of attempts to apply the concepts of computer science to generative linguistics (e.g. Zwicky and his colleagues [255], Petrick [181]). Given these historical origins, CL unwittingly inherited some of the goals for linguistic theory that we normally associate with Chomskyan linguistics. One such goal, for example, is to finitely describe *linguistic competence*, that is, the knowledge that underlies the human capacity for language by means of a set of universal principles that characterize the class of possible languages, and a set of descriptions for particular languages.

Accordingly, CL is concerned (and occasionally obsessed) with both the generative capacity and the descriptive efficiency of notation and the extent to which the notation associated with a theory, or 'grammar formalism', actually permits powerful generalisations to be expressed in ways that are linguistically parsimonious. All the usual arguments adduced in favour of

xiii

problem-oriented languages apply with vigour here (cf. Johnson and Rosner [99]), especially the observation that in CL the design and use of such formalisms are activities in a highly symbiotic relationship with each other.

The AI approach to language, on the other hand, might be characterized as the attempt to situate a theory of language use within a general computational theory of intelligence. Hence the areas of natural language processing most often addressed by AI theories (e.g. question answering, story comprehension, dialogue handling, etc.) are those that reflect a definite and necessary connection with other, basic aspects of intelligence. Now any such connection involves, explicitly or otherwise, taking a position on the *meaning* of utterances. For instance, a question answering program must embody a theory of question meaning to produce an answer; similarly, a story comprehension program requires a theory of story meaning to demonstrate understanding.

Now although the AI approach to language has apparently centred on semantic issues, there has never been any *consensus* as to the general character of semantic theory that might provide a framework for taking on these issues systematically. There is nothing, that is, to match the implicit consensus shared by computational linguists concerning a very general set of issues about syntax – that a grammar can describe a language, for example – that are due almost exclusively to Chomsky.

This lack of consensus is unfortunate for two reasons. One is that it renders difficult the task of calibrating and comparing different AI theories of language. The other is that it exacerbates the problem of building a complex theory of language processing that involves contributions from other disciplines and CL in particular.

The thesis of the project was that a theory of this kind requires the appropriate style of representational framework for the *contents* of utterances. Such a framework provides a natural point of communication between a CL-inspired component and an AI-inspired one, and in so doing, a kind of job specification for each. Once the representational framework is known the job of the CL component is to define effective computations between the domain of strings and the domain of representations; that of the AI component is, amongst other things, to provide interpretations for the representations. On this view, we can regard formal semantics as a 'tidy' subset of AI which is crucial if we are to investigate the notion of meaning with any precision.

The work of Montague provides an illustration of the way components of a theory start to fall into place once certain basic decisions about representation are taken. Higher order intensional logic is for many reasons the favourite of neither logicians nor linguists and, indeed, is the cause of many problems that subsequent theoreticians have sought to avoid, as we shall see below. However, Montague chose it as part of a larger package that took in an 'AI' component, i.e. possible worlds semantics, and a 'CL' one, i.e. Categorial Grammar, and, of course, a way of linking the two together with the mechanisms of the typed Lambda-Calculus. The quotation marks in the last sentence are there to remind the reader that these appellations would probably not have been accepted by either Montague or his contemporaries.

One of the main criticisms levelled against the Montagovian enterprise is that although it provides an organisation for a total system with interlocking, well-defined subcomponents, it is not clear to whom it ultimately appeals. Few are the linguists who actually *like* Categorial Grammar or who find it conducive to the discovery or statement of generalisations. Equally few are the philosophers who find that higher order intensional logic is the right vehicle for exploring the semantics of such 'natural' concepts as Intensionality. The Montague framework, in its original form, seems ultimately too *rigid* to be considered appropriate for dealing with a whole human language, and three papers look at various ways of coping with problems that derive from taking it too literally.

From a linguistic perspective, examples of such problems abound with respect to issues in type theory, type shifting, and the semantics of noun phrases. For Barbara Partee, in *Syntactic categories and semantic type*, the main issue is the apparent conflict between, on the one hand, a systematic correspondence between syntactic categories and semantic types, and on the other, the flexibility of natural languages. This conflict is exemplified by the shortcomings inherent to Montague's uniform treatment of all noun phrases as generalized quantifiers. This has the advantage of generality, but fails to account for the finer, more 'natural' correspondences that we intuitively feel to exist between, say, proper nouns and entities, or between common nouns and properties, and, in addition, between the verbs that take such entities as arguments and *their* corresponding semantic types.

By examining generalized conjunction, Partee provides some empirical evidence in favour of type multiplicity, with the suggestion that type should depend on context of occurrence, being fully determined in situ by allowing a kind of least effort principle – choosing the minimal type compatible with the context – to interact with a principled kind of type ambiguity.

A major contribution of the chapter deals specifically with the referential, predicative, and quantifier readings for NPs, and with a set of functors for shifting between these types, including some with names such as BE, THE and A. The claim here is that the functors defined purely formally as A and THE are natural and possibly universal. Partee concludes with the suggestion that the combination of a type hierarchy with type-shifting principles allows us to be both systematic and flexible in relating syntax and semantics.

Johan van Benthem's *Fine-structure in categorial semantics* attempts to present Montague Semantics as a complex artifact whose behaviour can be subjected to micro-adjustments. The chapter substantiates the claim that it is possible to formulate a set of principles for calibrating semantic theory that in some sense does for semantics what Chomsky's hierarchy does for syntax.

The power of a categorial parsing engine depends upon the inference rules present in the implicit *calculus of implication* that is used to drive derivations. Each categorial derivation of a type encodes a meaning that may also be expressed in a lambda term. However, the translation is not exclusively type-driven, since to a given transition may correspond several derivations, and therefore several readings. This raises the issue of how many readings exist for given type transitions and how far it is possible to tune the type system itself in order to contain ambiguity.

Another strategy for dealing with ambiguity is to filter out readings via an analysis of possible denotations. Van Benthem discusses the fine-tuning capacity of *denotational constraints* in this respect. These are general semantic properties that hold over the denotations of specific linguistic categories such as quantifiers and noun phrases.

There is also layering inherent to a semantics based on Lambda-Calculus, in particular with respect to restrictions on the number of variable occurrences bound by the lambda operator and the addition of an identity predicate over arbitrary types. The interaction between the choice of such restrictions and the number of readings obtained is also discussed. A further section is devoted to extensions and modifications of Montague's basic theory concerning, in particular, enrichments to the flat structure of the individual domain, additional truth values (for expressing partial information), extensions to the type system and the use of richer categorial logics admitting additional type-forming operators. The final appendices contain a number of relevant technical observations.

A third Montague-related chapter, Raymond Turner's *Properties, propositions and semantic theory*, introduces property-theoretic semantics, which, amongst other things, is intended to provide an account of intensional notions like knowledge and belief that does not suffer from either the defects of possible worlds semantics (i.e. omniscience), or those typified by so-called 'syntactical' approaches that view propositions as sentences in some semantic representation language. In the latter, conflicts typically arise between expressive power and consistency: either there will be propositions that cannot be represented, or the semantic theory will include inconsistent propositions.

Now although Turner adopts an expressively rich formal representation language that employs terms of the untyped Lambda-Calculus, he avoids such conflicts by defining the syntactic category of proposition as a *subset* of its well-formed formulae. The axiomatic theory itself comprises definitions for the notions of *proposition* ('P') and *truth* over propositions ('T'), the first of which is used to provide further definitions of *properties* and *relations*. The exposition of the basic theory is completed by the introduction of predicates for the abstract notions of determiner and quantifier, and it is shown how quantifiers obtain their natural truth conditions when applied to properties.

The next section illustrates an extension of the basic theory to handle modality: of particular interest is the distinction between intensional and extensional notions of equivalent terms. The former is sufficient to guarantee that substitution into modal contexts preserves truth. This does not hold for extensional equivalence.

The last two sections of the chapter are devoted to showing how the theory provides an adequate framework for a Montague-style semantics in general and the PTQ fragment in particular without any need to build the type theory into the syntax of the formal language. Instead of higher order functions, types are simply predicates in first order logic that classify objects as propositions, properties, quantifiers, determiners etc. Type checking can therefore be performed using purely first order proof techniques.

Implicit in the approach to intensionality exemplified by Property Theory is the assumption that belief or knowledge states are *incomplete* collections of propositions. This is important for several reasons. First, it eliminates omniscience: an agent will only believe those propositions that are sanctioned by the axioms. Second, it provides a starting point for a theory of incomplete knowledge and incomplete reasoning. However elegant and however well understood the techniques of classical logic are, the requirements of completeness are simply unrealistic when it comes to modelling human knowledge and belief. Human knowledge is *partial*, and typically we exploit techniques for moving between different states of partial knowledge. Partiality of description, representation and interpretation is the theme that unites the next four contributions.

Attribute-value structures are a fundamental part of AI programming going back to the association lists of Lisp; the idea that *features* can be used to construct partial descriptions is equally established in linguistics, particularly through phonology (cf. Jakobson [96]). Put the two ideas together and we have the basic ingredients of *feature structures*. One of the pioneers of feature structures, Martin Kay, gives his account in *Unification* of the rationale and development of feature-based descriptions and the associated operation of unification, showing how they can be used to solve in an elegant, declarative way many of the traditional problems of grammatical description.

Jens Erik Fenstad, Tore Langholm and Espen Vestre continue the theme in *Representations and interpretations*, whose point of departure is the claim that computational semantics lies at the intersection of linguistics, logic and computer science, and that therefore the study of natural language *systems* needs to admit contributions from all three disciplines. Their contribution can be read in three parts. In the first, they give an informal characterisation of feature structures and their role in various theories of language, followed by a review of a number of attempts to provide a mathematically precise formulation, including discussion of some of the well-known thorny problems like disjunction, negation and set-valued features. The second part addresses the relationship between meaning representations expressed in terms of feature structures and their interpretations within some model. The formal apparatus used is an adaptation of Situation Theory (Barwise and Perry [15]) in which interpretable representations are a particular subset of feature structures called *Situation Schemata* (Fenstad et. al [56]). They conclude with an application of the theory to the representation and interpretation of direct questions.

Two other contributions, Per-Kristian Halvorsen in *Algorithms for semantic interpretation* and C.J. Rupp, Roderick Johnson and Michael Rosner in *Situation schemata and linguistic representation*, also propose Situation Schemata as an intermediate representation on which to base semantic interpretation. Halvorsen is particularly concerned with the greater flexibility of unification-based interpretation strategies compared to the sequential, strictly compositional interpretation algorithms characteristic of the Montagovian paradigm. Within a particular descriptive framework he shows how the projection mechanisms of Lexical Functional Grammar [79] can be applied to formulate novel semantic analyses.

Rupp et al. also address the problem of relating text to Situation Schemata, in the belief that Situation Schemata offer not only a sound basis for semantic interpretation but also a representational form which is particularly suitable for linguistic computation. In support of this view they describe an implementation of an analyser for German with very wide coverage, together with the kinds of linguistic abstraction which were useful in constructing the analysis. An important aspect of the discussion concerns some modifications to the original definition of Situation Schemata arising out of the requirements of broad linguistic coverage.

Sergei Nirenburg and Christine Defrise are also concerned with wide coverage, within the context of building a semantic theory for natural language processing. Their approach, however, is very much in the AI tradition, organized around the central idea of the language user as an intelligent agent which participates in communication by instantiating constructs from a variety of knowledge sources. The paper discusses various knowledge representation needs involved in modelling such an agent, including a world model, or *ontology*, a meaning representation language and a number of *microtheories* of linguistic usage.

Lest we become too fixated with the problems associated with supplying a formal semantics for natural languages, Yorick Wilks, in characteristic iconoclastic mode, reminds us that it is by no means given that the formal enterprise is a useful way of studying language behaviour by computer. He uses a critique of the perspectives on 'Logic in AI' of Lifschitz [136] and McDermott [143, 144, 145] to re-emphasize his own position that for AI and CL formal semantics is in the last analysis irrelevant and that what counts is the relation between language utterances and associated behaviours.

In conclusion, Margaret King does an excellent job of summing up the salient issues, just as she did in the original conference. We are grateful to her and to all the other authors for their help and support throughout the preparation of the book.

We are particularly indebted to Catherine Max and her colleagues at Cambridge University Press, who have shown exceptional patience in the face of many delays. We also want to thank our colleagues and friends in the Fondazione Dalle Molle and in IDSIA for their understanding and for providing the stimulating working environment which is a prerequisite for any serious academic activity. We are grateful to them all, but would like to single out four names in particular for special mention: to C.J. Rupp who worked closely with us throughout, in the preparation of the workshop and of the book; to Angelo Dalle Molle and Franco Boschetti, whose vision and commitment turned IDSIA from a series of ideas into a reality. The last word of thanks, however, must go to Ken Ferschweiler, whose skill, persistence and good humour turned a motley collection of computer files into copy ready for the camera of the publisher.

1 Unification

Martin Kay

1.1 INTRODUCTION

This paper stands in marked contrast to many of the others in this volume
in that it is intended to be entirely tutorial in nature, presupposing little
on the part of the reader but a user's knowledge of English, a modicum of
good will, and the desire to learn something about the notion of unification
as it has come to be used in theoretical and computational linguistics.
Most of the ideas I shall be talking about were first introduced to the
study of ordinary language by computational linguists and their adoption
by a notable, if by no means representative, subset of theoretical linguists
represents an important milestone in our field, for it is the first occasion on
which the computationalists have had an important impact on linguistic
theory. Before going further, there may be some value in pursuing briefly
why this rapprochement between these two branches has taken so long to
come about. After all, the flow of information in the other direction – from
theoretician to computationalist – has continued steadily from the start.

1.2 PRODUCTIVITY

The aspects of ordinary language that have proved most fascinating to its
students all have something to do with its productivity, that is, with the
fact that there appears to be no limit to the different utterances that can
be made and understood in any of the languages of the world. Certainly,
speakers can make and understand utterances that they have never made
or understood before, and it is presumably largely in this fact that the
immense power and flexibility of human language resides. If language is
indeed a productive system in this sense, then it follows that what the
speakers of a language must know in order to use it is a system of rules,
relations, or abstractions of some sort, and not simply an inventory of

utterances. Further investigation suggests that these rules, relations, or abstractions have some interesting properties, important among which are the following:

- They differ remarkably little from one language to another.

- They are not easily accessible to introspection on the part of a language speaker.

- Their exact nature is greatly underdetermined by the facts of language use.

None of these properties is entirely uncontroversial. The last of them, however, has had the effect of diverting the main stream of linguistics, but notably not computational linguistics, into a particular course.

Following Chomsky, American – and many other – linguists took these three properties of language as a basis for an argument that goes somewhat as follows: if the linguistic system is complex and yet underdetermined by facts of usage, then language users presumably do not learn it by simply observing usage in themselves and others. They are presumably born with much of the system already intact, and this is supported by the observation that the particular language that a person learns seems to have little to do with the basic underlying system. I take it that this line of argument is familiar to most readers because, to the wholly uninitiated, the notion that the logical principles that organize the linguistic knowledge of, say, an Englishman and a Chinese are fundamentally the same would require more argument than we have time for here. For the moment, I simply want to draw attention to the fact that theoretical linguists have been led by considerations like these to concentrate a large part of their attention on the question of what it is about language that a baby knows at birth, what he or she acquires later and, in general, how the material is organized so as to make it possible for children to acquire it as effortlessly and as quickly as they apparently do.

The facts about language productivity pose other problems which are in some ways more immediate than that of accounting for the acquisition of the system. Foremost among these is the question of how the system works, and in particular, how it is that a person can compose utterances that have never been composed before – actually or essentially – so as to encapsulate a message that another person can then extract. We know something of how this is done in some very simple productive symbol systems, such as the language of integers written in decimal notation, or the languages used for writing computer programs. For the most part, computational linguists have been motivated more by this question than by the acquisition problem. The reason, I believe, is not far to seek. It is the business of the computational linguist – as opposed to the linguistic technologist – to build working models of human linguistic activities in the hope that some of them will prove revealing about how people do what they do. In principle, such a program could presumably be directed as well towards the acquisition as towards the communication problem. The result of the acquisition process is itself a working model of the understanding process, so that, before any understanding model has been built, we do not even have a good idea what kind of result an acquisition model should produce. In short, from the point of view of a model builder, production and understanding are logically prior to acquisition.

There is, of course, a more radical view according to which the only way in which a production and understanding model could be constructed is by acquiring it in the way humans acquire it. According to this view, whether or not any macro-structure is discernible in language, there are no components that correspond to its parts and that are responsible for maintaining it. The brain is indeed as it initially seems to be – an essentially undifferentiated mass of neurons and whatever the system learns suffuses and pervades it. Like an ant colony, it has only an emergent macro-structure. This view has gained a considerable amount of ground in recent years, but it has had little effect on the thinking of most linguists, computational or not. I shall have no more to say about it.

For the most part then, computational linguists have been captivated by the notion of language as a tool rather than language as a body of knowledge. They take as primary the fact that natural language works and have set themselves to discover something of how. There is another way in which this sets them apart from the great fraternity of linguists, at least in America, for many of whom language has become something that does not work in any essential sense. What a baby acquires when learning a language is not how to communicate needs, curiosities and observations using words and sentences, nor how to unpack words and sentences so as to learn about the mental states of others. Instead a baby learns how to distinguish the sentences of his or her language from other strings of words that are not sentences, how to put sentences into equivalence classes according to their logical properties, how to give a quantifier its proper scope, and the like. It is, after all, not necessarily the case that language has taken on its present form as the result of evolutionary processes that have fitted it to the needs of human communication any more than that it is necessarily the case that the survival value of flight played any role in the evolution of a bird's wings.

According to my rational reconstruction of the history of our field, then, one reason that computational linguists have concentrated on adult language as a medium of communication is that this has seemed to them to be logically prior to the acquisition problem. But there is a second reason that surely cannot be denied, namely that just about every computational linguist lives a double life as a linguistic technologist, that is, as at least an aspiring architect of well crafted, elegant, and efficient devices that will do useful things for people with language. This, after all, is the interest that has put them in the way of a little support from time to time from the government and industry. This, of course, has served only to reinforce their disposition to view language as a tool.

1.3   PHRASE STRUCTURE

One of the most robust conceptions that came from the realization that languages are indefinitely productive is what has come to be known as *phrase structure.* As I remarked earlier, it follows from the fact of productivity that utterances are generally not remembered; they are constructed. There must be some process by which they are assembled out of parts which must often be assembled themselves, and so on. The construction must be made both by the speaker and the listener. And, if it is really true that the productivity of language knows no bounds, then the process must be a *recursive* one. We can get an idea of what this means in the following way. The whole point of introducing the notion of a procedure is that it will be statable in a finite space whereas the utterances it is used to characterize will not. Notice that this means that, in principle at least, there could be utterances many times the length of the procedure that it would nevertheless be able to treat. It follows from this that there must be parts of the procedure that are being used several times. This is the heart of what it means for a procedure to be recursive and this is why it is important here. If there is no limit to the number of sentences that a language allows, even though the language only contains a finite set of words, then there can be no limit on the length of a sentence. A procedure for constructing sentences must therefore be recursive, however long it is.

The particular solution to the problem of providing a procedure to characterize an infinite set of sentences was motivated by an idea that has played a central role in both linguistics and computer science, namely that the strings that make up a language – call them utterances, sentences, programs, or whatever – are made up of interchangeable parts. Each part belongs to one or more equivalence classes. A class can, and in interesting cases does, contain infinitely many members, but the number of classes is finite. A simple declarative sentence consists of two main parts, a subject and a predicate. The subject can be any one of the infinite class of noun phrases and the predicate any member of the infinite class of verb phrases.

Noun phrases, like sentences, can be constituted in a variety of ways. For example, a member of the class of articles followed by a member of the class of nouns constitutes a noun phrase. The first component of the idea, then, is the common notion of a *part of speech*. The equivalence classes are the parts of speech and the members of a class are equivalent in that the substitution of one member for another in a string leaves its grammatical status unchanged.

This, then, is the second part of the idea – the notion of interchangeability. If a sentence is analysed into its parts, and the parts into their parts, and so on, then any one of those parts can be replaced by any other part belonging to the same class – a noun phrase by a noun phrase, a noun by a noun, and so on. Now, it is important to note that this can only be done when the sentence has been analysed completely. Consider the sentences

(1.1)   John plays

(1.2)   John wins

(1.3)   Mary writes plays

(1.4)   Mary writes novels

They each consist of a noun phrase followed by a verb phrase, and by interchanging members of these classes we get other sentences, such as

(1.5)   Mary plays

(1.6)   Mary wins

(1.7)   John writes plays

(1.8)   John writes novels

But 'plays' is both a noun and an intransitive verb, so that one might expect the principle of interchangeability to give us also

(1.9)   *Mary novels

(1.10)   *John novels

Examples (1.9) and (1.10) illustrate the linguistic usage of placing an asterisk before an unacceptable, or ungrammatical, string. All we have done is to start with sentence (1.1) and to replace its second word, which sentence (1.3) assures us is a noun, by another noun, namely 'novels'. The point is really an obvious one. The word 'plays' in (1.1) can be replaced only by another verb because the word figures in this sentence by virtue of being a verb. This is why we must have a complete analysis of a sentence before starting to make substitutions.

The idea of breaking strings into substrings, these into further substrings, and so on, according to some specified procedure or set of principles, gives us the key notion of phrase structure. The complete analysis, from the sentence down to the basic words, gives the structure of the sentence and of the phrases that make it up, in terms of other phrases. This is its *phrase structure*. The notion of interchangeability gives us a refinement, namely the notion of *context-free phrase structure*, or *context-free phrase structure grammar*, or simply *context-free grammar*. The term 'context-free' is not intended to suggest that we are not involved with context for, clearly, the object of the enterprise we are engaged in is precisely that of determining the allowable contexts for words and strings of words in a language. What it refers to is the fact that the interchangeability of the members of an equivalence class is not constrained in any way by the context in which the member occurs. It is enough to know that a string occupies its place in a sentence by virtue of its membership in the class of noun phrases, to be able to replace it by another noun phrase without compromising the sentencehood of the string as a whole.

The word 'grammar' in the phrase 'context-free grammar' refers to a set of statements or rules which say how the members of the various classes may be made up in terms of members of other classes. For example, rule (1.11)

(1.11)   S → NP VP

says that when a member of the class of noun phrases (NP) is followed by a member of the class of verb phrases (VP) the result is a sentence (S).

We started from the notion that the set of strings that constituted a fully productive, infinite language could be specified only by means of a recursive procedure, and proceeded from there to the notions of phrase structure and context-free grammars, which are not procedures. However, these notions also clearly presuppose the existence of procedures to verify that a particular string belongs to the set specified by the grammar. To verify that a string is a sentence, for example, the strategy is to consider all the rules like (1.11) above that have the symbol S to the left of the arrow. For each of these, we attempt to show that the string can be broken down in the manner specified to the right of the arrow, in this case into a noun phrase and a verb phrase. One way to do this would be to consider all the places at which the string could be broken into two and to apply this same recursive procedure to the two parts, taking NP as the goal for the first part, and VP for the second. There are in fact many different strategies all of which can be shown to produce the same result and our present purposes do not call for us to give their details or to choose among them. For our purposes, two points are worthy of note. First, a set of phrase classes and a set of rules, taken together with a sound strategy for their application, constitute the procedure we require. Second, the articulation of the information into a grammar and the procedure proper that applies it corresponds, in large measure, to the distinction between what we expect to differ as we move from one language to another, namely the grammar, and what we expect to remain constant, namely the procedure.

For the practical business of communication that I have claimed has provided computational linguists with their main source of motivation, the question of just where the dividing line lies between the sentences and the nonsentences is not the centre of interest. The point is to know how a given string of words is to be interpreted. The same line of argument that led us from the notion of productive languages to that of a recursive procedure for characterizing them leads to a recursive procedure for assigning them interpretations. The simplest hypothesis is that the procedures are the same. Each phrase has an interpretation and the rules that state how phrases can be assembled from other phrases are enriched so as to say how the interpretation of the phrase is related to those of the smaller phrases that make it up. This hypothesis is as natural as it is simple. What it suggests, of course, is that the strings of words that belong to the language will be precisely those that have interpretations. This is in fact a matter about which it is possible to argue at length; we shall give it only a passing glance.

Chomsky [34] claimed that the string (1.12) is clearly a sentence but is, just as clearly, meaningless.

(1.12)   Colorless green ideas sleep furiously.

The argument that it is meaningless is easy to make. Nothing can be both colourless and green, so that the phrase 'colorless green ideas', though undoubtedly a noun phrase, has no meaning. This is enough to make the point. But, of course, the argument can be continued. It makes no sense to speak of ideas sleeping, or of anything sleeping furiously.

Notice how this same argument could be used to claim that these phrases *do* have meaning. We do indeed know what properties a thing would have to have to be colourless and green. Independently, we believe that these sets of properties are contradictory so that we expect the set of objects in the world that have them to be empty. In other words, the meaning is unexceptionable; the terms simply fail to refer. Likewise for 'sleep' and 'furiously'.

The string in (1.13) (also from Chomsky [34]) is not a sentence. It is also meaningless, but the kind of argument that we made for the meaninglessness of (1.12) cannot be made for it because it simply does not contain phrases, like 'green ideas' and 'sleep furiously', whose absurdity we can point to.

(1.13)   Furiously sleep ideas green colorless

1.4   MULTIPLE STRUCTURES

The notion of phrase structure and of context-free grammar have continued to play a key role in linguistics despite the discovery of evidence suggesting that the original ideas need to be replaced, embellished, or at least argued for more carefully. Even those who would replace them, however, continue to derive some inspiration from the original idea.

Consider the following sentences:

(1.14)   the dog runs

(1.15)   the dogs run

The point they make is simply that noun phrases do not in fact constitute an equivalence class, and neither do the verb phrases. Otherwise (1.16) and (1.17) would be sentences, which they clearly are not.

(1.16)   *the dog run

(1.17)   *the dogs runs

The problem seems about as easy to remedy as it is to recognize. Instead of a class of noun phrases, we need to recognize a class of singular, and a class of plural, noun phrases and likewise for verb phrases. This move will propagate through the complete system of phrases, requiring classes of singular and plural nouns, articles, verbs, and so forth, to be acknowledged.

Parallel examples in other languages would lead the number of classes that must be recognized, and the number of rules in a corresponding context-free grammar, to be multiplied by a much larger factor. Consider, for example, the Latin sentences (1.18) and (1.19):

(1.18)   Puer puellam amat (the boy loves the girl).

(1.19)   Puerum puella amat (the girl loves the boy).

'Puer' (boy) can take the place it has in (1.18) only by virtue of being singular and in the nominative case. Though the number of 'puellam' (girl) is not important for objects in Latin any more than it is in modern European languages, it fits into this sentence only because it is in the accusative case. Replacing 'puer' by 'puerum' in (1.19) requires 'puellam' to be replaced by 'puella' in order to maintain sentencehood, and also meaningfulness.

Sentence (1.19) has an additional problem in that it does not contain a sequence of words that constitute a verb phrase. The verb phrase in this sentence is 'puerum...amat'. So perhaps the notion of verb phrase will have to be abandoned, in Latin at least, in favour of a description of sentences in terms of subjects, verbs and objects.

Parallel problems to the one posed by sentence (1.19) are also to be found in English. Consider (1.20)–(1.22):

(1.20) Write everything down that she tells you.

(1.21) The students all surprised me that gave papers.

(1.22) Greater love hath no man than this.

In (1.20), what you are presumably being exhorted to 'write down' is 'everything she tells you' but, in the string we actually have in (1.20), these phrases are intermixed with one another. We have a similar situation in (1.21). What surprised me was 'all the students that gave papers'. And again in (1.22), what 'no man hath' is 'greater love than this'. This seems to be a greater challenge for context-free grammar than the agreement of subjects with verbs, or the use of cases in Latin.

The real problem that examples like these pose – and there are many more troublesome than these – is not that they make context-free grammar completely unworkable, as was commonly claimed when Chomsky's theories were just taking hold, as that they eat away at the original simple intuition that there are certain phrases that can be the subjects of sentences and certain that can be predicates. Some phrases are relative clauses and can be placed after nouns which they modify, and so on. As soon as we say that there are singular noun phrases and plural noun phrases which are related only through a partial overlap in their names, we are denying something that our intuition tells us is true. In most scientific enterprises, this would surely be no cause for concern. But, if linguists try to educate their intuitions it is because they are often the only things they have to go on. Furthermore, more is at stake than the linguist's intuitions. Once we agree to recognize singular noun phrases as distinct from plural noun phrases, we must write distinct sets of rules to say that singular articles can form singular noun phrases when they occur before singular nouns. A similar rule, not systematically related, says something parallel about plural noun phrases, and so on for many other pairs of rules. But the parallelism of singular and plural noun phrases surely does not arise by chance and we therefore almost certainly fail to capture something important when we are forced to write separate rules for the two cases. So, yes, we are able to make the system work, but only by ignoring much of its real structure and by introducing a great amount of redundancy into it. To increase redundancy is to reduce perspicuity.

Linguists have addressed these problems in two ways, both preserving the initial phrase-structure intuition. The first approach is that of *transformational* grammar. In its simplest form, which is the only one we shall consider, this keeps the original conception of context-free grammar entirely intact, but reduces its responsibility to that of characterizing only a particularly well behaved subset of the sentences in the language. The sentencehood of each of the remainder is assured by a set of transformational rules that permit the given sentence to be derived from one of the core set. We can, for example, imagine a rule that allows a relative clause in a core sentence to be moved to the end in suitable circumstances. In particular, it would allow 'that she tells you' in (1.23) to be moved to the end, giving (1.24).

(1.23)   Write everything that she tells you down.

(1.24)   Write everything down that she tells you.

The same rule would derive (1.26) from (1.25).

(1.25)   The students that gave papers all surprised me.

(1.26)   The students all surprised me that gave papers.

However, while this shows how the relative clause is related to the noun it modifies, it still leaves the word 'all' in a position that we should not expect it to occupy in a core sentence. However, the transformational scheme provides for a sentence to be derived from a core sentence, directly or indirectly. So we assume that there is another transformational rule that enables us to get (1.25) from (1.27).

(1.27)   All the students that gave papers surprised me.

In like manner, we take it that there is a rule that moves the 'than' phrase associated with a comparative adjective to the end of a sentence like (1.22).

(1.22)   Greater love hath no man than this.

1.5   DESCRIPTIONS

The other way in which phrase-structure grammar has been adapted to the more particular properties of natural language is more in keeping with the original phrase-structure ideas. In particular, the distinction made between core sentences and the rest is not required – all sentences are accounted for by the same set of rules. The linguistic facts suggest (1) that the number of equivalence classes of strings is very large, but that (2) various subsets of the classes need to be distinguished only for some purposes; for others they can be treated as a single larger class. This suggests a solution according to which the equivalence classes are named not by simple unanalyzable terms like 'S', 'NP' and 'VP', but by expressions that make explicit the salient features of the members of the class. Various notations have been used for writing these expressions. The one we shall use is exemplified in (1.28).

$$(1.28) \quad \begin{bmatrix} \text{cat} & = & \text{noun} \\ \text{number} & = & \text{sing} \end{bmatrix}$$

It is easier to think of this as a *description* of a class of objects than as the *name* of a class as we have been doing up to now. The word 'description' not only suggests the idea of a list of properties, but also something of the way in which we intend to operate on them. Before pursuing the idea of grammatical descriptions, we may find it useful to consider how the term description is used in more general contexts.

If we speak on the telephone and agree to meet somewhere, and if you do not know me, I will doubtless supply you with a description. I may say that I am about 5 feet 10 inches tall and have a beard. If we do not expect our meeting place to be very crowded, that may be sufficient. Otherwise I may add more detail, saying that I weigh about 170 pounds and will be wearing a blue striped suit. The more details I give you, the larger the crowd in which you can hope to distinguish me, because the larger a description is, the smaller the set of objects is that meet it.

My description can be written in the notation we are proposing to use for linguistic objects as in (1.29).

$$(1.29) \quad \begin{bmatrix} \text{height} & = & \text{5ft.10ins.} \\ \text{beard} & = & \text{yes} \\ \text{suit} & = & \begin{bmatrix} \text{colour} & = & \text{blue} \\ \text{stripes} & = & \text{yes} \end{bmatrix} \end{bmatrix}$$

Each individual piece of information is given of an *attribute*, written to the left of an '=' sign, and a *value* written to the right. Notice that values can be of two forms. Either they are simple names or numbers, or they are descriptions in their own right. This makes sense in the current example. One way to describe me is to describe the suit that I will be wearing. This description is therefore embedded in my description as the value of the attribute 'suit'.

A requirement that we place on descriptions is that they give at most one value for any attribute. So, if we include 'suit' as an attribute, its value describes something that we can appropriately refer to as '*the* suit' in the description. This is not to say that a description could not contain two different attributes, each with a description for its value, and such that both of these embedded descriptions has its own 'suit' description. This restriction makes of the description what mathematicians refer to as a *partial function*. Suppose we designate the description of me given above as F, and let $F(beard)$ be the value of the function F when applied to *beard*. Clearly $F(beard) = yes$. Since we allow attributes to have not more than one value, the value of $F(x)$, for any x, is never ambiguous. This is a property of all functions. However, for some – indeed, most – choices of x, $F(x)$ is not defined at all. This is what makes the function partial.

Now suppose that, when we go to our appointment, you arrive a little late and are concerned that I might have come and gone away again. You ask a bystander if they have seen anyone waiting there, and they say 'yes'; there was someone with the description (1.30).

$$
(1.30) \quad \begin{bmatrix} \text{age} & = & 45 \\ \text{beard} & = & \text{yes} \\ \text{suit} & = & [\text{fabric} & = & \text{tweed}] \end{bmatrix}
$$

This is not very helpful. There is nothing about this that contradicts the description I gave, and there is one piece of evidence suggesting that the person was me, because they both describe their subject as having a beard. If you later discover that the person the bystander saw was indeed me, you will know that you missed the appointment, but you will also have learnt some things about me that you did not know previously, namely that, on that occasion, I fit the description (1.31).

$$
(1.31) \quad \begin{bmatrix} \text{height} & = & \text{5ft.10ins.} \\ \text{beard} & = & \text{yes} \\ \text{suit} & = & \begin{bmatrix} \text{colour} & = & \text{blue} \\ \text{stripes} & = & \text{yes} \\ \text{fabric} & = & \text{tweed} \end{bmatrix} \\ \text{age} & = & 45 \end{bmatrix}
$$

This description is arrived at in the obvious way, namely by combining the sets of attribute-value pairs in the original descriptions, eliminating repetitions. This is the operation we refer to as *unification*.

Combining sets of attribute-value pairs does not always yield a result that meets our definition of a description. Suppose, for example, that the bystander had claimed to have seen somebody meeting the description (1.32).

$$
(1.32) \quad \begin{bmatrix} \text{age} & = & 45 \\ \text{height} & = & \text{6ft.2ins.} \end{bmatrix}
$$

Combining the sets would give two instances of the attribute 'height' which, however, do not count as duplicates one of which can be eliminated, because they have different values. Keeping both of them, on the other hand, would violate the requirement that the description be a partial function – that it contain at most one instance of a given attribute. When this happens, the unification operation is said to *fail*, and we conclude that the two descriptions could not be of the same person or thing.

The kind of description we have been considering corresponds to the everyday notion of a description in several ways:

- Descriptions are always essentially *partial* because new detail (attribute-value pairs) can always be added to them.

- Descriptions are related through a notion of *compatibility*. Incompatible descriptions cannot be of the same thing.

- Compatible descriptions can be combined (unified) to yield a generally more complete (less partial) one than either of the originals.

1.6 GRAMMAR RULES

We are now ready to consider how descriptions affect the business of writing grammar rules. In (1.33), we give an example of a grammar rule using the new notation for descriptions instead of symbols designating parts of speech.

$$(1.33) \quad [\text{cat} \ = \ \text{s}] \rightarrow \begin{bmatrix} \text{cat} & = & \text{np} \\ \text{num} & = & n \\ \text{pers} & = & p \end{bmatrix} \begin{bmatrix} \text{cat} & = & \text{vp} \\ \text{num} & = & n \\ \text{pers} & = & p \end{bmatrix}$$

The italicized letters in the description are variables, and they may take on any value. Each instance of a variable name refers to the same variable so that the effect of writing the same variable name in more than one place is to require the same values (if any) to occupy all those positions. So what rule (1.33) says is that a sentence – a phrase whose category is 's' – can consist of a noun phrase followed by a verb phrase, provided that the noun and verb phrases have the same number and person.

To be completely clear about how a rule of this sort would apply, consider once again sentences (1.14) and (1.15).

(1.14)   the dog runs

(1.15)   the dogs run

Let us assume that, by virtue of some other rule, 'the dog' and 'runs' are analyzable as (1.34a) and (1.34b), respectively.

(1.34)
$$
\begin{bmatrix}
\text{cat} & = & \text{noun} \\
\text{num} & = & \text{sing} \\
\text{pers} & = & 3 \\
\text{det} & = & \text{def} \\
\text{head} & = & \text{dog}
\end{bmatrix}
\quad
\begin{bmatrix}
\text{cat} & = & \text{verb} \\
\text{num} & = & \text{sing} \\
\text{pers} & = & 3 \\
\text{tense} & = & \text{pres} \\
\text{head} & = & \text{run}
\end{bmatrix}
$$
(a)   (b)

These can be unified with the two descriptions that make up the right-hand side of rule (1.33) giving (1.34a) and (1.34b) as the results. In the course of the unification, the variables n and p in the rule are instantiated to 'sing' and '3', respectively. The rule therefore applies and allows a sentence to be created with these two parts. The descriptions of 'the dogs' and 'run' are presumably (1.35a) and (1.35b).

(1.35)
$$
\begin{bmatrix}
\text{cat} & = & \text{noun} \\
\text{num} & = & \text{plur} \\
\text{pers} & = & 3 \\
\text{det} & = & \text{def} \\
\text{head} & = & \text{dog}
\end{bmatrix}
\quad
\begin{bmatrix}
\text{cat} & = & \text{verb} \\
\text{num} & = & \text{plur} \\
\text{pers} & = & 3 \\
\text{tense} & = & \text{pres} \\
\text{head} & = & \text{run}
\end{bmatrix}
$$
(a)   (b)

These also unify with the two descriptions in the rule but, this time, n is instantiated to 'plur'. The reason the strings (1.16) and (1.17) are not accepted as sentences by the rule is that they would require inconsistent assignments to the variable n in the rule.

(1.16)   *the dog run

(1.17)   *the dogs runs

For the computational linguist, rules like (1.33) clearly introduce some additional complexity. However, there are certain tasks which they actually make simpler, notably that of relating the application of rules to the association that they establish between a sentence and its structure. In fact this responsibility can be turned over to the rules themselves, and with more far-reaching consequences than may at first be apparent.

Consider the variant of rule (1.33) given as (1.36)

(1.36)
$$
\begin{bmatrix}
\text{cat} & = \text{s} \\
\text{subj} & = subj \\
\text{pred} & = pred
\end{bmatrix}
\rightarrow
\begin{bmatrix}
\text{cat} & = \text{np} \\
\text{num} & = n \\
\text{pers} & = p
\end{bmatrix}_{subj}
\begin{bmatrix}
\text{cat} & = \text{vp} \\
\text{num} & = n \\
\text{pers} & = p
\end{bmatrix}_{pred}
$$

We have made one minor addition to the formalism which allows us to subscript an attribute-value list with the name of a variable, and we assume that that variable takes on as its value the description to which it is subscripted. When the rule is applied, the descriptions on the right-hand side of the rule are unified with the descriptions of actual phrases, and the result of these unification procedures is also reflected in the values of the variables *subj* and *pred*. As a result, these descriptions come to be embedded in the description that is constructed for the sentence as a whole as the values of the attributes 'subj' and 'pred' respectively. Applied to sentence (1.14), for example, they give the result in (1.37).

$$(1.37) \quad \begin{bmatrix} \text{cat} & = & \text{s} \\ \text{subj} & = & \begin{bmatrix} \text{cat} & = & \text{noun} \\ \text{num} & = & \text{sing} \\ \text{pers} & = & 3 \\ \text{det} & = & \text{def} \\ \text{head} & = & \text{dog} \end{bmatrix} \\ \text{pred} & = & \begin{bmatrix} \text{cat} & = & \text{verb} \\ \text{num} & = & \text{sing} \\ \text{pers} & = & 3 \\ \text{tense} & = & \text{pres} \\ \text{head} & = & \text{run} \end{bmatrix} \end{bmatrix}$$

A point about unification that is not immediately obvious, but that deserves to be stressed, is that the use of variables is not simply a shorthand that could be dispensed with in principle. Variables, or some equivalent special device, are essential to the workings of a system that relies on unification in a non-trivial way. It would, for example, be a grave mistake to take (1.38) as being equivalent to (1.36)

$$(1.38) \quad \begin{bmatrix} \text{cat} & = \text{s} \\ \text{subj} & = \begin{bmatrix} \text{cat} & = \text{np} \\ \text{num} & = n \\ \text{pers} & = p \end{bmatrix} \\ \text{pred} & = \begin{bmatrix} \text{cat} & = \text{vp} \\ \text{num} & = n \\ \text{pers} & = p \end{bmatrix} \end{bmatrix} \longrightarrow \begin{bmatrix} \text{cat} & = \text{np} \\ \text{num} & = n \\ \text{pers} & = p \end{bmatrix} \begin{bmatrix} \text{cat} & = \text{vp} \\ \text{num} & = n \\ \text{pers} & = p \end{bmatrix}$$

Notice, in particular, that unifying the two descriptions that make up the right-hand side of rule (1.38) with some more complete descriptions, produces larger descriptions as we saw in (1.37). But there is no reason to suppose that the size of the descriptions that are embedded in the description on the left-hand side of the rule in (1.38) will be in any way affected by this, since no new attributes have been unified with them. In (1.36), however, one and the same description occurs as the first item on the right-hand side of the rule and as the value of the *subj* attribute in the sentence description on the left. In our notation, we are always careful to give the details of a particular description in only one place in a larger expression and to refer to this by means of a variable if it also occurs in other places.

1.7   AUGMENTED TRANSITION NETWORKS

The term 'unification' arose independently in linguistics and in the field of logic programming. Indeed, even the name was chosen independently, and it was only discovered considerably later that the operations were the same in all essentials. In linguistics, the original impulse to design something like the system we have begun to sketch came from people working with Augmented Transition Networks (ATNs). They noted, with some dismay, that the ATNs that were used to analyse even very simple sets of sentences to yield a structure for them, could not be used to derive the sentences from the structures. In other words, the ATN specified the translation in only one direction. A simple example will make this clear.

Consider the ATN whose transition diagram is sketched in figure 1.1. An ATN is an abstract machine which, for present purposes, can be thought of as very similar to a standard finite-state automaton (FSA). The difference is that the transitions – the arcs in the diagram – are labelled with instructions rather than simple symbols. At any given moment, the machine is in one of a given set of *states*, represented by the circles in the diagram. The machine makes discrete moves from one state to another, the possible moves being just those given by the transition arcs in the diagram. In the course of moving from the current state to a new one, the instructions associated with the corresponding transition are carried out. At the outset, the machine is in a particular designated *start* state – in the case of figure 1.1, state 1 on the left of the diagram. It can cease operation only when it is in a *final* state, that is, one shown with thick lines in the diagram.

The instructions on the transitions in figure 1.1 are shown somewhat impressionistically. The basic idea is that, as the machine moves from state to state, a string of words or phrases is also being examined, one word or phrase with each transition. The symbols in the instruction set on the transitions that are written all in upper case letters give the properties that these words and phrases must have. So, a string consisting of a noun phrase (NP) followed by a verb (V), followed by another noun phrase, will allow that machine to move from state 1, through states 2 and 3, to state 4. An instruction of the form $\alpha < \beta$ causes whatever β refers to to be 'put in the α register'. So, when the machine reaches state 4, the first noun phrase will have been put in the 'Subj' register, the verb in the 'Verb' register, and the second noun phrase in the 'Obj' register. The idea of the registers is the

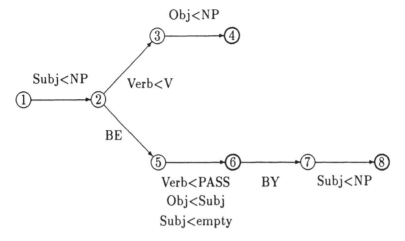

Figure 1.1. An Augmented Transition Network

obvious one. By examining their contents when the machine stops, we can identify the parts of a sentence that has just been examined.

The ATN in figure 1.1 will also accept a sentence like 'the cat was chased', or 'the cat was chased by the dog', following the route in the lower part of the diagram. There must be a noun phrase, followed by a finite form of the verb 'to be' (BE), followed by the past participle of a transitive verb (PASS). Such a sequence carries the machine into state 6. However, it may also continue to state 8 over the preposition 'by' (BY) and another noun phrase. Now, one of the advantages claimed for ATNs over previous parsing schemes was that much of the work required to parse different structures could be shared. In particular, the 'surface subject' – the initial noun phrase that agrees with the verb – can be recognized before any commitment is made to the voice of the sentence. Nevertheless, the constituent that the parser declares to be the subject of the sentence will be the ' deep subject', so that the distinction between an active sentence and its passive counterpart can be eliminated. The way it works is this: as the transition is taken from state 1 to state 2 (see figure 1.1), the noun phrase is stored in the *Subj* register on the hypothesis that it will turn out to be the 'deep' subject of an active sentence. However, if a part of the verb 'to be' is encountered next, followed by the past participle of a transitive verb, the active hypothesis is changed. It is now assumed that the first noun phrase was not a subject after all, but the 'deep' object of a passive verb. Accordingly, the contents of the *Subj* register are removed and placed in the *Obj* register.

The advantage of this scheme is not difficult to appreciate. The main point is that the initial noun phrase is analysed only once, and examined by the network in figure 1.1 only once. The disadvantage is that the scheme cannot be operated in reverse, so as to make it generate the same sentences it is able to analyse. Suppose it were supplied with an initial set of register contents as follows:

(1.39)

Register	Contents
Subj	John
Verb	expected
Obj	Mary

The active sentence can be produced without difficulty, following the upper route through the diagram as before. However, the attempt to produce the corresponding passive sentence, following the lower route, can only proceed as suggested in the following table:

(1.40)

Transition	Word
1–2	John
2–5	was
5–6	expected
6–7	by
7–8	???

The subject is put in the first position in the sentence. This is what the first transition calls for, and there is no obvious way to predict that the 5–6 transition changes the contents of the *Subj* register, effectively invalidating this move. The final transition (7–8) calls for the subject a second time, but the register has since been emptied so no word is available to place in the last position.

The property that makes ATNs irreversible is that they allow moves in which the contents of a register are replaced by new contents, effectively destroying some part of the history of the process. When history is destroyed, it cannot be retraced. It became clear, then, that the key to reversibility was to ensure that, once a register had been set, it could never be reset.[1] This seems to imply the abandonment of some techniques that tend to enhance efficiency, in particular that of using one transition to recognize

---

[1] In general, ATNs are nondeterministic and the restriction is only intended to refer to the current nondeterministic path through the control structure.

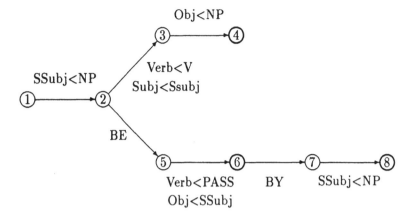

Figure 1.2. A restricted Augmented Transition Network

the subject of both transitive and intransitive sentences. But consider the transition diagram in figure 1.2.

We call this a *restricted* ATN because it does not change register values. The idea is simply that the first noun phrase is placed in the temporary register *SSubj* (for *surface subject*), from whence it is copied either to the *Subj* or the *Obj* register after the voice of the sentence has been determined. This device performs the recognition task just as well as the original. Under an appropriate interpretation, it can also be made to perform the generation task. When the 1–2 transition is made, the *SSubj* register has no contents, so that no word can be immediately assigned to the first position in the sentence. However, the name of the register can be associated with the first position, and its contents will occupy that position when they become known. In general, we cannot know if a given empty register will acquire contents but, at least, once it does they will not change, so that there will be no ambiguity about what should occupy the slot. Contents are indeed assigned to the *SSubj* register along both paths through the diagram, on the upper path from the *Subj*, and on the lower from the *Obj* register.

1.8 LOGICAL VARIABLES

What we have done in moving from figure 1.1 to figure 1.2 is to make the registers of the ATN less like *program variables*, and more like *logical variables*. Programmers are used to using the term 'variable' to refer to a storage location in a computer that can contain, now one value, and now another. In logic, and generally in mathematics, on the other hand, the term 'variable' refers to a specific quantity, which may or may not be known at certain of the times when it is used, but which does not change its value as the discussion proceeds. To put it another way, what we have done is to make the registers of the ATN for all the world like the attributes of our earlier structures.

One of the effects of observing the restriction that makes logical variables of program variables is to shift the emphasis in the design of a system from *process* and *temporal sequence* to *relations* and *constraints*. It is extremely striking that computational linguists, like computer scientists, whose subject matter *par excellence* is abstract processes and changes of state through time, seek to eliminate time dependencies wherever they are inessential. As the jargon has it, they seek *declarative* rather than *procedural* formulations of problems.

Theoretical linguists have tended to prefer procedural formalisms to declarative ones and, indeed, much of the discussion among linguists has concerned the fine adjustment of temporal sequences. In transformational grammar, for example, that we referred to earlier, the particular order in which transformational rules are applied has an important effect on the outcome and much has been made of this. As a consequence, however, transformational grammar is a system that has no known algorithm for analyzing sentences.

There is a fairly direct relationship between unification and the notion of a logical variable. It is natural to think of the descriptions we discussed earlier as conjunctions of logical variables, one for each of the attributes of the object described. The variables corresponding to attributes that have values are instantiated to those values and the remainder will be uninstantiated. In the notation for attribute-value unification introduced earlier, we did not mention variables. This is not because there is no role for them in that scheme, but because it shows up relatively rarely. As we have remarked, variables that correspond to attributes without values are not generally mentioned explicitly. We did not have any cause to introduce variables into these expressions because we had no instances of descriptions that had undergone unification. However, consider the following examples:

$$(1.41) \quad \begin{bmatrix} \text{cat} & = & s \\ \text{subj} & = & \alpha \\ \text{obj} & = & \alpha \end{bmatrix} \quad \begin{bmatrix} \text{cat} & = & s \\ \text{subj} & = & \alpha = \begin{bmatrix} \text{cat} & = & np \\ \dots & = & \dots \end{bmatrix} \\ \text{obj} & = & \alpha \end{bmatrix}$$

$$\qquad\qquad\qquad (a) \qquad\qquad\qquad\qquad (b)$$

These are both descriptions of passive sentences. In (1.41a), we know that the sentence is passive, and that its (deep) subject and object are therefore the same. However, the description says nothing about what the subject is like. In (1.41b), the subject and object are also the same, and we also have some details on the kind of constituent it is.

There are in fact alternatives to the explicit use of variable names that are frequently used in the attribute-value notation. The most often used convention is to choose one place in the description at which the variable would appear, and use a reference to this position in all the other places. The reference usually takes the form of a so-called *path*, that is, a list of attributes that can be followed from the outermost level of the description to the distinguished location. Using this convention, (1.41a) looks like (1.42a) or equivalently (1.42b).

$$(1.42) \quad \begin{bmatrix} \text{cat} & = & \text{s} \\ \text{obj} & = & \text{subj} \end{bmatrix} \quad \begin{bmatrix} \text{cat} & = & \text{s} \\ \text{subj} & = & \text{obj} \end{bmatrix}$$
$$\qquad\qquad\quad (a) \qquad\qquad\quad (b)$$

1.9 CLAUSAL FORM AND TERM UNIFICATION

A notation for descriptions that makes variables explicit is the one on which the languages of logic programming in general, and Prolog in particular, are based. In these languages, what we have been calling descriptions are expressed in so-called *clausal form*. Each description corresponds to a *term* and, in general, a term is a word, or *functor*, followed by a parenthesized list of arguments, each of which is either a variable or a term. The list of arguments can be empty, in which case the parentheses are not written. Following the Prolog convention for distinguishing variables from constants, we capitalize the names of the former, and begin the latter with lower-case letters. The following are examples:

(a)   john

(b)   np(Pers, sing)

(c)   np(3, Number)

(d)   np(3, sing)

(e)   np(3, sing, Case)

A functor that takes n arguments is said to be of *arity* n. In example (a), 'john' is an *atom*, that is, a functor of arity 0. In (b), (c) and (d), 'np' is a functor of arity 2, and in (e), 'np' is a functor of arity 3.

Functors with different arities are not systematically related to one another except perhaps mnemonically. But terms with the same names and arities are related in the sense that they are candidates for unification with one another. In fact, in the above examples, (d) is the expression that results from unifying (b) and (c). The rules for unification of these expressions are straightforward and, for the most part, obvious. If a and b are the expressions to be unified, then the result is given by the first of the following rules that applies:

- If a is a variable, it acquires the value b and the result of the unification is b.

- If b is a variable, it acquires the value a and the result of the unification is a.

- If a and b are of the forms $f(a_1, \ldots, a_n)$ and $f(b_1, \ldots, b_n)$ respectively, that is, they have the same functor and arity, the unification is $f(c_1, \ldots, c_n)$ where c_i is the result of unifying a_i with b_i for $0 < i \leq n$.

- If a and b are atoms, and $a = b$, the result is a.

Clausal form does away with explicit attribute names in favour of a place-valued scheme for identifying attributes. The two schemes are equivalent in many respects. However, one obvious and important difference is that clausal form provides only for those attributes to which positions have been assigned. Within this system there is therefore a notion of a *complete* description which is lacking when attributes are named explicitly. A term which contains no variables at any level in its structure can never be made more explicit by unification with other terms and is therefore complete. In this respect, the attribute-value notation comes closer to representing the everyday notion of a description.

Clausal form is used by a large community of computational linguists who work with logic programming systems. The fact that their systems work with a closed set of attributes is not a serious impediment for them because the set of attributes that are mentioned in a grammar is also closed. A simple grammar written in this notation is the following:

(1.43)   s   → np(X), vp(X)
          np(X)   → det(X), n(X)
          vp(X)   → v(X), np(_)
          det(f(3,_))   → the
          det(f(3, sing))   → a
          n(f(3, sing))   → cat
          n(f(3, plur))   → cats
          n(f(3, sing))   → dog
          n(f(3, plur))   → dogs
          n(f(3, _))   → sheep
          n(f(3, sing))   → chases
          v(f(3, _))   → chased

Following once again the standard conventions of Prolog, we have used the underline symbol ('_') to represent the so called *anonymous* variable. In the above examples, it behaves just like an ordinary variable. However, it is standard practice to use it where the variable is needed in only one place in an expression. If an expression contains more than one instance of the anonymous variable, each is treated as unrelated to the remainder – it is as though they had each been called by a unique, and different name.

The above example illustrates the use of logical variables and of term unification to control the agreement of subjects and predicates, and also of determiners (articles) with their nouns. The determiner 'a', for example, is a determiner that can be used only with singular nouns, and nouns, incidentally, are all third person. Accordingly, the argument to det is given as f(3, sing). The determiner 'the', on the other hand, can be used with both singular and plural nouns and is therefore annotated with the term f(3,_), where the position of number is taken by the anonymous variable. Nouns are treated similarly. The nouns 'cat' and 'cats' are marked singular and plural respectively, but 'sheep' is the same in the singular as in the plural, and the position of its number is therefore taken by the anonymous variable. The functor f has no particular significance. It serves only to collect the indicators of person and number into a single expression which will unify with the variable X in the rules at the beginning of the grammar.

Consider now what happens when some simple noun phrases are analysed. The following table shows four sentences with, written above the words, the result of applying rules to the individual words in them. Above this is the result of applying the second rule in the above grammar to these expressions. This involves unification of the arguments of the terms in the line below.

(1.44)   (a)   np(f(3, sing))
                     det(f(3, sing))   n(f(3, sing))
                     a   cat

         (b)   np(f(3, sing))
                     det(f(3, _))   n(f(3, sing))
                     the   cat

         (c)   np(f(3, sing))
                     det(f(3, sing))   n(f(3, _))
                     a   sheep

         (d)   np(f(3, _))
                     det(f(3, _))   n(f(3, _))
                     the   sheep

The result of applying the np rule in (a) is a description of a third person, singular noun phrase because the determiner and the noun agree on these attributes. When unification is applied to two identical copies of the expression np(f(3, sing)) it succeeds, producing that identical expression as the result. After all, the expression contains no variables that could be instantiated.

In (b), the two expressions that are unified are not identical. To make them so, the unification procedure must instantiate the anonymous variable in the expression corresponding to 'the', giving it the value 'sing'. Essentially the same thing happens in (c), except that the variable that must be instantiated is in the expression corresponding to the noun 'sheep'. Finally, in (d), the expressions are identical again, and no variables need to be instantiated to make them so.

The rules we have been considering have a strong family resemblance to the context-free rules familiar to linguists for decades. But the addition of arguments which may, in general, involve variables increases what can be done with them in many ways, extending far beyond verifying agreements of articles and nouns, or subjects and predicates. We will give one other example which has to do with the kinds of structure delivered by a program that conducts the syntactic analysis of a sentence. Generally speaking, such a program, which is referred to in the trade as a *parser*, must not only apply the rules of the grammar to the string, but must keep records of the structure that comes from applying them because this is the result that it must eventually return to its client. Now, it turns out that this second responsibility can be taken over by the grammar itself and, perhaps somewhat more surprisingly, there can be distinct advantages in doing this.

Consider the following variant of grammar (1.43):

```
(1.45)   s(s(NP, VP))              →  np(NP, X), vp(VP, X)
         np(np(D, N), X)           →  det(D, X), n(N, X)
         vp(vp(V, NP),X)           →  v(V, X), np(NP, _)
         det(det(the), f(3, _))    →  the
         det(det(a), f(3, sing))   →  a
         n(n(cat), f(3, sing))     →  cat
         n(n(cat), f(3, plur))     →  cats
         n(n(dog), f(3, sing))     →  dog
         n(n(dog), f(3, plur))     →  dogs
         n(n(sheep), f(3, _))      →  sheep
         v(v(chase), f(3, sing))   →  chases
         v(v(chase), f(3, _))      →  chased
```

Now let us consider what the descriptions of the noun phrases (1.44a)–(1.44d) would be like when constructed according to the rules of this grammar.

```
(1.46)  (a)  np(np(det(a), n(cat)),     f(3, sing))
                 det(det(a), f(3, sing)) n(n(cat), f(3, sing))
                 a                       cat

        (b)  np(np(det(the), n(cat)),   f(3, sing))
                 det(det(the), f(3, _)) n(n(cat), f(3, sing))
                 the                     cat

        (c)  np(np(det(a), n(sheep)),   f(3, sing))
                 det(det(a), f(3, sing)) n(n(sheep), f(3, _))
                 a                       sheep

        (d)  np(np(det(the), n(sheep)),f(3, _))
                 det(det(the), f(3, _)) n(n(sheep), f(3, _))
                 the                     sheep
```

Each of the rules in the latter part of the grammar effectively assigns a part of speech to a single word. In a real system, this function would be assigned to a different module than the main part of the grammar – one concerned only with the lexicon. Here, we simplify things by throwing the lexicon together with the grammar. Most of the terms in the grammar now have two arguments. The second performs the role of the single argument in the earlier grammar – that of monitoring agreement in number and person between articles and nouns and between subjects and predicates. The first argument contains an expression with a part of speech as functor and the word assigned to that part of speech as the only argument.

Now, consider the first three rules in the grammar. These are the rules that would indeed be part of the grammar in a more realistic system. The first argument of the term on the right-hand side of these rules also has a part of speech as its functor. Now, however, there are two arguments, because there are two terms making up the right-hand side of the rule. Each of these two arguments is a variable the value of which is obtained, by unification, from whatever a corresponding item of the right-hand side of the rule matches.

So, now consider (a) once again. The variables NP and VP in the expression s(NP, VP) on the left-hand side of the rule unify with det(a) and n(cat) respectively, giving the result np(det(a), n(cat)). This is simply a representation in the form of a term of the structure of the noun phrase.

We made the point at the beginning of this paper that the need for grammars arises from the fact that ordinary language admits an unlimited number of sentences. If the structures of these sentences are to be represented by single terms as we are now suggesting, then there can be no limit on the size and complexity of the terms. This is, of course, provided for in an entirely natural manner, because the language of terms has exactly the same recursive structures that natural languages presumably also have. A functor can have any number of arguments, and each of these can be a functor with arguments, and so on indefinitely.

1.10   PATH EQUATIONS

Any atomic value in an attribute-value matrix or in a term can be located by an expression known as a *path*, which is simply an ordered set of attribute names. To locate the value in question, we first locate the value of the first attribute in the path. If this is also the last member of the path, then we have the result. Otherwise, that value should itself be an attribute-value matrix or a term in which we now locate the second attribute in the path, and so on until either an attribute is called for in a structure for which it is not defined, or we reach the end of the path and retrieve the value. The ability to uniquely locate any value in this way comes, of course, from the functional property that these structures are required to have. Using it, we can specify any arbitrary attribute-value structure by means of a set of *path equations*, that is, pairs consisting of a path and the associated value. A plausible structure for the sentence 'The dog chased the cat' might be the one given by the following equations:

(1.47) $\langle \text{cat} \rangle$ = s
   $\langle \text{subj, cat} \rangle$ = np
   $\langle \text{subj, num} \rangle$ = sing
   $\langle \text{subj, pers} \rangle$ = 3
   $\langle \text{subj, lex} \rangle$ = dog
   $\langle \text{verb, lex} \rangle$ = chase
   $\langle \text{verb, tense} \rangle$ = past
   $\langle \text{obj, cat} \rangle$ = np
   $\langle \text{obj, num} \rangle$ = sing
   $\langle \text{obj, pers} \rangle$ = 3
   $\langle \text{obj, lex} \rangle$ = dog

Unification of a pair of equation sets consists in taking the union of the two sets and rejecting the result just in case it contains two instances of the same path with different values. Path equations have come to be the standard notation for specifying attribute-value structures in grammatical formalisms, such as Lexical Functional Grammar [105] and PATR II [210].

1.11   LONG-DISTANCE DEPENDENCY

There are a great many problems in syntax that can be treated by unification and for which more complex mechanisms were previously thought necessary. This is an important fact because unification makes for much more straightforward computational processes. Take the example of so-called *long-distance dependency*. This is a phenomenon that is demonstrated in examples like the following:

- This is the car I expected you to be able to persuade them to buy ◇.

- Everyone does not even claim ◇ to like garlic.

- This is the violin the sonatas are easy to play ◇ on ◇.

Each of these sentences contains a sentence fragment from which, however, something seems to have been deleted. Here are the fragments in question, with the missing parts replaced, as above, by a diamond (◇):

- to buy ◇.

- ◇ to like garlic

- to play ◇ on ◇.

There is an intuitive sense in which, to understand these fragments, we need to copy into the marked places some material from the enclosing context. If we do this, we get the following:

- to buy the car.

- everyone to like garlic

- to play the sonatas on the violin.

As the first two examples illustrate, there can be any number of intermediate-sized sentences (or sentence fragments) intervening between the outer one, from which the inserted material is taken, and the inner-most one where it is needed for proper interpretation. Hence the term *long-distance dependency*. Now consider the following grammar rule schemata:

(1.48) np( )   ⟶   X, s(... X, [] ...) :- X = np( )
        s(... X, Y ...)   ⟶   np( ), vp(... X, Y ...)
        vp(... X, Y ...)   ⟶   v( ), np(... X, Y ...)
        vp(... X, Y ...)   ⟶   vp(... X Z ...), pp(... Z Y ...)
        np(... X, [] ...)   :-   X = np( )

The first says that a noun phrase can be made up of something that we designate with the variable X and constrain to be a noun phrase, followed by a sentence which has as one of its arguments that same noun phrase. It also has another argument which is constrained to be an empty list.

The second and third rules show how the values of these arguments are passed down through the structure, from sentence to verb phrase, from verb phrase to noun phrase, and so on. The fourth rule, which allows a verb phrase to consist of a verb phrase and a prepositional phrase, associates the first argument of the larger verb phrase with the first argument of the smaller one, and the second of the relevant arguments of the prepositional phrase with the second argument of the larger verb phrase, and it unifies the second argument of the embedded verb phrase with the first argument of the prepositional phrase. If we think of these arguments as channels through which information can be passed, and of the first of the two distinguished variables as an 'input', and the second as an 'output' channel, then this rule can be seen as passing input to the first phrase, taking the output from there and passing it to the second phrase, and then returning the output it receives from there.

The last rule is unusual in having no right-hand side. What this rule means is that, at a place where a noun phrase would normally be required, it can be omitted, provided that the first of the two variables is bound to a noun phrase, and the second to an empty list.

The overall effect of this scheme is that the noun phrase that is bound to the 'input' channel variable by the first rule is passed from phrase to phrase, and from input to output, until a rule like the fifth one above is encountered. Now, for the first time, the output is different. Now it is an empty list, and it is this that continues to be passed from phrase to phrase until it emerges as the output in the first rule. Only if a rule like the fifth one above is found at some point will the output variable unify with the value required of it in the first rule. And the only way that the input in the first rule can be a noun phrase, and the output an empty list, is by using a rule like the fifth one at some point. For reasons that will be clear by now, this particular way of accounting for long-distance dependencies is known as *gap-threading*.

1.12 CONCLUSION

In this chapter I have tried to show how the cause of linguistic computing can be carried forward by what at first appears to be an unpromising approach, namely that of removing from the statement of linguistic facts all mention of process, of events and of time sequences. It turns out to be possible to do this by replacing these powerful things with one operation which is, itself, of quite unexpected power, namely unification. The reason for removing procedural statements from the statement of linguistic facts is so that they can be reintroduced in the ways, and in the places, that are dictated by good computational practice. Although this approach has caught on only in small enclaves of the linguistic community, it is more in line with the declared principles of the majority of linguists, at least in America, than what they themselves do. Processes and the ordering of events are clearly matters of performance. Competence, which is the domain of the theoretical linguist, is concerned with relations and constraints.

2 Representations and interpretations

Jens Erik Fenstad, Tore Langholm,
Espen Vestre

2.1 INTRODUCTION

Computational semantics lies at the intersection of three disciplines: linguistics, logic and computer science. A natural language system should provide a coherent framework for relating linguistic form and semantic content, and the relationship must be algorithmic.

There have been several important pairwise interactions, as detailed below, between linguistics and computer science, linguistics and logic, and logic and computer science. The point of computational semantics is the insistence on relating *all three* simultaneously. This is necessary from a cognitive as well as a knowledge engineering point of view.

2.1.1 LINGUISTICS AND COMPUTER SCIENCE

N. Chomsky's *Syntactic Structures* [34] signalled a renewal of theoretical linguistics, which for some of its theoretical tools drew upon automata and formal language theory. A link was soon established with the emerging computer science, leading to a vigorous field of computational linguistics, focusing on questions of linguistic form, i.e. syntax and morphology. This has proved to be of lasting value for the study of both natural and programming languages.

2.1.2 LINGUISTICS AND LOGIC

Language is more than linguistic form. R. Montague, in a series of papers starting from 1967 (see Thomason [219]), showed how to use the insights from logical semantics to 'tame' the meaning component of a natural language. Montague's tool was the model theory of higher order intensional logic. And he convincingly demonstrated how the use of this model theory could explain a wide range of linguistic phenomena. A further high point was the 'identity' which was established between noun phrases and generalized quantifiers.

2.1.3 LOGIC AND COMPUTER SCIENCE

Another important trend in 'applied logic' has been the use of model theory in the study of knowledge representation. In a certain sense, model theory *is* knowledge representation, but it took some time before the two professions, logicians and computer scientists, joined forces in developing a common field. Now the situation is vastly different; see for example Gurevich [73] and Makowsky [147] for a sample of some recent studies.

2.1.4 NATURAL LANGUAGE SYSTEMS

The study of natural language systems needs to learn from all three lines of development. Computing a representation in higher order intensional logic may throw light upon specific linguistic phenomena. But it is not the case that *any* computable representation may be a fruitful starting point for further processing, and this for several reasons. The representation may not be computationally tractable, which is the case if it is a formula in higher order logic, thus belonging to a system without a complete proof procedure. Also, we must pay equal attention to the representational forms developed in knowledge representation theory and choose our representation of linguistic information accordingly.

In retrospect, this was the important theoretical point behind the introduction of the format of *situation schemata* in Fenstad et al. [55], linking the functional structures of Lexical-Functional Grammar (LFG, Kaplan and Bresnan [105]) and basic facts as represented within the Situation Semantics of Barwise and Perry [15].

But the scope is wider than the linking of LFG and Situation Semantics. *Feature structures* or *attribute-value systems*, together with the associated unification algorithms, has emerged as a major candidate for representational forms; see also M. Kay [117, 116].

In this paper we will first review some topics in the general theory of feature structures; then we will turn to the question of how these representational forms must interact with the model theory in order to achieve a 'true' computational semantics.

2.2 REPRESENTATIONS

Common to the various unification-based grammar formalisms is the use of *attribute-value systems* or *feature structures*. Information contained in grammatical constituents is represented in corresponding feature structures; when two or more constituents are combined to form a larger constituent, the corresponding feature structures are *unified* to produce a new feature structure representing the information content of the larger constituent. At the same time, the unification process functions as a check on grammaticality: if the feature structures are incompatible and thus cannot be unified, then neither does the combination of the smaller constituents in fact produce a new grammatical constituent. See Kay[116, this volume] for the finer details.

2.2.1 FEATURE STRUCTURES

Characteristic to feature structures is the usefulness of a particular notational format for depicting them: an *attribute-value matrix* is a piece of notation of the form shown in (2.1)

$$(2.1) \quad \begin{bmatrix} l_1 & v_1 \\ \vdots & \vdots \\ l_n & v_n \end{bmatrix}$$

where $l_1, \ldots, l_n$ are *labels* or attribute names, and $v_1, \ldots, v_n$ are the corresponding *values*. Such values can be *simple* or *atomic*, as in (2.2),

$$(2.2) \quad \begin{bmatrix} \text{NUM} & \text{SG} \\ \text{PERS} & \text{THIRD} \end{bmatrix}$$

or they are *complex*, as is the latter value in (2.3).

$$(2.3) \quad \begin{bmatrix} \text{CAT} & \text{NP} \\ \text{AGR} & \begin{bmatrix} \text{NUM} & \text{SG} \\ \text{PERS} & \text{THIRD} \end{bmatrix} \end{bmatrix}$$

Values may also be shared, as in (2.4), where AGR and SUBJ have a common value, indicated by the matching numbers.

$$(2.4) \quad \begin{bmatrix} \text{CAT} & \text{NP} \\ \text{AGR} & [1]\begin{bmatrix} \text{NUM} & \text{SG} \\ \text{PERS} & \text{THIRD} \end{bmatrix} \\ \text{SUBJ} & [1] \end{bmatrix}$$

A *path* is a sequence of labels leading to some value, thus in the example above the path AGR.NUM has the value SG while the paths AGR and SUBJ are *structure-sharing*.

Subsumption

Subsumption is the ordering of feature structures in terms of information content. For example, in (2.5) the structure is *subsumed* by the larger structure (2.6).

(2.5) $\begin{bmatrix} \text{CAT} & \text{NP} \end{bmatrix}$

(2.6) $\begin{bmatrix} \text{CAT} & \text{NP} \\ \text{AGR} & \begin{bmatrix} \text{NUM} & \text{SG} \end{bmatrix} \end{bmatrix}$

If B subsumes[1] A, we write $A \sqsubseteq B$. In general

- For atomic A and B, $A \sqsubseteq B$ iff $A = B$.

- For complex A and B, $A \sqsubseteq B$ iff

  (i)   for every path in A, the same path exists in B, and its value in A is subsumed by its value in B, and

  (ii) for every pair of paths that are structure-sharing in A, the same pair is structure-sharing in B.

Unification

Unifying two feature structures, we obtain a new feature structure containing the combined information from the two original ones. Thus, unifying (2.7) and (2.8) we obtain (2.9).

(2.7) $\begin{bmatrix} \text{CAT} & \text{NP} \end{bmatrix}$

(2.8) $\begin{bmatrix} \text{AGR} & \begin{bmatrix} \text{NUM} & \text{SG} \end{bmatrix} \end{bmatrix}$

(2.9) $\begin{bmatrix} \text{CAT} & \text{NP} \\ \text{AGR} & \begin{bmatrix} \text{NUM} & \text{SG} \end{bmatrix} \end{bmatrix}$

More precisely, we define $A \sqcup B$ as the least upper bound of A and B with respect to $\sqsubseteq$. If no upper bound exists, as specified by (2.10) and (2.11),

(2.10) $A = \begin{bmatrix} \text{AGR} & \begin{bmatrix} \text{NUM} & \text{SG} \end{bmatrix} \end{bmatrix}$

(2.11) $B = \begin{bmatrix} \text{AGR} & \begin{bmatrix} \text{NUM} & \text{PL} \end{bmatrix} \end{bmatrix}$

then neither does there exist a least upper bound. Hence $A \sqcup B$ does not exist, and unification is said to *fail*.

---

[1] The reader is warned that in the literature *subsumption* sometimes refers to the inverse relation.

In (2.12) a few example unifications are listed, the last of which illustrates the concept of structure sharing.

$$(2.12) \qquad A \;=\; \left[\text{SUBJ}\quad \left[\text{AGR}\quad \left[\text{PERS}\quad \text{THIRD}\right]\right]\right]$$

$$B \;=\; \begin{bmatrix}\text{AGR} & \begin{bmatrix}\text{NUM} & \text{SG}\end{bmatrix} \\ \text{SUBJ} & \begin{bmatrix}\text{AGR} & \begin{bmatrix}\text{NUM} & \text{SG}\end{bmatrix}\end{bmatrix}\end{bmatrix}$$

$$C \;=\; \begin{bmatrix}\text{AGR} & [1]\begin{bmatrix}\text{NUM} & \text{SG}\end{bmatrix} \\ \text{SUBJ} & \begin{bmatrix}\text{AGR} & [1]\end{bmatrix}\end{bmatrix}$$

$$A \sqcup B \;=\; \begin{bmatrix}\text{AGR} & \begin{bmatrix}\text{NUM} & \text{SG}\end{bmatrix} \\ \text{SUBJ} & \begin{bmatrix}\text{AGR} & \begin{bmatrix}\text{NUM} & \text{SG} \\ \text{PERS} & \text{THIRD}\end{bmatrix}\end{bmatrix}\end{bmatrix}$$

$$A \sqcup C \;=\; \begin{bmatrix}\text{AGR} & [1]\begin{bmatrix}\text{NUM} & \text{SG} \\ \text{PERS} & \text{THIRD}\end{bmatrix} \\ \text{SUBJ} & \begin{bmatrix}\text{AGR} & [1]\end{bmatrix}\end{bmatrix}$$

We now turn to some examples to ground our theoretical discussion in linguistic theory. We have been somewhat selective in our choice of examples. For another approach see the TAG formalism developed by A. K. Joshi [101].

2.2.2 EXAMPLES FROM LINGUISTICS

Before plunging into the formal study of feature structures we shall recall three examples from linguistic theory. We assume that the reader will have some familiarity with these examples and therefore concentrate only on a few matters of importance from our present representational point of view.

Lexical-Functional Grammar

Our first example is the LFG theory due to J. Bresnan and R. Kaplan (see the collection Bresnan [20] as well as the lectures of P. Sells [209]). We recall that the *grammar* is determined by a *lexicon* and a simple syntactic structure, the *c-structure*. Information is basically given in the form of equational constraints, and a grammatical analysis leads up to a set of equations, the *f-description*, where the unknown entities are attribute-value structures.

Everyone's example of a c-structure is shown in (2.13):

(2.13)

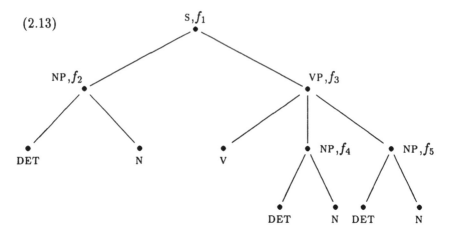

with the associated structural equations (2.14)–(2.17).

$$(2.14) \quad (f_1 \text{ SUBJ}) = f_2$$
$$(2.15) \quad (f_3 \text{ OBJ}) = f_4$$
$$(2.16) \quad (f_3 \text{ OBJ2}) = f_5$$
$$(2.17) \qquad f_1 = f_3$$

We read the meaning of this from the syntax tree and the set of equations: in virtue of (2.17) the S-node and the VP-node have a common associated attribute-value structure which has at least three attributes or features, SUBJ, OBJ, OBJ2, and possibly others. So far we get the representation (2.18)

$$(2.18) \quad f_1, f_3 \begin{bmatrix} \text{SUBJ} & f_2 \\ \text{OBJ} & f_4 \\ \text{OBJ2} & f_5 \\ \vdots & \vdots \end{bmatrix}$$

where the values f_2, f_4, f_5 are further attribute-value structures, atomic or complex.

Recalling the 'standard' example *a girl handed the baby a toy* the lexicon adds the following lexical constraint equations

$$(2.19) \quad (f_2 \text{ SPEC}) = \text{A}$$
$$\qquad\quad (f_4 \text{ NUM}) = \text{SG}$$
$$\qquad\quad (f_2 \text{ NUM}) = \text{SG}$$

$$(f_4 \text{ PRED}) = \text{'BABY'}$$
$$(f_2 \text{ NUM}) = \text{SG}$$
$$(f_5 \text{ SPEC}) = \text{A}$$
$$(f_2 \text{ PRED}) = \text{'GIRL'}$$
$$(f_5 \text{ NUM}) = \text{SG}$$
$$(f_3 \text{ TENSE}) = \text{PAST}$$
$$(f_5 \text{ NUM}) = \text{SG}$$
$$(f_4 \text{ SPEC}) = \text{THE}$$
$$(f_5 \text{ PRED}) = \text{'TOY'}$$
$$(f_3 \text{ PRED}) = \text{'HAND}\langle(\uparrow \text{ SUBJ})(\uparrow \text{ OBJ2})(\uparrow \text{ OBJ})\rangle\text{'}$$

A solution of the combined set of structural and lexical equations can be represented as the feature structure (2.20)

$$(2.20) \quad \begin{bmatrix} \text{SUBJ} & \begin{bmatrix} \text{SPEC} & \text{A} \\ \text{NUM} & \text{SG} \\ \text{PRED} & \text{'GIRL'} \end{bmatrix} \\ \text{OBJ} & \begin{bmatrix} \text{SPEC} & \text{THE} \\ \text{NUM} & \text{SG} \\ \text{PRED} & \text{'BABY'} \end{bmatrix} \\ \text{OBJ2} & \begin{bmatrix} \text{SPEC} & \text{A} \\ \text{NUM} & \text{SG} \\ \text{PRED} & \text{'TOY'} \end{bmatrix} \\ \text{TENSE} & \text{PAST} \\ \text{PRED} & \text{'HAND}\langle(\uparrow\text{SUBJ})(\uparrow\text{OBJ2})(\uparrow\text{OBJ})\rangle\text{'} \end{bmatrix}$$

Grammaticality of the given string is not guaranteed by the mere existence of an associated attribute-value structure. A *first condition of grammaticality* is to require that the string has a *valid c-structure* with an associated f-description (i.e. set of equations) that is both *consistent* (i.e. has a solution) and *determinate* (i.e. has a unique minimal solution). Obviously, the standard example satisfies this condition.

But how do we ensure that the final f-structure contains all and only those grammatical roles that the predicate calls for? We call an f-structure *locally complete* iff it contains all the governable grammatical functions that its predicate governs. We call it *complete* iff it and its subsidiary f-structures are locally complete. In a similar way, we call an f-structure *locally coherent* iff all the governable grammatical functions that it contains are governed by a local predicate. We call it *coherent* iff it and its subsidiary f-structures are locally coherent.

A *second condition of grammaticality* now requires that a string is grammatical only if it is assigned a complete and coherent f-structure. Again, the standard example fits the bill.

We used 'only if'; even adding the second condition on grammaticality is not enough to weed out all unacceptable strings. We shall return to this problem in connection with our third example.

Situation schemata

Situation schemata were introduced in Fenstad et al. [55, 56] in order to link the grammatical analysis of LFG with the Situation Semantics of Barwise and Perry. As we remarked in the introduction, the scope is wider than this particular linking. In the transition from f-structures to situation schemata we see a shift from grammatical to semantical roles. An example will bring this out. Let our sample sentence be *John married a girl*. The associated situation schema will be (2.21).

$$(2.21) \quad \begin{bmatrix} \text{REL} & marry \\ \text{ARG.1} & \begin{bmatrix} \text{IND} & John \end{bmatrix} \\ \text{ARG.2} & \begin{bmatrix} \text{IND} & \text{IND.1} \\ \text{SPEC} & a \\ \text{COND} & \begin{bmatrix} \text{REL} & girl \\ \text{ARG.1} & \text{IND.1} \\ \text{POL} & 1 \end{bmatrix} \end{bmatrix} \\ \text{LOC} & \begin{bmatrix} \text{IND} & \text{IND.2} \\ \text{COND} & \begin{bmatrix} \text{REL} & \prec \\ \text{ARG.1} & \text{IND.2} \\ \text{ARG.2} & \text{IND.0} \end{bmatrix} \end{bmatrix} \\ \text{POL} & 1 \end{bmatrix}$$

The 'mechanics' of how to arrive at the schema from the given string is explained in Fenstad et al. [56]; see also the ACAI '87 lectures by Fenstad [54]. Here we draw attention to two points:

(i)   The value of the ARG.2 feature is basically a notation for a generalized quantifier; hence our representational form is well suited to bring out the essential identity between noun phrases and generalized quantifiers.

(ii)   The shift from the TENSE-attribute of LFG to the LOC-attribute of a situation schema allows for a richer 'geometric' representation than merely recording the tense of verbs. This is of special importance in analyzing locatives of different kinds.

Our next example *John ran to the school* is meant to illustrate this point. Here the associated schema is (2.22).

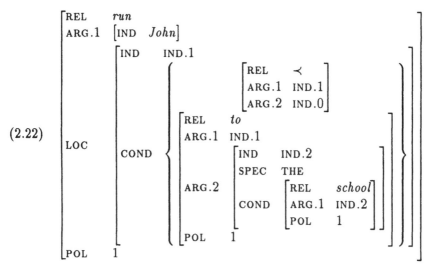

In this analysis IND.2 represents an object, *the school*, and IND.1 represents a trajectory in space-time which stands in the 'to-relation' to (i.e. ends at) the school. An analysis of *locative prepositional phrases* along these lines has been given by E. Colban [37].

We will return to the theory of situation schemata when we later discuss how representational form must interact with interpretations and model theory to give a full account of computational semantics. In particular, we will discuss how situation schemata can be used to build a theory of direct questions.

Other, but related questions of semantic representation are discussed by P.-K. Halvorsen in this volume [78] as well as in [77] and [79]. The format of situation schemata is also being used by C.J. Rupp, R. Johnson and M. Rosner [198], by H. Dyvik [51] at the University of Bergen, and by the KOLIBRI project led by D. Metzing [149] at the University of Bielefeld.

Head-driven Phrase Structure Grammar

Head-Driven Phrase Structure Grammar (HPSG) developed historically out of GPSG, but seen today from a somewhat different perspective it represents a 'purer' version of an attribute-value formalism than standard LFG. The basic text is C. Pollard and I. A. Sag [182].

HPSG can be seen as a *theory of signs* where a sign has the shape given by (2.23):

$$(2.23) \quad \begin{bmatrix} \text{PHON} \\ \\ \text{SYN} \quad \begin{bmatrix} \text{LOC} \quad \begin{bmatrix} \text{HEAD} \\ \text{SUBCAT} \\ \text{LEX} \end{bmatrix} \\ \text{BIND} \end{bmatrix} \\ \text{SEM} \end{bmatrix}$$

A sign can be *phrasal* or *lexical*, according to whether the LEX feature is unmarked or marked.

The minimal syntactic analysis of LFG is in the HPSG theory encoded directly into the sign or the attribute-value structure by using a special set of features. A sign can at a given level have a feature DTRS, daughters, with values HEAD-DTR, COMP-DTR, ... If you are at the sentence level, the path leading from DTRS to HEAD-DTR will take you down the branch of the corresponding syntax tree in LFG leading from the S-node to the VP-node. And the path leading from DTRS to COMP-DTR will take you down the branch leading from the S-node to the NP-node. Thus a saturated sign in HPSG will retain a complete copy of every step of the syntactic analysis, whereas in LFG the final f-structure will only display the predicate, the grammatical roles and the possible modifying circumstances.

The *head feature principle* is one of the basic principles of universal grammar in HPSG. It ensures the sharing of certain information between the HEAD attribute of one level and the HEAD attribute of HEAD-DTR of the next lower level, and corresponds to the '*up-arrow = down-arrow*' equation of LFG.

The *subcategorization principle* is another major principle of universal grammar according to HPSG. A complete sign must be *saturated*. A noun in itself is not saturated, but calls for a determiner to form a full sign, an NP. In the same way a VP subcategorizes for an NP in order to form a full sign, in this case a sign of category S. We see the relationship between this principle and the second condition of grammaticality in LFG, which requires completeness and coherence.

According to HPSG a language is given by an 'equation', say (2.24):

$$(2.24) \quad \text{ENGLISH} \quad = \quad P_1 \wedge \ldots \wedge P_n \wedge P_{n+1} \wedge \ldots \wedge P_{n+m}$$
$$\wedge (L_1 \vee \ldots L_p \vee R_1 \vee \ldots \vee R_q)$$

where

(i) $P_1, \ldots, P_n$ are the principles of universal grammar, e.g. the head feature principle, the subcategorization principle, etc.

(ii) $P_{n+1}, \ldots, P_{n+m}$ are the language-specific constraints.

(iii) $L_1, \ldots, L_p$ are the lexical signs.

(iv) $R_1, \ldots, R_q$ are the grammar rules.

The meaning of this 'equation' is rather straightforward. A sign S is a sign of English iff

(i)   it satisfies all principles of universal grammar, i.e. shares information according to the head feature principle, fills roles correctly according to the subcategorization principle, ...;

(ii)   it satisfies the language specific constraints such as special constituent ordering principles;

(iii)   it is either a lexical sign, or satisfies one of the grammar rules of the language.

It is very instructive to compare the syntactic analysis of LFG and the semantic analysis of the Situation Schema approach with the analysis of HPSG. The basic approach of HPSG is to encode everything into the sign. A different approach to attribute-value grammar formalisms, close in spirit to the original LFG analysis, has been given by M. Johnson [98] in his thesis.

Both Pollard and Sag [182] and Johnson [98] go beyond the grammatical analysis to a formal analysis. We also turn to a detailed study of the formal theory of feature structures.

2.2.3   FORMAL FRAMEWORKS

So far we have relied on a somewhat loose, intuitive understanding of what a feature structure is. In this section we discuss several attempts to formulate a mathematically precise notion. Such an exercise serves several purposes.

First and foremost, precise definitions are needed to get any substantial theory off the ground. Unless one knows exactly what one is talking about, it is hard to reach any decisions on the finer points of the theory, and impossible to make any enlightened choice when conflicting views are encountered.

Secondly, a precise mathematical framework may help to sharpen our intuitions and to weed out possible inconsistencies hidden in our informal thinking about the subject.

Thirdly, when all the formal details have been spelled out one is likely to discover similarities or even isomorphisms with mathematical structures for which a substantial theory already exists. Hence substantial work savings may result.

Such are the benefits of a precise mathematical definition – provided it is a well-chosen one. For the abstract mathematical theory to have any bearing on the issue at hand – natural language grammars – there must be a tight fit between intuitive notions and the formal framework. For such a fit to obtain, two major criteria must be satisfied.

(i)   *Right identity conditions*

A formal framework will give an account of which feature structures are identical, i.e. it will tell us when two different descriptions will pick out the same feature structure or two different ones. This account should match our informal notions as well as possible. For example, we want our formal framework to recognize that the two matrices (2.25) and (2.26) below are equivalent, i.e. that they depict the same feature structure.

(2.25) $\begin{bmatrix} \text{PERS} & \text{FIRST} \\ \text{NUM} & \text{SG} \end{bmatrix}$

(2.26) $\begin{bmatrix} \text{NUM} & \text{SG} \\ \text{PERS} & \text{FIRST} \end{bmatrix}$

(ii)   *Right essential properties*

The account built into the formal framework should match as well as possible our informal feelings (or the stipulations given by a semi-formal theory) of what it takes for something to be a feature structure. For example, the finite relation depicted by the matrix (2.27) below should not count as a feature structure.

(2.27) $\begin{bmatrix} \text{PERS} & \text{FIRST} \\ \text{PERS} & \text{SG} \end{bmatrix}$

Function structures and tree structures

According to the simplest conception, the class of feature structures is formed by an iteration according to which

(i)   *atomic values* from a given set V are feature structures, and

(ii)   if $A_1, \ldots, A_n$ are feature structures and $l_1, \ldots, l_n$ are distinct *labels* from a given set L, then the matrix (2.28):

$$(2.28) \quad \begin{bmatrix} l_1 & A_1 \\ \vdots & \vdots \\ l_n & A_n \end{bmatrix}$$

depicts a feature structure.

This can be represented by the use of finite partial functions: we define the set of *function structures* over V and L to be the smallest set F such that

(i) $V \subseteq F$, and

(ii)   if $A_1, \ldots, A_n$ are all in F and $l_1, \ldots, l_n$ are distinct members of L, then the finite partial function f with domain $\{l_1, \ldots l_n\}$, such that $f(l_i) = A_i$ for all $i, 1 \leq i \leq n$, is a member of F.

Tree structures represent an alternative to function structures. We can define a *tree domain* over L to be a finite set Δ of finite strings from L, satisfying

(i)   The empty string ϵ is in Δ.

(ii)   For $n \geq 1$, if the string $l_1 \ldots l_n$ is in Δ, then so is $l_1 \ldots l_{n-1}$.

The first condition ensures that Δ is non-empty, while the second condition ensures that initial segments of a string in Δ are also in Δ. Thus, if the string VCOMP.SUBJ.NUM is in Δ, then so is the string VCOMP.SUBJ, the string VCOMP and the empty string ϵ. The tree domain $\{\epsilon,$ SUBJ, SUBJ.NUM, OBJ.NUM, VCOMP, VCOMP.SUBJ, VCOMP.SUBJ.NUM$\}$ can be depicted graphically in (2.29):

The *terminal nodes* of a tree domain Δ are the strings in Δ which are not initial segments of any other string in Δ. Thus, the terminal nodes in the example above are SUBJ.NUM, OBJ.NUM and VCOMP.SUBJ.NUM. We now define a *tree structure* over V and L to be a pair $\langle \Delta, \alpha \rangle$ where Δ is a tree domain over L and α is a function from the terminal nodes of Δ into V.

Hence if Δ is the tree domain depicted above and if α is the constant function that maps all the three terminal nodes of Δ to SG, then the tree structure $\langle \Delta, \alpha \rangle$ is depicted by the matrix

$$(2.30) \quad \begin{bmatrix} \text{SUBJ} & [\text{NUM} \quad \text{SG}] \\ \text{OBJ} & [\text{NUM} \quad \text{SG}] \\ \text{VCOMP} & [\text{SUBJ} \quad [\text{NUM} \quad \text{SG}]] \end{bmatrix}$$

There is a simple 1:1 correspondence between function structures and tree structures, but still from a certain point of view there is a difference in flavour between the two. The feature structure depicted in (2.30) contains three instances of the simpler feature structure (2.31).

$$(2.31) \quad [\text{NUM} \quad \text{SG}]$$

In the function structure representation the three instances are all given by one and the same item, namely the finite partial function that maps NUM to SG. In the tree structure representation, on the other hand, the three instances are represented by three distinct subsets of Δ, namely

(i)   {SUBJ, SUBJ.NUM}

(ii)   {OBJ, OBJ.NUM}

(iii)   {VCOMP.SUBJ, VCOMP.SUBJ.NUM}

together with the appropriate parts of the function α.

Graph structures

The representation of similar substructures by the same or distinct items is significant for certain approaches. If we think of the feature structures as *partial* and *potentially uncompleted* objects, then we may recognize differences in possible growth patterns in addition to the differences displayed by the structures in their current manifestations. To make this somewhat less mysterious, consider again the example structure (2.30). In a typical application we may wish to express that the identities between the three substructures (2.31) are not all of the same variety; we may wish to express that the identity between the values associated with the SUBJ and OBJ labels are accidental and possibly transient, while the OBJ and VCOMP.SUBJ values are to remain identical even when more information is added to the structure. In this case we would allow

$$(2.32) \quad \begin{bmatrix} \text{SUBJ} & \begin{bmatrix} \text{NUM} & \text{SG} \\ \text{PERS} & \text{FIRST} \end{bmatrix} \\ \text{OBJ} & \begin{bmatrix} \text{NUM} & \text{SG} \end{bmatrix} \\ \text{VCOMP} & \begin{bmatrix} \text{SUBJ} & \begin{bmatrix} \text{NUM} & \text{SG} \end{bmatrix} \end{bmatrix} \end{bmatrix}$$

as a possible extension, but not

$$(2.33) \quad \begin{bmatrix} \text{SUBJ} & \begin{bmatrix} \text{NUM} & \text{SG} \end{bmatrix} \\ \text{OBJ} & \begin{bmatrix} \text{NUM} & \text{SG} \\ \text{PERS} & \text{FIRST} \end{bmatrix} \\ \text{VCOMP} & \begin{bmatrix} \text{SUBJ} & \begin{bmatrix} \text{NUM} & \text{SG} \end{bmatrix} \end{bmatrix} \end{bmatrix}$$

Neither the function nor the tree structure representation allows for such a distinction to be made. We turn therefore to a more expressive framework. What we need is a framework that gives us the choice of representing similar substructures by identical or distinct items, thus enabling us to distinguish between intended and accidental identities. This points towards the type of structure depicted in (2.34):

(2.34)

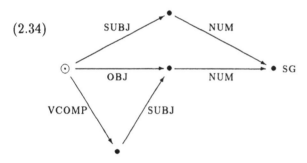

where the rightmost node is meant to represent the atomic value SG, while two of the other nodes are equivalent in having a single outgoing arch, labelled with NUM and pointing to the rightmost node. Both represent the feature structure (2.31). In a similar way, the encircled node represents the entire structure. From this node the SUBJ arch, the OBJ arch, and the path VCOMB.SUBJ, all lead to a node representing (2.31). But there is a difference between the resulting identities: if new label/value pairs are added to this structure at any point, i.e. if the structure is expanded with more nodes or transition arrows, then the OBJ/VCOMP.SUBJ identity will persist undisturbed, while the SUBJ/OBJ identity is unprotected, so to speak, and may very well perish.

To give precise expression to this somewhat vague idea, we shall use some constructs from automata theory, cf. Hopcroft and Ullman [90]. Thus we shall follow in the steps of Rounds and Kasper [193]. The definitions given here are not quite the same as those of Rounds and Kasper, however.

Definition: A *general graph structure* over V and L is a quadruple

(2.35) $\langle Q, q_0, \delta, \alpha \rangle$

where Q is a non-empty set, q_0 is a member of Q, δ is a partial function from $Q \times L$ into Q, and α is a partial, injective function from Q into V.

The members of Q are called *states* or *nodes*, while q_0 is the *initial state*, encircled in the graphical representation. To represent the structure depicted above, let Q be any set of five distinct elements, for instance the set $\{1, 2, 3, 4, 5\}$, $q_0 = 1$, and define δ and α as the smallest partial functions satisfying the equations

$$
\begin{aligned}
(2.36) \qquad \delta(1, \text{SUBJ}) &= 2 \\
\delta(2, \text{NUM}) &= 3 \\
\delta(1, \text{OBJ}) &= 4 \\
\delta(4, \text{NUM}) &= 3 \\
\delta(1, \text{VCOMP}) &= 5 \\
\delta(5, \text{SUBJ}) &= 4 \\
\alpha(3) &= \text{SG}
\end{aligned}
$$

The general graph structures are a little too general for our purposes, they include structures that we would not normally recognize as feature structures. We recall that in the definition of a tree structure, α was only defined on the terminal nodes. This is to say that the atomic values have no features defined on them. The analogue here is captured by the next definition.

Definition: A *graph structure* is a general graph structure $\langle Q, q_0, \delta, \alpha \rangle$ satisfying the additional requirement that for no $q \in Q$ and $l \in L$ are both $\delta(q, l)$ and $\alpha(l)$ defined.

Let L^* be the set of *strings* containing zero or more labels from L. The function δ is defined on elements of $Q \times L$, but can be extended to a larger subset of $Q \times L^*$ by the stipulations

$$
\begin{aligned}
(2.37) \qquad \delta(q, \epsilon) &= q \\
\delta(q, wl) &= \delta(\delta(q, w), l)
\end{aligned}
$$

In the latter case, $\delta(q, wl)$ is defined iff $\delta(q, w)$ and $\delta(\delta(q, w), l)$ are both defined. Here, w is used to range over arbitrary strings of labels, while wl is the result of a concatenation.

The new framework using graph structures allows for additional generality in more ways than one; observe that *cyclic* feature structures can now be represented:

$\langle Q, q_0, \delta, \alpha \rangle$ is *cyclic* if $\delta(q, w) = q$ for some $q \in Q$ and $w \in L^*$, $w \neq \epsilon$. An *acyclic* graph structure is a graph structure that is not cyclic.

The cyclic feature structure in (2.38) is used in an analysis of a sentence with a relative clause, and is borrowed from Johnson [98].

(2.38)

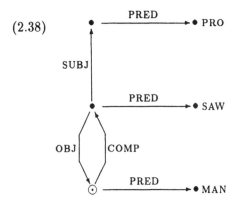

The structure (2.38) represents part of the syntactic information of the NP *the man that I saw.*. Several grammatical theories do not allow cyclic feature structures. From a computational point of view, acyclic feature structures are easier to deal with.

Another question of generality has to do with the relation between the set L of labels and the set V of atomic values. Some authors (Rounds and Kasper [193]) require these sets to be disjoint, i.e. nothing can appear both as an atomic value and as a label. LFG is more general in this respect; in the analysis of prepositional phrases (Kaplan and Bresnan [105]) feature structures of the following sort are used:

(2.39) $\begin{bmatrix} \text{TO} & [\text{PCASE} & \text{TO}] \end{bmatrix}$

See Colban [37] for an alternative analysis, however. Johnson allows for this generality, and then takes it a step further. Instead of defining the function δ on $Q \times L$, Johnson introduces a more general format where $L \cup V$ is put in correspondence with a subset of Q, and where δ is then defined on subsets of $Q \times Q$, with certain restrictions. This allows for feature structures of the type

(2.40) $\begin{bmatrix} [l_1 & l_2] & l_3 \end{bmatrix}$

where the complex feature structure

$$(2.41) \quad [l_1 \quad l_2]$$

is used as a label. We know of no linguistic application for such structures, however. In the following we shall consider graph structures and acyclic graph structures as already defined, without requiring $V \cap L = \emptyset$.

2.2.4   SUBSUMPTION AND UNIFICATION

'Possible growth patterns' were mentioned above. Such a notion is central to some approaches, hence we need a precise criterion of whether feature structure A 'may grow' into feature structure B.

Basically, there are three ways in which information could be added to a feature structure: the feature structure A in (2.42) may grow into each of B_1, B_2 and B_3.

$$(2.42)$$

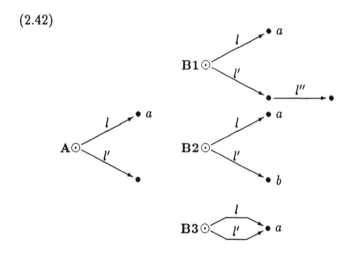

In the transition to B_1 one of the nodes acquires a new feature, in the transition to B_2 a terminal node with no value assigned to it acquires an atomic value, while in B_3 two nodes are identified. Below we define a *subsumption relation* that allows for these three types of growth. (From here on we use the notational convention that 'A' and '$\langle Q^A, q_0^A, \delta^A, \alpha^A \rangle$' refer to the same graph structure, unless there is a specification to the contrary. Similarly for other capital letters).

Definition: Let A and B be graph structures. We say that A is *subsumed by* B, and write $A \sqsubseteq B$, iff there exists a function h from Q^A into Q^B such that

(i) $h(q_0^A) = q_0^B$

(ii)   If $\delta^A(q, l)$ is defined, then $\delta^B(h(q), l)$ is defined, and $\delta^B(h(q), l) = h(\delta^A(q, l))$

(iii)   If $\alpha^A(q)$ is defined, then $\alpha^B(h(q))$ is defined, and $\alpha^B(h(q)) = \alpha^A(q)$.

This definition is adapted from Rounds and Kasper. The function h we call a *homomorphism*.

Possible growth corresponds to conditions that h does not have to meet, thus in the step from A to B_1 h is not surjective and δ^B is defined on more elements than δ^A is. In the step to B_2, α^B is defined on more elements than α^A, while in the step to B_3 h is not injective.

It is easy to check that $\sqsubseteq$ is reflexive and transitive. The subsumption relation gives us a way of comparing feature structures in terms of *information content*. We define $A \equiv B$ to hold iff $A \sqsubseteq B$ and $B \sqsubseteq A$. If $A \equiv B$ then A and B both have the same information content, and they are in a certain sense the same structure. According to the requirement of right identity conditions, we ought in fact to replace A and B both by some object representing a common equivalence class. We shall not do this here, however, but we do note that $\equiv$ is in fact an equivalence relation.

We say that a node q' is *reachable* from q in A if $\delta^A(q, w) = q'$ for some $w \in L^*$. Moreover, a graph structure is *rooted* if every node is reachable from the initial node. Finally, we say that w *exists* in A iff $\delta^A(q_0^A, w)$ is defined. The reader is invited to check that for any graph structures A and B, if A is rooted then $A \sqsubseteq B$ iff for all $w, w' \in L^*$

(i)   if w exists in A then w exists in B;

(ii)   if w exists in A and $\alpha^A(\delta^A(q_0^A, w))$ is defined, then so is $\alpha^B(\delta^B(q_0^B, w))$, and the values are equal;

(iii)   if w and w' both exist in A and $\delta^A(q_0^A, w) = \delta^A(q_0^A, w')$ then also $\delta^B(q_0^B, w) = \delta^B(q_0^B, w')$.

It can be seen that this matches rather closely the informal description given in the introduction.

When two structures are *unified*, the information present in the two structures is combined and a new structure is produced. In terms of subsumption, the new structure should be subsumed by exactly those structures that subsume both the original ones. Unifying A with C_i in (2.43) produces the corresponding B_i in (2.42).

Unification does not always succeed. The structures B_1–B_3 in (2.43) are pairwise non-unifiable. For instance, an attempt to unify B_1 and B_2 would produce something like (2.44):

(2.43)

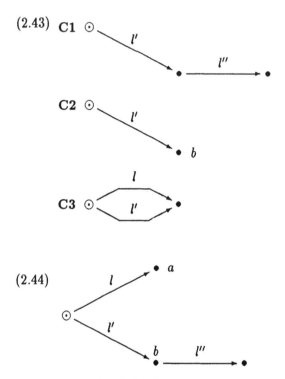

(2.44)

The structure in (2.44) is *not* a graph structure since it violates the condition on the interplay between α and δ, i.e. the requirement that features should not be defined on atomic values. On the other hand, if A and B are *compatible*, i.e. if there exists a structure C such that $A \sqsubseteq C$ and $B \sqsubseteq C$, then unification will succeed, i.e. there exists a structure D such that for all structures C,

(2.45) $D \sqsubseteq C$ iff both $A \sqsubseteq C$ and $B \sqsubseteq C$.

Suppose the graph structures A and B are compatible; we show how to define a structure $A \sqcup B$ with the property of such a D. We shall assume that Q^A and Q^B are disjoint sets. (When not initially true this can be achieved by *renaming*, i.e. by switching to equivalent structures A' and B' that are exactly like A and B in all respects except for the choice of node sets.)

    In informal terms, what we will do is to place the two graph structures alongside each other, and form a new structure containing the nodes of A and B. Then we *merge* those nodes that correspond to each other: the initial nodes correspond to each other, thus the two are merged. Similarly for any two nodes that represent the same atomic value. Then the following iteration is carried out: if q and r have been merged then also q' and r' are merged if for some label l there is an l-arch from q to q', and another one from r to r'.

For a precise formulation of this idea, let Q be $Q^A \cup Q^B$, let δ be $\delta^A \cup \delta^B$, and let α be $\alpha^A \cup \alpha^B$. Thus α is the partial function on Q that behaves like α^A on Q^A and like α^B on Q^B. Similarly for δ. Moreover, let $\approx$ be the smallest equivalence relation on Q such that

(i) $\quad q_0^A \approx q_0^B$;

(ii) $\quad$ if $\alpha(q)$ and $\alpha(r)$ are both defined and equal each other, then $q \approx r$;

(iii) $\quad$ for all l, if $q \approx r$, and $\delta(q,l)$ and $\delta(r,l)$ are both defined, then $\delta(q,l) \approx \delta(r,l)$.

Note that if $A \sqsubseteq C$ and $B \sqsubseteq C$, and h^A and h^B are corresponding homomorphisms, then we have the implication

(2.46) $\quad q \approx r \quad \longrightarrow \quad h(q) = h(r)$

where $h = h^A \cup h^B$.

Now let $Q^{A \cup B}$ be the set of equivalence classes from Q under $\approx$, let $q_0^{A \cup B}$ be $[q_0^A]$, the equivalence class of q_0^A under $\approx$, which is equal to $[q_0^B]$, and define $\delta^{A \cup B}$ and $\alpha^{A \cup B}$ as the smallest partial functions satisfying

(i) $\quad$ if $\delta(q,l)$ is defined, then $\delta^{A \cup B}([q],l) = [\delta(q,l)]$;

(ii) $\quad$ if $\alpha(q)$ is defined, then $\alpha^{A \cup B}([q]) = \alpha(q)$.

Since A and B are compatible, there exist C, h^A and h^B satisfying the implication above. Hence $\alpha^{A \cup B}$ is well-defined, i.e. $\alpha(q) = \alpha(r)$ if both are defined and $q \approx r$. For the same reason, there is no $[q]$ and l such that $\delta^{A \cup B}([q],l)$ and $\alpha^{A \cup B}([q])$ are both defined.

The proof that $A \sqcup B$ is in fact the least upper bound of A and B is straightforward but tedious; we consider instead an example. Suppose A is the graph structure (2.47):

(2.47)

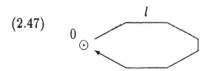

and B is the graph structure (2.48):

(2.48)

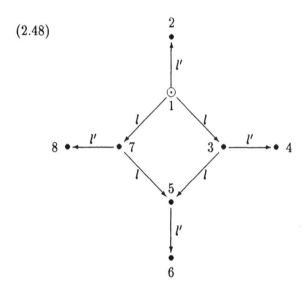

where this time the numbers annotating the nodes should be identified with the nodes themselves. Then the equivalence classes under $\approx$ on $\{0, 1, 2, 3, 4, 5, 6, 7, 8\}$ are the sets $\{0, 1, 3, 5\}$, $\{2, 4, 6\}$, $\{7\}$, $\{8\}$, and the resulting structure can be depicted as (2.49):

(2.49)

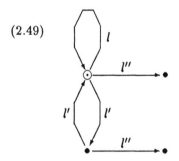

For finite A and B the definition of $A \sqcup B$ is essentially constructive and yields a *unification algorithm* in rough outline.

If A and B are incompatible and unification fails, this can be detected, either through conflicting instances of $\sqcup 2$, or because the resulting structure is not a proper graph structure. The details have been omitted.

In restricted cases one can formulate a concise, recursive algorithm. We define $\langle Q, q_0, \delta, \alpha \rangle$ to be *tree-like* if

(i)   for all $q \in Q$ there exists $w \in L^*$ such that $\delta(q_0, w) = q$, and

(ii)   if $\delta(q_0, w) = \delta(q_0, w')$ then either $w = w'$ or $\delta(q_0, w) \in dom(\alpha)$.

Thus a tree-like graph structure is a rooted graph structure satisfying the additional requirement that no two paths lead to the same node, unless they lead to an atomic value.

If $A = \langle Q, q_0, \delta, \alpha \rangle$ is a graph structure and $\delta(q_0, l)$ is defined, then let A/l be the structure $\langle Q', \delta(q_0, l), \delta', \alpha' \rangle$ where Q' is the set of nodes in Q reachable from $\delta(q_0, l)$, and δ' and α' are the appropriate restrictions of δ and α. Clearly, if A is tree-like then so is A/l.

For tree-like structures A and B, subsumption obeys the following recursive conditions:

(2.50) $A \sqsubseteq B$ iff

> (i)   if $\alpha^A(q_0^A) = a$ then $\alpha^B(q_0^B) = a$, and
>
> (ii)   for all l, if $\delta^A(q_0^A, l)$ is defined, then so is $\delta^B(q_0^B, l)$, and $A/l \sqsubseteq B/l$.

Thus the subsumption relation can be decomposed along matching labels, and much more efficient checking can be provided for. A check of compatibility, i.e. a check of whether A and B are unifiable, goes as follows (A is *complex*, *atomic* or *undefined*, depending on whether $\delta^A(q_0^A, l)$ is defined for some l, $\alpha^A(q_0^A)$ is defined, or neither):

(i)   If A is undefined, then unification succeeds. (Choose B.)

(ii)   If B is undefined, then unification succeeds. (Choose A.)

(iii)   If A is complex and B is atomic, or conversely, then unification fails.

(iv)   If A and B are both atomic, then unification succeeds iff $\alpha^A(q_0^A) = \alpha^B(q_0^B)$.

(v)   If A and B are both complex, then unification succeeds iff unification succeeds for each pair A/l, B/l such that $\delta^A(q_0^A, l)$ and $\delta^B(q_0^B, l)$ are both defined.

In fact a unification algorithm can be written along these lines, but we omit the details here.

2.2.5   DISJUNCTION

Disjunctive specifications have proved to be very useful when feature structures are applied in grammar formalisms. Example (2.51) is borrowed from

Karttunen [111], and is used to represent part of the syntactic information of the German article *die*.

$$(2.51) \quad \begin{bmatrix} \text{AGR} & \left\{ \begin{matrix} \begin{bmatrix} \text{NUM} & \text{SG} \\ \text{GEND} & \text{FEM} \end{bmatrix} \\ \begin{bmatrix} \text{NUM} & \text{PL} \end{bmatrix} \end{matrix} \right\} \\ \text{CASE} & \left\{ \begin{matrix} \text{NOM} \\ \text{ACC} \end{matrix} \right\} \end{bmatrix}$$

The structures inside the braces represent alternative values, hence in this structure the value associated with the AGR label is the *disjunction* between the structures

$$(2.52) \quad A = \begin{bmatrix} \text{NUM} & \text{SG} \\ \text{GEND} & \text{FEM} \end{bmatrix}$$

and

$$(2.53) \quad B = \begin{bmatrix} \text{NUM} & \text{PL} \end{bmatrix}$$

In terms of possible growth patterns, this means that the structure may grow into

$$(2.54) \quad \begin{bmatrix} \text{AGR} & \begin{bmatrix} \text{NUM} & \text{SG} \\ \text{GEND} & \text{FEM} \end{bmatrix} \\ \text{CASE} & \left\{ \begin{matrix} \text{NOM} \\ \text{ACC} \end{matrix} \right\} \end{bmatrix}$$

for instance, but not into

$$(2.55) \quad \begin{bmatrix} \text{AGR} & \begin{bmatrix} \text{NUM} & \text{SG} \\ \text{GEND} & \text{MASC} \end{bmatrix} \\ \text{CASE} & \left\{ \begin{matrix} \text{NOM} \\ \text{ACC} \end{matrix} \right\} \end{bmatrix}$$

since neither A nor B is subsumed by

$$(2.56) \quad \begin{bmatrix} \text{NUM} & \text{SG} \\ \text{GEND} & \text{MASC} \end{bmatrix}$$

Such structures do not fit the formal framework of graph structures. They would, however, if a given node could have more than one outgoing arc annotated with the same label, as in (2.57):

(2.57)

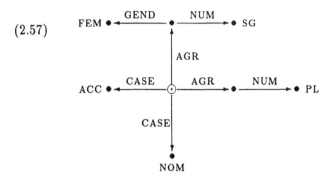

This is the same as allowing δ to be any subset of $(Q \times L) \times Q$, rather than a partial function from $Q \times L$ into Q. But there is more to be done: we must also provide a precise notion of subsumption to go with the generalized structures, and this latter task turns out to be a more challenging one. For instance, the following two structures would seem to be equivalent, and should therefore subsume each other.

$$(2.58) \quad \begin{bmatrix} \text{SUBJ} & \begin{bmatrix} \text{AGR} & \left\{ \begin{bmatrix} \text{NUM} & \text{SG} \\ \text{GEND} & \text{FEM} \end{bmatrix} \atop \begin{bmatrix} \text{NUM} & \text{PL} \end{bmatrix} \right\} \\ \text{CASE} & \text{NOM} \end{bmatrix} \end{bmatrix}$$

$$(2.59) \quad \begin{bmatrix} \text{SUBJ} & \left\{ \begin{bmatrix} \text{AGR} & \begin{bmatrix} \text{NUM} & \text{SG} \\ \text{GEND} & \text{FEM} \end{bmatrix} \\ \text{CASE} & \text{NOM} \end{bmatrix} \atop \begin{bmatrix} \text{AGR} & \begin{bmatrix} \text{NUM} & \text{PL} \end{bmatrix} \\ \text{CASE} & \text{NOM} \end{bmatrix} \right\} \end{bmatrix}$$

The problem is that there seems to be no straightforward generalization of our original definition of $\sqsubseteq$ that will provide such an equivalence in a reasonable way.

Pollard and Sag [182] seem to suggest an alternative treatment where both of the matrices above are considered as notational shorthand for the *set* consisting of the two structures in (2.60):

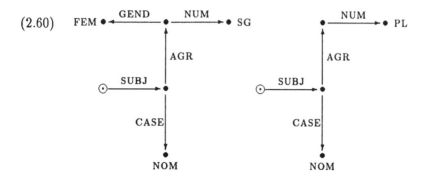

Generalizing subsumption to such disjunctive sets is straightforward. But clearly more needs to be said about how and why the two quite different matrices come to denote the same thing. Not least for computational purposes it will be of interest to develop a *calculus* of such matrices. We turn to this matter in the next subsection.

A totally different approach is outlined by Pereira and Shieber [179]. Instead of graph structures they use the domain theory of Dana Scott to define feature structures. In this context, power domain constructions can be used to give a treatment of indeterminacy and disjunction, but only at the cost of a considerable complexity. A treatment along the lines of domain theory is also quite different in spirit from the more algebraic approach considered here. In particular, the former does not in the same way as the latter provide us with a precise thought model for the feature structures. It will lead too far to attempt any general comparison between the two approaches here, however.

2.2.6 SYNTAX AND SEMANTICS

The difficulties with disjunctive feature structures can be traced back to an insufficient intuitive understanding of their ontological status. Merging two things into one – feature structures themselves and information that restrict their possible growth patterns – we have come up with a hybrid that can be quite useful as long as we can make sufficient sense out of it. But beyond a certain point the theory becomes conceptually simpler if we make the effort to separate the two ingredients explicitly. In particular, when we turn to disjunction we should have at our disposal a partition that enables us to locate this type of indeterminacy in our knowledge about the structures, rather than in the structures themselves.

Feature terms

In the framework of Rounds and Kasper [193] there are two domains: a semantic and a syntactic one. The semantic domain contains graph structures, while in the syntactic domain we find *feature terms* which are used to give partial descriptions of the graph structures. The outline given below is based on both Rounds and Kasper [193] and on Smolka [212].

In addition to the elements of V and L, feature terms may contain the symbols NIL, TOP, $\downarrow$, :, $\vee$, $\wedge$ and parentheses. The syntax is as follows:

(i)   NIL and TOP are feature terms.

(ii)   Any $a \in V$ is a feature term.

(iii)   If $w, w' \in L^*$ then $w \downarrow w'$ is a feature term.

(iv)   If σ is a feature term and $l \in L$, then $(l : \sigma)$ is a feature term.

(v)   If σ and τ are feature terms, then so are $(\sigma \wedge \tau)$ and $(\sigma \vee \tau)$.

When there is no risk of ambiguity we may drop some of the parentheses. A feature term describes a condition on feature structures, for instance the term

(2.61)   AGR:((NUM:SG)$\wedge$(GEND:FEM))

describes the condition satisfied by all and only the feature structures subsuming

(2.62)

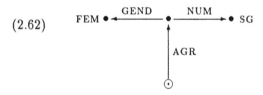

We now give a precise definition of what it means for a graph structure to satisfy a feature term:

(i) $A \models$ NIL for all A.

(ii) $A \models$ TOP for no A.

(iii) $A \models a$ for $a \in V$ iff $\alpha^A(q_0) = a$.

(iv) $A \models w \downarrow w'$ iff $\delta^A(q_0^A, w)$ and $\delta^A(q_0^A, w')$ are both defined and equal each other.

(v) $A \models (l : \sigma)$ iff $\delta^A(q_0^A, l)$ is defined and $A/l \models \sigma$.

(vi) $A \models (\sigma \wedge \tau)$ iff   both $A \models \sigma$ and $A \models \tau$.

(vii) $A \models (\sigma \vee \tau)$ iff   either $A \models \sigma$ or $A \models \tau$.

With this definition, the feature term NIL is totally uninformative. However, it can be quite useful as part of a larger feature term like (OBJ:NIL). The latter is satisfied by A iff $\delta^A(q_0^A, \text{OBJ})$ is defined. A feature term σ is *consistent* iff $A \models \sigma$ for some A. Otherwise σ is *inconsistent*.

The feature term σ *implies* the feature term τ, written $\sigma \gg \tau$, iff any structure that satisfies σ also satisfies τ. $\tau \ll \sigma$ will be used as a notational variant of $\sigma \gg \tau$, while σ and τ are *equivalent*, $\sigma \equiv \tau$, iff they are satisfied by exactly the same structures, i.e. iff both $\sigma \gg \tau$ and $\sigma \ll \tau$.

With this definition, the two feature terms

(2.63)   SUBJ:((AGR:(((NUM:SG) $\wedge$
                        (GEND:FEM)) $\vee$
                  (NUM:PL))) $\wedge$
               (CASE:NOM))

and

(2.64)   SUBJ:(((AGR:((NUM:SG) $\wedge$
                       (GEND:FEM))) $\wedge$
                 (CASE:NOM)) $\vee$
               ((AGR:(NUM:PL)) $\wedge$
                (CASE:NOM)))

are equivalent, since both are satisfied by exactly those graph structures that subsume one of the two structures at the end of the previous section.

There is a clear analogy between the subsumption relation $\sqsubseteq$ and the implication relation $\ll$. Also note that conjunction is to $\ll$ what unification is to $\sqsubseteq$. There is one difference, however. Unification may fail, while the conjunction of two feature terms is always a new feature term. Such feature terms can be inconsistent, however; the analogue of a failed unification is a conjunction producing an inconsistent feature term. If conjunction is to take over the role of unification, then we need an algorithm to check the consistency of feature terms. Rounds and Kasper [193] have designed a calculus of equivalences whereby one can transform any given term into an equivalent term in a certain normal form where inconsistency is displayed explicitly. By the use of equivalences approximately of the forms

$$(2.65) \qquad \varrho \wedge (\sigma \vee \tau) \ \equiv \ (\varrho \wedge \sigma) \vee (\varrho \wedge \tau)$$
$$l : (\sigma \vee \tau) \ \equiv \ (l : \sigma) \vee (l : \tau)$$
$$l : (w \downarrow w') \ \equiv \ lw \downarrow lw'$$
$$a \wedge a' \ \equiv \ \text{TOP}$$
$$a \wedge l : \sigma \ \equiv \ \text{TOP}$$
$$l : \text{TOP} \ \equiv \ \text{TOP}$$
$$(w : \sigma) \wedge (w \downarrow w') \ \equiv \ (w : \sigma) \wedge (w' : \sigma) \wedge (w \downarrow w')$$

etc, one reaches an end result that equals TOP if and only if the original term was inconsistent. The last of the above equivalences uses a metanotational convention whereby '$w : \sigma$', for $w \in L^*$, stands for a proper feature term as specified by the recursive rules (2.66) and (2.67):

$$(2.66) \quad \epsilon : \sigma = \sigma$$

$$(2.67) \quad wl : \sigma = w : (l : \sigma)$$

This calculus, which numbers quite a few more rules than the ones listed, is also complete, in the sense that equivalent terms are transformed to the same normal form. Recall, however, that the structures and feature terms of Rounds and Kasper are slightly different from those considered here.

Attribute-value formulas

In a somewhat different form, the syntactic/semantic division is also explicit in the LFG formalism put forth by Kaplan and Bresnan [105].

Functional descriptions are sets of equations as for instance

$$(2.68) \quad (f_1 \text{ SUBJ}) \ = \ f_2$$
$$(f_2 \text{ NUM}) \ = \ \text{SG}$$

while *functional structures* represent solutions to such equations, as in

$$(2.69) \quad [\text{SUBJ} \quad [\text{NUM} \quad \text{SG}]]$$

The attribute-value logic of Johnson [98] represents a similar approach. The present graph structures are of a less general format than the ones considered by Johnson; we shall restrict the syntax correspondingly:

Terms contain parentheses, labels and atomic values, in addition to *variables* x. The syntax is as follows:

(i)   Any $a \in V$ is a term.

(ii)   If x is a variable and $w \in L^*$, then $x(w)$ is a term.

For a variable x, the 'term' x is notational shorthand for $x(\epsilon)$. Also notice that *feature terms* and *terms* are two different things, and should not be confused with each other.

(i)   *True* and *False* are formulas.

(ii)   If t_1 and t_2 are terms, then $t_1 = t_2$ is a formula.

(iii)   If φ and ψ are formulas, then so are $(\varphi \wedge \psi)$ and $(\varphi \vee \psi)$.

Johnson's formalism also contains negation, but this we shall omit for the time being.

A *variable assignment* for a graph structure A is a function from the set of variables into Q^A.

The denotation $[\![t]\!]_A^\gamma$ of a term t relative to a graph structure A and a variable assignment γ is a node $q \in Q^A$. However, this denotation is not always defined, as seen from the following rules:

(i)   For $a \in V$, $[\![a]\!]_A^\gamma$ is the node $q \in Q^A$ such that $\alpha^A(q) = a$ if such a q exists. Otherwise $[\![a]\!]_A^\gamma$ is undefined. Note that this q is unique as α^A is injective.

(ii)   If x is a variable and $w \in L^*$, then $[\![x(w)]\!]_A^\gamma = \delta^A(\gamma(x), w)$ if $\delta^A(\gamma(x), w)$ is defined. Otherwise it is undefined.

(iii) $A, \gamma \models True$ always.

(iv) $A, \gamma \models False$ never.

(v) $A, \gamma \models t_1 = t_2$ iff $[\![t_1]\!]_A^\gamma$ and $[\![t_2]\!]_A^\gamma$ are both defined, and they equal each other.

(vi) $A, \gamma \models (\varphi \wedge \psi)$ iff $A, \gamma \models \varphi$ and $A, \gamma \models \psi$.

(vii) $A, \gamma \models (\varphi \vee \psi)$ iff $A, \gamma \models \varphi$ or $A, \gamma \models \psi$.

A comparison

The attribute-value formulas of Johnson are not directly comparable to the feature terms of Rounds and Kasper, among other things because of the variables, which have no counterparts in the feature terms. Also note that q_0^A plays no role in the definition of $A, \gamma \models \varphi$. Smolka [212] has explored the relationship between the formulas and the feature terms. Following Smolka in spirit if not in minute details, we define a *feature description* as a pair $x \mid \varphi$, where x is a variable and φ is a formula. Let A be a graph structure, we define $A \models x \mid \varphi$ to hold iff there exists some variable assignment γ such that $\gamma(x) = q_0^A$ and $A, \gamma \models \varphi$. Now there is a correspondence between feature descriptions and feature terms. For instance, the feature description

(2.70) $\quad x \mid x(l) = y \wedge y(l) = y$

and the feature term

(2.71) $\quad l : (\epsilon \downarrow l)$

are both satisfied by the graph structure in (2.72):

(2.72)

In fact, the two are satisfied by exactly the same graph structures, and are thus equivalent. Again following Smolka, we show how to translate a given feature term into an equivalent feature description.

Atomic feature terms can be translated according to the rules of (2.73):

(2.73)
$$
\begin{aligned}
\text{NIL} &\longrightarrow x \mid \textit{True} \\
\text{TOP} &\longrightarrow x \mid \textit{False} \\
a &\longrightarrow x \mid x = a \\
w \downarrow w' &\longrightarrow x \mid x(w) = x(w')
\end{aligned}
$$

In each case, any variable x will do the job. For complex formulas we use the rules of (2.74):

(2.74) $\quad$ If $\quad \sigma \longrightarrow x \mid \varphi$ and

$$\tau \longrightarrow x \mid \psi$$

then

$$(\sigma \wedge \tau) \longrightarrow x \mid (\varphi \wedge \psi)$$

$$(\sigma \lor \tau) \quad \rightarrow \quad x \mid (\varphi \lor \psi)$$
$$(l : \sigma) \quad \rightarrow \quad y \mid y(l) = x \land \varphi$$

provided φ and ψ have no other variables in common than x, and provided y is distinct from x and does not occur in φ. These conditions can easily be met, hence all feature terms are translatable into equivalent feature descriptions. On the other hand, there is no general translation procedure from feature descriptions to feature terms. Consider for instance the feature descriptions

(2.75) $x \mid a = a$

and

(2.76) $x \mid x(l) = a \land y(l) = b \land x(l') = y(l')$

which are satisfied by the graph structures (2.77) and (2.78) respectively.

(2.77) $\odot$ $\bullet \, a$

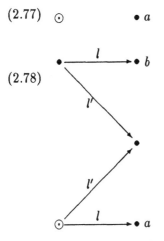

(2.78)

There are no corresponding feature terms. Note, however, that if we add to (2.76) the condition $x(l'') = y$ to get the (non-equivalent) feature description

(2.79) $x \mid x(l) = a \land y(l) = b \land x(l') = y(l') \land x(l'') = y$

which is equivalent to the feature description

(2.80) $x \mid x(l) = a \land x(l''l) = b \land x(l') = x(l''l')$

then we have an equivalent feature term

(2.81) $(l : a) \land (l''l : b) \land (l' \downarrow l''l')$.

Below we define a notion of *rooted* feature descriptions. (2.79) and (2.80) are rooted and therefore equivalent to feature terms, while (2.75) and (2.76) are neither.

Note that (2.80) is of the form $x \mid \varphi$ where φ contains no other variables than x, and contains no occurrences of $a = a$ for any $a \in V$. We first show that all feature descriptions of this type can be translated into feature terms.

If $a = a$ is prohibited and only one variable can be used, then a formula will be built up from atomic formulas of the types $True$, $False$, $x(w) = a$, $a = x(w)$, $x(w) = x(w')$, $a = b$. For the corresponding feature descriptions we have translation rules

$$(2.82) \qquad \begin{aligned} \text{NIL} \quad &\leftarrow \quad x \mid True \\ \text{TOP} \quad &\leftarrow \quad x \mid False \\ w : a \quad &\leftarrow \quad x \mid x(w) = a \\ w : a \quad &\leftarrow \quad x \mid a = x(w) \\ w \downarrow w' \quad &\leftarrow \quad x \mid x(w) = x(w') \\ \text{TOP} \quad &\leftarrow \quad x \mid a = b \end{aligned}$$

while for complex ones we have

$$(2.83) \qquad \begin{aligned} (\sigma \wedge \tau) \quad &\leftarrow \quad x \mid (\varphi \wedge \psi) \\ (\sigma \vee \tau) \quad &\leftarrow \quad x \mid (\varphi \vee \psi) \end{aligned}$$

if $\sigma \leftarrow x \mid \varphi$ and $\tau \leftarrow x \mid \psi$.

Thus we have a translation procedure for this restricted class of feature descriptions. In order to extend the procedure to a larger class, we need some new notions. These are again inspired by Smolka's work. Let φ be a conjunction of atomic formulas. Write

$$(2.84) \quad y \rightarrow_\varphi z$$

if for some $w \in L^*$, φ contains either the conjunct $y(w) = z$ or the conjunct $z = y(w)$. Let $\rightarrow_\varphi^*$ be the reflexive and transitive closure of $\rightarrow_\varphi$ on the set of variables. We say that $x \mid \varphi$ is *strongly rooted* if $x \rightarrow_\varphi^* y$ for all variables y occurring in φ, and φ does not contain a conjunct of the form $a = a$ for any $a \in V$.

For arbitrary formulas φ, we say that $x \mid \varphi$ is *rooted* if φ is equivalent to a formula $\varphi_1 \vee \ldots \vee \varphi_n$ where each φ_i is a conjunction of atomic formulas, and each $x \mid \varphi_i$ is strongly rooted.

In a strongly rooted feature description, occurrences of variables other than the designated one are in a certain sense superfluous. There is a simple procedure to reduce the number of such variables, one at a time, down to zero:

If the number is positive, i.e. if $x \mid \varphi$ contains a variable other than x, then there is a variable y distinct from x such that $x \rightarrow_\varphi y$, i.e. such that φ contains an atomic formula $x(w) = y$ or $y = x(w)$. For a single y there may be several such w; in that case we may pick any one of them. Now replace $x \mid \varphi$ by $x \mid \varphi(x(w)/y)$. The latter formula is derived from φ by substitution of $x(w)$ for all occurrences of y. In such a substitution, the term $y(w')$ will be replaced by $x(ww')$. The resulting feature description is equivalent to the original, has one variable less, and is strongly rooted. The procedure is then repeated until only x remains.

Connecting this up with the translation procedure outlined above, we get a procedure for translating strongly rooted feature descriptions into feature terms. Now, if $x \mid \varphi$ is rooted then $x \mid \varphi$ is equivalent to $x \mid \varphi_1 \vee \ldots \vee \varphi_n$, where each $x \mid \varphi_i$ is strongly rooted. Disjunctions (unlike conjunctions) can be 'pulled out' of a feature description, i.e. for any A

(2.85) $A, \gamma \models x \mid \varphi_1 \vee \ldots \vee \varphi_n$ iff $A, \gamma \models x \mid \varphi_i$ for some i.

Therefore, since each of the $x \mid \varphi_i$ is equivalent to a corresponding σ_i, also $x \mid \varphi_1 \vee \ldots \vee \varphi_n$ is equivalent to $\sigma_1 \vee \ldots \vee \sigma_n$. Hence to every rooted feature description there corresponds an equivalent feature term.

2.2.7 MONOTONICITY AND NEGATION

Feature terms as we have defined them so far are persistent or *monotonic* relative to the graph structures. This means that for any σ, A and B we have the implication

(2.86) $A \models \sigma \ \& \ A \sqsubseteq B \ \rightarrow \ B \models \sigma$

Moreover, for any feature term σ there exists a finite number (possibly zero) of finite graph structures $A_1^\sigma, \ldots, A_n^\sigma$ such that for any B,

(2.87) $B \models \sigma$ iff   for some i, $1 \le i \le n$, $A_i^\sigma \sqsubseteq B$.

Similar results hold for the formulas and feature descriptions considered so far. Rounds and Kasper [193] describe a procedure to find such a characterizing set $\{A_1^\sigma, \ldots, A_n^\sigma\}$ for any feature term σ. We note that if $\{A_1^\sigma, \ldots, A_n^\sigma\}$ characterizes σ and $\{A_1^\tau, \ldots, A_m^\tau\}$ characterizes τ, then

(2.88) $\{A_i^\sigma \sqcup A_j^\tau \mid 1 \le i \le n, \ 1 \le j \le m, \ A_i^\sigma \sqcup A_j^\tau \text{ exists}\}$

characterizes $(\sigma \wedge \tau)$. If one has a particularly efficient unification algorithm for graph structures, then this correspondence can be put to use, for instance in order to check mutual consistency of two feature terms σ and τ, since $(\sigma \wedge \tau)$ will be consistent iff there exist A_i^σ and A_j^τ which unify.

In some cases this type of checking can be more efficient than syntactic manipulations on the feature term $(\sigma \wedge \tau)$. However, in applications with substantial use of disjunction the sets $\{A_1^\sigma, \ldots, A_n^\sigma\}$ and $\{A_1^\tau, \ldots, A_m^\tau\}$ will tend to be large and the algorithm slow. (In the worst case, n will grow exponentially with the length of σ.) In this case well-chosen syntactic manipulations, or operations on data structures incorporating bits of feature terms as well as bits of graph structure, can be more efficient. See Kasper [113] for extensive discussions on this topic.

If σ is a feature term as defined above, and moreover is consistent and does not contain disjunction, then there exists a graph structure A^σ such that for any B, $A^\sigma \sqsubseteq B$ iff $B \models \sigma$. In checking the consistency of a set $\{\sigma_1, \ldots, \sigma_n\}$ of feature terms without occurrences of disjunction, one can find first the structure A^{σ_1}, then add more information to obtain $A^{\sigma_1 \wedge \sigma_2}$, and so on. If the procedure breaks down at any point, then $\sigma_1 \wedge \ldots \wedge \sigma_n$ is inconsistent. Otherwise it is consistent. Each σ_i is considered only once, and the ordering of $\sigma_1, \ldots, \sigma_n$ is without significance.

Classical negation

If we keep the graph structures as they are but add non-monotonic feature terms to the formalism, then things become more complex: if $A \models \sigma$ and $A' \not\models \sigma$ for some A and A' such that $A \sqsubseteq A'$, then clearly an algorithm of the above type will no longer work, since the step from $A^{\sigma_1 \wedge \ldots \wedge \sigma_i}$ to $A^{\sigma_1 \wedge \ldots \wedge \sigma_{i+1}}$ may produce a graph structure that does not satisfy all of $\sigma_1, \ldots, \sigma_i$. Briefly if not quite accurately put, information is no longer accumulative.

This is what happens if we add a classical negation symbol to the formalism, by allowing feature terms $\neg\sigma$ or formulas $\neg\varphi$ such that

(i) $A \models \neg\sigma$ iff *not* $A \models \sigma$

(ii) $A, \gamma \models \neg\varphi$ iff *not* $A, \gamma \models \varphi$

Both Johnson [98] and Smolka [212] consider such negation symbols. For an example, consider the graph structure (2.89):

(2.89)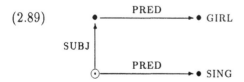

which will satisfy the feature term

(2.90) $\neg((\text{PRED}:\text{SING}) \wedge (\text{OBJ}:\text{NIL}))$

while the subsuming graph structure (2.91) will not.

(2.91)

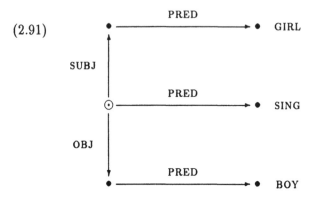

Such a feature term can be useful in some analyses of subcategorization phenomena: we need the ability to express that the first graph structure is acceptable and the second not, despite the fact that it subsumes the first.

In this example a particular type of growth is prohibited, namely the acquisition of an OBJ transition from the initial node. In other applications the restrictions may concern a different type of growth. In particular, one may want to ensure that the value associated with a particular label should be distinct from a certain atomic value, as in the example structure

$$(2.92) \quad [\text{CASE} \quad \neg\text{DAT}]$$

borrowed from Karttunen [111]. This is not an acceptable graph structure as we have defined it. Using feature terms, we would write (CASE:¬DAT). This feature term is satisfied by those graph structures that subsume (2.93) and at the same time do not subsume (2.94).

(2.93) $\odot \xrightarrow{\quad\text{CASE}\quad} \bullet$

(2.94) $\odot \xrightarrow{\quad\text{CASE}\quad} \bullet\text{DAT}$

Monotonic negation

Despite the observations about non-monotonicity, there is nothing intrinsically wrong with classical negation. In particular, when computation is carried out with formulas or feature terms rather than with feature structures, and conjunction takes over the role of unification while subsumption is put aside as a peripheral notion, then monotonicity becomes unimportant as well.

However, if one wishes to retain monotonicity, then it is still possible to have some form of negation. In fact, in restricted cases we can allow classical negation into our current framework without risking non-monotonicity. For instance, the structure (2.95):

(2.95)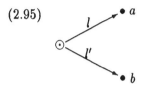

satisfies $\neg(l \downarrow l')$, and so does every structure that subsumes it. But in general we will have to revise the notion of a feature structure, so that more negative information can be represented in the structure. In other words, more knowledge about possible growth patterns will have to be integrated in the structure itself. This is done most explicitly by Moshier and Rounds [158], who give an account of negation along the lines of intuitionistic logic. In this treatment, graph structures are replaced by pairs $(A, \mathcal{K})$ of graph structures A and sets $\mathcal{K}$ of graph structures. The latter are to be thought of as the *acceptable* graph structures, the structures into which A may be allowed to grow.

$(A, \mathcal{K}) \models \neg\sigma$ is defined to hold iff there is no $B \in \mathcal{K}$ such that $A \sqsubseteq B$ and $(B, \mathcal{K}) \models \sigma$. For other connectives the definition of $\models$ is unchanged. Thus if A is the graph structure (2.96):

(2.96)

```
        PRED
  •----------------→• GIRL
  ↑
SUBJ |
  |     PRED
  ⊙----------------→• SING
```

and $\mathcal{K}$ contains no graph structure both subsuming A and with an OBJ-transition from the initial node, then

(2.97) $(A, \mathcal{K}) \models \neg((\text{PRED}:\text{SING}) \wedge (\text{OBJ}:\text{NIL}))$.

At the same time this definition ensures monotonicity in a sense, since for any $A, B \in \mathcal{K}$ and feature term σ, $(A, \mathcal{K}) \models \sigma$ and $A \sqsubseteq B$ imply $(B, \mathcal{K}) \models \sigma$. This suggests a definition of

(2.98) $(A, \mathcal{K}) \sqsubseteq (A', \mathcal{K}')$

by the condition

(2.99) $\mathcal{K} = \mathcal{K}' \& A, A' \in \mathcal{K} \& A \sqsubseteq A'$

but less restricted notions are possible and also more natural.

A feature term is defined to be consistent iff $(A, \mathcal{K}) \models \sigma$ for some A and $\mathcal{K}$. Moshier and Rounds present a complete tableau calculus for proving consistency of feature terms. If σ is consistent, a pair $(A, \mathcal{K})$ is produced such that $(A, \mathcal{K}) \models \sigma$.

Sketch of an alternative

A simpler if not quite so powerful technique is to mark each node in a graph structure with the labels that it may not acquire. In this case, we define an extended graph structure to be a quintuple $\langle Q, q_0, \delta, \alpha, \pi \rangle$, where Q, q_0, δ and α are as before, and where π is a function from Q to subsets of L, such that for any $q \in Q$ and $l \in L$, if $l \in \pi(q)$ then $\delta(q, l)$ is not defined. Now we may define

(2.100) $\langle Q, q_0, \delta, \alpha, \pi \rangle \models \neg(l : \sigma)$

to hold iff either

(i) $l \in \pi(q_0)$, or

(ii) $\delta(q_0, l)$ is defined and $\langle Q, \delta(q_0, l), \delta, \alpha, \pi \rangle \models \neg \sigma$.

Moreover, we let $A \models \neg(\sigma \wedge \tau)$ iff $A \models \neg \sigma$ or $A \models \neg \tau$, etc. Now consider (2.101):

(2.101)

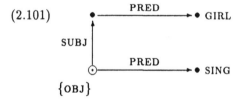

where the annotation $\{\text{OBJ}\}$ indicates that $\pi(q_0) = \{\text{OBJ}\}$. The graph structure depicted satisfies the feature term $\neg((\text{PRED:SING}) \wedge (\text{OBJ:NIL}))$. Moreover, if we add the requirement $\pi^A(q) \subseteq \pi^B(h(q))$ to our definition of $A \sqsubseteq B$, then we still have monotonicity. For a fuller account of this approach, see Langholm [134].

This does not give us a treatment of the feature term $(\text{CASE:}\neg\text{DAT})$, however. To represent such negations, we may introduce a complement-forming operation on the set of atomic values. In this case $A \models \neg a$ iff $\alpha(q_0) = \tilde{a}$, where $\tilde{a}$ is the complement of A. Once we have this, however, we would also want to say that $\widetilde{\text{DAT}}$ may grow into ACC, for instance. This points towards a treatment where even more structure is imposed on the atomic values, perhaps even a full Boolean algebra, somewhat in the same spirit that semilattices are used in Smolka [212].

2.2.8 FURTHER DIRECTIONS: SET VALUES AND FUNCTIONAL UNCERTAINTY

Set values

In preceding sections, set notations were used to depict feature structures with disjunctive values, as in

$$(2.102) \quad \begin{bmatrix} \text{AGR} & \left\{ \begin{bmatrix} \text{NUM} & \text{SG} \\ \text{GEND} & \text{FEM} \end{bmatrix} \\ \begin{bmatrix} \text{NUM} & \text{PL} \end{bmatrix} \right\} \\ \text{CASE} & \left\{ \begin{matrix} \text{NOM} \\ \text{ACC} \end{matrix} \right\} \end{bmatrix}$$

In other connections an extended format has been proposed where values can be *sets* of feature structures, as in (2.103), which is borrowed from Colban [37].

$$(2.103) \quad \begin{bmatrix} \text{IND} & \text{IND.2} \\ \text{COND} & \left\{ \begin{bmatrix} \text{REL} & \prec \\ \text{ARG.1} & \text{IND.2} \\ \text{ARG.2} & \text{IND.0} \end{bmatrix} \\ \begin{bmatrix} \text{REL} & on \\ \text{ARG.1} & \text{IND.2} \\ \text{ARG.2} & \begin{bmatrix} \text{IND} & \text{IND.4} \\ \text{COND} & \begin{bmatrix} \text{REL} & table \\ \text{ARG.1} & \text{IND.4} \\ \text{POL} & 1 \end{bmatrix} \\ \text{SPEC} & \text{THE} \end{bmatrix} \end{bmatrix} \right\} \end{bmatrix}$$

Superficially these look very much the same, but the intentions and interpretations are quite different. In the latter case, the use of set notations should be taken at face value; associated with the COND label is the *set* itself and not some unfinished object whose further history is constrained by a set of alternative values.

Suggested applications of set-valued feature structures in the area of grammar formalisms are analyses of adjuncts in LFG (Kaplan and Bresnan [105]) and situation schema theory (Colban [37]), and more recently constituent coordination in LFG, Kaplan and Maxwell [108]. Set values are also used extensively by Pollard and Sag [182].

An extended format of graph structures accommodating set values has been suggested by W. Rounds (forthcoming). The extended graph structures are quintuples $\langle Q, q_0, \delta, \alpha, \to_\epsilon \rangle$ where $\to_\epsilon$ is a binary relation on Q. The intended interpretation of $q \to_\epsilon q'$ is that q represents a set, one of the elements of which is represented by q'. From this we obtain graph structures of the type in (2.104):

(2.104)

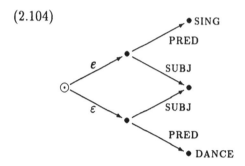

which represents part of the syntactic information in a sentence like *Mary sang and danced*. This would satisfy the feature description

$$(2.105) \quad x \mid y \in x \wedge z \in x \wedge y(\text{PRED}) \;=\; \text{SING}$$
$$\wedge z(\text{PRED}) \;=\; \text{DANCE}$$
$$\wedge y(\text{SUBJ}) \;=\; z(\text{SUBJ})$$

where $A, \gamma \models y \in x$ is defined to hold iff $\gamma(x) \rightarrow_\epsilon \gamma(y)$.

The syntax of feature terms is extended correspondingly. Different types of subsumption may be appropriate for different applications. Rounds considers *Hoare* subsumption and *Smyth* subsumption, which are derived from alternative power domain constructions in domain theory. Reportedly, yet other subsumption relations are currently being considered by C. Pollard and M. Moshier. For a discussion of subsumption relations between set expressions from a somewhat different but related perspective, see Langholm [133].

Functional uncertainty

Recently a quantificational mechanism has been introduced in the LFG formalism, motivated by so-called long-distance dependency phenomena, cf. Kaplan and Zaenen [109]. In the sentence

(2.106) *Mary John telephoned yesterday.*

borrowed from Kaplan and Zaenen, Mary is the *topic* of the sentence. There is no NP in the postverbal position where an object would normally be expected, and the topic is allowed to take over this function, as can be specified by the equation

(2.107) $x(\text{TOPIC}) = x(\text{OBJ})$.

However, this identity is not a necessary one, as seen from the sentence

(2.108) *Mary John claimed that Bill telephoned yesterday.*

where instead the topic is the complement's object, so that we should rather have a disjunction

(2.109) $x(\text{TOPIC}) = x(\text{OBJ}) \lor x(\text{TOPIC}) = x(\text{COMP.OBJ})$.

But this is not sufficient either, since we can easily iterate the construction to get a sentence like

(2.110) *Mary John claimed that Bill said that Henry telephoned yesterday.*

where we now have the identity

(2.111) $x(\text{TOPIC}) = x(\text{COMP.COMP.OBJ})$

and so on. This gives us an indeterminate disjunction

(2.112) $\quad x(\text{TOPIC}) \quad = \quad x(\text{COMP}) \lor$
$\qquad\quad x(\text{TOPIC}) \quad = \quad x(\text{COMP.OBJ}) \lor$
$$\vdots$$
$\qquad\quad x(\text{TOPIC}) \quad = \quad x(\text{COMP}^n.\text{OBJ}) \lor$
$$\vdots$$

which can be summed up as

(2.113) $\exists n \geq 0 (x(\text{TOPIC}) = x(\text{COMP}^n.\text{OBJ}))$.

What Kaplan and Zaenen propose is the use of set expressions in place of single paths; in the present formalism this would mean the introduction of terms of the type $x(p)$, where p stands for a (possibly infinite) set of paths. In the example considered, we would use the set expression 'COMP*OBJ', which denotes the infinite set

(2.114) $\{\text{OBJ}, \text{COMP.OBJ}, \text{COMP.COMP.OBJ}, \dots\}$.

The formula $x(\text{TOPIC}) = x(\text{COMP}^*\text{OBJ})$ is true iff there is some path $w \in \text{COMP}^*\text{OBJ}$ such that $x(\text{TOPIC}) = x(w)$.

It is assumed that the set denoted by p is drawn from the class of regular languages. The computational consequences of such an extension is explored by Kaplan and Maxwell [107].

2.3   REPRESENTATIONS AND INTERPRETATIONS

Representations must interact with the model theory, otherwise there will be no computational semantics. This was our claim in the introduction. We have at length studied the representational part of the enterprise; we now have an obligation to matters of interpretation and knowledge representation.

We have built a representational format which in a certain sense exhibits the 'logical form' of a linguistic utterance without ending up in the 'tightness' of a specific logical formalism. To formalize is perhaps an occupational hazard of the logician and could create a false ideal for those who want to use logic as a tool.

But this is a hazard to fight. It is always the model theory, the insight into some specific domain of knowledge, which should be the driving force. The formal language and the associated proof theory are only tools to 'tame' the meaning part, e.g. in constructing an efficient inference mechanism for the semantics.

Higher order logic may be a valuable tool in unravelling complexities of natural languages, but an alternative approach seems better adapted for our present task.

A *conceptual space* has a number of *quality dimensions*,

$$(2.115) \quad A = (D_1, D_2, \ldots, D_n),$$

where each D_i is a separate quality, e.g. colour, weight, space, time, temperature, mass, ... It is always assumed that each quality dimension has some topological or metrical structure.

The notion of a conceptual space has roots both in 'formal' physics, i.e., in the modelling process in natural sciences, and in 'naive' physics, i.e., in the modelling process in AI and knowledge representation theory. The importance of the present point of view has been argued by P. Gärdenfors [62]. It is also tied up with the renewed interest in many-sorted logic within AI, see A. Cohn [36]. We shall not aim at a full exposition of these topics, but turn to a two-sorted partial logic for space-time processes.

2.3.1   LOGICS OF SITUATIONS AND PARTIAL INFORMATION

First order logic is a theory of great elegance and depth. But as a knowledge representation tool it has its limitations. To cope with a mixture of quality dimensions we need a many-sorted theory. We also meet issues of partiality and problems concerning growth of information. We shall in this section describe a semantics better suited to deal with these matters.

Situations and basic facts

A central notion will be that of *basic facts*. These come in several varieties. Typically, a basic fact states that a certain relation holds (or does not hold) among certain individuals at some space-time location. This calls for three sets of primitives: *relations (R), locations (L) and individuals (D)*. We use the format

(2.116) $at\ l:\ r, a_1, \ldots, a_n; 1$

to express that at the location l in L the relation r in R holds of the individuals $a_1, \ldots, a_n$ in D. Substituting 0 for 1 we obtain the dual fact, that the relation does *not* hold among the given individuals at the specified location. The facts of this first variety we call *located*, since a location is specified. *Unlocated* facts are of the type

(2.117) $r, a_1, \ldots, a_n; i$

where i is 0 or 1. These typically involve a relation of a more permanent kind, such as that of a_1 being the mother of a_2. To such relations time and place are irrelevant, hence they do not enter into the corresponding facts.

Certainly these are not all the varieties of basic facts that can be envisaged. In this exposition we include a third type, to express relations between locations, viz. temporal overlap and temporal precedence. Thus, the location fact

(2.118) $l\ overlap\ l'$

states that the two space-time locations l and l' have a temporal overlap. Such a fact can be useful for analyzing sentences in the present tense.

A *situation* determines (or *contains*) a set of located and/or unlocated facts. We write

(2.119) $in\ s:\ at\ l:\ r, a_1, \ldots, a_n; 1$

or

(2.120) $in\ s:\ at\ l:\ r, a_1, \ldots, a_n; 0$

if the fact following the first colon is contained in the situation s. Similarly for unlocated facts.

A situation may be *partial* in the sense that many (or most) issues will not be settled either way by the situation, i.e. for several r and $a_1, \ldots, a_n$ the situation s may contain neither of the facts

(2.121) $r, a_1, \ldots, a_n; 1$

$r, a_1, \ldots, a_n; 0.$

Similar considerations hold for located facts. A situation is thus a kind of restricted, partial model (data base) containing a limited collection of facts.

The choice of basic attributes in a *situation schema* matches the structure of basic facts, as shown in (2.122):

$$
(2.122)\ (a)\ \begin{bmatrix} \text{REL} & - \\ \text{ARG.1} & - \\ \vdots & \vdots \\ \text{ARG.N} & - \\ \text{LOC} & - \\ \text{POL} & - \end{bmatrix} \quad (b)\ \begin{bmatrix} \text{REL} & - \\ \text{ARG.1} & - \\ \vdots & \vdots \\ \text{ARG.N} & - \\ \text{POL} & - \end{bmatrix} \quad (c)\ \begin{bmatrix} \text{REL} & - \\ \text{ARG.1} & - \\ \text{ARG.2} & - \end{bmatrix}
$$

In (2.122a) and (2.122b), the attributes REL, ARG.1, ..., ARG.n and LOC correspond to the primitives of relations, individuals and locations. POL, abbreviating polarity, takes the value 1 or 0. The values in the matrices are either atomic or embedded attribute-value matrices. The value of the attribute LOC is always complex.

The reader is referred to Fenstad et al. [56] for a complete exposition of the basic theory. The basic reference on Situation Theory is Barwise and Perry [15].

Meaning and interpretation

The interpretation of a situation schema in a situation structure is always relative to an 'utterance' situation u and a 'described' situation s. The utterance situation is further decomposed into a discourse situation d and a speaker's connection c. The former provides information about who the speaker is, who the addressee is, the sentence uttered, and the discourse location in space and time; the latter is a map which fixes the speaker's meaning of lexical items. The *meaning* of a sentence φ is a relation between an utterance situation d, c and a described situation s, and we use the situation schema computable from the syntactic form of φ to express this relation. We write this as

$(2.123)\ d, c[\![\text{SIT}.\varphi]\!]s,$

where SIT.φ is the situation schema computed from φ. We shall give a simple example to illustrate the above concepts. Our sample sentence will be

$(2.124)\ \varphi$: *John is running*.

The situation schema of this sentence is given by (2.125):

$$(2.125) \quad \text{SIT}.\varphi \quad \begin{bmatrix} \text{REL} & run \\ \text{ARG}.1 & John \\ \text{LOC} & \begin{bmatrix} \text{IND} & \text{IND}.1 \\ \text{COND} & \begin{bmatrix} \text{REL} & \circ \\ \text{ARG}.1 & \text{IND}.1 \\ \text{ARG}.2 & \text{IND}.0 \end{bmatrix} \end{bmatrix} \\ \text{POL} & 1 \end{bmatrix}$$

The atomic values IND.0 and IND.1 are called *indeterminates*. Let d, c be an utterance situation. A map g defined on the set of indeterminates of SIT.φ.LOC with values in the set L of locations is called an *anchor* on SIT.φ.LOC relative to d, c if

$(2.126) \quad g(\text{IND}.0) = l_d$

and

$(2.127) \quad g(\text{IND}.1) \ overlap \ l_d$

where l_d is the discourse location determined by d. (Hence the relation symbol $\circ$ is interpreted as *overlap*.) Relative to a described situation s we now have

$(2.128) \quad d, c [\![\text{SIT}.\varphi]\!] s$

if and only if there exists an anchor g on SIT.φ.LOC relative to d, c such that

$(2.129) \quad in \ s: \ at \ g(\text{IND}.1): \ c(run), \ c(John); \ 1.$

Observe that the speaker's connection is a map defined on the (morphological) parts of the expression φ and with values in the appropriate domains, i.e. $c(run)$ is an element of R and $c(John)$ is an element of D.

Formal logic

In Fenstad et al. [56] we carried through a rather complete mathematical study of model structures $\langle S, L, precede, R, D \rangle$, where S is some set of situations. (The two temporal relations were interpreted in such a way as to make *overlap* definable from *precede*, thus only one need be specified by any given model.) In particular, the reader will find several axiomatization theorems, providing complete inference systems for some two-sorted formal languages based on the above semantics of partial information. The basic language L_3 of the 1987 book has atomic formulas such as

$(2.130) \quad R(\ell, t_1, \ldots, t_n) \qquad R'(t_1, \ldots, t_n) \qquad \ell_1 \prec \ell_2$

where R, R' are relation symbols, ℓ, ℓ_1, ℓ_2 location variables or constants, and $t_1, \ldots, t_n$ individual variables or constants. Such formulas are evaluated relative to the situations s of S, and relative to interpretations ξ of the contained symbols. Thus $R(\ell, t_1, \ldots, t_n)$ is *supported* by s relative to ξ if s contains the fact

(2.131) $at\ \xi(\ell) : \xi(R), \xi(t_1), \ldots, \xi(t_n)$; 1.

and *refuted* if s contains the dual fact

(2.132) $at\ \xi(\ell) : \xi(R), \xi(t_1), \ldots, \xi(t_n)$; 0.

L_3 also contains *complex* formulas, which are built up from the atomic ones by a standard use of quantifiers $\forall, \exists$ and sentential connectives $\wedge, \vee, \neg, \sim$. Note that there are *two* negation symbols, the strong negation ($\neg$) and the weak negation ($\sim$). A situation supports $\neg\varphi$ iff it refutes φ, and supports $\sim \varphi$ iff it does not support φ. Because situations are partial, the two negations are not equivalent. Of the two, strong negation is the 'reliable' one. Weak negation is related to such notions as negation by failure. The relation between the two negation symbols is discussed further by Langholm [132].

A *Hilbert style* axiomatization was given to characterize the valid inferences *internal* to a situation, i.e. inferences of the form

(2.133) if s supports φ, then s supports ψ.

This can be expressed by the formula $\varphi \supset \psi$. The list of axiom schemata includes familiar ones like

(2.134) $\qquad (\varphi \wedge \psi) \quad \supset \quad \varphi$

$\qquad\qquad (\neg\varphi \wedge \neg\psi) \quad \supset \quad \neg(\varphi \vee \psi)$

$\qquad\qquad\qquad \varphi(t/x) \quad \supset \quad \exists x \varphi$

as well as schemata that reflect the partial perspective. Thus the axiom schema $\neg\varphi \supset \sim \psi$ captures the structural requirement that no situation shall both support and refute one and the same atomic formula, i.e. it shall not contain both a fact and its dual. Finally, there are special 'geometric' axiom schemata like $\sim (\ell \prec \ell)$, justified by corresponding structural conditions on the models. The relation symbol $\prec$ is interpreted as *precede*, thus the axiom says that no location shall precede itself temporally.

Together with the derivation rule of modus ponens and a pair of rules for the introduction of existential and universal quantifiers, the axioms provide a *complete* system, in the sense that all and only the formulas supported by all situations are theorems of the system. In theory, such an axiom system can be implemented on a computer, and programs can be written that will enumerate all the theorems in an infinite list. But for practical purposes this is worthless. Algorithms based on vastly different types of axiomatization are used by virtually all automated theorem provers for first order logic and its variants. In part, the reason can be traced to the very powerful rule of modus ponens, which says that ψ is a theorem if both φ and $\varphi \supset \psi$ are. Here the antecedent φ can be any formula whatsoever. In trying to prove ψ via modus ponens, we must choose a suitable antecedent φ, and then try to prove each of φ and $\varphi \supset \psi$. Most rule applications are in fact instances of modus ponens, thus the entire proof turns into little more than a series of enlightened choices for such antecedents. Consequently an automated theorem prover would have to include as its most important component a technique to choose the antecent formula in a profitable way. The axiom system itself says nothing about such techniques, however, and indeed all the complexities of first order logic would have to be involved.

Thus for computational reasons it is of interest to consider other forms of axiomatization as well. *Gentzen sequent calculi* are characterized by a very small number of axiom schemata (typically one) and a large number of rules, each of very limited applicability. Typically, a sequent calculus for classical first order logic is based on pairs Γ, Δ, where Γ and Δ are multisets of formulas. (Alternatively, they are sequences or ordinary sets. Multisets, or 'bags', are similar to sets, except that multiple memberships are counted.) Such pairs are called sequents. The idea is to capture in an axiom system the inference relation $\models$.

Definition: $\Gamma \models \Delta$ iff for every model M, if M supports all formulas of Γ then M supports some formula of Δ.

With this very general format, one can reduce a valid inference of the form

(2.135) $(\varphi \wedge \psi) \models (\psi \vee \chi)$

to

(2.136) $\varphi, \psi \models \psi, \chi.$

The whole derivation system is based on such reductions. Thus there are corresponding derivation rules

(2.137) $\quad \dfrac{\Gamma, \varphi, \psi \models \Delta}{\Gamma, (\varphi \wedge \psi) \models \Delta} \qquad \dfrac{\Gamma \models \Delta, \psi, \chi}{\Gamma \models \Delta, (\psi \vee \chi)}$

In each case, the lower sequent is valid if the upper is, for any choice of $\Gamma, \Delta, \varphi, \psi, \chi$. The notation Γ, φ, ψ is shorthand for $\Gamma \cup \{\varphi, \psi\}$, etc. Hence if we choose Γ to be $\{\varphi, \psi\}$ and Δ to be the empty set, then the second rule will take us from (2.136) to

(2.138) $\varphi, \psi \models (\psi \vee \chi)$

while a subsequent application of the first rule will take us one step further, to (2.135).

The axioms are of the form

(2.139) $\Gamma, \psi \models \Delta, \psi$

These are valid for the trivial reason that ψ is true whenever it is true. We observe that (2.136) is of this form Hence we have a *proof* of (2.135), from the axiom (2.136) through (2.138) by two applications of the inference rules.

Note that these rules are 'deterministic' in both directions in a way that modus ponens is not. In trying to prove (2.135) 'backwards' in the system outlined so far, we would have to choose which rule to try first, but beyond that the system itself would tell us what to do. In essence, that is why sequent calculi are better suited for automated theorem provers. As more and stronger rules are added, the freedom of choice increases and the old problems gradually reappear. Still, they do so in a better understood way. Note, by the way, that the two rules would not be fully 'deterministic' in both directions if Γ and Δ were *sets* rather than multisets.

In classical logic the models are complete. This means that a model refutes a formula iff it does not support it. Hence in classical logic there is an alternative, equivalent definition of $\models$.

Definition: $\Gamma \models \Delta$ iff for every model M, either M refutes some formula of Γ or M supports some formula of Δ.

Moreover, a model supports $\neg\varphi$ iff it refutes φ, and refutes $\neg\varphi$ iff it supports φ. Hence the following derivation rules are valid.

(2.140) $$\frac{\Gamma, \varphi \models \Delta}{\Gamma \models \Delta, \neg\varphi} \qquad \frac{\Gamma \models \Delta, \varphi}{\Gamma, \neg\varphi \models \Delta}$$

Indeed, these are the rules for negation given by G. Gentzen himself in the calculus *LK* for classical logic, cf. (Szabo [218]). It is the equivalence of the two definitions that allows for this very elegant treatment of negation. When we turn to situations or partial models, the two definitions are no longer equivalent, since it is possible for such a model neither to support nor refute a formula. Hence the first of the two derivation rules is no longer valid and cannot be used. Still, we need a rule approximately of this form, to prove relations like

(2.141) $\neg\varphi \models \neg(\varphi \wedge \psi)$

The solution is to expand the format of a sequent to obtain a common generalization of the two definitions above. Thus

(2.142) $$\frac{\Gamma \mid \Delta}{\Pi \mid \Sigma}$$

says that for every model M, if M supports all members of Γ and refutes all members of Π, then M supports some member of Δ or refutes some member of Σ. Now the first definition of $\Gamma \models \Delta$ corresponds to

$$(2.143) \quad \frac{\Gamma \mid \Delta}{\mid}$$

while the second definition of $\Gamma \models \Delta$ corresponds to

$$(2.144) \quad \frac{\mid \Delta}{\mid \Gamma}$$

Strong negation is treated by the following four rules

$$(2.145) \quad \frac{\Gamma \mid \Delta, \varphi}{\Pi \mid \Sigma} \qquad \frac{\Gamma \mid \Delta}{\Pi \mid \Sigma, \varphi} \qquad \frac{\Gamma, \varphi \mid \Delta}{\Pi \mid \Sigma} \qquad \frac{\Gamma \mid \Delta}{\Pi, \varphi \mid \Sigma}$$

$$\frac{\Gamma \mid \Delta}{\Pi \mid \Sigma, \neg\varphi} \qquad \frac{\Gamma \mid \Delta, \neg\varphi}{\Pi \mid \Sigma} \qquad \frac{\Gamma \mid \Delta}{\Pi, \neg\varphi \mid \Sigma} \qquad \frac{\Gamma, \neg\varphi \mid \Delta}{\Pi \mid \Sigma}$$

In general, there are four rules for each connective or quantifier – one for each of the four 'quadrants'. Before we proceed with the remaining derivation rules, however, we owe the reader a few more words about the model theory.

To simplify matters we shall leave the language L_3 and limit ourselves to a one-sorted language without the location variables and location constants. Hence only the unlocated facts can be expressed. The smaller language contains variables $x_1, x_2, \ldots$, constants $c_1, c_2, \ldots$ and relation symbols $R, R', \ldots$, each of which is assigned a natural number as its *arity*. The variables and constants together make up the *terms*; if R has arity n and $t_1, \ldots, t_n$ are terms, then $R(t_1, \ldots, t_n)$ is an atomic formula. We shall return to the connectives and quantifiers later.

We consider *partial models* that mimic situations. A model M is a pair $\langle D, \zeta \rangle$ where D is some non-empty set and ζ is a function that maps the constants into D. ζ is also defined on the relation symbols. If R has arity n then $\zeta(R)$ is a pair $\langle R_M^+, R_M^- \rangle$, where R_M^+ and R_M^- are disjoint subsets of D^n. A membership

$$(2.146) \quad \langle a_1, \ldots, a_n \rangle \in R_M^+$$

is our version of a positive fact

$$(2.147) \quad \zeta(R), a_1, \ldots, a_n; 1,$$

while a membership

$$(2.148) \quad \langle a_1, \ldots, a_n \rangle \in R_M^-$$

is our version of a negative fact

(2.149) $\zeta(R), a_1, \ldots, a_n; 0$.

Since R_M^+ and R_M^- are disjoint, a model never contains both a fact and its dual. To handle variables we introduce variable assignments; these are functions from the variables into D.

The interpretation t^{Mg} of a term t relative to the model M and the variable assignment g is $\zeta(t)$ if t is a constant and $g(t)$ if t is a variable. The pair M, g *supports* $R(t_1, \ldots, t_n)$, written

(2.150) $M \models^+ R(t_1, \ldots, t_n)[g]$, iff $\langle t_1^{Mg}, \ldots, t_n^{Mg} \rangle \in R_M^+$,

and *refutes* $R(t_1, \ldots, t_n)$, written

(2.151) $M \models^- R(t_1, \ldots, t_n)[g]$, iff $\langle t_1^{Mg}, \ldots, t_n^{Mg} \rangle \in R_M^-$.

The definition of

$$(2.152) \quad \frac{\Gamma \mid \Delta}{\Pi \mid \Sigma}$$

is the one above, only with the refinement that 'all pairs M, g' should be substituted for 'all M'.

We are now ready to list the axioms. This time they come in three different varieties, given by the three axiom schemata

$$(2.153) \quad \frac{\Gamma, \varphi \mid \Delta, \varphi}{\Pi \mid \Sigma} \qquad \frac{\Gamma \mid \Delta}{\Pi, \varphi \mid \Sigma, \varphi} \qquad \frac{\Gamma, \varphi \mid \Delta}{\Pi, \varphi \mid \Sigma}$$

where φ is an atomic formula. The first two are justified by the trivial implications

(2.154) $M \models^+ \varphi[g] \rightarrow M \models^+ \varphi[g] \qquad M \models^- \varphi[g] \rightarrow M \models^- \varphi[g]$,

while the third is slightly less trivial and rests on the observation that

(2.155) $M \models^+ \varphi[g]$ and $M \models^- \varphi[g]$

are mutually exclusive – this because of the requirement that R_M^+ and R_M^- be disjoint.

The negation symbols have the following semantics:

$$(2.156) \quad \begin{aligned} M &\models^+ \neg\varphi[g] & \text{iff} \quad M &\models^- \varphi[g] \\ M &\models^- \neg\varphi[g] & \text{iff} \quad M &\models^+ \varphi[g] \\ M &\models^+ \sim\varphi[g] & \text{iff} \quad M &\not\models^+ \varphi[g] \\ M &\models^- \sim\varphi[g] & \text{iff} \quad M &\models^+ \varphi[g] \end{aligned}$$

The derivation rules for strong negation we have already considered; for weak negation we get

$$(2.157) \quad \frac{\Gamma \mid \Delta, \varphi}{\Pi \mid \Sigma} \qquad \frac{\Gamma, \varphi \mid \Delta}{\Pi \mid \Sigma} \qquad \frac{\Gamma, \varphi \mid \Delta}{\Pi \mid \Sigma} \qquad \frac{\Gamma \mid \Delta, \varphi}{\Pi \mid \Sigma}$$

$$\frac{\Gamma \mid \Delta}{\Pi \mid \Sigma, \sim \varphi} \qquad \frac{\Gamma \mid \Delta, \sim \varphi}{\Pi \mid \Sigma} \qquad \frac{\Gamma \mid \Delta}{\Pi, \sim \varphi \mid \Sigma} \qquad \frac{\Gamma, \sim \varphi \mid \Delta}{\Pi \mid \Sigma}$$

For an atomic formula φ, we can now combine an axiom and two rules in a *proof*.

$$(2.158) \qquad \frac{\varphi \mid}{\varphi \mid}$$

$$\frac{\mid \sim \varphi}{\varphi \mid}$$

$$\frac{\neg \varphi \mid \sim \varphi}{\mid}$$

There is a close correspondence between the semantics of a connective and its derivation rules; here we shall include only one more to illustrate the point.

$(2.159) \quad M \models^+ (\varphi \wedge \psi)[g] \quad$ iff $\quad M \models^+ \varphi[g]$ and $M \models^+ \psi[g]$

Hence the rules

$$(2.160) \quad \frac{\Gamma, \varphi, \psi \mid \Delta}{\Pi \mid \Sigma} \qquad \frac{\Gamma \mid \Delta, \varphi}{\Pi \mid \Sigma} \qquad \frac{\Gamma \mid \Delta, \psi}{\Pi \mid \Sigma}$$

$$\frac{\Gamma, (\varphi \wedge \psi) \mid \Delta}{\Pi \mid \Sigma} \qquad \frac{\Gamma \mid \Delta, (\varphi \wedge \psi)}{\Pi \mid \Sigma}$$

The last rule has two conditions: the lower sequent is valid if *both* the upper ones are. For the negative half we get the mirror image:

$(2.161) \quad M \models^- (\varphi \wedge \psi)[g] \quad$ iff $\quad M \models^- \varphi[g]$ or $M \models^- \psi[g]$

$$(2.162) \quad \frac{\Gamma \quad \Big| \Delta}{\Pi, \varphi \Big| \Sigma} \qquad \frac{\Gamma \quad \Big| \Delta}{\Pi, \psi \Big| \Sigma} \qquad \frac{\Gamma \Big| \quad \Delta}{\Pi \Big| \Sigma, \varphi, \psi}$$

$$\frac{\Gamma \qquad \Big| \Delta}{\Pi, (\varphi \wedge \psi) \Big| \Sigma} \qquad \frac{\Gamma \Big| \quad \Delta}{\Pi \Big| \Sigma, (\varphi \wedge \psi)}$$

We also throw a brief glance at quantifiers. Ordinary first-order quantifiers can be treated in a way entirely analogous to the classical case; it is more interesting to consider a couple of generalized quantifiers. A binary universal quantifier is used in statements such as

(2.163) *all R's are Q's*

In a more formal syntax this can be written as

(2.164) $(A \, x \, R(x) \, Q(x))$

and more generally

(2.165) $(A \, x \, \varphi \, \psi)$

where φ and ψ are arbitrary formulas. The interpretation is not entirely clear. It could mean that all elements positively identified as R's by the situation are also identified as Q's. This can be expressed as $R_M^+ \subseteq Q_M^+$. Alternatively, there is a more cautious interpretation, namely that everything is either identified as a non-R or as a Q. This can be expressed as $R_M^- \cup Q_M^+ = D$. Note that the second interpretation implies the first.

Corresponding to the two interpretations we introduce the two quantifier symbols NPA (for 'non-persistent all') and PA (for 'persistent all'). If g is a variable assignment, $a \in D$ and x is a variable, then let $g(a/x)$ be the variable assignment that behaves exactly like g, except that $g(a/x)(x) = a$. We now give the 'positive' semantics of NPA and PA.

(i) $M \models^+ (\text{NPA} \; x \; \varphi \; \psi)[g]$ iff   for every $a \in D$, either $M \not\models^+ \varphi[g(a/x)]$ or $M \models^+ \psi[g(a/x)]$.

(ii) $M \models^+ (\text{PA} \; x \; \varphi \; \psi)[g]$ iff   for every $a \in D$, either $M \models^- \varphi[g(a/x)]$ or $M \models^+ \psi[g(a/x)]$.

The rules for occurrences in the upper right quadrant are now the following.

$$(2.166) \quad \frac{\Gamma, \varphi(c/x) \Big| \Delta, \psi(c/x)}{\Pi \qquad \Big| \quad \Sigma} \qquad \frac{\Gamma \Big| \Delta, \psi(c/x)}{\Pi \Big| \Sigma, \varphi(c/x)}$$

$$\frac{\Gamma \Big| \Delta, (\text{NPA} \; x \; \varphi \; \psi)}{\Pi \Big| \qquad \Sigma} \qquad \frac{\Gamma \Big| \Delta, (\text{PA} \; x \; \varphi \; \psi)}{\Pi \Big| \qquad \Sigma}$$

In both rules, the constant c must not occur in the lower sequent.

Rules would also have to be added for the analysis of occurrences in the upper right quadrant. And once a negative semantics is chosen, one would also need rules for occurrences in the two lower quadrants. A derivation system along these lines would not be *complete*, however, in the sense that valid yet non-derivable sequents would exist. This is rather obvious, since the semantics has at least the power of first order logic, hence there can exist no algorithm to check whether a given sequent is valid. Yet a derivational system of the type we have outlined would in fact be decidable, since any search for a proof of a given sequent would terminate in a finite number of steps. Hence validity and derivability are not the same.

There is a very interesting twist here, involving the use of multisets. Suppose Γ', Δ', Π' and Σ' are variants of Γ, Δ, Π and Σ, in the sense that each contains the same members as its counterpart. Then the two sequents

$$(2.167) \quad \frac{\Gamma \mid \Delta}{\Pi \mid \Sigma} \qquad \frac{\Gamma' \mid \Delta'}{\Pi' \mid \Sigma'}$$

would clearly be equivalent in the sense that one is valid iff the other is. When it comes to *derivability* they need not be equivalent, however. An example is the pair

$$(2.168) \quad \frac{\varphi_1 \mid \varphi_2}{ \mid } \qquad \frac{\varphi_1, \varphi_1 \mid \varphi_2, \varphi_2}{ \mid }$$

where φ_1 is

$$(2.169) \quad \text{(PA } x \ Q(x)$$
$$\text{(PA } y \ R(x,y) \ Q(y)))$$

and φ_2 is

$$(2.170) \quad \text{(PA } x \ Q(x)$$
$$\text{(PA } y \ R(x,y)$$
$$\text{(PA } z \ R(y,z) \ Q(z))))$$

The two sequents are clearly equivalent, yet the second is derivable while the first is not. If Γ is a multiset, let Γ^n be the multiset like Γ but with occurrences multiplied n times. With a slight reformulation of the rules, we would get the following: if

$$(2.171) \quad \frac{\Gamma \mid \Delta}{\Pi \mid \Sigma}$$

is valid, then for some n

(2.172) $\dfrac{\Gamma^n \mid \Delta^n}{\Pi^n \mid \Sigma^n}$

is derivable. (The reformulation hinted at would allow for the simultaneous application of a rule to two or more identical formula occurrences. The same cannot always be achieved by repeated applications of the original rules; cf. the condition on c in the above rules for NPA and PA.)

In Oslo a prototype theorem prover has been written in the programming language *Scheme*, that given a sequent will first check derivability of the sequent as it is. If no proof is found, an iteration is entered in which it will 'blow up' the sequent by adding more occurrences, and then check again. Given enough time, such a program will eventually come up with a proof if one exists. In practice, the program will be told to give up when the multisets exceed a certain size. Usually the length of execution time will be intolerable when more than a couple of 'blow-ups' are allowed. Since valid inferences involving short formulas often require proofs of considerable length and complexity, and hence call for more blow-ups than can be handled in 'real' time, it is clear that the system does not provide us with a workable all-round test of valid inference. But this is something we could not hope for in any case; first order logic is, after all, undecidable. Nevertheless, the present algorithm may not be entirely without interest; with the use of various heuristic strategies improved results may be achieved for certain restricted applications. This is clearly a subject for further research.

2.3.2 REPRESENTING DIRECT QUESTIONS

We have so far focused on the formal side of the theory. In this section we shall use the *format* of situation schemata to represent direct questions and the *interpretation* of the schemata to discuss what are relevant and informative answers. The ambition is a theory; what is done is still rather preliminary. But the point to stress is that any theory of questions and answers presupposes a semantics of direct questions.

Representing questions

A situation schema for an isolated sentence contains, as explained above, the restrictions on interpretations which can be deduced from the syntactic form of the sentence. When we construct situation schemata for *direct questions*, we do not necessarily want to interpret the question directly as some special semantic object. Instead, we will use the situation schema as a convenient *tool* for exploring the different aspects of direct questions. The situation schema will be used to generate answers, to characterize possible answers, and could also be used to obtain knowledge from the question itself (a question can bring new knowledge to the person supposed to answer it).

The Montague Grammar approach to questions started off with embedded questions (Hamblin [80], Karttunen [110]). The semantics for direct questions was then based on the semantics for the corresponding embedded questions (Engdahl [52]). This is typical of the compositionality requirements of the Montague framework. From our point of view we will rather start off with the simplest objects first, namely the direct questions.

A situation schema for a direct question will contain all constraints on possible answers that may be deduced from the syntactic form, and special quantifiers (SPEC-values) corresponding to the interrogatives. We introduce two new values for SPEC: WH and WH-n, where n is some natural number. WH-n is used in the cases where there is a presupposition that exactly n individuals will fill the given role, for instance WH-1 is used for typical which-questions. WH is used for the cases where there is no such presupposition, as in *who*-questions and in plural *which*-questions. WH indicates that information is wanted about the indeterminate that it binds, and could also be treated as a kind of existential quantifier. Our first example is the question

(2.173) *Who is running?*

which is given the following situation schema:

$$
(2.174) \quad
\begin{bmatrix}
\text{REL} & run & & & \\
\text{ARG.1} & \begin{bmatrix} \text{IND} & \text{IND.2} & \\ \text{SPEC} & \text{WH} & \\ \text{COND} & \begin{bmatrix} \text{REL} & person \\ \text{ARG.1} & \text{IND.2} \\ \text{POL} & 1 \end{bmatrix} \end{bmatrix} \\
\text{LOC} & \begin{bmatrix} \text{IND} & \text{IND.1} & \\ \text{COND} & \begin{bmatrix} \text{REL} & \circ \\ \text{ARG.1} & \text{IND.1} \\ \text{ARG.2} & \text{IND.0} \end{bmatrix} \end{bmatrix} \\
\text{POL} & 1 & & &
\end{bmatrix}
$$

This is – except for the SPEC WH – exactly the same schema that we would have given the sentence *a person is running*.

A schema for the question

(2.175) *To which school did Peter run?*

could be of the form:

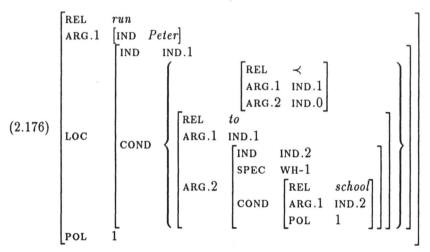

(2.176)

Note the WH-1 which indicates that we want to know *the* school to which Peter ran. This example is based upon work done by E. Colban [37].

An important feature of the situation schemata is that they may be scope ambiguous. This means that when universal quantifiers occur in questions, as in

(2.177) *Which woman does every Englishman admire?*

we simply generate one schema:

$$
(2.178)\quad
\begin{bmatrix}
\text{REL} & admire \\
\text{ARG.1} & \begin{bmatrix} \text{IND} & \text{IND.2} \\ \text{SPEC} & \text{EVERY} \\ \text{COND} & \begin{bmatrix} \text{REL} & Englishman \\ \text{ARG.1} & \text{IND.2} \\ \text{POL} & 1 \end{bmatrix} \end{bmatrix} \\
\text{ARG.2} & \begin{bmatrix} \text{IND} & \text{IND.3} \\ \text{SPEC} & \text{WH-1} \\ \text{COND} & \begin{bmatrix} \text{REL} & woman \\ \text{ARG.1} & \text{IND.3} \\ \text{POL} & 1 \end{bmatrix} \end{bmatrix} \\
\text{LOC} & \begin{bmatrix} \text{IND} & \text{IND.1} \\ \text{COND} & \begin{bmatrix} \text{REL} & \circ \\ \text{ARG.1} & \text{IND.1} \\ \text{ARG.2} & \text{IND.0} \end{bmatrix} \end{bmatrix} \\
\text{POL} & 1
\end{bmatrix}
$$

So far our analysis only covers questions which ask for individuals. This covers typical *who-* and *which*-questions, and those *what*-questions that ask for individuals.

It is easy to extend the framework to *locative* interrogatives, like *where* and *when*. But we cannot just add a SPEC WH inside the LOC, because this would not distinguish between spatial and temporal interrogatives. If we prefer to keep our 4-dimensional location intact, one solution could be to introduce two new values for SPEC: WH-TIME and WH-SPACE.

How should be possible to analyze as soon as we have a good analysis of adverbs and adjectives.

More general uses of *what* may be difficult to handle, simply because they require a good theory of e.g. attitudes. For instance

(2.179) *What did Peter see?*

requires a good understanding of to *see*.

The most challenging interrogative is probably *why*. Here we will need a good analysis of *conditionals and involvement*.

Observe that all these interrogatives can be handled in a way similar to the treatment of simple individual questions, provided we have the proper semantics for the corresponding declarative constructions.

Overview of the system

We have implemented a small prototype question-answering system using situation schemata. In general, we propose the following simplified general model of a question-answering system:

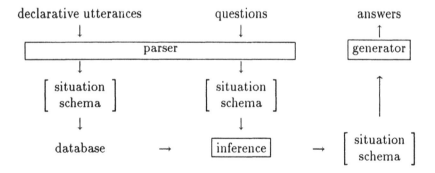

Here the box marked 'inference' may be any mechanism which is able to produce a situation schema representing an answer, given a situation schema representing a question and some database. The database may have any internal structure, but we would like to let the database and the inference mechanism be as close as possible to the level of situation schemata. In addition to a possible role inside the database and the inference mechanism, situation schemata are used in three different ways: to represent declarative utterances which are used to add information to the database, to represent questions which are executed as database queries, and as input to text generation algorithms generating answers and other messages from the system.

The key idea of our sample implementation is to use the logic L_3 in the inference part of the system. L_3 is by no means the ultimate language for describing situation structures. But it does provide us with a complete proof theory for a simple one-situation model. And it has another important feature: through the so-called L_4/L_2 reduction theorem (Fenstad et al. [56]) we are able to encode the logic into ordinary first-order logic. L_4 is the logic for possibly inconsistent situations, that is situations that may contain contradictory facts $r, a_1, \ldots, a_n; 1$ and $r, a_1, \ldots, a_n; 0$. The logic L_3 is obtained from L_4 by adding the axiom $\neg\varphi \supset \sim \varphi$ (φ atomic). Working inside L_4 we now perform the encoding by bringing a formula on *strong negation normal form* (see Fenstad et al. [56]), where every strong negation occurs with an atomic formula, and then introduce a pair of relation symbols P^+ and P for occurrences of P and $\neg P$. The resulting logic, which we call L_2, is ordinary two-sorted first order logic without identity.

The L_4/L_2 reduction theorem provides us with a set of certain L_3 formulas corresponding to Horn Clauses in L_2, thus in our sample implementation we have minimized implementation efforts by taking advantage of Prolog's parsing and inference capabilities. We have implemented the sample grammars in an extended Definite Clause Grammar (DCG) (Pereira and Warren [180]), and we use Prolog as our theorem prover in the inference part. The system has components as shown in figure 2.1.

The parser

The reader should note that we have no separate module for generating natural language text from situation schemata. The reason is that our DCG grammar is carefully constructed to make the parsing algorithm reversible. We take advantage of the rather fixed format of situation schemata which allows us to use functors of fixed arity to represent an attribute-value pair. Whenever there is a variable number of attributes, as in an argument-list, we lump these features together in a Prolog list. The grammar also contains a simple morphological analysis splitting words into stems and suffixes. The two-way approach works efficiently only if you are able to determine which part of the given schema corresponds to the leftmost category on the right-hand side of a rule. This may not be the case for topicalized sentences and questions, but in these cases the problem can be solved by providing the generator with a pointer to the schema corresponding to the topic phrase, thus avoiding unnecessary 'guessing'.

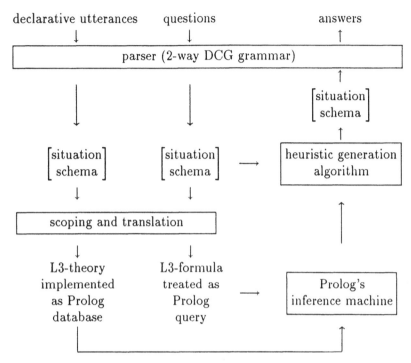

Figure 2.1. Prototype question-answering system

The scoping/translation module

This module translates a situation schema into a formula in the logic L_3. The determination of scope is left to the user: the system presents him with all possible non-equivalent translations and asks him to select the right one.

Translation and scoping are done simultaneously. The problem with equivalent scopings occur when two or more equivalent quantifiers occur in sequence:

(2.180) $\exists x(man(x) \wedge \exists y(woman(y) \wedge love(x, y))$

is equivalent to

(2.181) $\exists y(woman(y) \wedge \exists x(man(x) \wedge love(x, y))$

(and the corresponding for universal quantifiers). Using the situation schemata as input, it is fairly easy to generate only one such sequence, because we have a well-defined ordering on the indeterminates in our schemata (top to bottom). We also have to consider the problem of extracting existential quantifiers from relative clauses, but this occurs only if the quantifier is given a scope outside some universal quantifier. A more detailed description of the algorithm together with an example translation can be found in Vestre [235].

The theorem prover

As already mentioned, the formulas which the prover actually handles are formulas of the two-valued L_2 language. In our implementation we have used a syntax for L_2 closer to the traditional situation semantics syntax. A formula will typically look like:

(2.182) in(s,l0,laugh,[mickey],1)a

Using an extra argument to represent the polarity is an alternative to introducing a new relation (e.g. *laugh$^-$*). The reader should ignore the first argument of the *in*-predicate, which was included to allow for multiple databases (situations).

The theorem prover consists of Prolog's ordinary inference mechanism (operating on L_2 horn clauses) and extended by replacing the standard implementation of negation-by-failure by a small procedure defining weak negation:

(2.183) ~in(S,L,R,A,Pol)   :-   opposite_polarities(Pol,OPol),
                                  in(S,L,R,A,OPol).
         ~P   :-   ordinary_negation_by_failure(P).

Observe that the use of polarity as a parameter here turns out to be quite useful. The first clause of this procedure is a straightforward implementation of the axiom schema which extends L_4 to L_3.

Any L_3 formula can now be represented as a Prolog-query by translating into *Query Normal Form*: a formula is in QNF if it consists of atomic formulas (possibly with strong negation), $\exists$, $\wedge$ and $\sim$. Every L_3 formula can be translated to an equivalent QNF formula by the use of the strong negation normal form theorem, De Morgan's laws and similar principles for the quantifiers. Any QNF formula can be represented in Prolog. WH-specifiers give us special WH-quantifiers, which during execution of the query will have a 'procedural semantics': there is a wh-predicate which is responsible for generating the answers by first executing its range and scope as a query, then executing the heuristic generation algorithm (see the section below) with the given instantiation of Prolog variables.

Declarative sentences are translated into *Quasi Clausal Form*: a formula is in QCF if it is of the form H :- B, where H is a literal and B is empty or in QNF. 'Quasi' suggests that this is not a real Horn Clause, since it may contain negation on the right-hand side. Not every sentence can be translated into QCF.

Note that although every L_3 formula has a QNF-equivalent, the prover cannot correctly decide every QNF formula, because of the usual shortcomings of negation by failure. The output of the translation/scoping module, however, limits itself to formulas which usually do not cause problems: uninstantiated variables inside the scope of a weak negation will be bound by an existential quantifier.

The heuristic generation algorithm

This algorithm works in the following way: after the wh-procedure has executed its range and scope (thereby acting like an existential quantifier) the algorithm is given the original situation schema, which now possibly has some constants in place of variables as values for INDs. The algorithm then, for each such constant c, executes the query

(2.184) in(s,REL,LOC,[c],1)

trying to find a relation which holds for the individual. The relation with the lowest cardinality is chosen. If the cardinality is 1, we can use a definite description; if it is greater, we introduce subordinate SITSCHs (e.g. relative clauses) to possibly lower the cardinality of the set of individuals satisfying the description. If we find any relative clause narrowing the description, it is immediately chosen (although it might not be optimal) to reduce execution time. Recursion depth of relative clauses is restricted to 2. When the situation schema is ready, it is passed backwards through the parser, in the way described above.

What is a good answer?

Traditionally, questions have been given a semantics based on their generic answers, and the ill-understood field of *pragmatics* has been left with the task of explaining the vast number of alternative answers. In this section we show how situation schemata can be used as a tool for characterizing in a model-theoretic way a wider class of answers than the pure generic ones.

We assume that the schemata are interpreted in the way sketched in the beginning of this section, and that the WH-quantifier is given an existential quantifier reading. Following the terminology introduced in Fenstad et al. [56], we let $[\![Q(A)]\!]_{d,c,s,f}$, where Q is a SPEC-value and A is an abstract, be the generalized quantifier determined by Q and A with respect to some d, c, s and some partial anchoring f; i.e. it is some set of subsets of the domain of individuals D. For simplicity, the subscripts are usually left out. If n is some name, we let $[\![n]\!]$ be the generalized quantifier $\{X \subseteq D \mid c(n) \in X\}$. *Example.* Let the frame-situation s be determined by the following facts:

(2.185)   in s:*man, Peter; 1*
               man, John; 1
               woman, Mary; 1
               woman, Jane; 1
               dog, Pluto; 1
               politician, Mary; 1
               politician, Peter; 1

We assume that there is given a discourse situation d, c such that l_d overlaps with l:

(2.186)   in s: at l:*love, Peter, Mary; 1*
                   love, Peter, Jane; 1
                   love, John, Jane; 1
                   love, Jane, John; 1
                   pat, Peter, Pluto; 1

We also assume that a part $s_k \subseteq s$ is a known situation:

(2.187)   in s_k:*man, Peter; 1*
                 woman, Jane; 1
             in s_k:at l: *love, John, Jane; 1*

For simplicity, we let $c(n) = n$ for any name n.

Relevant answers

Let the question be

(2.188) ϕ: *Which men love Jane?*

We get the following schema SIT.ϕ:

$$
(2.189) \quad
\begin{bmatrix}
\text{REL} & run \\
\text{ARG}.1 & \begin{bmatrix} \text{IND} & \text{IND}.2 \\ \text{SPEC} & \text{WH} \\ \text{COND} & \begin{bmatrix} \text{REL} & man \\ \text{ARG}.1 & \text{IND}.2 \\ \text{POL} & 1 \end{bmatrix} \end{bmatrix} \\
\text{ARG}.2 & \begin{bmatrix} \text{IND} & Jane \end{bmatrix} \\
\text{LOC} & \begin{bmatrix} \text{IND} & \text{IND}.1 \\ \text{COND} & \begin{bmatrix} \text{REL} & \circ \\ \text{ARG}.1 & \text{IND}.1 \\ \text{ARG}.2 & \text{IND}.0 \end{bmatrix} \end{bmatrix} \\
\text{POL} & 1
\end{bmatrix}
$$

Consider the following answer:

(2.190) ψ_1: *Peter loves Jane.*

This answer is *relevant*, because:

(i)   it is true: $d, c[\![\text{SIT}.\phi]\!]s$;

(ii)   it is about the same relation as ϕ: $c(\text{SIT}.\psi_1.\text{REL}) = c(\text{SIT}.\phi.\text{REL})$

(iii) the actors in the answer are among the actors asked about; we check this by evaluating and comparing the generalized quantifiers corresponding to ARG.1 and ARG.2 of the question:

$$
\begin{aligned}
X_1 &= [\![\text{WH}(\langle x \mid \text{in } s : man, x; 1\rangle)]\!] \\
&= \{M \subseteq D \mid Peter \in M \vee John \in M\} \\
X_2 &= [\![Jane]\!] = \{M \subseteq D \mid Jane \in M\}
\end{aligned}
$$

and those of the answer:

$$
\begin{aligned}
Y_1 &= [\![Peter]\!] = \{M \subseteq D \mid Peter \in M\} \\
Y_2 &= [\![Jane]\!] = X_2
\end{aligned}
$$

We see that $Y_1 \subseteq X_1$ and $Y_2 \subseteq X_2$; i.e. the actors of the answer are among the actors asked about.

Let ψ_2 be the answer:

(2.191) ψ_2: *All men love Jane.*

This is also a relevant answer since (1) it is true in s; (2) it is about the same relation; and (3) $Y_1 \subseteq X_1$ and $Y_2 \subseteq X_2$ (in this case $Y_1 = \{M \subseteq D \mid \{Peter, John\} \subseteq M\}$). Also the answer

(2.192) ψ_3: *A politician loves all women.*

is relevant. In this case we must take into account that when *a politician* is used in the answer, we implicitly assume that this politician is also a man. So we compute Y_1 as follows:

$$
\begin{aligned}
(2.193) \quad Y_1 &= [\![A(\langle x \mid \text{in } s\colon man,\, x;\, 1 \wedge \text{in } s\colon politician,\, x;\, 1 \rangle)]\!] \\
&= \{ M \subseteq D \mid \\
&\qquad \{ x \mid \text{in } s\colon man,\, x;\, 1 \wedge \text{in } s\colon politician,\, x;\, 1 \} \cap M \neq \emptyset \} \\
&= \{ M \subseteq D \mid \{ Peter \} \cap M \neq \emptyset \}
\end{aligned}
$$

However, if the answer is

(2.194) ψ_4: *A dog loves Jane,*

this should not be counted as relevant, even if we assume that s is extended so as to make ψ_4 true. For ψ_4 we get:

$$
\begin{aligned}
(2.195) \quad Y_1 &= [\![A(\langle x \mid \text{in } s\colon man,\, x;\, 1 \wedge \text{in } s\colon dog,\, x;\, 1 \rangle)]\!] \\
&= \emptyset
\end{aligned}
$$

so we *do* have $Y_1 \subseteq X_1$. This means that we have to add the condition that each $Y_i \neq \emptyset$ in the definition of what constitutes a relevant answer.

Finally, let us look at an example where the inclusion criterion rejects an answer as irrelevant: let the question be *Which men love all women?*, where men is supposed to have wide scope. Let the answer be *Peter loves Jane.* This answer is not counted as relevant, even though it is true, because Jane is not the only woman. The reader may easily verify that this corresponds to failure of the inclusion $Y_2 \subseteq X_2$.

Informative answers

We conclude with a brief remark on *informative answers*. Let the question once more be

(2.196) ϕ: *Which men love Jane?*

And let SIT.ϕ be as above. A possible (and relevant) answer could be

(2.197) ψ: *Peter loves Jane.*

This answer we would count as informative relative to the 'known' situation s_k, since:

(i)   Knowledge is added to s_k, i.e.: not: $d, c[\![\text{SIT}.\phi]\!] s_k$;

(ii)   Let C_1 and C_2 be the fact schemata extracted from the questions, i.e.

C_1: *man, x*; 1
C_2: *love, x, Jane*; 1

There is an $a \in D$, such that $a = c(Peter)$ and

$d, c[\![C_1 \wedge C_2]\!]s, a$
not: $d, c[\![C_1 \wedge C_2]\!]s_k, a$.

Notice that in this simple example the interpretation of SIT.ϕ proceeds via the formula WH($\langle x|C1\rangle$)($\langle x|C2\rangle$); in other and more complicated examples the description in (2) is only part of the unravelling of SIT.ϕ, see Vestre [235].

Open problems

Extending the situation schema formalism to a wider class of questions is closely tied to the analysis of declarative sentences. One class of questions which deserves special attention are the highly problematic *why*-questions. The work on *conditionals* in Situation Semantics (see Barwise [14]) offers a promising start for a future theory.

     But representation is only part of the enterprise. We would also like to work out a more general theory for 'good answers'. In the long run, the aim of the model-theoretic work should be not only to *characterize* the answers, but to develop theoretically well founded procedures for *generating* the answers.

     We also aim to replace the language L_3 with something more powerful, allowing for generalized quantifiers and with general models containing more than one situation. But a more sophisticated logic requires a more sophisticated theorem prover. An immediate challenge would be to link a powerful parser for more general feature structure formalisms with a theorem prover based on a Gentzen type formalism as described above.

3 Syntactic categories and semantic type

Barbara H. Partee

3.1 INTRODUCTION

Before turning to some selected issues in type theory, type-shifting and the semantics of noun phrases, which form the main topic of this chapter, I will briefly mention some other, very exciting topics of current research in formal semantics that are relevant to the theme of this book, but which do not receive the attention they deserve in what follows.

One is the centrality of context dependence, context change, and a more dynamic view of the basic semantic values. This view of meanings, in terms of functions from contexts to contexts, is important both for the way it helps us make better sense of such things as temporal anaphora, and also for the way it solves some of the crucial foundational questions about presuppositions and the principles governing presupposition projection. The work of Irene Heim [86] is central in this area.

Another crucial area that will not be covered is the recently emerging emphasis on the algebraic structure of certain model-theoretic domains, such as entities, events or eventualities. As well as the work of Godehard Link [137] and Jan-Tore Lønning [140] in this area, referred to by Fenstad [54], I would also mention the attempt by Emmon Bach [6] to generalize the issue into questions about natural language metaphysics. An example of such a question is whether languages that grammaticize various semantic distinctions (such as mass versus count nouns) differently have different ontologies, or whether Link's use of Boolean algebras, which may be either atomic or not necessarily atomic, provides a framework in which to differentiate those structures that are shared from additional ones that only some languages express through grammar.

Another important issue concerns the parallels between count versus mass in the nominal domain and event versus process in the verbal domain. Although I will not say anything about that topic beyond these few sentences, it will be a pity if those issues are not brought to the fore in interdisciplinary discussions between computational linguists and formal semanticists, because explanations that rest on the structures of the domains that we use our language to talk about – the further structure that Link hypothesizes on the domain of entities, for instance – are interestingly different from explanations which are or can be cast in terms of properties of (language-like) representations.

The kinds of phenomena which seem most naturally to get a nice account in terms of the structure of the domains that the language is talking about, such as the similarities and differences in the behaviour of mass nouns and plurals, pose interesting challenges to typical computational models. These work almost exclusively on a representational level and try to capture both entailment relations, and similarities and differences in truth conditions, in terms of syntactic operations or manipulations on representations. I do not focus on this extremely important issue here, being unable to do it justice in a brief presentation.

The third important topic that I shall not deal with here is property theory: property theory as opposed to set theory in the foundations of the whole enterprise of formal semantics, the relation of recent new work by Raymond Turner, Gennaro Chierchia and others to the semantics of nominalizations (see for example [33, 254]), along with the related issue of recent revivals of interest in Davidsonian analyses of event-sentences. Turner's contribution to the present volume addresses some of those issues.

In this article, I want to focus on type theory and noun phrase semantics, and in particular on the relation between syntactic categories and semantic types, an issue which is one central part of the larger issue of compositionality. My principal point of departure is the fact that there is considerable tension between, on the one hand, the advantages of and evidence for a very systematic correspondence between syntactic categories and semantic types, and, on the other hand, evidence of the great flexibility and versatility of natural languages.

The second and related starting point is the evident fact that words and phrases can easily shift their meanings, either temporarily, as in metaphorical or figurative uses of language, or permanently, leading to families of meanings that appear to have families of types. As a formal analogy, if one thinks about the operation(s) denoted by '+' on integers and on the rationals, which we casually think of as the very same operation, it is clear that given those two different domains, they cannot actually be exactly the same operation. The explicit treatment of phenomena of this kind leads to notions of 'overloading' of certain symbols, of 'coercion', and of various kinds of polymorphism in the semantics of programming languages.

My goal here is to make some progress towards refining a notion of 'natural' families of meanings. That is, given that words can have a range of meanings, to say something about what kinds of meanings go together so that all such families are not treated as if they were instances of accidental homonymy. We also need to try to identify the most 'natural' rules for shifting from a given meaning of a word to some new meaning or meanings. This enterprise can be carried out in many sorts of domain for very particular domain-specific families of vocabulary. I shall focus on the structural aspects of this process which are more closely tied to the grammar itself, leading to the search for natural families of types and type-shifting principles, and for notions of natural functions shifting from meanings of one type to meanings of another.

Now, what is natural? Somehow we need to try to find both formal elegance and empirical generality. To make any kind of headway on such a question, it will take the cooperation of linguists, mathematicians and cognitive scientists to try to find some notion(s) of 'natural functions' in this area that are satisfying in some degree from all those perspectives.

An example from another domain might help convey the idea: a logician might suggest that the most natural function from the real numbers to the integers is obviously that which maps every real number onto zero. Most of us would not accept that. This is principally because that function 'ignores its input', and loses all the information about the argument in passing to the value. I would submit that we would all intuitively agree that the most natural function from the reals to the integers is rather some version of a rounding function – a function that maps from a given real number to the nearest integer. So let us try to analyse why we might all agree that such a function could be considered the most natural mapping between those two domains. For one thing, it preserves order, even though, when mapping from a larger domain to a smaller one we cannot preserve everything. And it comes as close as possible to preserving operations like addition and multiplication which are defined on both domains. So insofar as those two domains share a certain amount of structure, one can say that the most natural function from one to the other is the one that preserves most of the relevant structure that they share.

We can even take this example farther and ask what if anything we can say about the choice among the various different versions of rounding functions, which differ as to how to round off a number that ends with '.5'. It is illuminating to see how the choice depends on one's purposes and goals. If we want simplicity and maximal replicability then we choose some very simple rule like 'always round down'. On the other hand, a merchant wanting to maximize profits when computing prices will always round up.

But these are not the most natural rounding functions from the point of view of physics or other sciences, since always rounding up or always rounding down is bound to magnify errors under multiplication. So the strategy that is commonly taught in elementary physics is, 'If it's an even number, round down, and if it's an odd number, round up.' Assuming that even and odd numbers are randomly distributed in the inputs, this will come to minimizing the propagation of error and preserving the structure of the argument domain in applying operations that are defined on both domains.

We can pursue this example even farther. The last-mentioned function was still replicable and still a very definite algorithm. If we really want to be physically 'natural' we might imagine that we are modelling something like balls falling down from a space with a real-number distribution and being funnelled into discrete containers. To model a ball that is falling from a '.5'-type initial location, a good rule could then be to flip a coin to model which way it will go – that is, do something random to model the random part of the physical process, rather than make a deterministic algorithm out of it. This kind of solution is not taught in school because our teachers want to be able to check our computations and so they want us to have the same answers. Moreover, it also requires that we stretch the notion of function – though if it is indeed the most natural function for modelling a class of physical phenomena, then physicists should insist on being able to work with a notion of function that allows it. So even in a simple example like this, the question of what is the 'most natural' or the 'best' function of a certain general type is interestingly nontrivial[1]. While we can often give strong arguments that converge on identifying certain properties of such functions (in the example above, that it must be a rounding function), in some respects the choice of a most natural function may nonetheless depend on one's purposes and/or on empirical considerations.

A good example of a 'natural' meaning shift which is not primarily structural in nature, but is presumably based on some non-linguistic domain of our experience in the world, is the shift from count nouns to mass nouns that David Lewis christened the 'universal grinder' (see [178]). It is well known that for any count noun like 'potato' there is generally a corresponding mass noun like 'potato' paired with it. Lewis observed that for virtually any concrete common noun – take 'chair' for instance – we can

---

[1] I was recently informed of the existence of a doctoral dissertation in applied mathematics at Charles University in Prague concerned with the question of when one could and when one could not determine an optimal rounding function to minimize the propagation of error, given knowledge of what further operations were to be applied to the outputs; apparently the problem in general is NP-hard, and finding tractable subcases is an important and highly nontrivial area of research.

imagine subjecting an instance of its denotation to this universal grinder. You put a chair in one end and then you get chair, i.e. something denoted by the mass noun 'chair', all over the floor at the other end. In English such a shift from count to mass is certainly extremely easy to make, and I believe that most languages that differentiate mass and count nouns will similarly very easily allow any concrete count noun to shift to a mass meaning. Now that is not what I would call a 'formal' meaning shift; it has nothing particular to do with type theory, but it is an example in a domain-specific area of a natural shifting operation. In what follows I will focus on systematic meaning-shifting operations that are more closely bound up with the basic structure of syntactic categories and semantic types in the grammars of natural languages.

3.2 LINGUISTIC BACKGROUND

Most of the relevant linguistic background is relatively familiar. Briefly, Montague [154, abbreviated as 'PTQ'] employed a kind of extended categorial grammar and a syntax-semantics correspondence in which function-argument application plays a central role. For present purposes we can limit our attention to the purely extensional subpart of Montague's system, ignoring the otherwise central possible-worlds aspects of the semantics. Figure 3.1 lists some of the syntactic categories and their common abbreviations from Montague grammar, together with their (extensionalized) semantic types and example expressions.

Note in particular that in the syntactic category *e* and the corresponding semantic type *e*, one would expect to find proper names like *John*; but, as is well known, Montague did not treat the proper names that way but rather as generalized quantifiers. Similarly for simple transitive verbs like *kicks*: although the most natural assumption is that they are just relations between entities Montague again proposed a different treatment, as higher-order relations of the same type that he assigned to intensional verbs like *seeks*. Already here we see the tension between simplicity and generality, or between uniformity and flexibility. The unified treatment of natural language noun phrases as generalized quantifiers was one of Montague's great achievements but it also has seemed problematic in some respects. *John* and *every man* are both noun phrases in English; but in the old days when many logicians were inclined to dismiss natural language surface structure as not being anything to take very seriously, the fact that *John* and *every man* both showed up as noun phrases was just one more piece of evidence about how illogical ordinary language is. But Montague was convinced, as the title of his paper 'English as a Formal Language' [153] shows, that

Synt. Cat.	Abbrev.	Semantic Type (extensionalized)	Expressions (* = not in PTQ)
e	e	e	*names ('John')
t	t	t	sentences
t/e	IV	$\langle e,t\rangle$ or $e \to t$	verb phrases ('runs')
$t//e$	CN	$\langle e,t\rangle$ or $e \to t$	common noun phrases ('cat')
t/IV	T(or NP)	$\langle\langle e,t\rangle,t\rangle$ or $(e \to t) \to t$	term phrases as generalized quantifiers ('John', 'every man')
IV/e	TV_1	$\langle e,\langle e,t\rangle\rangle$	*simple transitive verbs ('kicks')
IV/T	TV_2	$\langle\text{type}(T),\text{type}(IV)\rangle$	transitive verbs ('kicks', 'seeks')

Figure 3.1.

natural languages can be described with just as systematic and rigorous a correspondence between form and structure as the logicians' formal languages, and in practice he stayed remarkably close to surface structure in doing so. As he showed, we can perfectly well get the interpretations of *John* and *every man* into the same type – the type of generalized quantifiers, $\langle\langle e,t\rangle,t\rangle$. So Montague treated *John* as denoting the set of all John's properties, as illustrated in (3.1).

$$(3.1) \qquad \text{John:} \qquad \lambda P.P(j)$$
$$\text{every man:} \qquad \lambda P.\forall x[\text{man}(x) \to P(x)]$$

$$\left\{ \begin{array}{c} \text{John} \\ \text{every man} \end{array} \right\} \quad + \quad \text{walks} \Rightarrow t$$
$$\qquad t/IV \qquad\qquad\qquad IV$$

So 'John walks' and 'every man walks' have the same basic syntactic category analysis and semantic type analysis in Montague's approach; in each case the noun phrase is the functor which takes the verb phrase as its argument. Montague's category-to-type correspondence as illustrated in PTQ – which of course is not essential to the 'Montague grammar' enterprise as defined in his earlier 'Universal Grammar' [152] but is the most familiar application of it – is uniform and general and treats all noun phrases as belonging to the same semantic type. But it is not simple in another sense: when starting to teach Montague grammar, having to explain how this set of properties is the interpretation of the name *John*, there is always a measure of initial resistance. A certain amount of work is required in order to convince people how beautiful the overall results are and to justify what appears in isolation to be a choice that is not so natural nor so simple.

This is just one example, but a representative one, of the tension between the uniformity and generality of Montague's system and the intuitive, case-by-case simplicity and flexibility of correspondence that one might be inclined to consider a more natural reflection of natural language.

3.3 Conjunction and type ambiguity

Starting from the cross-linguistic and cross-categorial uniformity of generalized conjunction observed by Gazdar [67], the real elegance of its recursive definition and its cross-linguistic universality, Mats Rooth and I [177] originally took it as established that Montague's treatment of cross-categorial conjunction was correct. However, there is direct empirical evidence for a non-uniform typing of English transitive verb phrases and for the existence of type-shifting rules to shift verb phrases of lower types to verb phrases of higher types by coercion when needed, as opposed to Montague's strategy of uniformly assigning all expressions of a given category to the highest type ever needed for the analysis of any of them.

Although the less uniform approach can be seen as a departure from or weakening of compositionality, it is in fact still compositional. It appeals to widespread systematic homonymy, but homonymy that is 'under control'.

3.3.1 Generalized conjunction

The central idea of generalized conjunction starts from the observation that in very many languages, with specific exceptions in specific languages, it is possible to conjoin not only sentences but noun phrases, intransitive verb phrases, transitive verb phrases, common noun phrases, adjective phrases, etc. The kind of conjunction that we are focusing on here is the Boolean *and* and *or* whose basic home is in the type t, the type of truth-value-denoting expressions, as opposed to the group-forming 'and' in 'John and Mary are a happy couple'.[2]

There are a number of different ways one can view the semantics of the Boolean *and* and *or* on type t. One can view it simply in terms of truth tables, or just think of them as operators in a two-element Boolean algebra. One can take the semantic values of sentences to be propositions

---

[2] In Partee and Rooth [177] we show how that occurrence of 'and' can be generalized a certain amount as well.

construed as sets of possible worlds, over which *and* and *or* just denote, respectively, intersection and union. Alternatively one can treat the basic semantic values as sets of assignment functions, which again leads to an interpretation in terms of intersection and union. All of these give the same familiar Boolean structure for *and* and *or* on sentences. The recursive definition for conjoinable types is given in (3.2).

(3.2)   Recursive definition of *conjoinable types*:

> (i) t, the type of sentences, is a conjoinable type.

> (ii)   if b is a conjoinable type, then for all a, the type $\langle a, b \rangle$, of functions from objects of type a to objects of type b, is a conjoinable type.

This definition extends the class of conjoinable types to all the other types where we find the same *and* and *or* showing up. It gives, in a sense, an index for the conjoinable types. From here we can define the full range of types for *and* and *or* as in (3.3), namely as functions from X's to functions from X's to X's, for all conjoinable types X. So when I call NP, say, a conjoinable type, I mean that *and* can conjoin two NPs to make an NP. The function shown in (3.3) is in the 'curried' form, where it takes one argument at a time, though in examples below conjoined structures are given in flat, uncurried two-argument form.

(3.3)   Types for *and, or*: $\langle X, \langle X, X \rangle \rangle$ for all conjoinable types X.

The semantics for this generalized *and*, written here with a square intersection sign ($\sqcap$), is given in (3.4).

(3.4)   Semantics for generalized *and* ($\sqcap$):

> (i)   for conjoinable type t, $\sqcap = \wedge$ (basic Boolean operation).

> (ii)   for f_1, f_2 of conjoinable type $\langle a, b \rangle$, $f_1 \sqcap f_2$ is defined by the condition $[f_1 \sqcap f_2](x) = f_1(x) \sqcap f_2(x)$.

This amounts to just pointwise lifting from the co-domain to the function space [177, page 364]. In other words, it is again a parallel recursive definition: we simply exploit the fact that once we have defined generalized conjunction over the range of a certain space of functions, i.e. on the domain of the things that are going to be the values of those functions, then we can just use that definition recursively to define generalized conjunction 'in the same way' (i.e. homomorphically) on the function space itself. Some examples of the effect of the definition are given in (3.5); verifying that they give the right results is left as an exercise for the reader.

(3.5)　(i)　$\langle e, t \rangle$:　　walk′ ⊓ talk′
　　　　　　　　　$= \lambda x[\text{walk}'(x) \sqcap \text{talk}'(x)]$

　　　(ii)　$\langle \langle e, t \rangle, t \rangle$:　(every man)′ ⊓ (some woman)′
　　　　　　　　　$= \lambda P[(\text{every man})'(P)$
　　　　　　　　　　　　　$\sqcap (\text{some woman})'(P)]$

　　　(iii)　$\langle \langle e, t \rangle, \langle e, t \rangle \rangle$:　old′ ⊓ useless′
　　　　　　　　　$= \lambda P[\text{old}'(P) \sqcap \text{useless}'(P)]$
　　　　　　　　　$= \lambda P[\lambda x[\text{old}'(P)(x) \sqcap \text{useless}'(P)(x)]]$

3.3.2　REPERCUSSIONS ON THE TYPE THEORY

This treatment of *and* – which differs only æsthetically from an earlier proposal by Gazdar [67] – is so elegant, applies so nicely to all the different conjoinable categories in English, and extends so readily to every language I have come across that has a generalized sentential conjunction, that it *must* to be essentially right, at least in its central generalization. If we accept that, then we have the basis for an empirical argument that it is not correct to treat all transitive verbs as being in the same type. Recall that Montague put the simple extensional verbs like *hits* and *kicks* in the same type as the intensional ones like *seeks*, making them all functions from the intensions of full generalized quantifiers to one-place predicates or sets of entities, whereas intuitively we would have thought that the extensional transitive verbs are just functions from entities to functions from entities to truth values.

　　Using this treatment of generalized conjunction as a premise, the empirical argument goes as follows. If the type of all transitive verbs is as Montague had it, i.e. functions from the full generalized quantifier type (the type of term phrases) to the type of verb phrases, which are just one-place predicates or sets of entities, then the predictions concerning the meaning of conjoined transitive verbs are spelled out in the formula in (3.6). (See Partee and Rooth [177] for more discussion on the following examples.)

(3.6)　If *TV* type is $\langle \text{type}(T), \text{type}(IV) \rangle$, then $[TV P_1 \text{ and } TV P_2] = \lambda \mathcal{P} \lambda x[TV P_1'(\mathcal{P})(x) \wedge TV P_2'(\mathcal{P})(x)].$

　　In particular (3.6), taken together with generalized conjunction, predicts that (3.7) (with normal intonation) means the same as 'John caught a fish and ate a fish', whereas in fact in English that is wrong: it has to be the same fish. Analogously, for (3.8) we get the prediction that John hugged three women and kissed three women, which is similarly wrong.

(3.7)   John caught and ate a fish.

(3.8)   John hugged and kissed three women.

So if we treat the simple extensional verbs in the same way Montague treated *seek*, generalized conjunction gives us the wrong result. On the other hand, Montague's type assignment gives us the right result for the intensional verbs, as in (3.9), where it correctly predicts the meaning that John wants two secretaries and needs two secretaries.

(3.9)   John wants and needs two secretaries.

It also gives us the right result when we conjoin an intensional verb and an extensional verb as in (3.10).

(3.10)   John needed and bought a new coat.

Sentence (3.10) is indeed equivalent to saying that John needed a new coat and he bought a new coat. From this we can also derive the entailment that there exists a particular coat that he bought but we, rightly, do not get any entailment that there was a particular coat that he needed. So using the higher type that Montague assigned to all the transitive verb phrases, we get the right result for conjoined intensional verbs and we get the right result if we conjoin an intensional and an extensional verb, but we get wrong results for conjoined extensional verbs.

Now what if we define the type of transitive verb as a function from entities to functions from entities to truth values? Given the generalized conjunction schema, we get the prediction that conjunction of two transitive verbs gives us the formula in (3.11).

(3.11)   If TV type is $\langle e, \text{type}(IV) \rangle$ (i.e. $\langle e, \langle e, t \rangle \rangle$) then
$$[TVP_1 \text{ and } TVP_2] = \lambda y \lambda x [TVP_1'(y)(x) \wedge TVP_2'(y)(x)]$$

This now yields the right result for (3.7) and (3.8) above, but the wrong result for (3.9) and (3.10). It would predict that (3.9) has to mean that there exist two secretaries such that John wants and needs them, and give a similar incorrect prediction for (3.10).

It is interesting to note how this difference between the two kinds of transitive verb phrases relates to the types that show up in Montague's meaning postulates for extensional transitive verbs. The simpler type for the transitive verbs given in (3.11) matches the first order relations *catch** and *eat** that are posited by Montague's meaning postulate for the first-order reducible transitive verbs. Montague assigned verbs like *catch* and *eat* to the higher type shown in (3.6), but then he wrote a meaning postulate that says that they behave with respect to their entailments as if they were just relations between entities; the corresponding relations projected by the meaning postulates were symbolized as *catch** and *eat**. What we are saying here is that the basic lexical interpretation of such verbs should be those relations between entities: we should not be assigning them the higher type and having to apply meaning postulates to get down to the lower type.[3]

The suggestion that comes from this state of affairs is that there is no single type that should be assigned uniformly to all transitive verbs once and for all, but rather that in the lexicon each verb should be entered in its minimal type (as defined below). We give up Montague's strategy of putting all of the items of a given syntactic category into the highest type needed for any of them. Rather we enter each item in the simplest type that is compatible with its semantics. The 'low-type' verbs, like extensional *kick*, *hit*, etc., all have predictable homonyms of higher types, and Partee and Rooth [177] discuss some of the principles that make that systematic; see the example in (3.12).

(3.12)   From buy_1 of type $\langle e, \langle e, t \rangle \rangle$ predict buy_2 of type $\langle type(T), \langle e, t \rangle \rangle$, where: $\text{buy}'_2 = \lambda \mathcal{P} \lambda x [\mathcal{P}(\lambda y [\text{buy}_1(y)(x)])]$

The relation is similar to that between *eat'* and *eat'$_*$* in PTQ.

So for instance from buy_1 as a relation between entities we can predict that there should be a buy_2 of the same type as *seek* or *need*. In fact to get the higher type buy_2 from the simpler one we are in effect going through the inverse of Montague's meaning postulate.

The rule, then, for interpreting conjoined expressions is always to interpret them at the lowest type that they both share. If we abbreviate these two different kinds of transitive verbs as TV_1 for the simpler relation-between-entities type in (3.6) and TV_2 for the higher type in (3.11), then we can illustrate the functioning of this principle as in (3.13).

(3.13)   Conjoined expressions are interpreted at the lowest type they both have.

---

[3] Readers who have ever taught or followed a course in Montague grammar might even want to argue for switching to this way of treating verbs because it was always pedagogically difficult to arrange that the more complicated verbs (such as the intensional ones) had the simpler translations and derivations, whereas for the intuitively simple ones it was necessary to go through all those applications of meaning postulates and lambda-conversions to get to the simple result. I reject that as a real argument though I am certainly pleased at the prospect of having the pedagogical task made easier if the present approach is the right one.

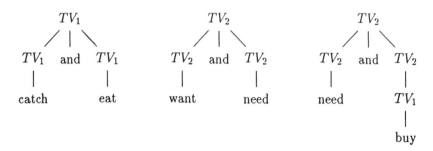

Two extensional verbs like *catch* and *eat* are lexically entered as TV_1s and
they both share the TV_1 relation-between-entity type (speaking loosely and
not carefully distinguishing syntax and semantics). That is the lowest type
they share, i.e. they are both extensional verbs, so conjoining at that level
the generalized conjunction rule yields the right result for (3.7). Similarly,
with two intensional verbs like *want* and *need* whose common intensional
type is the lowest type they share, conjoining them at that level once again
yields the right result from generalized conjunction. However, the case is different for *need* and *buy*, which are respectively intensional and extensional.
The semantics of these intensional verbs cannot be adequately captured
by relations between entities; that was part of what Montague's point in
arguing that 'John seeks a unicorn' has to be treated in terms of transitive
verbs taking intensions of generalized quantifiers as objects. Thus, *need*
does not share the lower type TV_1 of *buy*, but the low-type verbs do all
have higher type homonyms, so that *buy* can be 'lifted' to match the type
of *need*. I assume then that in this kind of mixed conjunction case, *buy*
is automatically lifted from its lexical TV_1 meaning to its potential TV_2
meaning, and the conjunction takes place at the TV_2 level. We can now
correctly predict that when we conjoin an intensional and an extensional
verb generalized conjunction gives the right results at the intensional type.
The reader is left to verify that all of the facts about examples (3.7–3.10)
are now correctly predicted.

The status of the principle enunciated in (3.13) about interpreting
conjoined expressions at their lowest common type can be regarded as
performance-related, a natural least effort strategy. There are parallel issues regarding intransitive verbs which I will mention more briefly; many
of the questions are familiar from the literature.

There has been a lot of debate about the type for verb phrases within the
Montague grammar tradition, where intransitive verb and verb phrase were
originally treated as the same notion. Montague in PTQ treated intransitive
verbs as one place predicates, type $\langle e, t \rangle$. Michael Bennett [16] did the
same, as I also did in my earlier work (see [176]). In PTQ it is always the
subject that takes the verb phrase as argument; the generalized quantifier

is interpreted as a set of properties, so it takes the verb phrase as argument and returns a truth value. But there have been various proposals to the effect that the intransitive verbs should take the subject as argument even if the subject is a generalized quantifier. Montague himself did it that way in the fragment he presented in 'Universal Grammar', as did Keenan and Faltz [119], as well as Bach and Partee [8] and Bach [7]. There are seemingly good arguments for doing it either way.

Looking at generalized conjunction again, it seems that sometimes we get the right result when the verb phrase is of one type, sometimes when it is of the other – although of course much more must be done to see whether such a claim is consistent with all of the evidence that has been presented in the literature. The relevant conjunction examples are given in (3.14) and (3.15); for further discussion see Partee and Rooth [177].

(3.14) lower type gives right result for:

(i) A fish walked and talked.

(ii) Every participant sent in an abstract or apologized.

(3.15) higher type gives right result for:

(i) An easy model theory textbook is badly needed and will surely be written within this decade. (both high type)

(ii) A tropical storm was expected to form off the coast of Florida and did form there within a few days of the forecast. (high type and low type)

3.3.3 INFINITE AMBIGUITY AND PROCESSING STRATEGIES

In principle, by positing some very general type raising rules of the sort that I have mentioned, I am positing infinite ambiguity. In practice we can live with this perfectly well as long as we have strategies about what to try first and as long as the total system is such that there are no ways of getting into infinite processing loops. What I hypothesize is a combination of potentially infinite ambiguity and a least effort principle.

Figures 3.2 and 3.3 graphically illustrate the phenomenon, though in fact I have never seen any examples that go more than a very small way up this hierarchy. Figure 3.2 is a kind of subject/predicate type-ladder, showing what happens when you start generating the different types the noun phrase subject and the intransitive verb may have. As the simplest

	NP	VP	Height
	$\vdots$	$\vdots$	$\vdots$
		$IV_3 : \langle \text{type}(T_2), t \rangle$	6
	$T_2 : \langle \text{type}(IV_2), t \rangle$		5
		$IV_2 : \langle \text{type}(T_1), t \rangle$	4
	$T_1 : \langle \langle e, t \rangle, t \rangle$		3
		$IV_1 : \langle e, t \rangle$	2
	e		1

Figure 3.2. The Subject-predicate type ladder (extensionalized)

Types of TV's (extensionalized)	Cost $(A + B)$	
	(i)$ht(A) + ht(B)$	(ii)$[ht(A)]^2 + [ht(B)]^2$
$TV_1 : e \rightarrow IV_1$	3	5
$TV_2 : T_1 \rightarrow IV_1$	5	13
$TV_3 : e \rightarrow IV_2$	5	17
$TV_4 : T_1 \rightarrow IV_2$	7	25
$TV_5 : T_2 \rightarrow IV_1$	7	29
$TV_6 : e \rightarrow IV_3$	7	37
$TV_7 : T_2 \rightarrow IV_2$	9	41
$\vdots$	$\vdots$	$\vdots$

Figure 3.3. TV Types

case is at the bottom of the type ladder, let us assume that a simple proper name like *John* is lexically of type e; then if we combine it with a simple verb phrase like *hits* which is of type $\langle e, t \rangle$, we get an IV_1 combined with an e-type NP, so the verb phrase is the function and the noun phrase is the argument. If on the other hand we have something like *every man* as a generalized quantifier subject, we may – unless empirical arguments require us to reject this possibility – say that in that case the subject takes the verb phrase as argument, so that we have T_1 applying to IV_1 as argument. If we found reason to suppose that the verb phrase can jump up another level, then it could again take the subject as argument. In general each time we do one of these type liftings we reverse the roles of function and argument. This is related to some earlier arguments that Thomas Ballmer [9] had with Keenan and Faltz over the possibility of establishing any general criteria to empirically identify function and argument in a given construction. There may very well be empirical arguments suggesting, for instance, that the verb phrase should always be the function and the subject should always be one of its arguments. In that case one should try to discover or at least impose constraints that make sure that the type shiftings are done a pair at a time. If there is a constraint on the directionality of the function-argument application, for instance, then that will itself be part of the input to the coercion process and will constrain what shifting can or must occur.

In the particular case illustrated in figure 3.2 it is very clear which are the simplest types, and for any given starting point of a lexical noun phrase and a lexical verb it is easy to figure out which are the simplest compatible types for the function-argument combination. For discussion of a wider range of cases from a related perspective, see the work of Klein and Sag [124] on type-driven translation.

Figure 3.3 is not meant to be taken strictly. It represents a completely ad-hoc illustration of the idea that in principle there could be measures of complexity for these types, and one could try to determine processing costs associated with type-shifting. For instance, if the cost of increasingly high type combinations were to increase only linearly as shown in the middle column, then we would expect to be able to reach relatively high types without an exorbitant processing load. If the cost goes up exponentially, on the other hand, then it would be more plausible that we rarely exploit this climbing ability very far. But there is absolutely no empirical data from which to make any conjectures about cost, so the table is purely hypothetical. As already implied, it is very natural to propose a similar type ambiguity for noun phrases (see also below). A reasonable general processing strategy might then be to use the simplest types which are consistent with the coherent typing of the entire sentence.

We can also find examples of noun phrase conjunction where coercion will force us to the higher types that we have predicted are available. Suppose that *John* is lexically of type *e* and that it is shiftable to the generalized quantifier meaning that Montague assigned to it. Suppose also that *every woman*, on the other hand, has only a generalized quantifier reading, as I will argue below. Then we cannot conjoin *John* with *every woman* at *John*'s lowest type, *e*, and so *John* would be type-shifted up to the interpretation that Montague originally assigned to it, making it also a generalized quantifier. Thus generalized conjunction would apply at the level of generalized quantifiers and we predict exactly the right interpretation.

Although the general processing strategy of using the simplest types consistent with coherent typing of the entire sentence is essentially the proposal for type-driven translation of Klein and Sag [124], it leads to the following query:

> What does it take to ensure that such a system of flexible typing and type-shifting will always yield a unique simplest result? Un-

der what conditions and by what measures does such a strategy really yield greater overall simplicity than Montague's strategy of generalising uniformly to the 'hardest case'?

The kind of strategy being proposed certainly makes the examples I have discussed look simpler, and I have argued empirically that we need to do something similar or the conjunction facts will not come out right. But in fact such a strategy could easily cause the processor to do a lot of potentially quite expensive pre-processing: what is simplest locally in some part of the sentence might lead to a processing path which would actually make things more complex later on when putting that part together with some other part. In general, maximizing local simplicity would not necessarily always result in maximum overall simplicity unless the total system has some special properties (which I do not know how to specify). The potentially expensive pre-processing required to determine overall type simplicity could easily cost more than it saves. At this stage we can be aware of the questions but we do not have the mathematical tools or the competence to know how to determine the answers.

3.4   NP TYPE MULTIPLICITY

3.4.1   BACKGROUND

In this section we will be talking more about NPs in particular and arguing for type multiplicity of NPs. In (3.16) we recall how Montague treated NPs uniformly as generalized quantifiers. Still simplifying to extensional types, all of these are of type $\langle\langle e,t\rangle, t\rangle$, i.e. (characteristic functions of) sets of properties of entities, or just sets of sets of entities in this extensional version.

(3.16)   Montague tradition: uniform treatment of NPs as generalized quantifiers, type $(e \mapsto t) \mapsto t$.[4]

John	$\lambda P[P(j)]$
a man	$\lambda P \exists x[\mathrm{man}'(x) \wedge P(x)]$
every man	$\lambda P \forall x[\mathrm{man}'(x) \rightarrow P(x)]$

I already remarked above that this uniform treatment, as important an achievement as it is, often meets with some resistance among linguists. There is often felt to be an intuitive type multiplicity of NPs in English and other languages, as illustrated in (3.17).

---

[4] Note the free alternation between two notations for functional types. Sometimes arrows are employed, which are more familiar to computer scientists, and sometimes angle brackets as used by Montague in PTQ.

(3.17)   Intuitive type multiplicity of NPs:

expression	use	representation	type
John	referential	j	e
a fool	predicative	fool$'$	$e \mapsto t$
every man	quantifier	see (3.16)	$(e \mapsto t) \mapsto t$

Although there is no single piece of evidence with the strength of the conjunction arguments for the transitive verbs, there do seem to be systematic linguistic phenomena which are easier to explain if we can appeal to type distinctions like those suggested in (3.17). For example, it is not only simpler but probably more correct to analyse most occurrences of proper names like *John* as being of type e, i.e. simply denoting entities. One kind of empirical argument for treating some occurrences of some NPs as having denotations of type e is used by Kamp [103] and Heim [85] in their work on discourse representation theory and discourse anaphora. Among the phenomena their theories are designed to account for is the fact that, while any singular NP can bind a singular pronoun in an appropriate local domain (c-command or f-command: see Bach and Partee [8]), only an e-type NP can normally license discourse anaphora with a singular pronoun, as illustrated in (3.18) and (3.19).

(3.18) $\left\{ \begin{array}{c} \text{John} \\ \text{the man} \\ \text{a man} \end{array} \right\}$ walked in. He looked tired.

(3.19) $\left\{ \begin{array}{c} \text{Every man} \\ \text{no man} \\ \text{more than one man} \end{array} \right\}$ walked in. *He looked tired.

The other principal type in which it seems NPs can sometimes be interpreted is the type $\langle e, t \rangle$, the type of predicates. When we study first order logic we immediately encounter examples with predicate nominals like 'John is a man', which just gets translated $man(j)$, with only the one-place predicate *man* interpreting the whole predicate phrase, and no overt trace of either the copula *is* or the indefinite article *a*. But that is not a direct, empirical linguistic argument for treating predicate nominal NPs as predicates, since as Montague showed with his analysis it is possible to analyse *is* in such a way that it in effect 'cancels out' the indefinite article, so that the predicate nominal NPs can be treated as normal generalized quantifiers. But there are in fact linguistic arguments for treating some NPs, including many or perhaps all predicate nominals, as really predicative in type; these arguments include the subcategorization of verbs like *consider* for predicative arguments and the conjoinability of predicative NPs and adjectives in such positions, as illustrated in (3.20) and (3.21) respectively.

(3.20)   Mary considers that $\left\{\begin{array}{l}\text{an island.} \\ \text{two islands.} \\ \text{many islands.} \\ \text{the prettiest island.} \\ \text{the harbor.} \\ \text{*every island.} \\ \text{*most islands.} \\ \text{*this island.} \\ \text{*?Schiermonnikoog.} \\ \text{Utopia.}\end{array}\right\}$

(3.21)   Mary considers John competent in semantics and an authority on unicorns.

Examples like (3.21) certainly suggest that predicative NPs should have the same type as the corresponding adjective phrases. In general, the evidence that many NPs can have e-type and/or $\langle e, t \rangle$-type interpretations appears to be very strong.

But not all NPs can have all these types of interpretations; *every man*, *each man*, *most men* really seem to have only the generalized quantifier type. They do not normally have referential uses, although a group reading can sometimes be forced on *most men* and *every man* – and is easily imposed on *everyone*, as noted by James McCawley (personal communication). They also do not normally have predicate uses.

It is possible to reconcile all the advantages of the uniformity of Montague's approach[5] with these arguments for type multiplicity by saying that the type $\langle \langle e, t \rangle, t \rangle$ of generalized quantifiers, assigned by Montague to NPs, is a type that all NPs can have, and is in fact the lowest type which all NPs share. Some but not all NPs also have one or more lower type meanings: some have meanings of type e, as in (16); some have meanings of type $\langle e, t \rangle$, as in (18); and in fact many can have both. If we can find general principles both for predicting which NPs have meanings of which types and for shifting where there is evidence that a given NP can have meanings of more than one type, then we can have the best of both worlds.

---

[5] I have not made explicit any of the positive aspects of Montague's uniform approach, since these have been taken for granted. The heart of the issue is being able to combine compositionality with faithfulness to natural-language syntax; see early works on Montague grammar such as Partee [176], Thomason's introduction to Montague [219], or Dowty, Wall and Peters [48].

One thing that becomes readily apparent once we adopt this general perspective is that particular natural language predicates may, semantically speaking, take arguments of type e, $\langle e, t \rangle$ or $\langle \langle e, t \rangle, t \rangle$, among others. The actual type choice in a particular case is ultimately determined by a combination of factors. None of this implies any violation of compositionality, since the kind of type multiplicity I am arguing for can be construed as involving a particular kind of ambiguity resolution. The factors that may resolve the ambiguity include coercion by the demands of particular predicates; for example the argument to *consider John X* has to be of predicate type (i.e., $\langle e, t \rangle$), so if we find an NP in that position we must be able to impose a predicate type reading on that NP. Another factor in resolving ambiguity is presumably the general strategy of trying simplest types first. And of course particular determiners have default preferences for the type of their NPs, even if they allow more than one possibility.

Note also that the 'essentially quantificational' NPs, i.e. those which have only the generalized quantifier type, of which *every man* is the paradigmatic example, do occur in e-type argument positions, for example as subjects and objects of ordinary extensional verbs like *hit* and *kick*. An essentially quantified NP may occur in an e-type argument position provided it is to be 'quantified in' (or whatever the corresponding mechanism of scope assignment is in a given theory). That, I think, is the part that is right about positing an obligatory QR ('quantifier raising') rule as Robert May [148] does within the Chomskyan GB framework. Whether we cast it in terms of obligatory quantifier raising or obligatory quantifying in or obligatory Cooper storage, what is right is the obligatoriness in the case of an essentially quantificational NP occurring in an essentially e-type argument position. But it is not right in general because there are predicates like *seek* which subcategorize for generalized quantifiers and there are NPs like 'John' which may be, but need not be, quantificational (that is, of type $\langle \langle e, t \rangle, t \rangle$) on a given occurrence, and in neither case is QR appropriate. In fact, to get the referentially opaque reading of 'John is seeking a unicorn', it is essential not to apply QR, since that generates the transparent reading.

3.4.2 SOME TYPE-SHIFTING FUNCTORS FOR NPS

A more detailed account of the topic of this section appears in 'Noun phrase interpretation and type-shifting principles' (Partee [174]), in which I try to show how NP interpretations of the three types just discussed can be systematically related to one another. Figure 3.4 presents a general overview of some of the formally definable type-shifting operations which I believe are both linguistically exploited in English and perhaps universal.

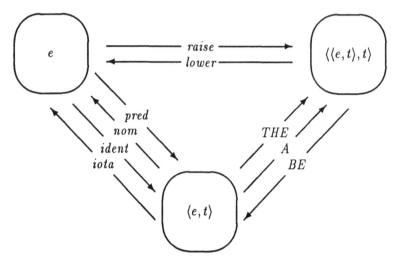

raise:	$j \mapsto \lambda P[P(j)]$	total; injective
lower:	principal ultrafilter $\mapsto$ its generator	partial; surjective
	$lower(raise(j)) = j$	
ident:	$j \mapsto \lambda x[x = j]$	total; injective
iota:	$P \mapsto x[P(x)]$	partial; surjective
	$iota(ident(j)) = j$	
nom:	$P \mapsto {}^\cap P$ (Chierchia)	almost total; injective
pred:	$x \mapsto {}^\cup x$ (Chierchia)	partial; surjective
	$pred(nom(P)) = P$	

Figure 3.4.

For the form of figure 3.4, I am indebted to Joseph Goguen and Jose Meseguer; the resemblance to the form of category-theoretic diagrams is not accidental, but it is they and not I who are knowledgeable about category theory. The three boxes represent the three domains: the domain of entities e (the upper left box); the domain of one-place predicates, corresponding to sets of individuals (the lower box); and the domain of generalized quantifiers, that is, sets of sets of entities (the upper right box). We are interested in some of the natural functions that would take us from a meaning in one of those domains to something that could reasonably be said to be a corresponding meaning in another.

Consider first the domains represented in the top two boxes, the entities and generalized quantifiers. The arrow labelled *raise* corresponds to what

Montague did to the meaning of *John*. It just takes us from an entity to the set of all properties[6] of that entity. This is a total function, since for any entity in the entity domain we can construct the set of all those sets that have that entity as a member; but it is also injective (i.e. 'into' rather than 'onto') because it maps the input domain onto only a proper subset of the bigger domain.[7] The arrow labelled *lower* represents an inverse of *raise* which is partial but surjective, that is an 'onto' map from part of the larger domain onto the smaller one. Intuitively, *lower* characterizes which generalized quantifiers have entity counterparts. More formally, it applies to any generalized quantifier which happens to be a principal ultrafilter and maps it onto its generator. A given generalized quantifier, or given NP with a generalized quantifier interpretation, is a principal ultrafilter if it denotes the set of all the properties of some one entity; if it does, then that generalized quantifier will have an entity correspondent; otherwise it will not. Although *lower* is a partial function, *raise* and *lower* are inverses in the sense that (3.22) always holds:

(3.22) $\mathrm{lower}(\mathrm{raise}(j)) = j$

One of the pairs of type-shifting operations between the domain of entities and that of sets of entities is the operation labelled *identity* and its inverse *iota*. *Identity* is a total, injective operation that maps *John* onto the property of being identical to *John*; it is the same as Quine's [184] 'pegasizing' operation, I believe. In a purely extensional subsystem it maps each entity onto its singleton set. I have called its (partial, surjective) inverse *iota* because that is the classic definite description operator that maps a property onto an entity which has that property. *Iota* is partial in that it takes a given property and if there is one and only one entity that has that property, it returns that entity as value; otherwise it is undefined. So these too form a natural pair which are inverses of each other in the same sense as above.

There is nothing substantial to say here about the pair labelled *nom* and *pred*, for which this completely extensional subsystem is a serious misrepresentation, because we really need properties rather than sets in the bottom box to represent it properly. The operations are Chierchia's [31, 32] nominalization operator and its inverse 'predicativizing' operator which maps 'entified' properties onto predicative or unsaturated ones. An example of what these operations do can be seen in the semantic side of the relation

---

[6] I frequently talk in terms of properties where these would be invoked in a full intensional model, although all that is represented here are extensional versions thereof, i.e. sets.

[7] Note that the $\langle\langle e, t\rangle, t\rangle$ domain is the power set of the $\langle e, t\rangle$ domain, which in turn is the power set of the e domain, so the cardinalities of the three domains are all different.

between *blue* as a noun naming a colour and *blue* as an adjective; of 'blue' as a property term and as the name of the colour blue.

The three pairs of operators discussed so far illustrate the heterogeneity of type-shifting principles. *Raise* is a matter of simple combinatorics that falls right out of the type system and would have an analogue between types a and $\langle\langle a, b \rangle, b \rangle$ for any a and b. *Lower* is not independently definable in combinatoric terms because it does not apply to the whole of the higher domain, but is definable as the (partial) inverse of *raise* or independently in terms of generators of ultrafilters. *Ident* and *iota* are not definable directly from the type theory but are still 'formal' insofar as they do not depend on any particular assumptions about the domain of entities (the primitive domain of which the other two are successive power sets). *Nom* and *pred* are more 'substantive' in that they depend on the inclusion of properties or property-correlates among the entities. (These are all still potentially universal in the sense of being exploited in some manner in all the world's languages or at least in all those in which these three types are used at all; others may be only language-particular, like the one which lets English use NPs like 'that size' or 'a nice colour' as predicates: see Partee [174] for discussion.)

The other three operations shown in figure 3.4 are discussed in the next section.

3.4.3 'NATURALNESS' ARGUMENTS: *THE, A* AND *BE*

When we consider possible functions mapping from $\langle e, t \rangle$ to $\langle \langle e, t \rangle, t \rangle$, the obvious candidates are all the meanings of the various determiners, since that is exactly their type. Natural language data suggest that *a* (and plural *some*) and *the* are particularly natural, since they are often not expressed by a separate word or morpheme but by constructional features, or not expressed at all. Can we find formal backing for the intuition that what *a* and *the* denote in English are particularly 'natural' type-shifting functors?

To approach a positive answer, let us consider the three functors labelled *THE, A* and *BE* in figure 3.4. They should be thought of simply as operations from one domain to the other, even though their names are mnemonic and come from Montague's treatment of the English words 'the', 'a', and 'be' in PTQ. *THE* maps a given property, e.g. the property expressed by *king*, to the set of all those properties which are such that (a) there is a unique individual who is the king and (b) he (or more carefully, some king) has those properties. This is written out in logical notation, along with the corresponding formulas for *A* and *BE*, in (3.23).

(3.23) THE: $Q \rightarrow \lambda P[\exists x[\forall y[Q(y) \leftrightarrow y = x]] \land P(x)]$

A: $Q \rightarrow \lambda P[\exists x[Q(x) \land P(x)]]$

BE: $\mathcal{P} \rightarrow \lambda x[\mathcal{P}(\lambda y[y = x])]$ or $\lambda x[\{x\} \in \mathcal{P}]$

Now although anything which is treated as a determiner in generalized quantifier theory is interpreted as a function from common noun meanings to generalized quantifier meanings and hence is in principle a candidate for being hypothesized as a type-shifting operator rather than (or as well as) a lexical meaning, what I am suggesting by taking just THE and A as type-shifting operations is that those two particular mappings are special and have rather widespread applications; they are not just the meanings of particular English morphemes. In English I think those functors are indeed encoded as the interpretations of the words 'the' and 'a', but the same functors may play a role in languages without determiners, being encoded in various ways or not being formally encoded at all.

THE

The argument offered in Partee [174] for the naturalness of THE comes largely from considering the interpretations of definite singular NPs like 'the king' in all three types. The main points are summarized here with the aid of figure 3.5.

Four of these mappings were described in the previous section: *raise*, *lower*, *ident* and *iota*. THE is the total function described above. Since THE is a total function, there are no presuppositions required for the use of definite descriptions as generalized quantifiers. If there is a unique king, THE(king') denotes the set of all his properties; otherwise it denotes the empty set of properties. *Iota*(king'), on the other hand, is defined if and only if there is exactly one king; if we assume that e is the unmarked type for subject position, this would help to explain the strong but not absolute preference for taking existence and uniqueness as presuppositions in subject position.

Iota and THE are related to each other by the fact that whenever *iota* is defined, i.e. whenever there is one and only one king, *raise*(*iota*(king')) = THE(king') and *lower*(THE (king')) = *iota*(king'), and furthermore whenever *iota* is not defined, THE(king') is vacuous in that it denotes the empty set of properties.

Now what about a possible predicative ($\langle e, t \rangle$) reading for *the king*? Suppose we start with the $\langle\langle e, t \rangle, t \rangle$ reading THE(king'). We know that one way of getting from a denotation of type $\langle\langle e, t \rangle, t \rangle$ to one of type $\langle e, t \rangle$

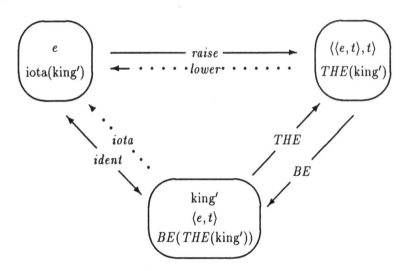

(Solid lines indicate total functions, dotted lines partial ones.)

Figure 3.5.

is to apply the function denoted by Montague's PTQ translation of English *be*, $\lambda \mathcal{P} \lambda x[\mathcal{P}(y[y = x])]$. This is the function called *BE* in the figure; I will argue further for its 'naturalness' in the next section. But let me anticipate that discussion with the two proposals in (3.24) and (3.25).

(3.24)   **Proposal about** *BE*: *BE* is not the meaning of English *be* but rather a type-shifting functor that is applied to the generalized quantifier meaning of an NP whenever we find the NP in an $\langle e, t \rangle$ position.

(3.25)   **Proposal about** *be*: (following Williams [248]) the English *be* subcategorizes semantically for an *e* argument and an $\langle e, t \rangle$ argument, and has as its meaning 'apply predicate', i.e. $\lambda P \lambda x[P(x)]$.

Then the predicative reading of 'the king' is as given in (3.26).

(3.26)   Predicative reading of *the king*: $BE(THE(\text{king}'))$

In terms of logical formulas, $BE(THE(\text{king}'))$ works out to be $\lambda x[\text{king}'(x) \land \forall y[\text{king}'(y) \leftrightarrow y = x]]$, or equivalently, $\lambda x[\exists y[\text{king}'(x) \leftrightarrow x = y]]$. This gives the singleton set of the unique king if there is one, the empty set otherwise. It is always defined, so the predicative reading also requires no presuppositions.

Note that if there is *at most* one king, then king′ =$BE(THE$(king′)), i.e. this predicative reading of *the king* has the same extension as the common noun *king* in that case, since both then pick out either the empty set or a singleton. The fact that the common noun and the predicative definite description agree modulo this 'at most one' presupposition may help explain why in English the definite article is sometimes but not always optional in predicative constructions, as illustrated in (3.27) and (3.28).

(3.27)   John is $\left\{ \begin{array}{l} \text{the president.} \\ \text{president.} \end{array} \right\}$

(3.28)   John is $\left\{ \begin{array}{l} \text{the teacher.} \\ \text{*teacher.} \end{array} \right\}$

It appears that the definite article is optional in such constructions just in case the presupposition that there is at most one such-and-such in any context is virtually built into the language, so that the conditions for the equivalence can be taken for granted.

The double-headed arrow on the ident mapping in figure 3.5 reflects the fact that for *iota* to be defined there must be one and only one king, hence

(3.29)   king′ =$BE(THE$(king′)) =$ident(iota$(king′)).

In fact, when *iota* is defined, the figure is fully commutative:

$$
\begin{aligned}
(3.30) \quad \text{king}' \;&=\; BE(THE(\text{king}')) \\
&=\; ident(iota(\text{king}')) \\
&=\; ident(lower(THE(\text{king}'))) \\
&=\; BE(lift(iota(\text{king}'))) \\
&\quad\ \text{etc.}
\end{aligned}
$$

This property of the mappings lends some formal support to the idea that there is a unity among the three meanings of *the king* in spite of the difference in type.

A and BE

Let *A* be the categorematic version of Montague's treatment of *a/an*: in intensional logic terms, $\lambda Q[\lambda P[\exists x[Q(x) \wedge P(x)]]]$. If we focus first on the naturalness of *BE*, we can then argue that *A* is natural in part by virtue of being an inverse of *BE*. The operation *BE* has some very nice formal properties that are summarized in (3.31) and (3.32).

(3.31) *Fact 1: BE* is a homomorphism from $\langle\langle e, t,\rangle t\rangle$ to $\langle e, t\rangle$ viewed
as Boolean structures, i.e:

$$BE(\mathcal{P}_1 \sqcap \mathcal{P}_2) = BE(\mathcal{P}_1) \sqcap BE(\mathcal{P}_2)$$
$$BE(\mathcal{P}_1 \sqcup \mathcal{P}_2) = BE(\mathcal{P}_1) \sqcup BE(\mathcal{P}_2)$$
$$BE(\neg\mathcal{P}_1) = \neg BE(\mathcal{P}_1)$$

(3.32) *Fact 2: BE* is the unique homomorphism that makes figure
3.6 commute. (There are other homomorphisms, and other
functors that make the figure commute, but no others that
do both.)

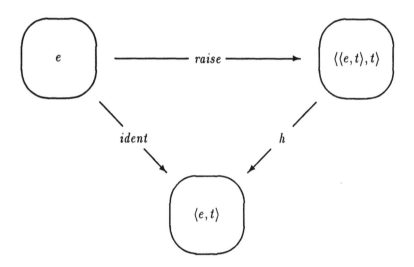

Figure 3.6.

Now what exactly does *BE* do? We can write an expression equivalent to
Montague's intensional logic formulation of his interpretation of English
be but in set-theoretical terms as follows: $\lambda\mathcal{P}[\lambda x[\{x\} \in \mathcal{P}_1]]$. That is, it
applies to a generalized quantifier, finds all the singletons therein, and
collects their elements into a set. The commutativity of figure 3.6 is then
straightforward. So *BE* is indeed a particularly nice, structure-preserving
mapping from $\langle\langle e, t\rangle, t\rangle$ to $\langle e, t\rangle$.

As mentioned in the previous subsection, *BE* should *not* be understood
as the meaning of the lexical item 'be' but as an implicit type-shifting
functor. At first sight, it seems that my proposal and Montague's original

treatment are exactly equivalent, but that is only true for the combinations of *be* + NP that Montague treated. The difference shows up when we consider predicative readings in other positions, such as with verbs like 'consider', and with other predicative complements to the copula *be*, in particular adjective phrases and predicative prepositional phrases. Montague would need additional mechanisms to account for the former and a second homonymous *be* (or some other mechanism) to account for the latter, whereas on the alternative proposal these are covered by the same principles that apply to predicate nominals after *be*, and with a single *be*.

Now *BE* is a *total* function from generalized quantifier interpretations to predicative interpretations, so we still have to explain why some NPs don't occur naturally after *be* or in other predicative positions. An explanation can be found in the fact that *be* ignores a lot of structure by looking only at the singletons in any generalized quantifier. *Most men*, for instance, will never contain any singletons, so *be most men* will always be empty. The NPs that do yield 'sensible' (non-degenerate) predicative readings fall into two categories: those formed with 'weak' determiners, and definite singular NPs. Since our *BE* has the same effect on a generalized quantifier as combining it with Montague's original interpretation of *be*, we can illustrate those results by reviewing the original Montague translations of various such combinations. It can be seen from the entries in (3.33) that the resulting combinations always have interpretations, that the interpretation of 'be no man' is identical to that of 'not be a man' (and languages seem to choose randomly which locution they prefer), and that the interpretation of 'be every man' is degenerate in that it will denote the empty set unless there is exactly one man, so that it is equivalent (only in predicative position) to 'the man'.

$$(3.33) \quad \text{(MG)} \quad \text{be}'(\text{a man}') \quad = \quad \text{be}'(\lambda P[\exists x[\text{man}'(x) \land P(x)]])$$
$$= \quad \lambda x[\text{man}'(x)]$$
$$= \quad \text{man}'$$

$$\text{(MG)} \quad \text{be}'(\text{John}') \quad = \quad \text{be}'(\lambda PP(j))$$
$$= \quad \lambda x[x = j]$$

$$\text{(MG)} \quad \text{be}'(\text{no man}') \quad = \quad \lambda x[\neg\text{man}'(x)]$$

$$\text{(MG)} \quad \text{be}'(\text{every man}') \quad = \quad \lambda x[\forall y[\text{man}'(y) \to y = x]]$$

Now, having given some grounds for claiming that *BE* is a 'natural' type-shifting functor, we can use that to support the naturalness of *A*, since it turns out that *A* is an inverse of *BE* in that $BE(A(\text{P})) = \text{P}$ for all P. But so are *exactly one* and *some*, so this is not a sufficient argument by itself. Two other potentially significant properties of *A* that I mention only briefly here are that it is symmetric and that it is monotonically increasing in both arguments; I conjecture that these are both 'nice' properties. I would conjecture, in fact, that among all possible DET-type functors, A (which combines English *a* and *some*) and THE are the most 'natural' and hence the most likely to operate syncategorematically in natural languages.

The general enterprise hinted at here, for which there is still a great deal more work to be done, involves trying to find arguments for singling out designated operations between particular domains as being particularly natural ones, and using this to make sense of such facts as that very many languages do not express *a* and *the* with determiners. I would like to be able to find solid evidence for more specifically linguistic generalisations: for example, if in some language certain determiners are left implicit and encoded, say, in the verb morphology or even not at all, then the indefinite and definite article are the two most likely candidates for that kind of treatment. And of course the investigation could be extended into many other domains besides noun phrases and determiners: the encoding of aspectual information seems another particularly promising area to investigate from this perspective.

3.5   GENERAL ISSUES

The general picture that begins to emerge from this kind of work is that natural languages are, arguably, not only strongly typed but also highly polymorphic. One important caveat is that everything I have said in terms of type theory could equally well be said in terms of sorts, at least if one imposes a structure on the sorts that is comparable in relevant respects to the type structure exploited here. I have no absolute arguments for a type theory as opposed to a theory of sorts, and in many ways sorts are more flexible since, for example, they do not necessarily have to be disjoint. But the function-argument structure which is encoded in the type theory does do a lot of work in helping us connect the syntax to the semantics. I believe that we do not go very far up the type hierarchy unless there is good reason to, but that structure, together with the type-shifting principles, is available and these allow us to be very systematic and very flexible at the same time. So I think we can say that syntactic categories correspond to natural type families, though I would not claim that this follows from the notions 'natural' and 'type' in any existing theory.

Another important general point has been emphasized in the work of Keenan and Stavi [121]: the open-ended lexical classes, the lexical nouns, verbs, adjectives, etc., nearly all have interpretations that are virtually never higher than first or second order in the type hierarchy. Natural language expressions which seem to call for an analysis in higher types than first or second order, or recursive types such as the type I proposed in section 3.3 for generalized conjunction, tend to belong to small closed syntactic categories whose members seem very close to being universal. Examples are determiners, conjunctions, words like 'only', 'almost', 'very', the 'more than' construction, etc. These function words that belong to small closed classes typically involve the most lambdas when their meaning is spelt out explicitly. That suggests that in acquiring those items that really involve the higher types, children do not have to find their way through the whole domain of possible meanings. In the higher types we presumably do not conceptualize full domains, since we not only lack open-class lexical items but also anaphora, quantification, or question-words. Rather there seem just to be certain very useful particular meanings of higher types that we have evolved into our language faculty. The domains that really seem to be open-ended and fully exploited all involve 'low' types: entities, first-order predicates and relations, and second-order predicates, relations and modifiers.

Another general point concerns the acquisition of type distinctions by children and the distribution of type distinctions across languages. Children do not immediately distinguish proper and common nouns, and many languages make a much less sharp distinction between them than English makes. The distinction between nouns (both proper and common) and verbs seems to be acquired earlier and to be more universal. This certainly goes against the standard treatment of common nouns and verbs as one-place predicates versus proper names as entity-denoting, and needs further study and explanation.

The last general point I want to make relates to some of the important lines of current research that I had to leave out of this presentation. We really need more investigation of various notions of types or sorts to find out what is optimal for natural language semantics, surely going beyond just the functional types of Montague's classical theory. While I disagree strongly with some of the criticisms that have been levelled at the use of a type theory like Montague's, I would certainly agree with him that the analysis of natural languages may require something more versatile than just the building of functional types as a means of getting more complex types from simpler ones. For instance, the algebraic approach to partially ordered types of Goguen and Meseguer [69] might give us a way to help capture the similarities and differences among count NPs and mass NPs, where (cf. Link) count nouns seem to be associated with an atomic Boolean semilattice structure, mass nouns with a *non-atomic* but otherwise similar structure. Some determiners (*all, some, no, the, most*) make sense with both, some come in similar pairs (*many, much; few, little*), and some make sense only for one or the other domain (*three, every*). It would be nice to be able to give them both a common type to capture their similarity and their conjoinability (*meat and potatoes*) and different types reflecting their differences. It is important to note in this regard that 'non-atomic' above means 'not necessarily atomic', so that the two kinds of structures as defined are not disjoint; the count noun domains simply require a more highly articulated structure, whereas the mass noun domains can be either different or unspecified. Trying to give two categories both a common type (reflecting the structure they have in common) and different types (to capture their differences) would be incoherent in a system like Montague's where the types are disjoint, but not incoherent in a system like Goguen and Meseguer's where the types themselves form a partially ordered structure.

Wherever the answers to such questions may lie, it is clear that progress in identifying the kinds of structures that are most appropriate for the description of natural language semantics is being made, and that further progress can benefit from cooperation among as many different kinds of research strategies as possible, in order to take into account both empirical facts about the richness of the variety of human languages and formal characterizations of the kinds of structures that might be contributing to that richness.

ACKNOWLEDGEMENTS

The present paper corresponds to the first of two tutorial lectures given at the Lugano workshop. I am grateful to the organizers not only for arranging a very stimulating and productive meeting but also for their invaluable assistance in recording and transcribing the lectures and providing me with a written transcript to work from. Ms. Kathleen Adamczyk of my home department made a separate transcript from the tapes, which was also invaluable, since each deciphered some things the other didn't. The reader should see Partee and Rooth [177] and Partee [174] for fuller technical detail of some of the material presented here. The research reported here was supported in part by a grant from the System Development Foundation and more recently by NSF Grant BNS-8719999.

4 Fine-structure in categorial semantics

Johan van Benthem

4.1 INTRODUCTION

In the linguistic study of syntax, various formats have been developed for measuring the combinatorial power of natural languages. In particular, there is Chomsky's well-known hierarchy of grammars which can be employed to calibrate syntactic complexity. No similar tradition exists in linguistic semantics, however. Existing powerful formalisms for stating truth conditions, such as Montague Semantics, are usually presented as monoliths like Set Theory or Intensional Type Theory, without any obvious way of expressive *fine-tuning*. The purpose of this chapter is to show how semantics has its fine-structure too, when viewed from a proper logical angle.

The framework used to demonstrate this claim is that of Categorial Grammar (see Buszkowski et al. [24] or Oehrle et al. [173] for details). In this linguistic paradigm, syntactic sensitivity resides in the landscape of logical *calculi of implication*, which manipulate functional types as conditional propositions. The landscape starts from a classical Ajdukiewicz system with modus ponens only and then ascends to intuitionistic conditional logic, which allows also subproofs with conditionalisation. A well-known intermediate system is the Lambek Calculus (Moortgat [156], van Benthem [232]), which takes special care in handling occurrences of propositions or types. These calculi represent various 'engines' for driving categorial parsing, which can be studied as to their formal properties by employing the tools of logical proof theory.

Such categorial logics also come with a systematic *semantics*. Each categorial derivation corresponds effectively to a type-theoretic term encoding its intended semantic reading (van Benthem [227, chapter 7]). This so-called 'Curry-Howard isomorphism' again reveals a landscape, this time of different *fragments* of a full type-theoretic language employing function application and lambda abstraction, a standard medium of expression in model-theoretic semantics. Thus there is a *semantic* hierarchy of richer or poorer vehicles for expressing denotations of linguistic expressions, which may be studied by employing the tools of logical model theory (van Benthem [232]). If Montagovian compositionality is the dogma which says that Type Theory provides enough 'abstract' glue to make Frege's Principle work for natural language, the issue now becomes just how much of this substance is needed for specific linguistic phenomena.

The further organization of this paper is as follows. Section 4.2 presents standard lambda semantics, and the notion of possible readings for linguistic expressions. Section 4.3 introduces a first sense of fine-structure, namely the interaction between this general mechanism and various semantic phenomena that have been discovered in specific linguistic categories. Fine-structure in the sense of care for fragments is then elaborated in section 4.4. Section 4.5 reviews some variations on the standard approach, to indicate how the perspective so far transfers to more complex linguistic facts. Finally, some relevant technical observations have been collected in an appendix that constitutes section 4.6.

4.2   TYPE-THEORETICAL SEMANTICS FOR CATEGORIAL GRAMMAR

4.2.1   DERIVATIONS AND MEANINGS

We shall be using a standard type theory, including the primitive types

(4.1) e (entity) and t (truth value),

with at least this rule for forming complex function types:

(4.2) (a, b) (functions from a-type to b-type objects).

These refer to semantic function hierarchies built up as follows:

(4.3) D_e is some initial universe of individuals;
           D_t is the truth value domain $\{0,1\}$;
           $D_{(a,b)} = \{f \mid f : D_a \rightarrow D_b\}$.

Further types may be added as the need arises, such as an intensional basic type s (possible worlds) or a complex operation like the formation of product types.

A suitably expressive type-theoretic companion language then has variables and constants of each type, as well as (at least) the following ways of building complex terms:

(4.4) **Application:** if A is a term of type (a, b) and B of type a, then $A(B)$ is a term of type b.

(4.5) **Abstraction:** if A is a term of type b, and x a variable of type a, then $\lambda x \cdot A$ is a term of type (a, b).

(Again, suitable operations of *pairing* or *projection* may be added in practice to handle further types.) Interpretation of this language in the above structures is standard. Various extensions of its resources are possible, such as adding an *identity* predicate '=' for arbitrary types with its proper meaning. This reflects a move from Lambda-Calculus (Barendregt [10]) to genuine Type Theory.

Recently, various modifications of this framework have been proposed, including many-sorted prunings of overcrowded function hierarchies, as well as more partial, information-oriented versions of the latter (Muskens [159]). But the standard format adopted here will suffice for illustrating the main issues of importance.

Terms in this Lambda-Calculus may be assigned systematically to *derivations* in Categorial Grammar. This may be illustrated as follows, using a running example in several categorial calculi. We start with the simplest Ajdukiewicz system, moving up in two steps.

Example: reflexives I

Reflexives like 'self' (and even bound pronouns) may be viewed as argument reducers on binary relations, living in type

(4.6) $((e, (e, t)), (e, t))$ ('[despise] oneself').

A categorial derivation exemplifying this use, with its matching type-theoretic meaning computed analogously, is shown in figure 4.1.

Note how function applications reflect occurrences of modus ponens, and how, by invoking the denotation of the reflexive operator, viz.

(4.7) $\lambda R_{(e,(e,t))} \cdot \lambda y_e \cdot R(y)(y)$,

the last formula may be converted into the intended meaning

(4.8) $\text{DESPISE}(\text{MARY})(\text{MARY})$.

Example: reflexives II

Reflexives may also occur in more complex 'parametrized' contexts like '[teach] oneself [a lesson]', whose relevant type is

(4.9) $((e, (e, (e, t))), (e, (e, t)))$.

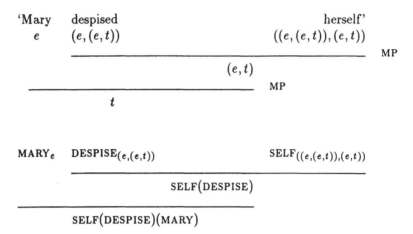

Figure 4.1. 'Mary despised herself.'

A categorial derivation must now invoke a stronger calculus of implication, involving the deduction rule of conditionalisation, as in figure 4.2.

Note how lambda abstraction encodes the conditionalisation step in this categorial derivation. Again, the ordinary definition of reflexives may be plugged in to obtain the intended meaning

$$(4.10) \quad \lambda x_e \cdot \lambda y_e \cdot \text{TEACH}_{(e,(e,(e,t)))}(x)(y)(y).$$

Example: reflexives III

Even reflexivization in prepositional phrases, seemingly different, follows the same pattern. The words 'to' (type $(e,((e,t),(e,t)))$) and 'oneself' (type $((e,(e,t)),(e,t))$) combine categorially into 'to oneself' of type $((e,t),(e,t))$ with the appropriate meaning as shown in figure 4.3.

By the definition of REF again, this reduces to the intended meaning

$$(4.11) \quad \lambda P_{(e,t)} \cdot \lambda x_e \cdot \text{TO}(x)(\text{P})(x).$$

These examples of reflexivization demonstrate an important issue. A type-theoretic framework is useful in semantics because it supports maximal *generality* for phenomena discovered in one context across different linguistic categories. Further illustrations, involving Boolean particles, will be found below. Next, we shall develop some general logical semantic themes. The reader might compare our selection of topics with that in Gallin [61], which represents the classical stage of theorizing in the Montagovian paradigm.

$$e^1 \qquad\qquad (e,(e,(e,t)))$$

$$\overline{\qquad\qquad\qquad\qquad\qquad\qquad\qquad} \text{ MP}$$

$$(e,(e,t)) \qquad\qquad\qquad ((e,(e,t)),(e,t))$$

$$\overline{\qquad\qquad\qquad\qquad\qquad\qquad\qquad\qquad} \text{ MP}$$

$$(e,t)$$

$$\overline{\qquad\qquad\qquad} \qquad\qquad \text{COND, withdrawing 1}$$

$$(e,(e,t))$$

$$x_e \qquad\qquad \text{TEACH}_{(e,(e,(e,t)))}$$

$$\overline{\qquad\qquad\qquad\qquad\qquad\qquad}$$

$$\text{TEACH}(x) \qquad\qquad\qquad \text{SELF}_{((e,(e,t)),(e,t))}$$

$$\overline{\qquad\qquad\qquad\qquad\qquad\qquad\qquad\qquad}$$

$$\text{SELF}(\text{TEACH}(x))$$

$$\overline{\qquad\qquad\qquad\qquad\qquad}$$

$$\lambda x_e \cdot \text{SELF}(\text{TEACH}(x))$$

Figure 4.2. 'teach oneself a lesson'

4.2.2 ENUMERATING POSSIBLE READINGS

As we have seen, each categorial derivation of a type b from some type sequence A encodes a meaning which may also be expressed in a lambda term (4.12)

$$(4.12) \quad \tau_b[\{x_a \mid a \in A\}]$$

of type b having parameters x_a for each type occurrence $a \in A$. This translation is not exclusively type-driven: a single derivable transition

$$(4.13) \quad A \Rightarrow b$$

may have different derivations, and hence possibly different readings. Thus it is the *derivation* which is the unit of linguistic meaning, rather than the surface string. On the other hand, not every difference in derivational structure must cause a detectable difference in semantic meaning.

Example: varying numbers of readings

$$(4.14) \quad e \;\; (e,t) \Rightarrow t.$$

This derivable sequent has only one meaning, expressible in the form

$$(4.15) \quad x_{(e,t)}(y_e),$$

$$
\cfrac{
  \cfrac{
    e^1 \qquad\qquad\qquad (e,((e,t),(e,t)))
  }{
    \cfrac{(e,t)^2 \qquad\qquad ((e,t),(e,t))}{
      \cfrac{(e,t)}{(e,(e,t))}\ \text{COND, withdrawing 1}
      \qquad\qquad ((e,(e,t)),(e,t))
    }\ \text{MP}
  }\ \text{MP}
}{
  \cfrac{(e,t)}{((e,t),(e,t))}\ \text{COND, withdrawing 2}
}
$$

$$
\cfrac{
  \cfrac{
    \cfrac{
      x_e \qquad\qquad\qquad \text{TO}_{(e,((e,t),(e,t)))}
    }{
      \cfrac{P_{(e,t)} \qquad\qquad \text{TO}(x)}{\text{TO}(x)(P)}
    }
  }{\lambda x_e \cdot \text{TO}(x)(P) \qquad\qquad \text{REF}_{((e,(e,t)),(e,t))}}
}{
  \cfrac{\text{REF}(\lambda x_e \cdot \text{TO}(x)(P))}{\lambda P_{(e,t)} \cdot \text{REF}(\lambda x_e \cdot \text{TO}(x)(P))}
}
$$

Figure 4.3. 'to oneself'

corresponding to one single modus ponens step. Of course, different categorial derivations do exist here:

$$
\cfrac{
  \cfrac{e^1 \qquad\qquad\qquad (e,t)}{t}\ \text{MP}
}{
  \cfrac{\dfrac{t}{((e,t),t)}\ \text{COND, withdrawing 1} \qquad\qquad (e,t)}{t}\ \text{MP}
}
$$

But this can be *reduced* to the simpler one using normalisation, a proof-theoretic technique which does not affect meaning, to remove the obvious detour:

(4.16) $e \Rightarrow ((e, e), e)$.

Here, genuinely different meanings exist: witness such non-equivalent derivations as

$$
\dfrac{e \qquad (e,e)^1}{\dfrac{e}{\dfrac{}{((e,e),e)}\ \text{COND, -1}}}\ \text{MP}
$$

$$
\lambda x_{(e,e)} \cdot x_{(e,e)}(y_e)
$$

$$
\dfrac{\dfrac{e \qquad (e,e)^1}{e \qquad\qquad (e,e)^1}\ \text{MP}}{\dfrac{e}{\dfrac{}{((e,e),e)}\ \text{COND, -1}}}
$$

$$
\lambda x_{(e,e)} \cdot x_{(e,e)}(x_{(e,e)}(y_e))
$$

and so on to further repetitions.

(4.17) (t, t) t $(t, t) \Rightarrow t$.

This case is ambiguous too, leading to different scope orders:

(4.18) $x_{(t,t)}(z_{(t,t)}(y_t))$ versus $z_{(t,t)}(x_{(t,t)}(y_t))$.

In fact, cases with exactly n non-equivalent readings may easily be constructed for each finite number n.

Finally, more complex examples may be found in van Benthem [231, 232] concerning the possible ways of construing transitive sentences with complex noun phrases:

(4.19) $((e, t), t)$ $(e, (e, t))$ $((e, t), t) \Rightarrow t$,

or deriving binary determiners from unary quantifiers.

This diversity of readings for linguistic expressions raises several systematic questions. One is *how many readings* exist for given type transitions. No algorithm is known for computing this number in general. Statman [215] characterizes precisely those derivable transitions in a typed Lambda-Calculus with one basic type that has finitely many readings. In our case, there are more primitive types than just one and each may also be subject to additional restrictions (see below). But Statman's result can probably be extended.

Moreover, special cases are of interest: in particular, the *non-ambiguous* type transitions having just one reading – or in other words, those logical laws which have essentially just *one proof*.

Example: non-ambiguous transitions

Well-known unambiguous sequents are such type change 'laws' as the Montague Rule for lifting denotations

$$(4.20) \quad a \Rightarrow ((a, b), b).$$

Up to normalisation by successive conversions, it has only one corresponding lambda term in normal form (by a simple syntactic argument about possible shapes; cf. van Benthem [232]):

$$(4.21) \quad \lambda x_{(a,b)} \cdot x(u_a).$$

Likewise, the so-called Geach Rule for composing denotations

$$(4.22) \quad (a, b) \ (b, c) \Rightarrow (a, c)$$

has essentially just the lambda normal form

$$(4.23) \quad \lambda x_a \cdot u_{(b,c)}(v_{(a,b)}(x_a)).$$

Thus for some key principles of current flexible categorial grammars, the difference between derivations and mere transitions on type strings turns out to be inessential. One obvious general question is whether this notion of non-ambiguity is *decidable*.

Can one describe all possible readings in a more systematic manner? What we have to offer here is a method based on the use of grammars and automata (see van Benthem [232] for further details).

Example: complex transitive sentences

Sentences of the form $NP_1 - \text{TV} - - NP_2$ have categorial derivations corresponding to the obvious scope possibilities with the transitive verb or its passive form:

$$(4.24) \quad \begin{array}{ll} NP_1(\lambda x \cdot NP_2(TV(x))) & \text{('every boy loves a girl')} \\ NP_2(\lambda x \cdot NP_1(TV(x))) & \text{('a girl loves every boy')} \\ NP_1(\lambda x \cdot NP_2(\lambda y \cdot TV(y)(x))) & \text{('every boy is loved by a girl')} \\ NP_2(\lambda x \cdot NP_1(\lambda y \cdot TV(y)(x))) & \text{('a girl is loved by every boy')} \end{array}$$

But in general, further cases arise, such as the reflexive form

$$(4.25) \quad NP_1(\lambda x \cdot TV(x)(x)).$$

All possibilities are generated here by the finite state automaton shown in figure 4.4, traversal of which generates traces by lambda terms in normal form representing all possible readings. Appendix 4.6.1 shows how such automata can be constructed from a context-free rewrite grammar induced by

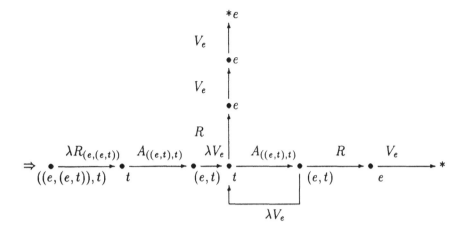

Figure 4.4.

the relevant type transitions. Note that traversing this scheme will produce an infinity of non-equivalent lambda normal forms for the above transition. This example also introduces a further twist to our query. Although the number of possible readings for the transitive sentence pattern is infinite in a global sense, it is finite in a local sense: inside each specific model. The reason is the special structure of the truth value domain D_t, which was finite, and indeed two-valued. By an additional argument (cf. van Benthem [232]), it may be shown that:

(4.26) Given any two objects A, B in the domain $D_{((e,t),t)}$ of some fixed model, the only items in the domain $D_{((e,(e,t)),t)}$ which are application/lambda definable from these are generated by forms $\lambda R\cdot$ followed by a matrix in the following list (with 'N' for A or B, and '$(\neg)$' indicating an optional negation):

(i) $(\neg)N(\lambda x_e \cdot (\neg)R(x)(x))$

(ii) $(\neg)N(\lambda x_e \cdot (\neg)N((\neg)R(x)))$

(iii) $(\neg)N(\lambda x_e \cdot (\neg)N(\lambda y_e \cdot (\neg)R(y)(x)))$.

Whatever constraints have been considered so far, the above calculus produces too many readings for most ordinary linguistic expressions. For instance, of the above four scope readings for complex transitive sentences only two are really plausible. Also, an intuitively unambiguous expression like 'Every dinosaur died' would still obtain two readings, being the inclusion of DINOSAUR in DIED, and also the converse. There are various strategies for coping with this over-generation. One is to impose some filter on admissible categorial derivations, for instance, banning derivations with an overly high computational cost. Another is to encode more syntax into the type structure, as is done in the *directional calculi* of Lambek and Bar-Hillel (see Moortgat [156] for an up-to-date presentation). But in semantic terms it is more attractive to filter out readings via an analysis of possible denotations: in particular, Keenan [118] proposes some empirically motivated universal constraints on quantifier scoping. More generally, the type-theoretic semantics for categorial derivations maps out a logical space of a priori denotational possibilities, out of which natural language only realizes those satisfying certain additional denotational constraints. What we want to show next is another aspect of fine-structure, namely how such specific semantic phenomena interact with general type-theoretic structure.

4.3 DENOTATIONAL CONSTRAINTS AND CATEGORIAL COMBINATION

4.3.1 COMPUTING DENOTATIONAL CONSTRAINTS

In various linguistic categories of expression, one encounters so-called 'denotational constraints', being general semantic properties possessed by all, or at least many, important denotations for the relevant expressions. Prominent examples have arisen in the study of *generalized quantifiers* (cf. van Benthem [227]), where all determiners turned out to be *conservative*, while many important ones are *logical* or *monotone*. A type theory provides a convenient mechanism for making such notions quite general across arbitrary categories of expression.

One major source of denotational constraints are *Boolean operators*, which provide many concepts with a universal import (cf. Keenan and Faltz [120]). For instance, here is a notion of general inference across all categories. There exists a general relation of hereditary *inclusion* (Boolean implication) defined as follows:

(4.27) $\leq_t$ is $\leq$
        $\leq_e$ is $=$
        $f \leq_{(a,b)} g$ if *for all* $x \in D_a$, $f(x) \leq_b g(x)$.

Now, an object $f \in D_{(a,b)}$ is *monotone* in its a-argument if

(4.28) $x \leq_a y$ implies $f(x) \leq_b f(y)$, for all x, $y \in D_a$.

More general versions of this notion are possible, referring to other argument types waiting inside b. This generalizes the well-known notion of monotonicity found with generalized quantifiers, expressing a certain inferential parallelism between an expression and some of its parts. We shall return to this phenomenon of monotonicity below.

Another example of Boolean structure arises with the already mentioned general constraint of Conservativity. In other words, for determiners D, the first argument turns out to restrict the second:

(4.29) $D\ AB$ iff $D\ A(B \cap A)$.

In the earlier process of categorial combination, this phenomenon turns out to proliferate.

Example: computing Conservativity I

The denotation of a complex transitive sentence with two NPs

(4.30) $Q_1\ A\ R\ Q_2\ B$

may be computed as follows, in accordance with the simplest categorial derivation of its associated type transition:

(4.31) $Q_1(A, \lambda x \cdot Q_2(B, R(x)))$ iff
$Q_1(A, \lambda x \cdot Q_2(B, \lambda y \cdot (R(x)(y) \wedge B(y)) \wedge A(x)))$ iff
$Q_1(A, \lambda x \cdot Q_2(B, \lambda y \cdot (R(x)(y) \wedge B(y) \wedge A(x)) \wedge A(x)))$ iff
$Q_1(A, \lambda x \cdot Q_2(B, \lambda y \cdot (R(x)(y) \wedge B(y)) \wedge A(x)))$.

I.e., $Q_1\ A\ R\ Q_2\ B$ holds iff $Q_1\ A\ R \cap (A \times B)\ Q_2\ B$ does.

Similar phenomena occur in other linguistic contexts. For instance, in the expression 'Wendy walks to every city', the common noun 'city' will come to restrict the individual argument of the preposition 'to', whose type may be taken to be $(e, ((e, t), (e, t)))$, as in section 4.2.1. A full calculation goes as follows.

Example: computing Conservativity II

One categorial derivation for the above prepositional phrase has the tree and associated lambda term shown in figure 4.5.
Here, by ordinary Conservativity, the last line may replace its part $\lambda x_e \cdot \text{TO}(x)(\text{WALK})(\text{WENDY})$ by $\lambda x_e \cdot (\text{TO}(x)(\text{WALK})(\text{WENDY}) \wedge \text{CITY}(x))$.

There are also different categorial derivations for the above expression. Its type transition also has unintended readings such as

(4.32) $\text{EVERY CITY}_{((e,t),t)}(\text{TO}_{(e,((e,t),(e,t)))}\ (\text{WENDY}_e)(\text{WALK}_{(e,t)}))$,

saying that 'Every city walks to Wendy'. Even so, the latter has its appropriate form of Conservativity too, computed as above.

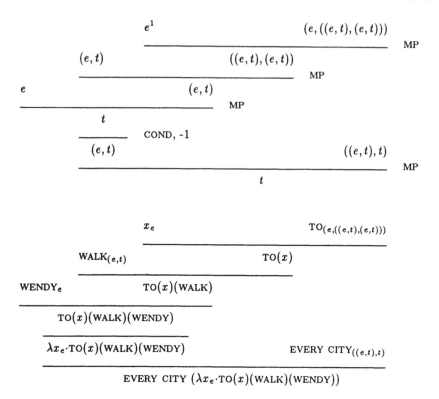

Figure 4.5. 'Wendy walks to every city.'

By this mechanism of categorial evaluation of expressions, each common noun in a quantifier phrase will come to restrict at least one individual argument position, in an algorithmic manner. This gives us a general principle of *Domain Restriction* across the whole language, explaining the difference in function between common nouns and verbs: the former serve to restrict frames of predication set up by the latter.

Conservativity also provides one way in which denotational constraints may rule out undesired but type-theoretically possible readings. For instance, an expression of the form *determiner – common-noun – verb-phrase* (say, 'every sinner repented') will only be conservative with the arguments of the determiner applied in the order given. A reading in the converse order, although a priori possible, will in general violate conservativity: witness the non-conservative converse of 'all', being 'only'.

There are various further kinds of semantic behaviour for specific linguistic expressions that can be analyzed in this categorial fashion. One important example are so-called *logical* quantifiers, like 'all' or 'no'. In our general perspective, these suggest an explanation of the general linguistic phenomenon of logicality as topic neutrality, which amounts to *permutation invariance* in the typed universe. Van Benthem [227, 232] shows how this notion applies equally to quantifiers, propositional operators, or even relation reducers like the earlier reflexivization.

4.3.2 Semantic behaviour under polymorphism

Categorial derivation with its associated semantic interpretation may be viewed as a general mechanism for the pooling of denotational constraints contributed by the various components of an expression into the eventual semantic behaviour of the whole. One suggestive focus for this phenomenon arises in the study of what is often called *polymorphism* – the ability of natural language expressions to modify their types in different environments, as required by the needs of interpretation. The above semantic account may also be viewed as a theory of polymorphism, explaining how items in one type can migrate to another one, with a systematic transfer of meaning:

(4.33)   derivation of $a \Rightarrow b$: lambda term $\tau_b[\{x_a\}]$.

In this perspective, a central question is one of dynamics. How are the earlier denotational constraints affected by type changing? Or more generally, how does one constraint manifest itself across polymorphic type jumps? Here are some answers.

Type change preserves *logicality*, in that permutation-invariant items in type a transform into permutation-invariant items in the derived type b. But, for example, a *monotone* item in type a can lose its monotonicity in derived types. Any individual A_e is trivially monotone – whereas the following lifted form, for instance, is not:

(4.34) $\lambda x_{(e,t)} \cdot \lambda y_{((e,t),(e,t))} \cdot y(x)(A_e)$.

In general, of course, there need not be exact reproduction of the original semantic property, but rather the emergence of some new variant of it. For instance, section 4.3.1 showed how the property of *conservativity* for subject NPs, in type $((e,t),t)$, transfers to a suitable new version for object NPs in type $((e,(e,t)),(e,t))$.

In addition to transmitting or modifying existing denotational constraints, polymorphism can also *create* new semantic properties of interest. For instance, the transition $e \Rightarrow ((e,t),t)$ transforms plain individuals A_e into *Boolean homomorphisms* in the NP type $((e,t),t)$, by the lambda recipe

(4.35) $\lambda x_{(e,t)} \cdot x(A_e)$ 'individual lifting'.

All this semantic behaviour of lambda terms may be investigated systematically in logical model theory. Many phenomena are in fact visible by their *syntactic form.* For example in individual lifting it is the occurrence of the variable x in syntactic head position which explains the homomorphic behaviour of the resulting function.

Another natural perspective is to ask, not which *properties* of old denotations are preserved under polymorphism, but which *relations* between them continue to hold after the change.

To start with, which polymorphic changes reproduce the old items exactly, in that they establish a *one-to-one* map from some old type domain D_a into a new domain D_b? For instance, individual lifting is indeed one-to-one, when viewed as a map from objects in the domain D_e to values in $D_{((e,t),t)}$. In other words,

(4.36)   the lambda term $\lambda y_e \cdot \lambda x_{(e,t)} \cdot x(y)$ defines a one-to-one function in the domain of type $(e, ((e,t),t))$.

But the earlier reflexivization, for example, behaves differently:

(4.37) $\lambda x_{(e,(e,t))} \cdot \lambda y_e \cdot x(y)(y)$ is not a one-to-one function in the domain of type $((e,(e,t)),(e,t))$.

The question as to an effective syntactic characterization of lambda terms defining one-to-one functions seems open at present. One general reason for interest in one-to-one definable maps as such is the possibility of *recreating* the typed hierarchy within itself at some higher level. For instance, current semantic accounts of *plurality* tend to switch from individuals in type e to sets of individuals, in type (e,t), as their basic objects. This can be done without loss of earlier structure by mapping old individuals uniquely to their *singletons* in the new type via the instruction $\lambda x_e \cdot \lambda y_e \cdot y = x$.

There are two equivalent ways of looking at these issues. From a semantic point of view, there is no difference between studying definable type transitions $a \Rightarrow b$ or simply definable maps in a functional type (a,b). An interest in the fine-structure of polymorphic shifts is also an interest in classifying denotations as to their logical complexity of definition. Thus, focusing on lambda terms $\tau[u]$ with parameters, or rather on the corresponding closed terms $\lambda x \cdot \tau[x]$, is largely a matter of convenience.

Our final example of transfer concerns the earlier relation of general *inclusion.* How does Boolean inference fare under polymorphism? If a polymorphic transition $a \Rightarrow b$ is to respect this, then the following implication must hold for its associated term τ (written with a harmless abuse of notation):

(4.38) $x_a \leq y_a$ *only if* $\tau_b[x_a] \leq \tau_b[y_a]$.

What this says is that τ, when viewed as a map from D_a to D_b, must be *monotone* in the earlier sense. Again, whether this is so will depend on its actual form.

Example: preservation of Boolean inclusion

Typically monotone is the map lifting one-place sentence operators to one-place predicate operators, via the following term:

(4.39) $\lambda x_{(e,t)} \cdot \lambda y_e \cdot u_{(t,(t,t))}(x(y))$.

Typically non-monotone is individual lifting: $\lambda x_{((e,t),t)} \cdot x(u_{(e,t)})$.

Thus, the logical question arises of characterizing just those lambda terms which induce monotone transitions. A sufficient condition is the following: τ will define a monotone map if u occurs positively, that is in syntactic head position. This condition may be relaxed, however, in the presence of Boolean parameters in our Lambda-Calculus. A precise characterization is open at present. (Van Benthem [232] reviews results so far, linking up with the preservation theorems of logical model theory.)

This concludes our discussion of dynamic transfer of semantic behaviour under polymorphism.

Actually, there are more metamorphoses in natural language than have appeared so far. Our concern has been with *derivational* polymorphism, arising in the process of grammatical construction. But there is also evidence for *variable* polymorphism, reflecting indeterminacies in initial type assignment (cf. section 4.5.3.) And yet further forms of type change may occur: witness the various notions of *collectivization* in current accounts of plurality (cf. section 4.5.1.)

4.4 THE SEMANTIC HIERARCHY

4.4.1 FRAGMENTS

Categorial Grammar comes with a landscape of weaker or stronger calculi of implication as its combinatorial apparatus. And these calculi form a hierarchy of different proof-theoretic strength, which can be stratified according to various natural principles. But at present we are interested in the *semantics* behind the enterprise, as provided by our Lambda-Calculus. (There are other semantics for conditional logics, cf. Gabbay & Guenthner [60], but these will not concern us here.) Now, this medium too admits of a significant layering. For example, as with other logical formalisms, one could classify lambda terms by special syntactic patterns of their logical operators. A case in point are the pure combinators of the form

(4.40)   prefix of lambdas – lambda-free application term,

of which several have figured in preceding sections. These are reminiscent of *universal* formulas in predicate logic. For present purposes, however, another principle of classification is more relevant, namely by patterns of *variable binding*.

In section 4.2.2 it was shown how numbers of *occurrences* of variables in lambda terms reflect significant facts about semantic construction. In the full type-theoretic language, a lambda operator can bind any number of variables, but it is natural to look at more restricted formats too. For instance, one basic candidate is the fragment where each lambda binds *exactly one* variable, something which turns out to correspond to the basic categorial calculus of Lambek [128], which has become a landmark in the area. (Some technical details about the exact Lambek terms are omitted here.) Thus, a basic hierarchy in categorial semantics is that of ascending fragments of Lambda-Calculus with increasing numbers of bindings allowed per lambda operator. Many of the illustrations in section 4.2 already belonged to the single-bond Lambek fragment of the kind illustrated in (4.41):

Example: multiplicity of binding for lambda recipes

(4.41) $\lambda x_{(e,t)} \cdot x(u_e)$ individual lifting;
         $\lambda x_{(e,t)} \cdot \lambda y_e \cdot u_{(t,(t,t))}(x(y))$ parametrizing unary
                                                       sentence operators.

By contrast, the following typically require multiple binding:

(4.42) $\lambda R_{(e,(e,t))} \cdot \lambda x_e \cdot R(x)(x)$ reflexivization;
         $\lambda x_{(e,t)} \cdot \lambda y_{(e,t)} \cdot \lambda z_e \cdot u_{(t,(t,t))}(x(z))(y(z))$
                                                       parametrizing binary
                                                       sentence operators.

Arbitrary binding multiplicity is displayed by the earlier terms

(4.43) $\lambda x_{(e,e)} \cdot x_{(e,e)}(\ldots x_{(e,e)}(y_e) \ldots)$.

Alternative principles of division

Different styles of classification by binding patterns are possible too – such as restricting the total number of available variables in advance. The latter has turned out fundamental in Modal Logic, but it seems less useful here.

The role of identity

Consider the richer formalism which arises by adding *identity* in arbitrary types to the above Lambda-Calculus. Given the great expressive power of this Type Theory, it stands in even more need of fine-structuring into fragments. Nevertheless, the presence of identity affects the earlier binding hierarchy, as it may be used to simulate multiple variable binding. For instance, already in first-order predicate logic with identity, lambdas need never bind more than *three* variable occurrences. The reason is the following trick. Any formula of the form $\phi(x, x, x, x)$ can be rewritten to

(4.44) $\quad \exists y_1 \exists y_2 \exists y_3 (\phi(x, y_1, y_2, y_3) \ \& \ x = y_1 \ \& \ y_1 = y_2 \ \& \ y_2 = y_3)$.

As is well-known in contemporary Logic, parts of formalisms may be much more pleasant than the whole. After all, standard first-order predicate logic started its career as a fragment of a full Type Theory, obtained by restricting attention to lower type levels. And within first-order logic again, fragments such as universal Horn clauses have proved their mettle in logic programming, precisely because of their special semantic characteristics. We shall encounter similar phenomena in section 4.4.2.

For the moment, we turn to a more general question, namely, in which sense the above proposal can be said to yield a genuinely *semantic* hierarchy. Here, a distinction is needed. Our main concern so far has been with *compositional* semantics, which merely studies the 'semantic glue' needed to merge component meanings into wholes. And by looking at weakest lambda fragments needed to perform this task, we are determining the price of compositionality. In addition, however, there is the matter of providing a *lexical* semantics, giving denotations to expressions in specific categories. And the latter may come with their own special purpose classifications of semantic complexity, such as the *semantic automata* hierarchy for determiners (cf. van Benthem [227, 228]). Even so, the border between the two concerns is fluid. For instance, purely type-theoretically definable items at least form an important *logical* subclass inside many specific categories: and to them, the above classification applies directly.

Example: classifying logical objects

The domain of each constructively provable type contains lambda-definable objects, and hence, in principle, an ascending hierarchy of various multiplicities of lambda binding. Thus, in type $((e, (e, t)), (e, (e, t)))$, relational operators include

(4.45) single bond $\lambda R_{(e,(e,t))} \cdot \lambda x_e \cdot \lambda y_e \cdot R(x)(y)$ Converse
       double bond $\lambda R_{(e,(e,t))} \cdot \lambda x_e \cdot \lambda y_e \cdot R(x)(x)$ Diagonal

To conclude, here is one more illustration of our binding hierarchy, having to do with the earlier distinction between compositional and lexical semantics. Natural language has invisible mechanisms for certain compositional tasks, so to speak, whereas other tasks have to be explicitly *lexicalized*. At least to a first approximation, single-bond Lambek-type transitions seem freely available, whereas procedures performing multiple binding have to be lexically expressed: witness the reflexivizer 'self'. Here is a technical illustration of this division of labour.

Example: Quinean predicate logic

The *predicate-functor* formalism for predicate logic of Quine [185] has no variables, but only logical constants plus 'book-keeping' operators on predicates performing identification and permutation. Now, under the appropriate categorial view of Boolean operators and logical quantifiers, predicate logic becomes a small fragment of Type Theory, which can be written in the following style:

(4.46)   usual notation $\forall x(\exists y\ Rxy\ \&\ \neg Sxx)$
          categorially $\forall(\lambda x\ \cdot\ \&(\exists(R(x))\ (\neg(S(x)(x)))))$.

A restriction to single lambda binding will then produce a small fragment of predicate logic. The role of explicit Reflexivization now becomes particularly vivid in the following observation:

(4.47)   Single-bond predicate logic with an additional reflexivizer of type $((e,(e,t)),(e,t))$ is expressively equivalent with all of predicate logic.

For the full type-theoretical language, no similar result holds.

There is still room for speculation here on the border line of logic and linguistics. Natural language lacks arbitrary reflexivizers, even where these would be a priori possible. For instance, there might be a higher-order reflexivizer **self** on binary determiner relations over unary predicates, so that 'every **self** dog' would stand for 'every dog is a dog'. Why has this linguistic facility failed to emerge in reality?

4.4.2 EXPRESSIVE POWER

Next, various theoretical issues arise in the new finer-grained perspective. Notably, what happens to the semantic themes of section 4.2 across the different fragments introduced above?

First, the number of *readings* for expressions will be affected by the expressive power of the semantics.

Example: readings revisited

Returning to the main example of section 4.2.2, here are some new outcomes, listed in the following table (with the full Lambda-Calculus corresponding to intuitionistic derivation, and its pure application fragment to the categorial grammar of Ajdukiewicz):

Transition	Number of Readings		
	Ajdukiewicz	Lambek	Intuitionist
$e \quad (e,t) \Rightarrow t$	1	1	1
$e \Rightarrow ((e,e),e)$	0	1	∞
$(t,t) \quad t \quad (t,t) \Rightarrow t$	2	2	∞
$e \quad e \Rightarrow e$	0	0	2
$((e,t),t) \quad (e,(e,t)) \quad ((e,t),t) \Rightarrow t$	0	4	∞

The full Lambda-Calculus provides an *infinity* of readings in some cases, whereas this did not happen in the Lambek fragment. Here is an explanation.

(4.48)   Proposition: For any Lambek-derivable transition $A \Rightarrow b$, the number of single-bond lambda terms $\tau_b[\{x_a \mid a \in A\}]$ is *finite* up to logical equivalence.

The proof of the latter result is constructive (cf. van Benthem [227]): one can display representatives of each equivalence class. As a corollary, in this fragment, one can also effectively characterize such special cases as the earlier unambiguous transitions having a *unique reading*. Even so, the number of Lambek readings is still subject to combinatorial explosion. It would be of interest to have more precise numerical information in this field, which could then be measured against general computational intuitions concerning the semantic complexity of natural language.

Another area of interest is the earlier *polymorphic transfer* and related preservation results. For instance, the natural syntactic characterization for *monotonicity* of lambda terms (namely, having the relevant parameter only in head position) which failed for the full Lambda-Calculus, does in fact hold for the Lambek fragment (cf. van Benthem [232]). And other improvements over earlier outcomes exist too.

Despite such positive findings, one objection to the present semantic approach might be that we are still doing *syntax*, no longer of the natural language being described, but nevertheless of its semantic representation language. To some extent this is true: after all, even model theory is crucially concerned with the interplay between logical syntax and abstract denotations. But a more radical acceptance of the criticism is possible too.

Perhaps the perspective of meanings for derivations has really changed the traditional notion of semantics, by making *complexity* of truth conditions, or their associated verification procedures, an integral part of the enterprise.

If this is so, then there ought to be significant differences in complexity between, say, the Lambek fragment and the full lambda formalism. And in one sense this is what the earlier observations indicate. But how do we substantiate such claims by means of some formal interpretative procedure? One approach derives from the model-theoretic notion of 'Ehrenfeucht-Fraïssé Games', which may be modified so as to analyze the significance of binding restrictions (appendix 4.6.3 provides further elaboration). But complexity is a notion which can be conceptualized in many different ways. And therefore outcomes need not always be unambiguous. In particular, the Lambek system will not do better than the full intuitionistic one on *every* count of derivational complexity (cf. van Benthem [230]).

4.5 Variations and Extensions

The above has been concerned with the fine-structure of extensional type-theoretic semantics as originated by Richard Montague, a theory which is undergoing considerable modification at present. In this section some extensions or modifications will be considered, to show how our considerations may be generalized.

4.5.1 Shifting individuals

For many descriptive purposes, the bare structure of the individual domain D_e cannot suffice. For example, a viable account of *mass terms* requires individuals structured by some form of *non-Boolean inclusion*. Likewise, collective quantification involves *groups* in addition to single individuals. One conservative move, which already provides much useful additional structure, is to replace the individual type e by the type (e, t) of sets of individuals in a number of categorizations. Notably, *intransitive verbs* will then receive type $((e, t), t)$, formerly that of *noun phrases*, rather than (e, t) – with the old type (e, t) remaining for *common nouns*.

As was observed in section 4.3.2, such one-to-one self-embeddings of the universe preserve a lot of the original structure. Even so, they also involve adjustment of previous denotational constraints for lexical items. But then the earlier general derivational apparatus will work in the same fashion.

Example: adjusting generalized quantifiers

Plural determiners may now be taken to live in the type

(4.49) $((e, t), (((e, t), t), t))$,

relating sets to families of sets. Truth conditions which have been proposed then exhibit such forms as

(4.50)   All AB 1 $A \subseteq \cup\{X \cap A \mid X \in B\}$ van Benthem [227]
         2   $A \subseteq \cup\{X \subseteq A \mid X \in B\}$ Hendriks [87]

In fact, these exemplify lifting strategies for the old determiners:

(4.51)   (i) D_{old} goes to $\lambda A_{(e,t)} \cdot \lambda B_{((e,t),t)} \cdot D_{old}(A, \cup B \upharpoonright A)$
         (ii) D_{old} goes to $\lambda A_{(e,t)} \cdot \lambda B_{((e,t),t)} \cdot D_{old}(A, \cup(B \cap \text{pow}(A)))$.

Earlier denotational constraints also return. In particular, Conservativity has even been built into the above truth conditions (see van der Does [234] for an up-to-date treatment). But the additional structure on the new individual domain becomes important too: in this case, mainly concerning the role of *set inclusion*. For instance, Logicality of determiners now comes to mean invariance not for arbitrary permutations of the new individuals (possibly disrupting their relative location), but only with respect to *inclusion automorphisms* of $D_{(e,t)}$ satisfying the equivalence

(4.52) $\pi(X) \subseteq \pi(Y)$ iff $X \subseteq Y$.

The latter may still be represented as induced by *arbitrary* permutations $\pi*$ on old individuals, obtainable as follows:

(4.53) $\pi * (x) = \pi(\{x\})$.

Thus the earlier notion of Logicality has essentially survived. Nevertheless, the additional structure can be more interesting too. For instance, *Monotonicity* will now come in several variants, because there are other natural relations between families of sets than mere set inclusion. The above two clauses for D_{new} both satisfy the 'straightforward' variant of monotonicity in the B argument: if true, they remain true for larger families of sets B. But one could also define another notion of inclusion:

(4.54) $B_1 \leq B_2$ iff $\forall X \in B_1 \exists Y \in B_2 X \subseteq Y$.

Reading (4.51i) is monotone with respect to this relation too, whereas reading (4.51ii) is not. Thus, new semantic variety emerges.

Another useful perspective on the polymorphism occurring here is the so-called 'Partee Triangle' of related basic types, with various semantic interconnections indicated:

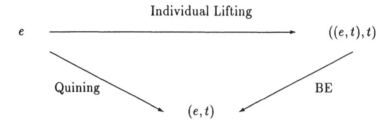

Individual Lifting

'Quining' is the earlier operation of forming singletons. See Partee [174][1], or van Benthem [227, chapter 3], on applications and theory of this schema. For instance, the various polymorphic operations in the Triangle commute. Other such 'corners' of the type universe exist too, for instance between (e,t), $((e,t),t)$ and $(((e,t),t),t)$ (see van Benthem [230] on 'Verkuyl's corner', involving a lowering map $\lambda x_e \cdot u_{(((e,t),t),t)}(\lambda z_{(e,t)} \cdot z(x))$ from $D_{(((e,t),t),t)}$ to $D_{(e,t)}$).

4.5.2 ADDITIONAL TRUTH VALUES

Another source of variation lies in the truth value domain $\{0,1\}$. For instance, recent *partial semantics* employ three or four truth values (cf. Muskens [159]). Again, such a move does not affect the earlier categorial apparatus as such – although it may engender more sophisticated versions of earlier semantic notions. (See Fenstad et al. [56] or van Benthem [229] on some issues in partial Type Theory, and Ketting [122] on the theory of many-valued fuzzy generalized quantifiers.)

But even the intensionality in Montague's original framework may be said to involve re-interpretation of the old type t. This now becomes a domain of *propositions*, which can be represented as sets of possible worlds in a new type (s,t), where

(4.55) D_t is again $\{0,1\}$ in the old sense,
        D_s is a new base domain of 'worlds', 'situations' or 'states'.

This time there is a new issue of categorial combination, namely how freely the new type may participate in semantic composition. Apparently, no Lambek single-bond restrictions apply to bindings of the form λx_s. For example, an intensionalized reading of the sentence

(4.56) 'all   elephants   dance'
        $((e,t),((e,t),t))$ $(s,(e,t))$ $(s,(e,t))$ $\Rightarrow$ (s,t),

might end up with the following double binding

(4.57) $\lambda x_s \cdot \text{ALL}(\text{ELEPHANT}(x))(\text{DANCE}(x))$.

---

[1] See also Partee [175, this volume] – eds.

As before, perhaps the more interesting semantic issues arise from the intricacies of the new semantic situation as such. Examples in this case are the proper definition of 'extensionality' in this setting, or the description of more dynamic intensional structures in *programming languages* (cf. van Benthem [232, chapter 12] as well as Harel [81]).

4.5.3 ADDITIONAL TYPES

Many recent theories have employed entirely *new* kinds of semantic type. Examples are *event-based* frameworks, where individuals and events are treated on a par, occupying separate (though formally similar) primitive domains D_e and D_E. This extension need not invalidate the earlier categorial approach; it rather suggests new questions. For instance, with the new basic sentential pattern

$$(4.58) \quad \begin{array}{cccc} \text{Det} & \text{CN} & \text{VP} & \\ ((e,t),((e,t),t)) & (e,t) & (E,t) & \Rightarrow \quad t, \end{array}$$

what will be the proper 'temporalized' account of generalized quantification and its denotational constraints?

But also, various new modes of categorial combination have been proposed. For instance, in event-based frameworks it has been suggested that a new combinatory mechanism should be envisaged in addition to the 'subordinating' function application – namely a form of 'coordinating conjunction'. Many relative clauses and adverbial or adjectival phrases might then be treated in the latter coordinating manner. This is indeed possible. But there is also an alternative, which is to stick with the old functional apparatus, enriched with suitable *denotational constraints*. For instance, an extensional coordinating adjective denotes a function A in type $((e,t),(e,t))$ which satisfies the following semantic conditions:

$$(4.59) \quad \begin{array}{ll} \text{introspection} & A(X) \subseteq X; \\ \text{continuity} & A(\cup_{i \in I} X_i) = \cup_{i \in I} A(X_i). \end{array}$$

And all such adjectives can be *represented* in the following conjunctive form (van Benthem [227]):

$$(4.60) \quad A(X) = X \cap A* \text{ for some predicate } A* \text{ of individuals.}$$

A more fundamental change would allow *variable types* in our set up – as has become widespread in computational linguistics, with *unification* serving as a preferred mechanism for building up and passing on information. Besides computational convenience, there may also be intrinsic semantic motivations for taking this line. For instance, in many cases $\{e,t,s\}$-based types are too rigid, even with the derivational polymorphism of section 4.2.

Consider the earlier example of collective expressions and plurality. One can start a sentence 'all bandits ...' thinking indeterminately of individual bandits or groups of these, letting a choice occur only after having encountered a subsequent predicate: distributive ('snored') or collective ('quarrelled'). Assigning a variable type

$$(4.61) \quad ((x,t),t)$$

to such a head noun phrase would leave the semantic choice open until the appropriate moment. Another example arises with intensionality. In the earlier intensional analysis of the sentence 'All elephants danced', the determiner retained its standard type $((e,t),((e,t),t))$, requiring it to capture extensionalized 'snapshots' of the two predicates of type $(s,(e,t))$. But in certain intensional contexts the determiner might have a stronger force, expressing a regularity across possible worlds, in type

$$(4.62) \quad ((s,(e,t)),((s,(e,t)),t)).$$

Again, an initial assignment employing an appropriate type variable would provide this intuitive latitude right from the start, postponing decisions until they are needed (for instance, in the course of an argument).

If this move is to be more than just a convenient computational trick, however, we shall have to devise an independent semantics for it. This might lead to category-theoretic approaches (cf. Lambek and Scott [129]) or the parametrized structures of Situation Semantics, which build indeterminates right into their semantic objects.

4.5.4 RICHER CATEGORIAL LOGICS

Finally, we consider the issue of additional type-forming operators in somewhat greater generality. Our Type Theory so far had only few connectives, namely 'implication' (function types) and at best 'conjunction' (product types). From a logical point of view, this makes it a rather poor system. Is there no use for other connectives, and hence a richer logic? Indeed, there have been various proposals in the categorial literature making linguistic use of additional type structure. For instance, *intersection* types would enable us to say that an expression belongs to two categories at the same time, while *disjunction* types would encode an expression's belonging to one of a number of possible categories. Finally, Moortgat [156] has various 'infixation operators' for categorial encoding of linguistic expressions with gaps.

A more systematic linguistic perspective on these matters arises in the theory of formal languages. A calculus like Lambek's may be seen as referring to concatenation of expressions in different *languages* (sets of expressions of different categories, cf. Buszkowski [23]), including their concatenation product as well as its left- and right-inverses. But many further candidates qualify, such as Boolean operations of intersection, union and complement, or the infinitary Kleene iteration. As with the original implication and product, a proof calculus may be set up for the new connectives. The resulting systems come very close to Relevance Logic or Linear Logic (cf. Avron [5], Girard [68]). Morrill [157] is a conscious quest for linguistic applications of this new variety of categorial operations. As systems of logic, such calculi are noticeable for the absence of the usual structural rules such as Monotonicity or Contraction on premise sequences – as was the case already with Lambek-style categorial logic. (See van Benthem [232] for a general development of this theme).

This convergence between grammatical and logical concerns may be understood as follows. 'Categorial grammarians' are looking for systems describing syntactic structures, whilst also insisting on some principled semantic motivation. This leads to calculi taking a somewhat liberal attitude towards every last syntactic detail. Thus, from the Ajdukiewicz system upward, one ascends toward stronger logical calculi of types. 'Linear logicians', on the other hand, are beginning to take the actual structure of premises more seriously. This takes them on a downward road from full standard systems to weaker ones, more sensitive to syntactic detail, but hence also to new distinctions between logical constants. Thus the two movements reach a common ground.

What remains less well-understood about the newer categorial logics is their intrinsic *semantic motivation*. To be sure, one can expand the Lambda-Calculus so as to include analogues for the new logical constants. But, in a sense, this is just a direct encoding of proof theory. A genuine modelling which may at least point in the right direction takes the view that categorial logics are about *processing* in some broad sense. To a first approximation, this might be modelled abstractly by making propositions or types *binary transition relations* over a set of information states, much like programs in computation. Then the eventual framework for our computational linguistics becomes rather one of Relational Algebra and Dynamic Logic, with categorial operations becoming operations of 'dynamic control'. (Van Benthem [232] attempts a synthesis of this approach with the main concerns of this paper.) In this manner, the declarative logic of linguistic *structure* and the procedural logic of language *use* may be related in the end.

4.6 APPENDICES

4.6.1 GENERATING ALL POSSIBLE READINGS

We present one method for enumerating readings of expressions, demonstrated at work on a somewhat more general issue of definability in the theory of generalized quantifiers. Consider the linguistic category of *determiners:*

(4.63)   When is a determiner denotation, in type $((e,t),((e,t),t))$, lambda-definable from objects in lower types, i.e., e, t, (e,t), $((e,t),t)$?

All possible lambda normal forms may be generated here using a *context-free grammar* having auxiliary symbols X_a, $X_a{}^*$, C_a, V_a for each of the relevant types a. Here, V_a stands for a variable of type a, C_a for a constant (parameter), X_a for any term of type a and $X_a{}^*$ for such a term which does not start with a lambda. The point of this division will become clear from the following rewrite rules for terms in normal form, for all types a. One starts with the obvious connections

(4.64) $X_a \Rightarrow X_a{}^*$ $X_a{}^* \Rightarrow C_a$ $X_a{}^* \Rightarrow V_a$.

Next, rules for applications or lambda abstractions depend on the actual types involved[2].

$$(4.65) \quad \begin{aligned} X_{((e,t),((e,t),t))} &\longrightarrow \lambda V_{(e,t)} \cdot X_{((e,t),t)} \\ X_{((e,t),t)} &\longrightarrow \lambda V_{(e,t)} \cdot X_t \\ X_t &\longrightarrow X_{(e,t)}{}^*(X_e) \\ X_t &\longrightarrow X_{((e,t),t)}{}^*(X_{(e,t)}) \\ X_{(e,t)} &\longrightarrow \lambda V_e \cdot X_t. \end{aligned}$$

The description of possible readings is much facilitated here because we can make this grammar *regular*. This may be visualized in the following finite state machine for producing definitions (where 'D_a' stands for C_a or V_a, wherever applicable):

---

[2]Note that lambda *normal forms* contain no more 'redexes' of the form $(\lambda x \cdot \alpha)(\beta)$, while the types of all variables occurring in them must be subtypes of either the resulting type or of one of the parameter types.

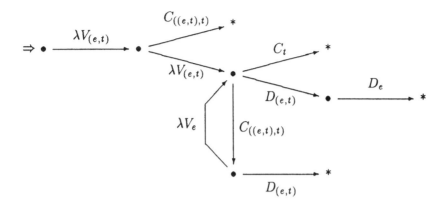

This scheme generates such determiner denotations as

(4.66) 1 $\lambda x_{(e,t)} \cdot c_{((e,t),t)}$

     2   $\lambda x_{(e,t)} \cdot \lambda y_{(e,t)} \cdot c_{((e,t),t)}(x)$

     3   $\lambda x_{(e,t)} \cdot \lambda y_{(e,t)} \cdot x(c_e)$

     4   $\lambda x_{(e,t)} \cdot \lambda y_{(e,t)} \cdot c_{((e,t),t)}(\lambda z_e \cdot c'_{((e,t),t)}(\lambda u_e \cdot x(z)))$

The latter kind is iterative, producing infinitely many forms by repeating the $c'_{((e,t),t)}(\lambda u_e \cdot$ subroutine. Thus globally there are *infinitely* many distinct possibilities for defining determiners. The reason for this behaviour lies in the above 'cycles'. This leads us to the following conjecture:

(4.67)   Conjecture: A derivable transition has *finitely* many readings if and only if its associated context-free grammar is *acyclic*.

Nevertheless, for determiners, the observed global infinity is still *locally* finite. In any fixed model, all these forms are equivalent to only some *finite* number. The reason is as follows. Any scheme of definition will start with a prefix $\lambda x_{(e,t)}\cdot$, and then some further term τ of type $((e,t),t)$. If the latter contains no free occurrences of the variable $x_{(e,t)}$, then it defines some fixed object, which has one parameter $c_{((e,t),t)}$ denoting it, corresponding to the above case 1. Next, if the variable $x_{(e,t)}$ does occur in τ, then, analyzing the latter term one step further, one can rewrite the whole scheme of definition to

(4.68) $\lambda x_{(e,t)} \cdot \lambda y_{(e,t)} \cdot [(\lambda z_{(e,t)} \cdot \tau[z/x])(x)],$

where the subterm $\lambda z_{(e,t)} \cdot \tau[z/x]$ contains no more free occurrences of the variable $y_{(e,t)}$. (To see this, check the exit routes in the above machine diagram.) Now, this subterm again denotes some fixed object in the $((e,t),t)$ type domain, which is the above case 2. So terms of the first two kinds listed above always suffice.

A proof of the local finiteness for polyadic quantifier readings mentioned in section 4.2.2 requires a more careful analysis of the potential infinity of lambda forms, relying on Boolean reductions to arrive at a finite list (van Benthem [232]).

The outcome of our analysis is that determiner relations admit of no non-trivial reductions to lower types: they are a genuinely new semantic category. Evidently, this is just one of many questions about reducibility in type domains which may be investigated. Whether for this purpose or for others, the grammar-based approach to the description of type-theoretic readings may be of independent interest.

4.6.2   FROM LANGUAGE RECOGNITION TO SEMANTIC DEFINABILITY

A first encounter with occurrences

Section 4.2.2 still omitted some subtleties concerning expressibility of readings for linguistic expressions. One is given an expression with, say, n components of types $a_1, \ldots, a_n$, and the question is if and how these may be composed into a meaning of type b. This statement of the problem already seems to convey some restrictions on admissible type-theoretic forms of definition $\tau_b[\{u_{a_1}, \ldots, u_{a_n}\}]$. For instance, it seems reasonable to demand that

(4.69)   Each type a_i should have at least one corresponding parameter u_{a_i} occurring in τ.

This would already rule out some of the cases considered earlier on. Thus, conditions on the *format* of truth conditions come to the fore, in particular concerning *occurrences* of terms within these. Here is another example. Intuitively, it would seem that the parameters u_{a_i} standing for the component expressions can be used just once, as happens in actual sentence construction. But then there is another demand:

(4.70)   Free parameters u_{a_i} should occur only once in the schema τ.

Again, this has repercussions for the earlier examples. For instance, in the given schema for transitive sentences, only finitely many readings remain, as only two N positions can be filled. But there remains an infinity of admissible readings for the earlier transition $e \Rightarrow ((e, e), e)$.

It might seem that this new requirement can be circumvented quite easily. For if τ contains two occurrences of some parameter u, then it may be rewritten to an equivalent term $\lambda x \cdot [x/u]\tau(u)$, which obeys the letter of the above requirement. But evidently this move violates its spirit; and hence we have been led to consider normal form lambda terms obeying certain restrictions on lambda binding throughout in section 4.4. Thus we have encountered a reasonable source of 'fine-structure' for truth conditions.

Disregarding occurrences

But there are also natural occasions when an emphasis on occurrences seems quite inappropriate. For instance, within some given model there are natural questions of *definability*:

(4.71)   Let objects $u_1, \ldots, u_n$ be given in domains of types $a_1, \ldots, a_n$. Which objects in some target domain D_b are lambda-definable from these?

In this second case, one is not concerned with any particular piece of syntax awaiting interpretation. And in fact no constraints on occurrences of parameters in definitions for the b-type objects seem implied. Therefore, the question can be of high complexity. For instance, given some function u_1 on the natural numbers and some natural number u_2, the question whether some other natural number v is definable from these two is in general undecidable. On *finite* base domains, however, the above question may in fact be decidable. The statement that it does amounts to a general form of what is known in the literature as 'Plotkin's Conjecture' (cf. Statman [216]).

This second kind of question has a more linguistic counterpart after all in terms of *language recognition*. A *language* is a set of admissible strings over some finite alphabet, and the recognition problem is to see if an arbitrary string belongs to the set. Here, items in the alphabet correspond to the above parameters and, in principle, strings in the language can have arbitrary numbers of occurrences of these. Now, semantic problems like the above arise by generalizing from recognizing strings to *objects denoted by strings*. For instance, given a context-free grammar and some map from its symbols to objects, as well as some interpretation schema for its rewrite rules, one can ask of an arbitrary object in the relevant semantic domain whether it belongs to the obvious denotation class of this grammar. The original language recognition problem is then that special case where the interpretation map is the syntactic identity function, with mere concatenation for the rules. In this general form, the *semantic* recognition problem for context-free grammars is undecidable. The above natural numbers example shows this, with respect to the grammar $\{N \Rightarrow u_2, N \Rightarrow u_1 N\}$. But again we have an interesting question: is the semantic recognition problem for context-free grammars decidable on all *finite* models?

This digression shows how the usual concerns of mathematical linguistics may be transferred from pure syntax to semantics.

4.6.3   MODEL COMPARISON GAMES FOR BINDING FRAGMENTS

One natural model-theoretic tool for analyzing variable restrictions are 'Ehrenfeucht Games' of model comparison, suitably augmented with fur-

ther structure, such as the *pebbling* used in Immerman [93] for characterizing variable-restricted fragments of predicate logic. We shall illustrate this
for single-bond predicate logic.

In an Ehrenfeucht Game, two players are comparing two models, with
player I trying to establish their difference and player II their similarity.
The game proceeds in rounds, started by I who picks an object in one
of the models, and followed by II who picks a (matching) object in the
opposite model. After some pre-arranged number of rounds, a comparison is
made between the two finite submodels obtained, by collecting the matched
objects chosen on each side. If the total matching is isomorphic then player
II has won, otherwise the win is for player I. The basic result here is given
in (4.72).

(4.72)   Two models verify the same predicate-logical sentences up
         to quantifier depth n if and only if player II has a winning
         strategy in their Ehrenfeucht Game over n rounds.

The final comparison may itself be pictured as another game: player I is
allowed to choose any fact involving the objects selected, whose truth value
is then compared in both models. All comparisons must match if player II
is to have a guaranteed win here.

Immerman's characterization of restricted variable fragments of predicate logic involves influencing the course of the main game by allowing
selection of objects only through some fixed supply of *pebbles* which can be
put on them. When these run out, earlier selections will have to be undone
by removing a pebble.

By contrast, in order to characterize the single-bond fragment, a restriction is needed, not on the main game, but on the comparison to be
performed during the end game:

(4.73)   The fact selected can only involve *distinct occurrences* of ob-
         jects selected in the course of the main game (represented,
         say, by their 'stage numbers').

(4.74)   This fact has to be selected by I *beforehand*.

Here, the first condition is inspired by the actual mechanics of verification.
Because of it, players will typically not be able to see the difference between a reflexive model, satisfying the double-bond property $\forall x\, Rxx$, and
one which is not reflexive. The second condition, on the other hand, serves
to break any Boolean connection between atoms in the matrix, thus removing another source of multiple binding (exemplified in formulas like
$\forall x(Px \wedge Qx)$). Call this new convention the 'Linear Token Game'. Then
the following can be proved by an obvious induction:

(4.75)   Two models verify the same single-bond formulas up to quantifier depth n if and only if player II has a winning strategy in the n-round Linear Token Game on these models.

There are further possibilities for playing around with Ehrenfeucht games. For instance, the joint effect of the first condition with fact selection postponed until the end yields another interesting fragment of predicate logic.

Of course, this analysis is to be extended to general Lambda-Calculus in order to make it applicable to our semantic hierarchy. Possibly, this can be done in terms of players picking corresponding objects on either side, so that all possible equalities between their application compounds will match on both sides in the final comparison. But other semantic games might be worth exploring in this context too, such as Hintikka-style verification games on single type models.

5 Properties, propositions and semantic theory

Raymond Turner

5.1 INTRODUCTION

This paper is a tutorial on property-theoretic semantics: our aim is to provide an accessible account of property theory and its application to the formal semantics of natural language. We develop a simple version of property theory and provide the semantics for a fragment of English in the theory. We shall say more about the particular form of the theory in the next section but to begin with we outline the main reasons why we believe property-theoretic semantics to be worthy of attention.

5.2 INTENSIONALITY

The main motivation for the development of a theory of propositions and properties stems from the desire to develop an adequate account of *intensionality* in natural language. In this section we briefly review some possible approaches to intensionality in order to motivate the approach we shall eventually adopt.

5.2.1 INTENSIONALITY VIA POSSIBLE WORLDS

Traditional approaches to intensionality employ the notion of *possible world*. Propositions are taken to be sets of possible worlds and properties to be functions from individuals to propositions. The modal and doxastic operators are then unpacked as functions from propositions to propositions. For example, the modal operator of necessity is analysed as that function which maps a proposition P to that proposition which consists of all those worlds whose accessible worlds are elements of P. Different choices of the relation of accessibility between worlds yield different modal and doxastic notions. Kripke [127] introduced the possible world analysis of necessity and possibility while Hintikka [88] extended the analysis to deal with belief and knowledge. The possible world analysis, while not pinpointing one correct account of the various modal notions, nevertheless provides a clear semantic perspective from which the formal differences between the possible options can be clearly articulated.

Despite its success the possible world analysis of intensionality has recently come under attack. The crucial point seems to be that the notion of proposition as a set of possible worlds is not sufficiently *fine-grained* to serve as the foundation on which to hang intensional meaning. In particular, propositions as sets of possible worlds are too *coarse-grained* to serve as arguments to the doxastic operators of knowledge and belief: if two sentences denote exactly the same set of possible worlds then an agent who believes one is committed to believing the other. While this may be acceptable for certain notions of belief (e.g. rational belief) it does not seem persuasive for all notions. Mathematical belief seems to be a case in point. Since mathematical assertions are naturally taken to be necessarily true or necessarily false, under this account of belief an agent who believes one true assertion of mathematics is thereby committed to believing all true assertions of mathematics. This seems not to supply an adequate account of mathematical belief.

This criticism of the possible world approach to the attitudes of belief and knowledge naturally leads to the demand for a notion of proposition that will not commit an agent to believing all the logical consequences of his basic beliefs.

5.2.2   PROPOSITIONS AS SENTENCES:
THE OBJECT/METALANGUAGE HIERARCHY

One approach which meets this demand and which emanates from the artificial intelligence community seeks to view propositions as sentences in some language of semantic representation. Properties are then unpacked as λ-abstractions on such sentences. This certainly addresses the fact that propositions need to be fine-grained, but there are obvious philosophical objections to such an approach.

Intuitively, what is believed, known, desired, deemed to be possible etc. are not sentences in some language. Sentences are just collections of symbols arranged according to some grammatical principles, whereas the objects of desire, knowledge or belief have *semantic content*. One cannot be said to believe a sentence but rather one stands in relation to its semantic content.

Whatever the merits of this criticism, there appear to be more devastating problems for this syntactic analysis of propositions and properties.

To pinpoint the problem, let L be the language in which such propositions are to be constructed. Informally writing $x \in L$ to indicate that x is a sentence of the language L, we can express (5.1) as (5.2).

(5.1)   John believes something false.

(5.2) $\exists x (x \in L \wedge bel(\text{John}, x) \wedge false(x))$

This looks promising in that we have expressed the fact that John believes something false or believes a proposition which is false where propositions are identified with the sentences of L. But now we face a problem with regard to the language in which (5.2) is expressed. Suppose there are two believers, John and Peter, and Peter wishes to express the assertion that John believes something false. Then Peter's language must be expressive enough to express (5.2) and consequently must have access to the *propositions* of John's language in that its variables of quantification must range over the sentences of L. One way of achieving this is to employ the Tarskian object/metalanguage distinction: Peter's language becomes the metalanguage of John's and in Peter's language the well formed formulae (*wff*) of John's language occur as terms.

The main problem with such an approach concerns its expressive power. Consider the sentences:

(5.3) A believes that everything that B believes is true.

(5.4) B believes that everything that A believes is true.

Let $O_A (= M_{O_B})$ be the object language of A which is also to serve as the metalanguage for the object language O_B Of B. Then we can attempt to express (5.3) as (5.5)

(5.5) $bel(A, \forall x \in O_B(bel(B, x) \rightarrow True(x)))$

where $x \in O_B$ has its obvious interpretation and facilitates quantification over the wff of B's language. In order to express (5.4), however, we require a language which has the facility to quantify over the wff that are the beliefs of A. This cannot be achieved in O_B or O_A since we now wish to quantify over A's beliefs. We must resort to a metalanguage M_{O_A}. We can then attempt a statement of (5.4) as (5.6).

(5.6) $bel(B, \forall x \in O_A(bel(A, x) \rightarrow True(x)))$

But now observe that the quantification in (5.5) does not include the belief of B expressed by (5.6) since in O_A we can only quantify over those beliefs expressible in O_B. The belief expressed by (5.6) is only expressible in a further metalanguage M_{O_A}. We can, of course, replace (5.5) with (5.7):

(5.7) $bel(A, \forall x \in M_{O_A}(bel(B, x) \rightarrow True(x)))$

but then (5.6) does not express what we think it does. Indeed, no matter how far we climb up the object/metalanguage hierarchy we will not be able to capture the intuitive content of (5.3) and (5.4); some of the beliefs of A or B will always be left out.

    This appears to be a rather devastating criticism of the *syntactical* approach. However, one cannot immediately draw the conclusion that no such approach will work. All we have actually established is that the object/metalanguage hierarchy approach is too restrictive in that the logical content of certain sentences cannot be naturally expressed.

5.2.3   THE PARADOXES

One way out of this impasse is to remove the object/metalanguage distinction and identify the languages. The modal and truth operators now take sentences of the language (or their quoted relations) as arguments. This would certainly deal with the problem of the expressive power of the language. Indeed, this approach is too expressive in that it admits too liberal a notion of proposition. Consequently, we run into severe foundational difficulties. In order to see this we need to be a little more explicit about the structure of the language and theory we envisage.

    We assume a first order language in which the truth and modal operators are predicates and the sentences of the language can occur as terms. Propositions are identified as the sentences of the language. In addition, if we wish our language to serve as the language of semantic representation for natural language, properties have to be part of the basic ontology, and so we require the language to be rich enough to support the definition of properties through λ-abstraction: as we previously indicated, properties are unpacked as propositional functions and, given that sentences are to serve as propositions, it is natural to unpack properties as the λ-abstracts on such. All this can be simply achieved by including the Lambda-Calculus as part of the syntax of terms. Indeed, once the Lambda-Calculus is included in the language the wff can be coded as terms using the facilities of the Calculus.

Unfortunately, once the natural axioms for the truth predicate are added to the theory, in the form of the Tarski biconditionals, the theory becomes inconsistent. The problem arises because the facilities of the Lambda-Calculus which seem crucial for the application at hand enable the derivation of a wff which says of itself that it is false. This together with the Tarski biconditionals leads to inconsistency. More explicitly, we have the *Liar sentence* (5.8) and the *Tarski Biconditional* (5.9).

$$(5.8) \qquad A \ \leftrightarrow \ \sim true(A)$$
$$(5.9) \qquad A \ \leftrightarrow \ true(A)$$

In classical logic these two assertions are formally inconsistent. Even if we had no truth predicate in the language we would not be entirely safe since similar problems arise with the modal predicates if anything like the standard systems of modal logic are employed.

This seems to indicate that the syntactical approach will not work. This is independent of any philosophical scruples we might have about the very idea of propositions being taken to be sentences. However, there is still one route we might explore. It is still open to us to maintain that although propositions are not sentences they are systematically related to them in that the structure of propositions exactly mirrors the structure of the sentences in some language of semantic representation. This is a weak *representationalist* view. Not only does this perspective address some of the philosophical objections raised against the simple-minded view of propositions as sentences but there is much to be said in favour of such a stance. The fine-grained notion of proposition we require certainly seems to demand that the identity criteria for propositions be as stringent as those for sentences. So we might still be able to maintain this weak representational view of propositions. However, Thomason [220] has shown conclusively that even this option is not available to us. Paradoxes still arise even under the guise of this more sophisticated representationalist view.

We have to proceed with care in drawing conclusions from these reflections on the syntactical approach to intensionality. What the paradoxes establish is not that we cannot have a representationalist view of propositions but rather that *not all* sentences of our formal language can be representations of propositions. The language is too rich in its expressive power.

5.2.4 THE AXIOMATIC APPROACH

The way out, and the one that we shall explore, is to develop an axiomatic theory of propositions, truth and modality. Propositions will be delineated by sentences in our formal language and formally the syntactic category of propositions will be a subset of the class of well-formed formulae but the propositions are no more to be identified with the sentences or well-formed formulae than the sets of Zermelo-Frankel set theory are to be identified with the expressions in the formal language of set theory which delineate them. It is naive to believe that the objects of any axiomatic theory must be identified with the syntactic expressions which delineate them.

5.3 A THEORY OF PROPERTIES, RELATIONS AND PROPOSITIONS

The principal concern of the present paper is to illustrate the main ideas behind property-theoretic semantics. There are several theories of properties which might be employed for our purposes including Feferman [53], Turner [223] and Aczel [1]. All these theories could be pursued for the purposes of natural language semantics. Indeed, Chierchia and Turner [33] apply the theory of Turner [223] to the semantics of a fairly large fragment of English, while Kamareddine [102] employs Aczel's [1] *Frege Structures*. The theories of Feferman have not yet been explicitly exploited for semantic purposes. Frege Structures are formally contained in the other two theories mentioned and moreover are formally the simplest to describe. For pedagogical purposes it therefore seems prudent to illustrate the main ideas behind property-theoretic semantics by employing the notion of a Frege Structure. The thesis of Kamareddine contains a slightly different approach to the one adopted here and contains many more details about the construction and underlying theory of Frege Structures. Rather than employ the set-theoretic notion of a Frege Structure we shall develop the formal theory of these structures as a theory of propositions, properties and truth.

5.3.1 THE LAMBDA-CALCULUS

The formal language of the theory is in essence the language of the untyped Lambda-Calculus, in which all objects will be represented, whether they be individuals, propositions, properties, relations, quantifiers or determiners. A basic definition of the language is given in figure 5.1. This formal language should be seen in contrast to Montague's intensional logic where every expression is explicitly typed, whereas the Lambda-Calculus supports only minimal explicit typing. In the present theory the categorization of objects as individuals, propositions, properties, relations, quantifiers, etc. will be achieved axiomatically or proof-theoretically rather than explicitly through the syntax.

Basic vocabulary

individual variables $x, y, z, \ldots$
individual constants $c, d, e, \ldots$
logical constants $\wedge, \vee, \neg, \Rightarrow, \Leftrightarrow, \Xi, \theta, \approx$

Inductive definition of terms

(i) Every variable or constant is a term.
(ii) If t is a term and x is a variable then $(\lambda x.t)$ is a term.
(iii) If t and t' are terms then (tt') is a term.

Axioms

(i) $\lambda x.t = \lambda y.t[y/x]$ for y not free in t
(ii) $(\lambda x.t)t' = t[t'/x]$

Figure 5.1. The language of terms

One can view the language as a flat version of Montague's intensional logic with all the type information and restrictions removed. The distinguished constants $\wedge, \vee, \neg, \Rightarrow, \Leftrightarrow, \Xi, \theta, \approx$ stand for the intensional analogues of conjunction, disjunction, negation, implication, equivalence, existential quantification, universal quantification and equality, respectively. We shall write $\wedge st$ as $s \wedge t$ etc. The intensional connectives and quantifiers are thus combinators in the Lambda-Calculus and as such they inherit its highly intensional properties: the notion of equality belongs to the Calculus itself.

This language needs to be given some interpretation; we need to spell out the truth conditions for the logical connectives and quantifiers. Of course, not all the expressions can be assigned truth values but only those which are propositions. To this end we introduce the formal theory of propositions and truth.

5.3.2 Propositions and truth

In order to unpack the notions of proposition and truth we introduce a simple first order language which has the Lambda-Calculus as the language of terms. The complete language of the formal theory has just two categories, *terms* and *wff*. The terms are those of the Lambda-Calculus together with basic combinators for the logical connectives and quantifiers. The wff are those of standard first order logic together with three forms of atomic wff: the equality of two terms, the assertion that a term is true, and the assertion that a term is a proposition. This is summarized in figure 5.2.

(i)   If t and s are terms then $s = t$, $P(t)$ and $T(t)$ are (atomic) wff.
(ii)   If Φ and Φ' are wff then $\Phi \,\&\, \Phi'$, $\Phi \vee \Phi'$, $\Phi \rightarrow \Phi'$, $\sim \Phi$ are wff.
(iii)   If Φ is a wff and x a variable then $\exists x \Phi$ and $\forall x \Phi$ are wff.

Figure 5.2. Inductive definition of wff

The actual theory concerns the predicates P, which asserts that something is a proposition, and T, which asserts that it is a true proposition. These predicates are governed by the *axioms of propositions* and the *axioms of truth*. These appear in figure 5.3 and figure 5.4 respectively.

(i) $(P(t) \,\&\, P(s))$ $\rightarrow$ $P(t \wedge s)$
(ii) $(P(t) \,\&\, P(s))$ $\rightarrow$ $P(t \vee s)$
(iii) $(P(t) \,\&\, P(s))$ $\rightarrow$ $P(t \Rightarrow s)$
(iv) $P(t)$ $\rightarrow$ $P(\neg t)$
(v) $\forall x P(t)$ $\rightarrow$ $P(\theta \lambda x.t)$ [1]
(vi) $\forall x P(t)$ $\rightarrow$ $P(\Xi \lambda x.t)$
(vii) $P(s \approx t)$

Figure 5.3. Axioms of propositions

(i) $P(t) \,\&\, P(s)$ $\rightarrow$ $(T(t \wedge s) \leftrightarrow T(t) \,\&\, T(s))$
(ii) $P(t) \,\&\, P(s)$ $\rightarrow$ $(T(t \vee s) \leftrightarrow T(t) \vee T(s))$
(iii) $P(t) \,\&\, P(s)$ $\rightarrow$ $(T(t \Rightarrow s) \leftrightarrow (T(t) \rightarrow T(s)))$
(iv) $P(t)$ $\rightarrow$ $(T(\neg t) \leftrightarrow \sim T(t))$
(v) $\forall x P(t)$ $\rightarrow$ $(T(\theta x t) \leftrightarrow \forall x T(t))$
(vi) $\forall x P(t)$ $\rightarrow$ $(T(\Xi x t) \leftrightarrow \exists x T(t))$
(vii) $T(s \approx t)$ $\leftrightarrow$ $s = t$
(viii) $T(t)$ $\rightarrow$ $P(t)$

Figure 5.4. Axioms of truth

Most of the axioms of propositions are self-explanatory and together simply state that the notion of proposition is closed under the intensional connec-

---
[1] For convenience we shall abbreviate $\theta \lambda x.t$ as $\theta x.t$ and $\Xi \lambda x.t$ as $\Xi x.t$.

tives and quantifiers. The last axiom insists that the assertion of intensional equality constitutes a proposition.

The axioms of truth apply only to those objects which are propositions but on the class of propositions they yield the standard Tarski truth conditions. The axioms thus provide us with a formal version of the notion of proposition and its standard Tarski truth conditions. The last axiom informs us that everything which is true is a proposition. These axioms are slightly weaker than those of a Frege Structure.

5.3.3 PROPERTIES AND RELATIONS

The main concern of property theory is with the development of notions of proposition, property and relation. The first notion is taken as primitive while the other two are derived. Essentially, properties are to be unpacked as propositional functions where the notion of function is inherited from that of the Lambda-Calculus. Definition (D1) shows how relations are defined in curried form by recursion.

definition D1

(i)^2 $Rel_1(f)$ $\equiv$ $\forall x(P(fx))$
(ii) $Rel_{n+1}(f)$ $\equiv$ $\forall x(Rel_n(fx))$

The notion of property is closed under the standard Boolean operations.

definition D2

(i) $\cap$ $\equiv$ $\lambda f.\lambda g.\{x : fx \wedge gx\}$
(ii) $\cup$ $\equiv$ $\lambda f.\lambda g.\{x : fx \vee gx\}$
(iii) $-$ $\equiv$ $\lambda f.\lambda g.\{x : fx \wedge \neg (gx)\}$

These combinators correspond to union, intersection and complementation. We can derive the following axioms for these constructors where we shall write $\cap xy$ as $x \cap y$ etc.

theorem TM1

For $\mathcal{O}$ any of the combinators $\cap, \cup, -: Pty(t) \rightarrow (Pty(s) \rightarrow Pty(t \mathcal{O} s))$

proof: All the results follow from the axioms of propositions (see figure 5.3) and are straightforward if tedious to check. ∎

---

^{2}We shall subsequently write Pty (property) for Rel_1. Also, we shall often write $\lambda x.t$ as $\{x : t\}$ and $T(tx)$ as $x \in t$ especially when t is a property.

theorem TM2

For $Pty(s)$ and $Pty(t)$

(i) $z \in t \cap s \quad \leftrightarrow \quad z \in t \,\&\, z \in s$
(ii) $z \in t \cup s \quad \leftrightarrow \quad z \in t \,v\, z \in s$
(iii) $z \in t - s \quad \leftrightarrow \quad z \in t \,\&\, \sim (z \in s)$

proof: We employ definition (D1) part (i) together with the observation that s and t are properties; we then apply the axioms of truth. ∎

The combinators mentioned by definition (D3) provide the universal and empty property respectively. These may seem somewhat surprising to someone familiar with classical set theory.

definition D3

(i) $\nabla \quad \equiv \quad \{x : (x \approx x)\}$
(ii) $\Omega \quad \equiv \quad \{x : \neg\, (x \approx x)\}$

theorem TM3

$Pty(\nabla) \,\&\, Pty(\Omega)$

proof: These follow from the propositional nature of intensional equality and the axiom of negation (see figure 5.3 part (i)) for propositions. ∎

The standard determiners are easily definable as follows.

definition D4

(i)   **every** $\equiv \quad \lambda x.\lambda y.[\theta z(xz \Rightarrow yz)]$
(ii)   **some** $\equiv \quad \lambda x.\lambda y.[\Xi z(xz \wedge yz)]$
(iii)   **no** $\equiv \quad \lambda x.\lambda y.[\theta z(xz \Rightarrow \neg(yz))]$
(iv)   **not all** $\equiv \quad \lambda x.\lambda y.[\Xi z(xz \wedge \neg (yz))]$
(v)   **the** $\equiv \quad \lambda x.\lambda y.[\Xi z(xz \wedge yz \wedge \theta u(xu \Rightarrow u \approx z))]$

theorem TM4

For **d** any of the above determiners $Pty(s) \rightarrow (Pty(t) \rightarrow P(\mathbf{d}st))$.

proof: The result follows directly from the axioms of propositions. For example, consider (i). If x and y are properties then for every z, $xz \Rightarrow yz$ is a proposition. It follows that for every z, $\theta z(xz \Rightarrow yz)$ is a proposition. ∎

theorem TM5

For $Pty(s)$ and $Pty(t)$ we have:

(i) $T(\textbf{every } st)$ $\leftrightarrow$ $\forall x(x \in s \rightarrow x \in t)$
(ii) $T(\textbf{some } st)$ $\leftrightarrow$ $\exists x(x \in s \,\&\, x \in t)$
(iii) $T(\textbf{no } st)$ $\leftrightarrow$ $\forall x(x \in s \rightarrow \sim (x \in t))$
(iv) $T(\textbf{not all } st)$ $\leftrightarrow$ $\exists x(x \in s \,\&\, \sim (x \in t))$
(v) $T(\textbf{the } st)$ $\leftrightarrow$ $\exists x(x \in s \,\&\, x \in t \,\&\, \forall u(u \in s \rightarrow u = x))$

proof: The fact that $Pty(s)$ and $Pty(t)$ ensures that all the atomic assertions are propositions; the theorem follows immediately from the axioms of P and T. ∎

Hence the quantifiers obtain their natural truth conditions when applied to properties. Finally, we introduce the predicates that capture the abstract notions of determiner and quantifier.

definition D5

(i) $Det(f)$ $\equiv$ $\forall x(Pty(x) \rightarrow Quant(fx))$
(ii) $Quant(f)$ $\equiv$ $\forall x(Pty(x) \rightarrow P(fx))$

theorem TM6

$$Quant(f) \,\&\, Quant(g) \rightarrow Quant(f \cap g) \,\&\, Quant(f \cup g) \,\&\, Quant(f - g)$$

Theorem (TM6) is straightforward to check. This completes the basic exposition of the theory. We now turn to a simple extension.

5.3.4   MODALITY AND TRUTH

The theory has been largely motivated by the need to provide an adequate treatment of intensionality but thus far we have said little about one aspect of intensionality, namely modality itself. Even the language of the present theory has no explicit modal operators. To remedy this the language of the theory is extended by the addition of two new operators, ■ and □, where the former is a new term and the latter a new sentential connective. The logical constants now have the form $\wedge, \vee, \neg, \Rightarrow, \Leftrightarrow, \Xi, \theta, \approx, \blacksquare$, and the class of wff is extended by the clause (5.10):

(5.10)   If Φ is a wff then $\square\Phi$ is a wff

The new term-forming operator is the intensional modal ■. The natural axioms for these new constructs are given by (5.11) and (5.12).

(5.11) $\Box(P(t)) \rightarrow P(\blacksquare\, t)$

(5.12) $\Box(P(t)) \rightarrow (T(\blacksquare\, t) \leftrightarrow \Box(T(t)))$

Axiom (5.11) states that if it is necessary that t is a proposition then $\blacksquare\, t$ is a proposition while axiom (5.12) states that, under such conditions, $\blacksquare\, t$ is true precisely when $T(t)$ is necessarily true (or is known to be true or is believed to be true depending on the interpretation of the operator).

We could extend the theory to include an intensional truth predicate $\mathcal{T}$ with axioms (5.13) and (5.14), but we shall not employ this extension in the fragment discussed below. We need only notice that some of our original examples required such an extension.

(5.13) $P(t) \rightarrow P(\mathcal{T}t)$

(5.14) $P(t) \rightarrow (T(\mathcal{T}t) \leftrightarrow T(t))$

The logic and model theory of the extensional modal is dictated by the intended interpretation in the standard way. We shall not pursue this topic any further here, but see Turner [224] for details of the formal aspects of such an addition. However, one point is crucial. Observe that the principle (5.15) is derivable from the axioms of equality.

(5.15) $T(t \approx s) \rightarrow [T(\blacksquare\, t) \leftrightarrow T(\blacksquare\, s)]$

The intensional equality of the two terms (and in particular propositions) is sufficient for substitution in modal contexts to preserve truth. In contrast, the principle (5.16) is *not* derivable.

(5.16) $T(t) \leftrightarrow T(s) \rightarrow [T(\blacksquare\, t) \leftrightarrow T(\blacksquare\, s)]$

The extensional equivalence of the two terms is not sufficient to guarantee that substitution in modal contexts preserves truth. Propositions are permitted to be sufficiently fine-grained to block such derivations. Even the principle (5.17) is not derivable.

(5.17) $\Box[T(t) \leftrightarrow T(s)] \rightarrow [T(\blacksquare\, t) \leftrightarrow T(\blacksquare\, s)]$

5.4   TYPES AS PREDICATES

The rich structure of the theory of properties, relations and propositions provides a framework in which the semantics of natural language in the style of Montague can be carried through pretty much intact. What is missing is any notion of *type*. Montague's intensional logic has the type theory built into the syntax of the language. In contrast, our language of semantic representation is the untyped Lambda-Calculus and no type information is present. However, the formal theory does allow us to characterize certain objects as propositions, relations, quantifiers and determiners etc. In the present type regime, sentences in the fragment of English addressed in Montague's [154] *Proper treatment of quantification* (PTQ) will denote propositions, intransitive verbs and nouns will denote properties and term phrases quantifiers etc. However, to carry this out systematically for the whole PTQ fragment we need a more general approach.

5.4.1 THE TYPE HIERARCHY

Initially, we define a version of the classical hierarchy of types in which the types are predicates in our language of wff. In definition (D6), **U** is the type of everything, **P** the type of those objects which are propositions and **R** ⫤ **S** the type of functions from objects of type **R** to those of type **S**.

definition D6

(i) $\mathbf{U}(x)$ $\equiv$ $x = x$
(ii) $\mathbf{P}(x)$ $\equiv$ $P(x)$
(iii) $\mathbf{R} \dashv \mathbf{S}(f)$ $\equiv$ $\forall x (\mathbf{R}(x) \to \mathbf{S}(fx))$

In particular, the type of properties, *Pty*, is **U** ⫤ **P**; *Quant*, the type of quantifiers, is **Pty** ⫤ **P** and that of determiners is **Pty** ⫤ **Quant**. We summarize the relation between syntactic categories and semantic types in figure 5.5. For pedagogical reasons we shall employ the framework of Dowty, Wall and Peters [48].

Figure 5.5 should be self-explanatory. It merely sets out the correspondence between the various syntactic categories as presented in Dowty, Wall and Peters [48] and their types as first-order predicates. The important difference between this notion of type and that of intensional logic is that these types do not refer to higher-order functions but are simple first-order predicates and are governed by the proof theory of first-order logic. Indeed the type-checking rules can be expressed as simple rules of proof in a natural deduction style as shown in (5.18).

category name	categorial definition	semantic type
t	t	P
CN	CN	Pty
IV	IV	Pty
T	t/IV	$Quant$
IAV	IV/IV	$Pty \dashv Pty$
TV	IV/T	$Quant \dashv Pty$
T/CN	(t/IV)/CN	$Pty \dashv Quant$
t/t	t/t	$P \dashv P$
IV/t	IV/t	$P \dashv Pty$
IV/IV	IV/IV	$Pty \dashv Pty$
IAV/T	(IV/IV)/T	$Quant \dashv (Pty \dashv Pty)$

Figure 5.5. Correspondences between categories and type

(5.18)

$$\frac{\begin{array}{c}[\mathbf{R}(x)]\\\vdots\\\mathbf{S}(t[x])\end{array}}{\mathbf{R}\dashv\mathbf{S}(\lambda x.t)} \qquad \frac{\mathbf{R}(a)\quad \mathbf{R}\dashv\mathbf{S}(f)}{\mathbf{S}(fa)}$$

The reader should note that this is a theory of *variable* types, so that objects can live in more than one type. The theory is not *strictly typed* as is, for example, intensional logic. Types in this theory are predicates which classify the objects in the domain of individuals as propositions, properties, quantifiers or determiners etc., but an object can possess more than one type. The only constraint is that they must conform to the type discipline defined by the above proof rules.

5.5   A FRAGMENT OF ENGLISH AND ITS SEMANTICS

We now illustrate the application of the present theory to natural language semantics. In this section of the paper we provide a semantics for the PTQ fragment and for pedagogical reasons we shall follow the exposition in Dowty, Wall and Peters [48]. We shall go through most of the fragment and provide its semantics in the present theory. As we proceed we shall comment upon the differences between the present treatment and that of Montague[3].

5.5.1 DETERMINER-NOUN RULE

(S2) If D is an element of T/CN
and N is an element of CN
then $F_2(D, N)$ is an element of T
where $F_2(D, N) = DN$.

(T2) If D is an element of T/CN
and N is an element of CN
then $Trans(F_2(D, N)) = Trans(D)\,Trans(N)$.

For simplicity we have ignored morphological complications in the statement of this rule. The translation rule (T2) differs from Montague's in terms of its treatment of intensionality. In Montague's intensional logic, intensionality is presented as a derived notion: intensional contexts are induced by the employment of the operator ' ^ ' and are furnished semantically in terms of possible worlds. Here properties are inherently intensional notions and are taken as primitive.

An example should help to clarify the issues: 'every man' translates to **every**(m') which yields, via beta reduction, $\lambda y.[\theta z(m'z \Rightarrow yz)]$. This differs from the representation in Montague's intensional logic. Since *man* is represented as a property and properties are intensional notions there is no need to employ the intensional operator ' ^ ' in the representation.

As regards the role of types, note that if the type of $Trans(D)$ is *Det* and that of $Trans(N)$ is *Pty* the result will be of type *Quant*, as required.

5.5.2 SUBJECT-PREDICATE RULE

(S4) If A is in T and D is in IV
then $F_4(A, D)$ is an element of t
where $F_4(A, D) = AD$.

(T4) If A is in T and D is in IV
then $Trans(F_4(A, D)) = Trans(A)\,Trans(D)$.

---

[3]The reader should note that we shall in general retain the rule names established by Montague and also the convention whereby a syntactic rule Sn is associated with a translation rule Tn.

We have once again ignored morphological complications in the statement of these rules. The translation rule (T4) also differs from Montague's in the treatment of intensionality. We shall not labour this point further. Once again it is easy to see that the rule obeys the type regime: if $Trans(A)$ is of type $Quant$ and $Trans(D)$ of type Pty then the result will be of type P. Table 5.1 illustrates rule (T4) in conjunction with rule (T2).

string		translation	type
Every	$\mapsto$	$\lambda x.\lambda y.[\theta z(xz \Rightarrow yz)]$	Det
man	$\mapsto$	m'	Pty
Every man	$\mapsto$	$\lambda y.[\theta z(m'z \Rightarrow yz)]$	$Quant$(by T2)
talk	$\mapsto$	t'	Pty
Every man talks	$\mapsto$	$\theta z(m'z \Rightarrow t'z)$	P (by T4)

Table 5.1. Every man talks.

The truth conditions for the sentence in table 5.1 are given by (5.19). The fact that these are the standard Tarski ones follows from the result in section 5.3 which provides the truth conditions for determiners under the assumption that m' and t' are properties.

(5.19) $T(\theta z(m'z \Rightarrow t'z)) \leftrightarrow \forall z(z \in m' \rightarrow z \in t')$

5.5.3   Conjoined sentences, verb-phrases and term-phrases

The rules for sentence conjunction (S11a and T11a) are identical to those of PTQ. From the basic axioms for propositions, $Trans(S) \wedge Trans(S')$ is a proposition provided that $Trans(S)$ and $Trans(S')$ are both propositions. So the type regime is again left intact.

(S11a)   If S and S' are in t
then $F_8(S, S')$ (i.e. S *and* S') is in t.

(T11a)   If S and S' are in t
then $Trans(F_8(S, S')) = Trans(S) \wedge Trans(S')$

Rules (S12a) and (T12a) for IV-conjunction are similar, and the result is of type Pty since the intersection operation preserves Pty.

(S12a)   If D and D' are in IV
then $F_8(D, D')$ is in IV.

(T12a) If D and D' are in IV
then $Trans(F_8(D, D')) = Trans(D) \cap Trans(D')$

For term-phrase disjunction we proceed in a similar fashion with (S13) and (T13). Once again the type regime is obeyed since intersection and union preserve the type *Quant*.

(S13) If A and B are in T
then $F_9(A, B)$ is in T.

(T13) If A, B are in T
then $Trans(F_9(A, B)) = Trans(A) \cup Trans(B)$

5.5.4 ANAPHORIC PRONOUNS AS BOUND VARIABLES; SCOPE AMBIGUITIES AND RELATIVE CLAUSES

To deal with these topics we must first unpack the translation of the basic term phrases. The basic term phrases are he_0, he_1, he_2 etc., whose general schema for translation is given by (5.20)

(5.20) $Trans(he_n) = \lambda z.(zx_n)$

Observe that $\lambda z.(zx_n)$ is of type *Quant*: given $Pty(z)$, zx is a proposition for each z. Once the translation for basic term phrases is in place we can proceed to the rule of quantification (S14) and the corresponding translation rule.

(S14) If A is in T and S is in t
then $F_{10,n}(A, S)$ is in t.

(T14) If A is in T and S is in t
then $Trans(F_{10,n}(A, S)) = Trans(A)(\lambda x_n . Trans(S))$.

It is easy to establish that the type regime is obeyed: if $Trans(A)$ is of type *Quant* and $Trans(S)$ is of type P, then $\lambda x_n . Trans(S)$ is of type *Pty* and the result of type P. This is illustrated by table 5.2.

The truth conditions for the sentence of table 5.2 are given by (5.21).

(5.21) $T(\exists x(s'x \wedge w'x \wedge t'x)) \leftrightarrow \exists x(x \in s' \mathbin{\&} x \in w' \mathbin{\&} x \in t')$

Following the presentation in Dowty, Wall and Peters [48] we next illustrate how (T14) accounts for *de dicto/de re* ambiguities in the complements of intensional verbs like *believe*. First we require rules (S7) and (T7).

(S7) If A is in IV/t and S is in t
then $F_{11}(A, S)$ is in IV
where $F_{11}(A, S) = A$ **that** S.

string	translation	type
1. he_2	$\mapsto$ $\lambda z.(x_2 \in z)$	*Quant*
2. walk	$\mapsto$ w'	*Pty*
3. talk	$\mapsto$ t'	*Pty*
4. he_2 walks	$\mapsto$ $w'x_2$ (by 1,2, and T4)	*P*
5. he_2 talks	$\mapsto$ $t'x_2$ (by 1,3, and T4)	*P*
6. he_2 walks and he_2 talks	$\mapsto$ $w'x_2 \wedge t'x_2$ (by T11a)	*P*
7. A woman	$\mapsto$ $\lambda y.\Xi x(s'x \wedge yx)$	*Quant*
8. A woman walks and she talks	$\mapsto$ $\Xi x(s'x \wedge ((\lambda x_2.[w'x_2 \wedge t'x_2])x))$ (by T14)	
9.	$\mapsto$ $\Xi x(s'x \wedge w'x \wedge t'x)$ (by λ-conversion)	*P*

Table 5.2. A woman walks and she talks.

(T7)   If A is in IV/t and S is in t
       then $Trans(F_{11}(A,S)) = Trans(A)\,Trans(S)$.

Observe that the proposition $Trans(S)$ is the argument of the verb. For example, *believes that a fish walks* , translates to: $believe'(\Xi x(f'x \wedge w'x))$. So the object of belief is the proposition expressed by the sentence following the *that* clause. Subsequently, the *de dicto* reading of *John believes that a fish walks* would get the representation $believe'[\Xi x(f'x \wedge w'x)]j'$. The truth conditions for the sentence, i.e. $T(believe'[\Xi x(f'x \wedge w'x)]j')$, cannot be further elaborated without more details regarding the truth-conditions for *believe*. If treated as a modal operator then the logic of the extensional modal would dictate matters. On the other hand, using T14 the *de re* reading would obtain the representation $\Xi x(f'x \wedge believe'[w'x]j')$ whose truth conditions would unpack as $\exists x(x \in f' \,\&\, T(believe'[w'x]j'))$.

Relative clauses are governed by PTQ's rule (S3) for which S' comes from S by replacing each occurrence of he_n or him_n by *he* or *him*, *she* or *her*, or *it* according to gender.

(S3)   If E is in CN and S is in t
       then $F_{3,n}(E,S)$ is in CN
       where $F_{3,n}(E,S) = E$ such that S'

(T3) If E is in CN and S is in t
then $Trans(F_{3,n}(E, S)) = \lambda x_n.[(Trans(E)x_n) \wedge \mathrm{trans}(S)]$.

The functioning of (S3) and (T3) is illustrated in table 5.3.

string	translation
1. he$_5$ walks	$\longmapsto$ $w'x_5$
2. fish such that it walks	$\longmapsto$ $\lambda x_5.[f'x_5 \wedge w'x_5]$ (by T3)
3. Every fish such that it walks	$\longmapsto$ $\lambda y.[\theta x((f'x \wedge w'x) \Rightarrow yx)]$
4. Every fish such that it walks, talks	$\longmapsto$ $[\theta x((f'x \wedge w'x) \Rightarrow t'x)]$

Table 5.3. Every fish such that it walks, talks.

5.5.5 TRANSITIVE VERBS, MEANING POSTULATES, AND NON-SPECIFIC READINGS

All this is quite straightforward but for the sake of completeness we will continue with rule (S5) that combines a transitive verb with a term-phrase to give an IV phrase.

(S5) If D is in TV and B is in T
then $F_5(D, B)$ is in IV
where $F_5(D, B) = DB$.

(T5) If D is in TV and B is in T
then $Trans(F_5(D, B)) = Trans(D) Trans(B)$.

Under (T5) we obtain the analysis given in table 5.4. As regards the type regime we have only to note that if $Trans(D)$ is of type $Quant \dashv Pty$ and $Trans(T)$ is of type $Quant$, then the result is a property.

string	translation
1. seek	$\longmapsto$ s'
2. a unicorn	$\longmapsto$ $\lambda y.[\exists z(u'z \wedge yz)]$
3. seek a unicorn	$\longmapsto$ $s'(\lambda y.[\exists z(u'z \wedge yz)])$
4. John seeks a unicorn	$\longmapsto$ $(\lambda p.[pj'])(s'(\lambda y.[\exists z(u'z \wedge yz)]))$
5.	$s'(\lambda y.[\exists z(u'z \wedge yz)])j'$
	(by λ conversion)

Table 5.4. John seeks a unicorn.

The treatment of extensional verbs such as *find* parallels that of PTQ, so that to force the equivalence of the two semantic representations of *John finds a unicorn* we follow PTQ and add a *meaning postulate* such as (5.22).

(5.22) $fxa \approx a(\lambda y.[f_* xy])$ *where* $f_* = \lambda y.\lambda x.[f(\lambda u.[uy])x]$

for such verbs. We could develop a modal version of the postulate but we assign this as an exercise to the interested reader.

5.5.6   THE VERB *be*

The verb *be* is treated as in PTQ by (5.23),

(5.23) $Trans(be) = \lambda y.\lambda x.(y[\lambda z.(x \approx z)])$

and just a little reflection should be sufficient to convince the reader that this has type $Quant \rightharpoondown Pty$. Table 5.5 shows how this is used in calculating the truth conditions for the sentence *John is Bill*.

	string		translation
1.	be Bill	$\mapsto$	$(\lambda y.\lambda x.(y[\lambda z.(x \approx z)]))(\lambda u.[ub'])$
			$\lambda x.(x \approx b')$ (by λ-conversion)
2.	John is Bill	$\mapsto$	$(\lambda u.[uj'])(\lambda x.(x \approx b'))$
			$j' \approx b'$ (by λ-conversion)

Table 5.5. John is Bill.

The reader should note that the truth conditions for the last step yield $j' = b'$ as expected.

5.5.7   ADVERBS AND INFINITIVE COMPLEMENT VERBS

Here we consider sentential adverbs such as *necessarily* and verb phrase adverbs such as *slowly*. We deal first with sentential adverbs. Translating the adverb *necessarily* as ■, we use rules (S9) and (T9) to obtain the translation for *necessarily John walks*, as shown in table 5.6.

(S9)   If D is in t/t and S is in t
         then $F_6(D, S)$ is in t
         where $F_6(D, S) = DS$.

(T9)   If D is in t/t and S is in t
         then $Trans(F_6(D, S)) = Trans(D)\,Trans(S)$.

string	translation
1. John walks	$\mapsto$ $w'j'$
2. Necessarily John walks	$\mapsto$ $\blacksquare(w'j')$ (by T9)

Table 5.6. Necessarily John walks.

The truth conditions are then unpacked as (5.24).

$$(5.24) \qquad T(\blacksquare(w'j')) \leftrightarrow \Box(T(w'j'))$$

For verb-phrase adverbs we proceed in much the same way as Montague, using rules (S10) and (T10). The analysis of infinitive complement verbs is also identical to that of PTQ.

(S10) If D is in IV/IV and B is in IV
then $F_7(D, B)$ is in IV
where $F_7(D, B) = DB$.

(T10) If D is in IV/IV and B is in IV
then $Trans(F_7(D, B)) = Trans(D)\,Trans(B)$.

5.5.8 DE DICTO PRONOUNS AND SOME PRONOUN PROBLEMS

The case where the antecedent of a pronoun has a de dicto reading is covered by rule (S16):

(S16) If A is in T and D is in IV
then $F_{10,n}(A, D)$ is in IV.

(T16) If A is in T and D is in IV
then $Trans(F_{10,n}(A, D)) = \lambda y.[Trans(A)(\lambda x_n[Trans(D)y])]$.

If the type of $Trans(A)$ is *Quant* and that of $Trans(D)$ is *Pty* then $\lambda x_n[Trans(D)y]$ has type *Pty*; $[Trans(A)(\lambda x_n[Trans(D)y])]$ has type P and $\lambda y.[Trans(A)(\lambda x_n[Trans(D)y])]$ is of type *Pty*, as required. The reader should by now be able to see how the type rules shown in (5.18) enable us to check that the expressions are all correctly typed without the need for the type information to be explicit in the syntax.

5.5.9 PREPOSITIONS

Prepositional phrases are produced by rule S6, which follows the treatment of PTQ.

(S6)   If D is in IAV/T and A is in T
then $F_5(D, A)$ is in IAV.

(T6)   If D is in IAV/T and A is in T
then $Trans(F_5(D, E)) = Trans(D) Trans(A)$.

5.5.10 NOMINALIZATION

Finally, in this section we consider the phenomenon of nominalization. In particular, rules $(S_{Nom}1)$ and $(T_{Nom}1)$ provide a semantics for infinitives, thus going beyond the approach of Dowty, Wall and Peters. We follow the approach of Chierchia [31].

$(S_{Nom}1)$ If A is in IV
then $\mathbf{To}(A)$ is in T.

$(T_{Nom}1)$ If A is in IV
then $Trans(\mathbf{To}(A)) = \lambda z.[z\ Trans(A)]$.

	string		translation
1.	seek a unicorn	$\mapsto$	$s'(\lambda y.[\Xi z(u'z \wedge yz)])$
2.	To seek a unicorn	$\mapsto$	$\lambda z.[z(s'(\lambda y.[\Xi z(u'z \wedge yz)]))]$
3.	To seek a unicorn is foolish	$\mapsto$	$f'(s'(\lambda y.[\Xi z(u'z \wedge yz)]))$

Table 5.7. To seek a unicorn is foolish.

Table 5.7 completes our semantics for the fragment. There are many issues not covered but that is to be expected. Moreover, the semantic and syntactic treatment of many constructs leaves much to be desired, but our intention has not been to carry out detailed syntactic or semantic analysis but rather to establish the viability and advantages of the property-theoretic approach to semantics.

6 Algorithms for semantic interpretation

Per-Kristian Halvorsen

6.1 INTRODUCTION

The integration of syntactic and semantic processing has prompted a number of different architectures for natural language systems, such as rule-by-rule interpretation [221], semantic grammars [22] and cascaded ATNs [253]. The relationship between syntax and semantics has also been of central concern in theoretical linguistics, particularly following Richard Montague's work. Also, with the recent rapprochement between theoretical and computational linguistics, Montague's interpretation scheme has made its way into natural language systems. Variations on Montague's interpretation scheme have been adopted and implemented in several syntactic theories with a significant following in computational linguistic circles. The first steps in this direction were taken by Hobbs and Rosenschein [89]. A parser for LFG was augmented with a Montagovian semantics by Halvorsen [76]. GPSG has been similarly augmented by Gawron et al. [65], and Schubert and Pelletier [206] followed with a compositional interpretation scheme using a first order logic rather than Montague's computationally intractable higher-order intensional logic.

In parallel with these developments in the syntax/semantics interface, unification-based mechanisms for linguistic description had significant impact both on syntactic theory and syntactic description. But the Montagovian view of compositionality in semantics and the architectures for configuring the syntax/semantics interface were slower to achieve a similar reevaluation in view of unification and the new possibilities for composition which it brought.

Unification is first and foremost a technique for combining pieces of information given certain facts about how the individual pieces relate to each other. The task of semantic composition is exactly of this nature. It is concerned with the combination of semantic information based on the relationship between the constituents in a phrase-structure tree or some other syntactic representation. The method for combination of information used in Montague grammar was function application and set formation, or equivalently, the reflexes of these operations in the Lambda-Calculus. This choice imposed certain restrictions on the manner of combination of information in the interpretation (or translation) step. Specifically, it required that the informational substructures to be combined be contiguous in the structure being interpreted. Unification, supplemented with the flexible addressing scheme usually associated with it in computational linguistics, permits a loosening of this restriction on contiguity. This again allows interesting new choices for interpretation algorithms.[1]

In this paper I present a proposal for a unification/constraint-based interpretation algorithm where interpretation is accomplished through successive approximation. The algorithm is stated using an extension of the rule language for lexical-functional grammars (LFGs). This extension permits the statement of semantic rules on a par with rules for the derivation of functional structures. In fact, an arbitrary number of *projections* can be described using this new rule language. In addition to the functional structure and the semantic structure, interesting other projections might include *discourse structure* and *thematic structure*. The discourse structure would provide the appropriate level for statement of generalizations concerning inter- or intra-sentential anaphora and the information structure of the discourse. The thematic structure would make explicit the representation of the pseudo-semantic thematic roles which determine such phenomena as the range of syntactic constructions particular verbs partake in.[2]

The proposed interpretation mechanism allows functional structures and semantic structures to be constructed in parallel. This proposal differs from previous ones in that it does not take functional structures to be the input to semantic interpretation, and consequently all semantically relevant information does not have to be funnelled through the f-structure. Yet it permits the dependencies between functional and semantic information to be captured through the association of functional and semantic annotations on constituents in the phrase-structure rules. The projection mechanism itself does not impose a pivotal role on the f-structure any more than on the semantic structure. In fact, the f-structure could be viewed as a projection

---

[1] Unification-based semantic descriptions were first introduced in the tradition of logic grammars, e.g. Pereira and Warren [180], but no connection was made there to the work on compositional semantics in linguistics.

[2] Dalrymple [43] employs the projection-mechanism in an investigation of anaphoric binding phenomena.

from the semantic structure, or as a combined projection from c-structure and semantic structure. The projections are functions from structural level to structural level and can be composed and inverted to model these complex dependencies.[3]

6.2 COMPOSITIONALITY

A clearly desirable trait of any interpretation mechanism is that it be systematic. By this I simply mean that the interpretation of the utterance should be mechanically and deterministically derivable given a (semantic) dictionary and the rules (or principles) of the interpretation scheme. One would also like the interpretation mechanism to be complete. This means that all meaningful utterances in the fragment described should have an interpretation.

Compositionality is an additional requirement often viewed as important. Under a strict interpretation a compositional semantics is one where the interpretation algorithm is recursive on the syntactic tree assigned to the utterance, and the meaning of a constituent is required to be a function of the meaning of its immediate constituents.

Strict compositionality is not necessarily entailed by systematicity and/or completeness as defined here. However, as long as the mechanism for composition of information is limited to the devices available in Montague Grammar, strict compositionality does follow from the systematicity requirement. But with new methods for composition of information, such as unification or even more general constraint satisfaction techniques, noncompositional alternatives which do not necessarily sacrifice systematicity become available.

The utility of the compositionality hypothesis is also brought into question when we turn our attention from *meanings* to *interpretations*, that is from the consideration of the semantic potential of sentences or utterance types (meaning), to the impact of an utterance in a specific context. This calls for integration of information from various kinds of sources (e.g. *context* as well as text) for which the structured semantic representations and the unification-based constraint-satisfaction techniques I employ are well-suited.

---

[3] See Halvorsen and Kaplan [79] for a more detailed discussion of the notion of projections

6.3   TRANSLATION AND INTERPRETATION

Our interpretation process is indirect in that it relies on a level of semantic representation. The interpretation algorithms I am concerned with here relate utterances or analyses of utterances to these semantic representations. In other words, they address what in Montague grammar is known as *translation*.

The exact nature of the representations depends on the purpose of the semantic analysis. In Fenstad et al. [56], the focus was on providing interpretations in the context of situation theory (Barwise-and-Perry:83), and on relating this to traditional, model-theoretic semantic frameworks. For this purpose we designed the language of situation schemata defined by the rules below.

SITSCHEMA	$\rightarrow$	(SIT)(FOCUS) REL^n ARG^n LOC POL
SIT	$\rightarrow$	$\langle$*situation indeterminate*$\rangle$
FOCUS	$\rightarrow$	{IND | IND_e}
REL_I	$\rightarrow$	$\langle$*n-ary relation constant*$\rangle$
ARG.i	$\rightarrow$	{IND_e | IND (SPEC) COND $(\text{SITSCHEMA})^n$ (FOCUS)}
LOC	$\rightarrow$	IND COND_{loc}
POL	$\rightarrow$	{1 | 0}
IND_e	$\rightarrow$	$\langle$*entity*$\rangle$
IND	$\rightarrow$	$\langle$*indeterminate*$\rangle$
SPEC	$\rightarrow$	$\langle$*quantifier*$\rangle$
COND	$\rightarrow$	(SIT) REL ARG'.1 POL
COND_{loc}	$\rightarrow$	REL_{loc} ARG'.1 ARG'.2
ARG'.i	$\rightarrow$	{IND_e | IND}

More recently, we have explored the notion of deduction in situation theory using a language we call PROSIT (for *P*rogramming in *Si*tuation *T*heory) [161].

The constraint-based interpretation schemes are equally well-suited to either formalism, the only requirement being that the semantic representations provide objects whose internal constituents are individually addressable.

6.4   THE PROJECTION MECHANISM

Previous proposals for semantic interpretation of LFGs took functional structures as input to the semantic component.[4] The semantic representa-

---

[4] The following material is also covered in Halvorsen and Kaplan [79].

tions were described based on an analysis of the level of functional structure, and I therefore call this technique 'description by analysis'. The first examples of this approach are Halvorsen [75, 76]. There, LFGs were interpreted with four interpretation principles which applied to f-structure configurations in any order, provided the configuration matched the pattern specified in the interpretation principle. The patterns corresponded to semantically significant aspects of the f-structure. These interpretation principles licensed the introduction of a set of semantic equations. The complete set of semantic equations had been found when all the semantically significant f-structure configurations had been matched by an interpretation principle. The semantic equations could be solved using the same extended unification algorithms used in the construction of the functional structure itself. Other examples of semantic interpretation using the 'description by analysis' approach are Frey and Reyle [59] and Reyle [189]. They defined a set of 'transfer rules' which mapped functional structures into semantic representations by means of a modified Lambda-Calculus.

All interpretation schemes based on 'description by analysis' assume that the functional structure, or fragments of it, has been constructed prior to interpretation, and they require that all semantically relevant information be encoded in the functional structure. The approach makes it impossible to write semantic interpretation rules which are tailored to specific constructions, unless these constructions have different functional structures. There are two reasons for this: (1) The connection between syntactic rules and interpretation principles is severed by stating the interpretation rules on f-structures; (2) no semantic rule language is provided.

The proposal for semantic description set forth here is based on the general notion of *structural correspondence* in the LFG theory ([104], [105]). Under this view a variety of structures representing different systems, or *projections*, of linguistic information (phrasal, functional, semantic, discourse and prosodic) are connected through piecewise mapping functions. This proposal also contrasts with the approach to the specification of semantic structures in unification grammars using distinguished attributes in a single level of representation (e.g. **SYNTAX** and **SEMANTICS**) as in Fenstad et al. [55, 56], Karttunen [112], Shieber [210], Pollard and Sag [182]. With distinguished attributes, functional and semantic properties are collapsed into a single information complex. Although this does, of course, permit an account of both syntactic and semantic generalizations, it is limiting in several ways. It assumes that all levels of representation are mapped off a single base structure (typically the c-structure), even though the informational dependencies may be more elegantly stated as constraints between more abstract structures. It also does not suggest some of the useful extensions to which the correspondence view naturally leads. On the correspondence view semantic structures can be based on a direct mapping from c-structure, while semantic generalizations based on information that is independently expressed in functional structure can be stated by composing the semantic correspondence with the inverse of the functional correspondence (i.e. $\sigma \circ \phi^{-1}$) in terms of the notation introduced below and in Kaplan [104] and Halvorsen and Kaplan [79].

6.5 NOTATION FOR SEMANTIC RULES

The point of departure for the semantic extensions to the rule language is the notation for syntactic rules in LFG. In the standard version of this formalism the phrase-structure rules are annotated with constraints, also called functional descriptions. In our implementation, each term in the right-hand side of a phrase-structure rule has two parts. The first part, preceding the colon, (':'), must be a symbol representing a syntactic category. The second part, following ':', contains equational constraints. In the equations, ↑ and ↓ refer to functional structures corresponding to specific nodes of the phrase-structure tree. The relational character of the annotated phrase-structure rules is obvious: they connect phrase-structure and functional structure, with the functional descriptions (the constraints) attributing properties to the latter.

The functional structure is, however, but one of many possible *projections* from the sentence string and the phrase-structure tree. Each projection represents a different aspect of the analysis of the sentence. Here I am particularly interested in the projection describing the content of the utterance, or, following Barwise and Perry [15], the *described situation*. To be better able to use the equations to describe this projection, I introduce some new symbols into the vocabulary of our constraint language: * refers to the current node in the phrase-structure tree (*not* the functional structure of the current node), and $\mathcal{M}$, a function which when applied to a node gives us its mother. We also introduce ϕ and σ. We call these symbols *projectors*. The σ-projector maps *into* semantic structures. Depending on how the theory is configured the σ-projection can relate semantic structures to another single level of structure (e.g. f-structure, or c-structure). But this approach also permits the semantic structure to be related directly to a *set* of other structures (e.g. the semantic structure can be expressed as a composite function of the information in the c-structure and in the f-structure, see below). The ϕ-projector maps *into* functional structures. Typically, ϕ has been taken to define a mapping between c-structure and functional structure, but the projection mechanism can also open up other possibilities if they prove to be empirically motivated.

For the moment, let ϕ be defined as a mapping between c-structure nodes and functional structures. It is now possible to decompose $\uparrow$ and $\downarrow$ in terms of $\mathcal{M}$, $*$ and ϕ: $\uparrow$ is equivalent to $\phi\mathcal{M}*$, and $\phi*$ corresponds to $\downarrow$.

Let us also assume that the σ-projection is defined on c-structure nodes. In this configuration, either projector can be prefixed to any expression denoting a c-structure node. The following are both well-formed expressions of the extended equational language: $\sigma\mathcal{M}*$, $\sigma*$. In combinations, the $\mathcal{M}$-function binds most tightly with $*$, whereafter the projectors, ϕ and σ, take precedence over other combinators. Consequently, $(\sigma\mathcal{M} * \text{ARG1})$ denotes the value of the ARG1 attribute in the semantic structure corresponding to $\mathcal{M}*$.

The projectors, being functions, also permit us to work with their inverses. In the current setup, the inverse of a projector, for example ϕ^{-1}, will denote the set of c-structure nodes corresponding to a given element in the projection (here the set of c-structure nodes corresponding to a given f-structure). ϕ^{-1} can be prefixed to any expression denoting an element in the functional projection; for example $(\phi^{-1}(\phi\mathcal{M} * \text{SUBJ}))$ denotes the set of nodes contributing information to the SUBJ function in the f-structure for the node referred to by the expression $\mathcal{M}*$.

The composition of the σ-projection with the inverse of the ϕ-projection can now be used to express the fact that the functional object and the second argument (or theme) in an active sentence coincide even if the information about the object is scattered throughout the sentence, as in the Latin example *Scriba tabulam habet rasam*, where the object *tabulam rasam* is discontinuous. This is done by letting the semantic structure of the theme be a function from the full set of c-structure nodes contributing information about the functional object. The semantic structure corresponding to the object of the f-structure, f_i, is then denoted by $(\sigma(\phi^{-1}(\phi(f_i \text{ OBJ}))))$.

The projector can, in principle, occur in any equation (i.e. in the lexicon or in the phrase-structure rules). Where a particular equation occurs depends on the nature of the semantic generalization it expresses. The following is a typical lexical item with semantic equations.

KICK   V   S-ED $(\phi\mathcal{M}* \text{ PRED})=\text{'KICK'}$
                          $(\sigma\mathcal{M}* \text{ REL})=\text{KICK}$
                          $(\sigma\mathcal{M}* \text{ ARG1})=\sigma(\phi^{-1}\phi\mathcal{M}* \text{ SUBJ})$
                          $(\sigma\mathcal{M}* \text{ ARG2})=\sigma(\phi^{-1}\phi\mathcal{M}* \text{ OBJ})$

This lexical entry contains two kinds of equations. First, there is a pure functional description:

$(\phi\mathcal{M}* \text{ PRED})=\text{'KICK'}$

Second, there are inter-module equations constraining the relationship between the semantic interpretation and the functional properties of the phrase. The inter-modular constraint:

$$(\sigma\mathcal{M}* \ \mathtt{ARG1}) = \sigma(\phi^{-1}\phi\mathcal{M}* \ \mathtt{SUBJ})$$

asserts that the first argument role of the relation 'kick' is covered by the interpretation which, by force of other equations, is associated with the functional subject.

The extended rule language permits a third type of equation as well. This is the pure semantic equation. The lexical entry for the tense marker illustrates this type of equation (cf. any σ-equation in this entry), which is adapted from Fenstad et al. [55, 56].

```
-ED  AFF  (φM* TENSE) = PAST
          (σM* LOC) = σ*
          (σ* IND ID) = IND-loc
          (σ* COND RELATION) = ≺
          (σ* COND ARG'1) = (σ* IND)
          (σ* ARG'2) = LOC-D
          (σ* POL) = 1
```

The analyses the notation makes possible exhibit several improvements over earlier treatments. First, one can now explicate in equational terms the mixture of functional and semantic information hiding behind the original representation of semantic forms in LFG, where the association between functional entities (SUBJ, OBJ etc.) and unspecified semantic (or rather thematic) roles was implicit in the order of arguments, as in the semantic form below.

```
'kick⟨(↑SUBJ),(↑OBJ)⟩'
```

By bringing these factors under 'equational' treatment, one can make the trade-offs between a functional and a semantic analysis of completeness, coherence etc. on empirical grounds, and not have these decisions be dictated by notation. Second, the correct assignment of interpretations to roles in passive constructions and other constructions involving lexical rules is achieved without further stipulations and without modification of the lexical rules. The standard version of the passive rule in LFG

```
SUBJ → BY-OBJ;
OBJ → SUBJ
```

can be applied directly to the lexical form for *kick* with the desired result. This contrasts with the proposals of Cooper [40, 38] and Gawron [64], where more elaborate mechanisms are introduced to cope with the effects of relation changing rules, and with the analysis given by Barwise and Perry [15], where no allowances are made for the effects of such rules.

6.6 THE TREATMENT OF SCOPE

The preferred mechanism for scope analysis both in formal linguistic treatments and in the natural language systems built on them has long been the so-called Cooper-storage [39]. This approach combines a compositional interpretation of a syntax tree with the ability to pass around in the tree the interpretation of the quantified noun phrase and an indexed variable which will eventually be bound by the quantifier in the noun phrase. Different scope interpretations are achieved by discharging the quantifier expression at different points in the process of putting together the interpretation of the rest of the sentence. The theory of interpretation and the rule-language which is presented here makes it possible to handle scope ambiguities without recourse to a storage mechanism.

The generalization underlying the use of Cooper-storage is that the quantifier associated with a quantified noun phrase can take scope over a number of different constituents of the interpretation of the sentence. For simplicity, let us initially restrict our attention to subject noun phrases, and let us assume that a noun phrase NP_k in a sentence constituent S_j, where j corresponds to the level of embedding, can be quantified in at the level of any constituent S_i, where $i < j$. Stated in these terms one can see that the problem of scope ambiguity could be analyzed by the 'functional uncertainty' mechanism (Kaplan and Maxwell [107]) which implements unification of structures characterizable by path specification in any regular language. Specifically, the generalization about scope possibilities for subjects stated above can be captured in the following equation attached to any N which is the head of a quantified subject NP:

$$(\sigma\phi^{-1}(\text{VCOMP}^* \text{ SUBJ } \uparrow) \text{ QP}) = \sigma\mathcal{M}*$$

The equation states that the quantifier attribute (QP) of the semantic structure of a sentence can be filled by the semantic structure of the SUBJ of that sentence, or by the SUBJ of the VCOMP of the sentence (i.e. the interpretation of the subject of the immediately embedded sentence), or by the SUBJ of the VCOMP's VCOMP, and so on. Conditions on the extractability of quantifiers from embedded positions, such as the purported semantic reflections of the complex NP-constraint (Rodman [191]) can be formulated in terms of conditions on the functional or semantic aspects of the path characterized in the 'functional uncertainty' equation.

This illustrates how this approach makes possible a treatment of quantifier scope ambiguities without any mechanism other than 'functional uncertainty', which is independently motivated by the treatment of unbounded dependency phenomena in the syntax. Functional uncertainty also has an efficient implementation based on incremental decomposition of finite-state machines (Kaplan and Maxwell [107]).

6.7 SUMMARY

We have shown how to formulate a semantic interpretation mechanism for LFGs which permits the statement of semantic rules using a simple extension of the language for functional descriptions. While previous proposals have taken functional structures as input to the semantic interpretation component requiring all semantically relevant information to be reflected in the functional structure, this proposal coordinates the characterization of the functional and semantic properties of a construction (i.e. co-description). This allows us to simplify the functional representations by the elimination of functionally irrelevant, but semantically significant, material. It also puts at our disposal the full power of the rule language of LFG, including functional uncertainty. This, in turn, makes it possible to formulate novel semantic analyses, such as the treatment of quantifier scope ambiguities which avoids the use of any storage mechanism. Finally, the notion of projections as functional mappings makes it possible to characterize a wider set of dependencies between c-structural, f-structural and semantic information.

7 Situation Schemata and linguistic representation

C.J. Rupp, Roderick Johnson, Michael Rosner

7.1 INTRODUCTION

This chapter concerns experiments with *Situation Schemata* as a linguistic representation language, in the first instance for Machine Translation purposes but not exclusively so. The work reported is primarily concerned with the adaptation of the Situation Schemata language presented by Fenstad et al. [56] (but see also Fenstad et al. in this volume) to an *implementation* within grammars having interestingly broad linguistic coverage. We shall also consider the computational tools required for such an implementation and our underlying motivation. The chapter is therefore not solely concerned with the *form* of the representation language and its relation to any eventual interpretation language, but also with practical and methodological issues associated with the implementation of current theories in Computational Linguistics. A key theme is the interplay between linguistic information, representation and appropriate mechanisms for abstraction.

The rest of the chapter is divided into three further sections. Section 7.2 suggests that the problem of translation can shed light on a range of representational issues on the syntax/semantics border; it contains a brief introduction to Situation Semantics and the original version of Situation Schemata. Section 7.3 outlines the design of a computational toolkit for experimenting with unification-based descriptions, concentrating on details of the grammar formalism and its abstraction mechanisms. Section 7.4 considers the form of Situation Schemata that has been implemented within a grammar of German and some related representational issues that arise out of this work.

7.2 MOTIVATION

Our immediate concern has been with the design and implementation of an environment that is suitable for developing both tools and prototypes for machine translation. Most of this paper concerns that enterprise. However, we do not wish to exclude other applications, such as database enquiries, question answering and computer-aided language teaching. It is important, therefore, to establish that the approach we adopt to translation does not lose sight of the requirements imposed by these other domains.

7.2.1 REPRESENTATIONS

The project has a strongly developmental flavour, but this does not exclude the fact that if we are to fit various applications together, a number of research problems remain to be solved. One point of intersection where a number of issues from different areas collect is the notion of representation, which sits between language and interpretation, as shown in figure 7.1.

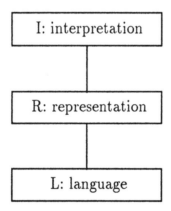

Figure 7.1. Representation

There are two obvious, and related, questions which arise as soon as a level of representation is introduced between a language and its interpretation. Why is the representation necessary and what type of representation is required? There may well be theoretical arguments for some level of semantic representation, such as psychological plausibility or the need to provide discourse referents, but the most common motivations for maintaining a level of semantic representation are more technical and practical. Whatever form of semantic interpretation is assumed, and here differences may arise out of philosophical preference, it will be useful to have a *syntactically precise metalanguage* for talking about those interpretations, independently of the original linguistic forms, and if possible, of the nature of the intended interpretation, for example whether the objects referred to are in the world or in the mind. Even assuming a particular type of interpretation, it may be desirable to *decouple* the development of the representational semantics from that of interpretative semantics. The detailed elaboration of the semantic interpretation of specific phenomena characteristically moves very slowly, often through a range of similar proposals, whereas the representation of such phenomena can progress quite rapidly once the general form of the treatment is determined. The primary role of a semantic representation is therefore as an *interface* between different ways of working on the semantics of natural language. It should modularize the task in such a way that different specialists can take away topics to work on according to their native methodology. It should also be borne in mind that it must be possible to interface semantic representations with other components of a linguistic description.

If the primary role of semantic representations is to act as an interface between linguistic description and semantic interpretation, there still remain a large range of options as to the nature of such representations. Some constraints will of course be provided by the underlying semantic theory that is assumed, but these primarily affect the content of representations. The key questions when defining a representation language for an application are the form of representations and the level of abstraction provided by the representation language – the precise relation between representations and interpretations – and in particular the distribution of labour between these two domains.

The main constraint on the form of representations is the necessity to efficiently compute representations from any given natural language input. The appropriate level of abstraction will vary according to the nature of the application – issues such as quantifier scope and anaphoric binding may have different priorities in querying a database than they would in translation between two natural languages. If tools are to be developed that are adaptable to various tasks then it may be appropriate to support variation in this type of content.

7.2.2 TRANSLATION AS A TEST CASE

Translation between two natural languages may actually provide an interesting test for the general linguistic adequacy of a form of semantic representation. Whereas many applications mimic the theoretical structure of the semantic domain, as given in figure 7.1, in that they map language first to a representation and then to some form of interpretation, which in practice is usually another symbolic representation in a machine friendly form, translation, when performed by computer systems, provides independent motivations for a level of representation. The reason for this is most easily seen by considering the classical view of Machine Translation (MT) and the way that this view arises.

The key to the functioning of a translation system is obviously the notion of translational equivalence between linguistic forms. The system must encode knowledge about this equivalence relation. The encoding and processing of this information would be impractical, and perhaps even impossible, if it were reduced to a mass of special cases. A common approach to this problem is to encode a more abstract relation between representations of classes of texts, rather than the direct translational equivalence between individual texts. Figure 7.2 presents a schematic representation of this quite common view of MT.

The relation Rep between the language domain and the representation domain is described by means of a grammar and lexicon. The relation TR corresponds to the internal, 'machine' theory of translation expressed with respect to the representation domain R.

The quality of translation, that is, the extent to which TL matches our intuitions about the translational equivalence of sentence pairs, depends crucially on TR. Clearly, a great deal is going to depend on the structure and contents of R itself.

This is where a relationship between semantic representation in general and linguistic representations in MT can be established. Translation as an application provides an independent motivation for a particular level of representation, which may not be provided either by the form of the semantic representations or by the underlying semantic theory. The precise level of abstraction required for R and the kind of information that influences the relation TR, are still largely a domain for experimentation as indicated in Kay [114]. Nevertheless, it should be clear that the prime content of the representations R, and therefore the prime concern of the relation TR, will be the informational content of the text, precisely the information that semantic representations should be concerned with.

An experimental approach to this issue seems appropriate, because a system of representation that is geared to translation will only arise through the interaction of different disciplines. There is no reason why a semantic theory that is specifically oriented to translation should come into being, nor why semanticists should concentrate on topics that are the source of difficulties in translation. Linguists, both computational and theoretical, have also tended to focus on similarities between languages in attempting to understand the human language faculty, rather than on the obvious diverse differences of use between languages that are often quite close in both

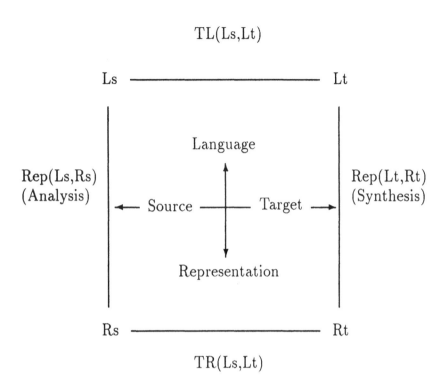

Figure 7.2. Relations between classes of text

their descent and geographical distribution. The development of a representational theory for translation must therefore depend on compromise and finding, borrowing and adapting techniques and analyses from more theoretically oriented work. This type of development will in all probability not progress in an orderly fashion. In fact the most reasonable methodology would appear to be to start with a basic coverage of a limited, but reliable, fragment and to extend this incrementally, perhaps with periodic adjustments to the existing treatments. This requires very flexible tools, such as the grammar development environment to be considered below. It also places considerable constraints on the type of semantic framework that may be assumed to underly this work.

While some of these constraints have been noted above, others are particular to this method of development. For instance we must assume that any such framework can offer:

- sufficient *flexibility* to permit incremental extension;

- enough *internal structure* to give suggestive guidance for the treatment of new phenomena;

- relative *independence* from the morphology and syntax, to allow a comparable degree of incremental flexibility in the development of the morphology and syntax;

- a reasonable guarantee of *computational feasibility* when used in large-scale language processing applications.

7.2.3   TRANSLATION AND SEMANTIC THEORIES

We have just stated a number of constraints on the kind of semantic framework that would be appropriate for experimentation with representations for MT, but a representational framework is by no means the only thing required of a semantic theory. It should be noted that the failure of one of the most successful semantic paradigms to be truly appropriate as a representation for translation, arises not from inadequacies in the representational theories and linguistic theories associated with it, but from the notion of interpretation adopted by the theory in the first place. Montague Semantics (see [152, 154]) is typically associated with a number of assumptions regarding semantic representation and linguistic processing. These amount to a set of fundamental choices with respect to:

- *semantic representation language:* a higher order intensional logic;

- *syntactic theory:* categorial grammar;

- *syntax-semantics interface:* strictly compositional, by the use of homomorphic syntactic and semantic algebras (the rule-to-rule hypothesis);

- *semantic interpretation:* truth conditions in possible worlds.

Although Montague's approach *has* been used as the theoretical basis for practical MT (see Landsbergen [130, 131]), Fenstad et al. [56] and Halvorsen [77] have presented cogent arguments against the linguistic component of the framework. Although rigorously defined, it fails to take into account the role of linguistic behaviour in a sufficiently overt manner. It is therefore unable to account for the primary role of the kind of natural language text that typically requires translation, namely the conveyance of information. Symptoms of this deficiency can be seen in the lack of any account of discourse reference and in the failure to distinguish between the interpretations of logically equivalent utterances. There is obviously very little to be gained by modifying the representational framework if the underlying theory is impervious to the processes to be treated.

7.2.4 SITUATION SEMANTICS

Within Situation Semantics (Barwise and Perry [15]), the distinguishing mark of meaningful utterances is taken to be *conveyance of information* rather than a set of truth conditions. This view, combined with other primitive notions, may open some new representational perspectives, for translation as well as for other applications. The most apparent benefits of Situation Semantics as a semantic theory arise out of its more prominent features, for example:

- *partiality*, which places emphasis on informational content;

- a *relational view* of both interpretation and meaning, where this relation involves context, content and linguistic form;[1]
  $d, c[\![\phi]\!]s$ (Barwise and Perry [15])
  $\mathcal{C}_R(S, c) = P$ (Barwise [12])

---

[1] In the first formulation the meaning relation associated with a linguistic form, ϕ, holds between a content, in the form of a described situation, s, and a context, which mainly consists of a discourse situation, d. In the later formulation the linguistic form is denoted by S, the content by P and the context by the circumstances, c. In each case the meaning relation is also dependent on another factor: in the first case 'speaker connections', c, form part of the context, in the second the relation $\mathcal{C}$ is dependent on a set of conventional constraints, R. In fact these represent two different types of convention governing the use of language, but the fact that they are made explicit in the formulation of the meaning relation makes them comparable.

- the use of *various types* of semantic objects: situations, individuals, locations, relations.

However, we believe that the more explicit role assigned to linguistic expressions in this theory will prove one of its most useful aspects in an application such as translation.

Situation Semantics makes explicit not only the role of linguistic forms (ϕ/S), but also the context (d/c) in which they are used and the mechanisms by which they may relate to their interpretations (c/R). In applications that are primarily linguistic, such as translation, this provides not only mechanisms for representing the required relations, but also explanatory power in supporting the way that a formal model may correspond to human behaviour. For instance, one of the more recent approaches to MT (Whitelock [238]) can be explained in terms of the connection between lexical items and the uniformities that a speaker may individuate, or at least this is the point of view advanced in Rupp [195, 196].

7.2.5 SITUATION SCHEMATA

While Situation Semantics provides an interesting theoretical framework for exploring issues relating to translation it does not, of itself, provide a representation language that is suited to the development of (prototype) MT systems. There is however a framework for semantic representation that is inspired by Situation Semantics, but which explicitly sets out to fulfill some of the most basic requirements on semantic representation languages stated in section 7.2.2 above. This is the framework of Situation Schemata proposed by Fenstad et al. [56]. Not only do Situation Schemata have the form of feature structures, but the framework also explicitly espouses a technique of *constraint propagation* across different levels of linguistic representation, which is effectively an extension of the more common use of unification. This is a property it shares with current linguistic theories such as HPSG (Pollard and Sag [182]). These purely formal properties of the representation language virtually guarantee that the constructs used to represent semantic content will be efficiently computable from natural language inputs and that the technology will exist for the incremental development of extensive linguistic descriptions using semantic representations of this form.

The remainder of the chapter will be concerned with an instance of the type of technology required for this task and with issues relating to the content of the representation language.

7.3 THE DESCRIPTION LANGUAGE UD

We now turn to the description language used to define a grammar that relates a form of Situation Schemata to texts. It was noted above that the form of Situation Schemata, as feature structures, or DAGs (Directed Acyclic Graphs), facilitates their computation from input strings, as a number of environments exist for such linguistic processing. This is, however, not the only criterion that must be fulfilled. It must also be possible to develop the grammar *incrementally*, in conjunction with incremental developments in other domains of linguistic representation, such as syntax and morphology. This is a more difficult goal to achieve and for this reason the grammar was developed within a home-grown environment and language known as UD. Further details on the implementation of UD are provided in Johnson and Rosner [100].

As there are now a number of environments and formalisms for treating linguistic information expressed in the form of constraints, the most concise way of presenting the essential features of the description language is by comparison with other existing notations and formalisms. This will apply not only to the description language, but also to conventions adopted in defining the grammar.

7.3.1 PRINCIPAL FEATURES OF THE LANGUAGE

- a rich set of *representational types*, including atoms, terms, lists, user-defined sub-DAG types, as well as variables and disjunctions ranging over all of these;

- an *abstraction mechanism* similar to Prolog 'predicates', but implemented in a fully declarative way;

- a completely *declarative* semantics;

- an acceptably *efficient* implementation.

Figures 7.3 and 7.5 provide a comparison of a typical PATR lexical entry for *has* (taken from Shieber [210]) with a fairly direct translation into UD. This should help to give an impression of the capabilities of the language. Figures 7.4 and 7.6 show the corresponding lexical representations.

```
Lexicon root.
     ⋮
Word has: <cat> = V
          <head form> = finite
          <syncat first cat> = VP
          <syncat first head form> = pastpart
          <syncat first syncat rest> = end
          <syncat first syncat first> = <syncat rest first>
          <syncat rest first cat> = NP
          <syncat rest first head agreement number> = singular
          <syncat rest first head agreement person> = third
          <syncat rest rest> = end
          <head trans pred> = perfective
          <head trans arg1> = <syncat first head trans>.
```

Figure 7.3. PATR notation

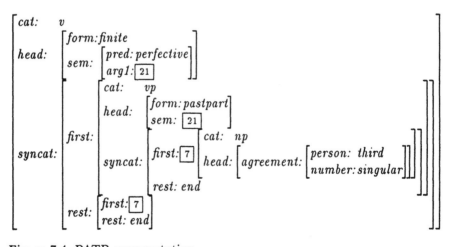

Figure 7.4. PATR representation

```
# Lexicon root
       ⋮
has      v   <* head form> = finite
             <* syncat> = [Vcomp,Subj]
             <Vcomp cat> = vp
             <Vcomp head form> = pastpart
             <Vcomp syncat> = [Subj]
             <Subj cat> = np
             !Agree(Subj,3,singular)
             <* head trans pred> = perfective
             !Arg(1,Vcomp)
       ⋮
# Define relations

Agree(X,<X head agreement person>,<X head agreement number)

Arg(N,X)    <* trans arg N> = <X head trans>
```

Figure 7.5. UD notation

$$\begin{bmatrix} \textit{cat:} & v \\ \textit{head:} & \begin{bmatrix} \textit{form:} & \textit{finite} \\ \textit{trans:} & \begin{bmatrix} \textit{pred:} & \textit{perfective} \\ \textit{arg:} & \begin{bmatrix} \textit{1:} \boxed{22} \end{bmatrix} \end{bmatrix} \end{bmatrix} \\ \textit{syncat:} & \left\{ \begin{bmatrix} \textit{cat:} & \textit{vp} \\ \textit{head:} & \begin{bmatrix} \textit{form:} & \textit{pastpart} \\ \textit{trans:} & \boxed{22} \end{bmatrix} \\ \textit{syncat:} & \left\{ \boxed{4} \begin{bmatrix} \textit{cat:} & \textit{np} \\ \textit{head:} & \begin{bmatrix} \textit{agreement:} & \begin{bmatrix} \textit{person:} & 3 \\ \textit{number:} & \textit{singular} \end{bmatrix} \end{bmatrix} \end{bmatrix} \right\} \end{bmatrix} \; \boxed{4} \right\} \end{bmatrix}$$

Figure 7.6. UD representation

7.3.2 REMARKS ON THE NOTATION

The comparison between the PATR and the UD notations for the same
description provides a basis for explaining the basic features of the UD
notation. A more detailed exposition of the description language is provided
in Rupp [196]).

It should be obvious from the examples given above that the UD notation
is generally more compact than PATR-II, but it is also much more powerful
and the added features require extensive additions to the syntax. These are
largely adopted either from DCGs, or rather Edinburgh syntax Prolog, or
from the LFG formalism (Kaplan and Bresnan [105]), as instantiated in
the Grammar Writer's Workbench (Kaplan and Kiparsky [106]). As noted
in section 7.3.1, two of the major extensions to the PATR format are the
inclusion of a range of different data-types and of a general abstraction
mechanism. The latter is most useful in defining large scale grammars and
will be the main concern of section 7.3.3. Of the additional data types the
most widely used are lists, but Prolog-style terms have also proved useful
in defining a semantic representation language.

The definition of abstractions or of additional data types requires the
general ability to refer to any piece of structure, an ability which is not
a property of more primitive linguistic formalisms where the relevance of
constraints must be determined by the context in which they occur. While
the PATR example (figure 7.3) contains a large number of unrooted paths,
because the only object they can possibly refer to is the current lexical
entry, the UD example (figure 7.5) makes use of variables to root paths in
elements of the entry's substructure. The syntax for variables is essentially
that of Prolog. The UD equation

```
<Subj cat> = np
```

carries the same information as the PATR equation:

```
<syncat rest first cat> = NP
```

The position of the object denoted by the variable 'Subj' in the list is given
by another equation:

```
<* syncat> = [Vcomp,Subj]
```

Lists are also annotated in a similar manner to Prolog lists, including the
bar notation to separate heads and tails:

```
[Head|Tail]
```

There are however also other operators defined over lists, including membership (--):

```
List = Remainder -- Member
```

and append (++):

```
List = Front ++ Back
```

These are useful as the environment does not support sets as a data type. It should be obvious from the examples above that explicit encoding of lists is more concise than the standard 'first/rest' list emulation found in PATR. It should perhaps be noted that this notation is interpreted as a lower level list implementation rather than as syntactic sugar for the PATR approach. This marks a general approach to polymorphic unification and, in conjunction with the extensive use of abstractions, a viable and more pragmatic approach to linguistic descriptions. The notation of 'terms' similarly denotes a class of tree-structured objects that have their own form of unification. These are broadly similar to Prolog structures, except that any class of object may occur in the 'predicate' position. The argument structure of the auxiliary 'has' might equally have been expressed by the term:

```
<* head trans> = perfective(<Vcomp head trans>)
```

7.3.3 ABSTRACTIONS AND THEIR USE IN GRAMMAR DEVELOPMENT

PATR-II contains a most basic form of abstraction of linguistic information, in that sets of equations may be collected into predefined packages, termed 'templates', which may be used in various contexts in a description. A simple illustration of the use of templates is given by the following, which are taken from Shieber [210, page 57] and involve information contained in the above example.

```
ThirdPerson
<subcat first head agreement person> = third

Singular
<subcat first head agreement number> = singular

ThirdSing
ThirdPerson
Singular
```

These templates are very restricted in their expressive power. The UD notation, on the other hand, provides a very powerful abstraction mechanism, which is tantamount to the inclusion of a form of pure Prolog within the description language. We call these constructs 'relational abstractions' and the notation adopted for them is similar to that for Prolog predicates. The examples given in figure 7.5 show the notation used.[2] The following agreement abstraction is defined very simply, as there are no equations in the body of its definition.

```
Agree(X,<X head agreement person>,<X head agreement number>)
```

The notation of its invocation must be preceded by an exclamation mark, which distinguishes abstraction invocations from terms:

```
!Agree(Subj,3,singular)
```

The argument assignment abstraction provides a more usual form of definition:

```
Arg(N,X) <* head trans arg N> = <X head trans>
```

These examples display the concise nature of the notation provided but do not exhibit the full power of relational abstractions. On a checklist of properties desirable in an abstraction mechanism they score very highly, as they are relational, disjunctive and recursive. Rupp [197] provides a more detailed comparison of the various abstraction mechanisms available in current linguistic formalisms.

The motivation for such a powerful mechanism again arises out of the pragmatic approach adopted to grammar development. An extensive grammar will involve the collaboration of different linguists over a range of levels of description. Hence it is necessary that they maintain a shared vocabulary of primitives.

In a low level formalism this requires that the entire feature system be determined in advance. Alternatively, one might define a compiler from a high level linguistic formalism to a more computationally tractable form: this permits progress to be made through modifications to the compiler but it is not particularly flexible.

Abstractions, however, provide both flexibility and modularity. A morphological description may, for instance, invoke the agreed form of a semantic abstraction without making assumptions about its current definition.

---

[2] We have also taken the liberty of expressing Shieber's examples of templates in UD notation. This shows that templates are equivalent to a primitive form of relational abstractions. We trust that this is not intrusive, as the notations are very similar.

The assumption is that if you knew what the 'true' linguistic formalism was you would have implemented it in the first place. In fact the mechanism used to define 'linguistic principles' in HPSG has many of the same properties as relational abstractions.

As the notion of relational abstraction has been introduced here, the subsequent presentation of the semantic representation language will attempt to emphasise the semantic abstractions used and the effect of the need to define abstractions on the form of the representation language. Hopefully it has been made clear that the purpose of such abstraction mechanisms is to prevent large grammars from degenerating into a mass of repetitive and incomprehensible equations, and to provide instead an ultimate structure of more or less linguistically plausible constructs.

7.3.4 SOME COMMENTS ON THE GRAMMAR

Having introduced the basic notational constructs provided for linguistic description, it is worth providing a few comments on the nature of the grammar of German used to implement the Situation Schemata language. The main focus of this section will be the relation between the conventions adopted and more familiar linguistic formalisms, as section 7.4 provides a detailed presentation of the form and usage of the semantic representations. The details of the syntactic analyses adopted are of limited relevance to the concerns of this paper. It should suffice to say that the starting point for the syntactic description was an analysis of basic clause structure adapted from early GPSG grammars of German (Uszkoreit [226], Russell [199]). This skeleton was fleshed out with analyses of a variety of constructions, so as to provide a testing ground for the semantic representation language. Rupp [196] provides a more detailed presentation of all aspects of this grammar, including syntactic and semantic analyses, and their implementation in the UD environment. A major part of this implementation was concerned with the use of the UD abstraction mechanism to encode constructs from other formalisms. This amounts to an eclectic approach to the general notion of a linguistic formalism, which was based on the observation that there are now a number of constraint-based linguistic formalisms which offer broadly equivalent though not identical syntactic coverage and none of which exhibit any obvious monopoly on 'the truth'. The definition of an intermediate level of linguistic formalism, within an extensible notational formalism, therefore seemed a viable alternative to the wholesale adoption of one of a number of competing theories.

An eclectic approach turns out to be quite interesting, in a context which emphasises semantic representation over syntax, and which also emphasises the various relationships between different levels of analysis rather

than a strict ordering over them. In practice the result is quite similar to a
form of the HPSG formalism, relying heavily on the use of lists to specify
'completeness' and 'coherence' constraints, though the treatment of control
is more like that of LFG, in relating syntactic and semantic representations. The general approach to modifiers is also modelled on polymorphic,
exocentric categories in categorial grammar or its constraint-based cousins
(Karttunen [112], Zeevat et al. [254]). The use of abstractions comes into
play in the definition of general linguistic principles, such as mechanisms
to deal with 'extraction' phenomena and passivisation, where a disjunctive abstraction is used rather than a lexical rule. In fact there is no need
for a lexical rule construction, as the morphology has direct access to any
abstraction or other feature information it may require. The most extensive use of abstractions is however in the definition of lexical entries, and
in particular of verbs, where a description language is implemented that
bears only a passing relation to the actual representations associated with
an actual word form in the lexicon. This notation is in effect interpreted
by a sequence of abstractions, which unpack such details as passivisation
and subcategorisation.

For example, an invocation of a Subcat abstraction might appear in the
lexical entry of a transitive verb such as *sehen*, 'to see'.

```
!Subcat(np(nom),np(acc))
```

This specifies the category and case of the arguments the verb subcategorizes for and the argument positions of the semantic arguments they
provide, in the default case. It is important to note that a description in
terms of this abstraction provides the kind of information that it is easy
to agree on, but does not predetermine in any way the structure of the
representation that will result from its invocation. The definition of this
abstraction includes a clause which treats transitive verbs.

```
Subcat(np(nom),np(acc))  !Verb(norm)
                         !Assigntr(<* subcat>,_)
```

This in turn invokes an abstraction, which generates distinct subcategorisation lists for passive and active forms of the verb. The expansion of this
latter abstraction obviously interacts with the morphology of the verb form.

```
Assigntr([X,Y],[X,Y])   !Voice(*,active)
                        !Form(*, pas)
                        !Argn(<X sem desc>,<* sem desc>,1)
                        !Subj(X)
                        !Argn(<Y sem desc>,<* sem desc>,2)
                        !Obj(Y,acc)
```

```
Assigntr([X,Y],[X],[Z,X])    !Voice(*,passive)
                             !Vform(*,pas)
                             !Subj(X)
                             !Argn(<X sem desc>,<* sem desc>,2)
                             !Obl(Y,von,dat,Z)
                             !Argn(Z,<* sem desc>,1)
```

The grammar is strongly lexicalist, as all information about subcategorisation and semantic structuring is encoded on the lexical entries of individual words. This results in a relatively small grammar with very general rules: a division of labour that has come to be accepted as the norm in most of the formalisms mentioned above.

For this particular application the lexicalist approach has added advantages in that it allows us in principle to isolate the constraints on the use of a particular word. This is essentially the same notion as speaker connections in Situation Semantics. The next step will be to compare the constraints on words in different languages in the hope of developing definitions for lexical transfer based on speaker connections.

7.4 SEMANTIC REPRESENTATION

The semantic representation language that we have implemented is a variant of the Situation Schemata language presented in SLL [56]. We will present this language in three stages:

- the syntax of the semantic representation language;

- a direct comparison between an example of an SLL representation and one of our representations;

- examples of representations in our language that extend the coverage of the SLL fragment.

As the available space is limited, it will be necessary to assume some familiarity with SLL and some recent form of Situation Semantics notation (e.g. Barwise [12], Devlin [45, 46]).

7.4.1 THE SYNTAX OF SEMANTIC REPRESENTATIONS

The system of domain equations in figure 7.7 gives an abstract syntax for the set of possible semantic representations which appear as values of a SEM feature. We assume that Situation Schemata are in fact partial representations of constructs in an interpretation language. The description of

SEM	=	DESC $\otimes$ REF $\otimes$ DISC
REF	=	LOC
DISC	=	LOC
DESC	=	FACT $\oplus$ OBJ
FACT	=	REL $\otimes$ LOC $\otimes$ ARG $\otimes$ POL
REL	=	RELOBJ $\oplus$ WORD
LOC	=	LOCOBJ
ARG	=	ARG-POS*
ARG-POS	=	$Z \rightarrow$ OBJ
OBJ	=	IND $\otimes$ COND
COND	=	CONSTRAINT*
CONSTRAINT	=	FACT $\oplus$ STRUCT
STRUCT	=	S-REL.n $\otimes$ OBJ^n
OBJ	=	SITOBJ $\oplus$ ENTOBJ $\oplus$ RELOBJ $\oplus$ LOCOBJ
SITOBJ	=	SITIND $\otimes$ COND
ENTOBJ	=	ENTIND $\otimes$ COND
RELOBJ	=	RELIND $\otimes$ COND
LOCOBJ	=	LOCIND $\otimes$ COND
IND	=	SITIND $\oplus$ ENTIND $\oplus$ RELIND $\oplus$ LOCIND
POL	=	1,0
SITIND	=	A set of situation type indeterminates
ENTIND	=	A set of entity type indeterminates
RELIND	=	A set of relation type indeterminates
LOCIND	=	A set of location type indeterminates
S-RELn	=	A set of structural relations of arity n
Z	=	natural numbers (probably between 1 and 3)
WORD	=	The words of the language

Figure 7.7. An abstract syntax for Situation Schemata

their syntax is expressed in terms of the kind of thing they can be representations of. It therefore equally describes the kind of construct expected in any interpretation language.

This semantic representation language contains certain extensions and modifications to the Situation Schemata language of SLL. The modifications are directed towards two of the primary goals of this paper: the application of Situation Schemata to a wider linguistic coverage and the systematic development of a linguistic description that achieves that task. The necessity to modify the existing form of Situation Schemata therefore arises when the syntax of that language is either too restrictive or too complex for application in a larger grammar.

The main extension to the Situation Schemata language is in making more explicit the different types of information contained in the representation. A semantic representation, SEM, consists of three types of information: reference information derived from the resource situation, discourse information from the discourse situation, and the described semantics. This is essentially an extension of the format given in SLL [56, page 77] and repeated below:

$$
\begin{bmatrix}
DESCRIBED\ SITUATION & SIT.\varphi \\
\\
UTTERANCE\ SITUATION & \begin{bmatrix} QMODE \\ RMODE \\ \cdots \\ \cdots \end{bmatrix}
\end{bmatrix}
$$

This shows a semantic representation structured according to the binary version of the meaning relation, involving a content component, the described situation and a contextual component, the utterance situation. This format is, however, only partially elaborated in SLL, in the consideration of modes of quantification (QMODE) and reference (RMODE).

In contrast to the SLL approach we base our representations on the ternary version of the meaning relation, with the slight modification that resource situations play a direct role in the meaning relation, but the role of connections is made more implicit. We also assume that the other types of semantic information will be represented in the same type of notation as the described situation, rather than in terms of QMODE and RMODE statements. This latter assumption is in keeping with the subsequent development of a strong notion of 'circumstances' (Barwise [12]) that is exploited in Gawron and Peters [66]. For the purposes of this paper, however, the only interesting components of the resource and described situations are the locations that they contribute to representation of tense information.

The actual representations proposed for situational constructs only really become apparent when considering the representation of the described semantics of an expression. In this domain two basic types of representation are distinguished: *facts* and *objects*.[3]

A fact is a combination of a relation, a location, some arguments and a polarity. This construct has the same structure as the basic form of Situation Schema in SLL, with none of its optional constituents realised. Its structure also suggests that it would be an appropriate representation for the basic informational constructs of Situation Semantics, variously known as infons, states of affairs or (possible) facts.

The polarity is a truth value taken from the set of one and zero. This permits the representation of both positive and negative facts. A relation may be a relational object or be represented by a word of the language. In most cases only words will appear in the relation slot, but in certain contexts complex objects may occur as relations, or a relation may be underspecified. A location must be a locational object. Both the notion of object typing and the role of the location will be elaborated below. Each position in the block of arguments consists of a mapping from a (small) natural number to an object. This method of representing arguments bears some similarity to the argument assignments used in more recent work by Barwise [12], where the ordering and significance of argument roles is not made explicit. It is, however, in marked contrast to another unification-based representation of situational constructs in HPSG where argument roles are made explicit and dependent on the value of the relation. The numerical designation is retained from SLL, because the intended application of this language is multilingual and therefore does not want to be hide-bound by explicitly monolingual structure. The incorporation of an explicit mapping from numbers to argument roles is incorporated as a generalisation of the numerical suffixing of argument positions. This also permits a general abstraction to cover all argument assignments, in which the numbering of the position can also occur as an argument.[4]

The other basic type of semantic representation is referred to as an object representation and is the type of representation which may occur in the argument positions of a fact. An object consists of an indeterminate and a *condition* on the way that indeterminate may be anchored. The application of such a condition requires that the situation in which the indeterminate is anchored support all of the facts in the condition. This type of object representation corresponds to the basic form of the construct

---

[3]As these two constructs are defined in terms of each other, it is not possible to provide a fully self-contained description of either. We present facts first as they are closer to the form of Situation Schemata in SLL.

[4]This type of abstraction has been shown in section 7.3.3 and figure 7.5.

filling argument positions in the SLL formulation of Situation Schemata, in that none of the optional constituents are realised. This formulation of objects is also an extension of the original form in that the condition is a set[5] of constraints rather than a single constraint of a restricted form. This in turn is an extension of the use of sets of constraints on locations, introduced by Colban [37].

Constraints in a condition may be facts or they may have the form of *structural constraints*, which represent a generalisation of the special form of condition applied to locations in the SLL formulation. It is assumed that certain structural relations are constituents of the theory and that these are used to form constraints, whose truth is not dependent on any particular situation. An obvious example of such relations are those that impose structure over a particular domain, such as the temporal ordering relations over locations used to express tense information. Other notable examples of this type of relation are the 'supports' relation ($\models$) that forms the basis of 'propositions' in Barwise and Etchemendy [13] and the 'is-of-type' (:) relation used in Gawron and Peters [66]. The information provided by structural constraints is consistently independent of any described situation. Some of these structural constraints correspond to propositions, provided that they are formed by the appropriate structural relations. In the current context these constructs arise not from any theory of propositions, but out of the need to make a systematic distinction between structural constraints, which are not partial and typically have a fixed arity, and partial facts of often indeterminate arity. Structural constraints are, therefore, not represented by feature structures, but by tree structures which have the same appearance as Prolog terms or 'predicate-argument structures' in LFG. It is perhaps also interesting that structural constraints in semantic representations are generally provided either by mechanisms that are morphologically encoded or by closed class grammatical words, whereas open class content words generally contribute to facts.

Object representations are classified in two ways in the definition in figure 7.7. Their structure, consisting of a distinguished indeterminate and a set of constraints, makes them appropriate representations for either types or restricted parameters in an interpretation language. They are however horizontally partitioned into different basic types of object, according to the taxonomy of primitive objects offered by Situation Semantics: Situations, Entities,[6] Locations and Relations. Object typing is performed by typing

---

[5] While conditions are defined as sets and the values of the COND feature will appear between brace brackets, they are in fact implemented as lists. This is due to the technical difficulty of implementing set-valued features.

[6] This is just an alternative characterisation of the set of individuals, prompted by the need for an alternative mnemonic in the feature system because 'ind' for indeterminate

the distinguished indeterminate of the object representation, according to which type of object it may be anchored to. The typed indeterminates are, therefore, among the basic domains of the definition, as are the structural relations of the theory and the words of the language.

In presenting a definition of the syntax of the semantic representation language it has been possible to explain some of the structural modifications to the form of Situation Schemata presented in SLL. These can be summarized as:

• explicit top-level information;

• set-valued conditions;

• distinct representations for structural relations;

• explicit argument mappings.

The use of these constructs will be demonstrated in some examples presented in the remainder of this section. The main purpose of such examples is to exhibit distinctions between the usage and coverage of this representation language and the SLL form of Situation Schemata. The first such example is therefore presented in direct comparison to a representation in the SLL format.

$$
\begin{bmatrix}
REL & kick \\
ARG1 & John \\
ARG2 & Pluto \\
\\
LOC & \begin{bmatrix} IND & \boxed{1} \\ \\ COND & \begin{bmatrix} REL & overlap \\ ARG1 & \boxed{1} \\ ARG2 & Ld \end{bmatrix} \end{bmatrix} \\
\\
POL & 1
\end{bmatrix}
$$

Figure 7.8. John kicks Pluto.

7.4.2   COMPARING TWO VERSIONS OF SITUATION SCHEMATA

Figure 7.8 is based on a Situation Schema given in SLL [56, page 25]. This schema represents the described semantics of the sentence 'John kicks Pluto'. It can be compared with the semantic representation in figure 7.9

_____

might be confused with 'ind' for individual. Of course the semantic theory then promptly changed its terminology for variable type objects to 'parameter'.

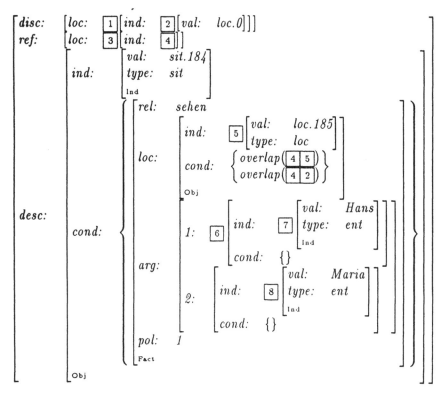

Figure 7.9. Hans sieht Maria.

that is assigned to the sentence *Hans sieht Maria* ('Hans sees Maria'), which has a similar syntactic structure.

While both of these schemata are representations of trivially simple sentences, consisting of only a transitive verb with proper name arguments, these examples are sufficient to show most of the syntactic modifications described in section 7.4.1. The additional level of structure in the second representation means that in fact the Situation Schema in figure 7.8 might be more directly compared with the value of the DESC feature in figure 7.9, as it represents only the described semantics, or content of the sentence. As the contextual and referential components of our representations remain underexploited, by far the major part of our schemata are taken up with content representations, so this shift in emphasis is hardly necessary.

As both of these examples are sentence representations, their comparison highlights a major modification in the use of Situation Schemata, namely the type of object used to represent the content of a sentence. In SLL the Situation Schema is the primary form of representation and is used to represent the content of sentences. In this role it is effectively representing a situation type: the type of the described situation. While situation types may be regarded as sets of facts, it has become more common to represent them in a form similar to that adopted for other object types, following Devlin [46]. This also provides a potential, if slight, distinction between situation types and complex infons. We have therefore found it useful to make the representation of the situational indeterminate explicit in sentence representations. This also provides a potential reference marker for sentential anaphora. Representations of situation types do however differ slightly from other object representations in that it will not generally be required for an argument position in the condition to be bound to the distinguished indeterminate. This indeterminate may instead be anchored to, or abstracted over, situations supporting the facts in the condition.

7.4.3 MODIFICATIONS AND EXTENSIONS IN THE USE OF SITUATION SCHEMATA

The comparison of simple examples of our representations and Situation Schemata in the SLL format should have clarified the simplifications and generalisations in the syntax of the representation language, but this comparison will also have made it clear that individual representations in our format are more complex objects. The modifications in the syntax are motivated partly by the descriptive and processing needs of a sophisticated grammar development environment, but mostly by major extensions in the range of linguistic phenomena to be covered. This section will consider three areas in which coverage has been extended and offer examples of the major types of representations that result.

A SIMPLE REPRESENTATION OF TENSE

E = event time = location of fact = loc
R = reference time = reference location = lref
S = speech time = discourse location = ld

PRESENT	overlap(R,E) overlap(R,S)	PERFECT	precede(E,R) overlap(R,S)
PAST	overlap(R,E) precede(R,S)	PLUPERFECT	precede(E,R) precede(R,S)
FUTURE	overlap(R,E) precede(S,R)	FUTURE PERFECT	precede(E,R) precede(S,R)

The representation of tense information

In the first case it is possible to reuse the example offered in figure 7.9, as even the most trivial example of a sentence representation also provides an example of the use of structural constraints to represent tense. The treatment of tense provided by the grammar is a slight extension of that presented in the SLL fragment and Barwise and Perry [15]. The range of tenses covered has been extended by the use of a reference location, so that the same two structural relations can be used to represent six tenses. This is essentially a basic Reichenbach [188] treatment of tense, which does not include some of the more interesting features of tense representation, such as aspectual classes (Cooper [40]) and modal approaches to future tense, but the purpose of the inclusion of these tense representations is to indicate that it is possible to utilize abstractions which concentrate basic notions of tense structure in the linguistic description. The six representational forms can be divided into two sets of three representations, according to the presence or absence of perfective aspect. This means that notions such as 'past' or 'perfect' are associated with specific abstractions in the grammar.

```
Past(X,precede(<X lref ind>,<X ld ind>))
```

We assume that any more sophisticated treatment of tense phenomena would preserve this approach to the intuitive notions which will relate to other levels of linguistic analysis, such as morphology.

Modification

One of the major goals in attempting to extend the coverage of the SLL fragment has been the obvious need to represent various forms of modification. Most natural language texts are replete with modified constituents and so this extension to the representation language should provide an automatic explosion in coverage with very little cost at the level of semantic theory. The primary contribution to the coverage of multiple modifiers is the use of more complex conditions on object representations. This is first exemplified by the use of sets of constraints on locational objects in Colban's treatment of prepositional phrases. We have attempted to generalize this approach to all the other types of possible objects, though we use lists of constraints rather than sets for technical reasons. It is actually quite difficult to find a general definition of operations over sets in a unification environment, whereas the inclusion of simple membership and append operations over lists provides essentially the same functionality as the set operations described in HPSG. The use of list-valued constraints makes it relatively easy to treat, for instance, multiple adjectives, adjectival phrases,

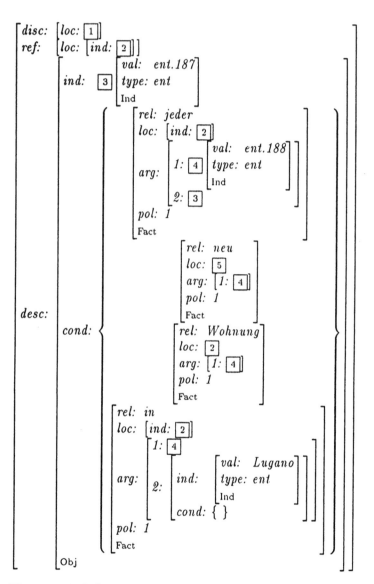

Figure 7.10. Jede neue Wohnung in Lugano

prepositional phrases and relative clauses in a systematic manner in noun phrase representations. German presents some particularly interesting cases of this in the use of both deverbal adjectival phrases and relative clauses. Figure 7.10 is the representation for the noun phrase *Jede neue Wohnung in Lugano* ('every new apartment in Lugano'), which contains both an adjectival and prepositional modifier.

In a similar manner to Colban's treatment, locational adverbial modifiers can be treated as adding constraints to the location of the fact provided by the verb, but other adverbial modifiers may be treated as constraining the type of relation that is individuated. This is demonstrated by the representation in figure 7.11: the representation of the sentence *Der Hund läuft schnell* ('The dog walks quickly').

This last type of modification would give rise to complex relational objects. In the current context such examples are useful, mainly to exemplify the fact that they are not, necessarily, higher order constructs, as relations are just another type of object. The use of such objects in the general case does however raise questions associated with the individuation of relational uniformities and their relation to lexical items. In a translational context it may be safer to consider only relations that may be associated with specific lexical items, rather than with more complex, potentially discontinuous forms.

The presentation of an NP representation also makes it clear that we take a slightly different approach to determiner relations than that of SLL. Rather than using a specifier attribute, as in LFG f-structures, and relying on the process of constructing Fact Schemata to make the function of determiners explicit, we prefer to associate determiners with relations, in the manner of generalized quantifier theory, at the representational level, although the actual scoping of these relations may not be explicit in the representations. This is not intended as a mechanism for immediately dispensing with Fact Schemata as a level of representation, but rather we would wish to make other levels of representation optional, according to the amount of information expressed in the Situation Schemata. This should also permit alternative methods of interpretation, such as an embedding in a larger structure, in the manner of DRT [103] interpretations.

Subordinate clauses

The final range of extensions to the coverage of the grammar that will be considered here are the representations of controlled and embedded verbal and sentential constructs. The approach we have taken is the most obvious one. Given sentential representations of the same form as the object representations that are assigned to argument positions, there is no syntactic

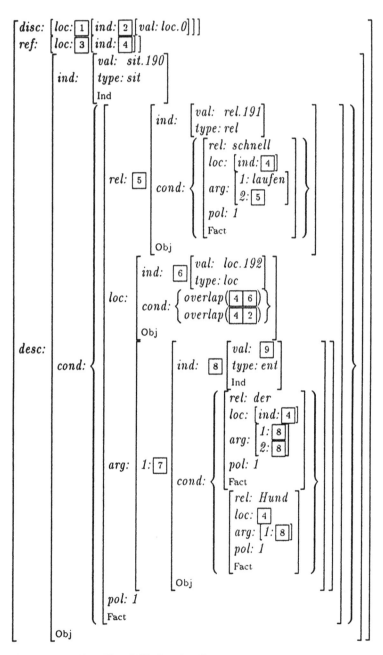

Figure 7.11. Der Hund läuft schnell.

constraint in the representation language to prevent sentential constructs from being arguments to verbs. Figure 7.12 shows just such a representation which would be assigned to the sentence *Hans weiß, daß Maria den Brief übersetzt hat* ('Hans knows that Maria has translated the letter').

In traditional terms controlled verbal constructions can also be regarded as reduced forms of sentences and be represented accordingly. This permits situations to occur as arguments in other situations and begs a number of questions, which comprise a large part of Barwise and Perry [15]. It may also make an appeal to one of the resolutions of some of these problems, the use of a non-wellfounded set theory (Barwise and Etchemendy [13]), if situations are ever represented as containing themselves. Where there remain problems with this direct approach to the representation of one of the most basic forms of recursion in natural language, we will assume that these are interpretative concerns rather than representational ones.

7.4.4 FURTHER DIRECTIONS

There are three obvious directions in which extensions to the current form of this Situation Schemata language might be explored:

- the structure of specific domains;

- the inclusion of more 'circumstantial' information;

- experimentation with dynamic techniques of representation and interpretation.

An example of this kind of domain structure might be seen in the considerable amount of work that has been devoted to the logic of plurals and mass terms (Link [137, 138], Lønning [139, 140], inter alia). These results could easily be emulated in terms of structural relations over the domain of individuals. One of the most interesting developments in recent Situation Semantics has been the extended notion of contextual information, known as 'circumstances'. This notion was put forward in Barwise [12] and exploited heavily in Gawron and Peters [66]. A more developed theory of circumstances would help to flesh out the currently underpopulated sections of the representations. A number of dynamic approaches to the interpretation of natural language have been put forward recently (Barwise [11], Rooth [192], Groenendijk and Stokhof [71, 72]). These offer an interesting approach to the treatment of discourse reference, but it remains to be seen whether such techniques are appropriate to constraint-based representations or whether the same effects can be achieved by a more explicitly representational technique, such as that presented in Johnson and

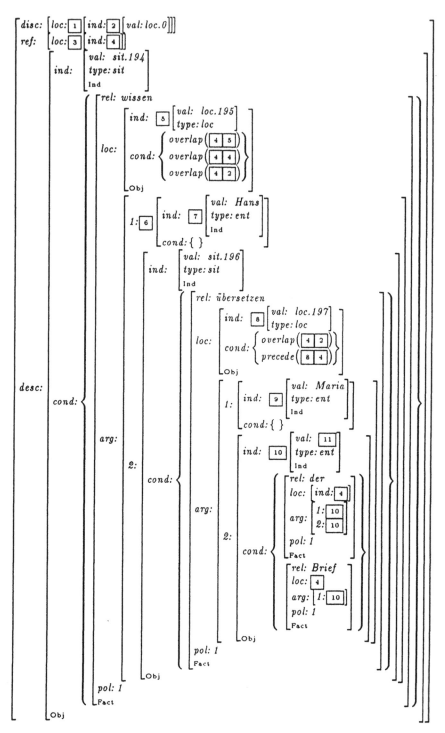

Figure 7.12. Hans weiß, daß Maria den Brief übersetzt hat.

Klein [97]. The exploration of these issues is currently under way and some preliminary results are provided in Rupp [196].

7.5 CONCLUSION

This paper has outlined the form of a constraint-based semantic representation language, based on the Situation Schemata of SLL. It has also presented the motivation for experimenting with this type of representation and the methodology governing the way it was put into use. While the examples of representations offered have been relatively trivial, it should be clear that this form of representation may contain very large amounts of information, at the expense of (human) readability. It should perhaps be emphasised that we see the major contribution of this type of research to be in the approach to the definition of linguistic descriptions which incorporate a representational semantic component, rather than particular semantic treatments, as many of the key issues in current formal semantics, representational or otherwise, situational or otherwise, remain to be addressed.

7.5.1 ACKNOWLEDGEMENTS

This chapter reports on work partially funded by an EEC COST13 grant carried out at IDSIA, Lugano in collaboration with the Department of Mathematics of the University of Oslo and BIM, Brussels. We would like to acknowledge the contribution of all active participants in the project, including Jens-Erik Fenstad, Jan-Tore Lønning, Espen Vestre, Tore Langholm, Erik Colban, Helle Sem, Jean-Louis Binot, Lieve Debille.

8 Application-oriented computational semantics

Sergei Nirenburg and Christine Defrise

8.1 INTRODUCTION

Large practical computational-linguistic applications, such as machine translation systems, require a large number of knowledge and processing modules to be put together in a single architecture and control environment. Comprehensive practical systems must have knowledge about speech situations, goal-directed communicative actions, rules of semantic and pragmatic inference over symbolic representations of discourse meanings and knowledge of syntactic and phonological/graphological properties of particular languages. Heuristic methods, extensive descriptive work on building world models, lexicons and grammars as well as a sound computational architecture are crucial to the success of this paradigm. In this paper we discuss some paradigmatic issues in building computer programs that understand and generate natural language. We then illustrate some of the foundations of our approach to practical computational linguistics by describing a language for representing text meaning and an approach to developing an ontological model of an intelligent agent. This approach has been tested in the DIONYSUS project at Carnegie Mellon University which involved designing and implementing a natural language understanding and generation system.

8.2 SEMANTICS AND APPLICATIONS

Natural language processing projects at the Center for Machine Translation of Carnegie Mellon University are geared toward designing and building large computational applications involving most crucial strata of language phenomena (syntactic, semantic, pragmatic, rhetorical, etc.) as well as major types of processing (morphological and syntactic parsing, semantic interpretation, text planning and generation, etc.). Our central application is machine translation which is in a sense the paradigmatic application of computational linguistics.

Our theoretical work in semantics is devoted to developing not a general semantic theory but rather a semantic theory for natural language processing. Therefore, issues of text meaning representation, semantic (and pragmatic) processing and the nature of background knowledge required for this processing are among the central topics of our effort. A number of differences exist between the mandates of general semantic theory and semantic theory for natural language processing. In what follows we suggest a number of points of such difference (this list is an extension of the discussion in Nirenburg and Raskin [169]; see also Raskin [187]).

- While it is agreed that both general and NLP-related theories must be formal, the nature of the formalisms can be quite different because different types of reasoning must be supported.

- A general linguistic theory must ensure a complete and equal grain-size coverage of every phenomenon in the language; an NLP-related theory analyzes only as much as is needed for the purposes of a particular application.

- The ultimate criterion of validity for a general linguistic theory is explanatory adequacy; for an NLP-related theory it is the success of the intended application.

- A general linguistic theory can avoid complete descriptions of phenomena once a general principle or method has been established. A small number of clarification examples will suffice. In NLP the entire set of phenomena present in the sublanguage of an application must be covered exhaustively.

- A general linguistic theory has to be concerned about the boundary between linguistic and encyclopædic knowledge. This distinction is spurious in NLP-oriented semantic theories because in order to make semantic (and pragmatic) decisions a system must have access equally to both types of data.

- While a general linguistic theory can be method-driven, that is, seek ways of applying a description technique developed for one phenomenon in the description of additional phenomena (this reflects the predominant view that *generalization* is the main methodology in building linguistic theories), an NLP-related theory should be task-driven – which means that adequacy and efficiency of description take precedence over generalization.

We also subscribe to a cognitivist approach to building NLP-related language processing theories, centred around the metaphor of the model of an intelligent agent. An NLP-related theory must account for such properties of intelligent agents as goal- and plan-directed activity, of which language activity is a part (verbal actions, together with perceptual, mental and physical actions, comprise the effector inventory of an intelligent agent). It must also take into account the knowledge of the agent's attitudes to the entities in the world model as well as to remembered instances of events and objects in its own episodic memory. Not only are these attitudes often the subject of a discourse but they also influence the form of discourse on other topics.

8.3 CONFIGURATION

A semantic theory for natural language processing must address issues connected with the meaning-related activities in both natural language understanding and generation. While the semantic processing in these two tasks is different in nature (in lexical semantics, for instance, understanding centrally involves resolution of ambiguity while generation deals with resolution of synonymy for lexical selection), the knowledge bases, knowledge representation approaches and the underlying system architecture and control structures can be shared.

For instance, in the DIONYSUS natural language processing project many of the static knowledge sources and the basic control architecture are, indeed, shared, while the type of processing is quite different in different components of the system.[1]

In this section we describe the current computational configuration for implementing our agent-oriented theory of natural language processing. Not all facets of the agent model are implemented in our systems at this point, though we plan to remedy this situation. The current configuration of DIONYSUS contains the following modules:

---

[1] In fact, our general attitude to computational processing of natural language extends to other projects, such as TRANSLATOR (Nirenburg et al. [171]), POPLAR (Nirenburg et al. [172]; see also Nirenburg and Lesser [165]), KBMT-89 (Goodman and Nirenburg [70]), ONTOS (Monarch and Nirenburg [151]), and KIWI (Brown and Nirenburg [21]).

1.   An *ontology*, a view of the intelligent agent's world, including both knowledge about types of things in the world and the so-called 'remembered instances' of these types; the ontology consists of

   • a model of the physical world;

   • a model of 'self', including knowledge of own goals and static attitudes to elements of the ontology and remembered instances of ontological objects;

   • knowledge about the language communication situation.

2.   A *lexicon* for each of the natural languages in the system. The lexicon contains the union of types of information required for analysis and generation.[2] The information in entries for polysemic lexical items includes knowledge supporting lexical disambiguation. The same type of information is used to resolve synonymy in lexical selection during generation. A more detailed description of the structure of the lexicon in DIONYSUS is given in Meyer et al. [150].

3.   A textual meaning representation formalism.

4.   Knowledge about semantic processing, including

   • structural mappings relating syntactic and semantic dependency structures;

   • reference treatment rules (anaphora, deixis, ellipsis);

   • unexpected input treatment rules (including metaphor and metonymy);

   • text structure planning rules;

   • knowledge about both representation (in analysis) and realization (in generation) of discourse and pragmatic phenomena, including cohesion, textual relations, producer attitudes, etc.[3]

---

[2] In our earlier systems (see, e.g., Nirenburg and Raskin [170]) we maintained that different lexicons have to be produced for analysis and generation. It seems now that this decision was in a large part induced by the logistics of knowledge acquisition in a large application project. In fact, the overlap of the knowledge in the two lexicons is quite considerable – even the collocation information that we once considered useful mostly in the lexical selection process of natural language generation appears to be valuable in certain situations in analysis.

[3] Some of the rules from this list can be physically a part of the lexicon; however, they are mentioned overtly here because in most computational dictionaries this type of knowledge is not used.

Text understanding consists in representing, using a specially designed notation, the semantic and pragmatic (discourse, attitude, intention) information encoded in each clause of a natural language input, augmented by the representation of domain-related and text-related connections (relations) among natural language clauses or sets thereof.

In fact, the final result of the process of text understanding includes some information not overtly present in the source text. For instance, it may include results of reasoning by the consumer, aimed at filling in elements required in the representation but not directly obtainable from the source text. It may also involve reconstructing the agenda of rhetorical goals and plans of the producer active at the time of text production and connecting its elements to chunks of meaning representation.

Early AI-related natural language understanding approaches were criticized for not paying attention to the halting condition of meaning representation. They were open to this criticism because they did not make a very clear distinction between the information relayed in the text and information retrieved from the understander's background knowledge about the entities mentioned in the text. This state of affairs occurs when it is decided that the program must apply all possible inferences to the results of the initial representation of text meaning.

For a given ontology, we define text understanding as detecting and representing a text component as an element of a script/plan (in Schank-Abelson-Cullingford-Wilensky's terms – see Schank and Abelson [203], Cullingford [42], Wilensky [239]) or determining which producer goals are furthered by the utterance of this text component. We stop the analysis process when, relative to a given ontology, we can find no more producer goals/plans which can be furthered by uttering the sentence. But first we extract the propositional meaning of an utterance using our knowledge about selectional restrictions and collocations among lexical units. If some semantic constraints are violated, we turn on metonymy, metaphor and other 'unexpected' input treatment means. After the propositional meaning is obtained, we actually proceed to determine the role of this utterance in script/plan/goal processing. In doing so, we extract speech act information, covert attitude meanings, and eventually irony, lying, etc.

There is a tempting belief among applied computational semanticists that in an application such as MT, the halting condition on representing the meaning of an input text can, in many cases, be less involved than the general one. The reason for this belief is the observation that when a target language text is generated from such a limited representation, one can in many cases expect the consumer to understand it by completing the understanding process given only partial information. Unfortunately, since without human involvement there is no way of knowing whether the complete understanding is, in fact, recoverable by humans, it is, in the general case, impossible to posit a shallower (and hence more attainable) level of understanding. To stretch the point further, humans can indeed correctly guess the meaning of many ungrammatical, fragmentary and otherwise irregular texts (e.g. Charniak's example of 'lecture, student, confusion, question' [28, page 159]). This, however, doesn't mean that an automatic analyzer, without specially designed extensions, will be capable of assigning meanings to such fragments – their semantic complexity is of the same order as that of 'regular' text.

8.3.1 THE CONCEPT OF MICROTHEORIES

Significant progress has been made recently in the field of computational linguistics with respect to the theories of syntax. Semantic and pragmatic phenomena have traditionally been less amenable to computational analysis. It does not seem plausible that an integrated semantic theory which would account for all lexical and compositional phenomena as well as the various pragmatic considerations will be formulated in the near future. This assessment becomes even more evident if one recognizes the necessity of providing heuristics for automatic recognition of the multiple meaning facets of natural language texts as a part of the theory. At the same time, linguistics has accumulated a significant body of knowledge about the various semantically laden phenomena in the natural languages (cf. Raskin [187] for a discussion of how this body of knowledge can be applied to computational analysis).

The above suggests that one of the more feasible ways toward building a comprehensive computational model of language understanding and generation behaviour in humans is to develop a large number of *microtheories* that deal with a particular linguistic phenomenon in a particular language or group of languages and then provide a computational architecture that allows the integration of the operation of all the modules based on these microtheories. Thus, one can envisage a microtheory of time, modality, speech act, causality, etc. In our work on DIONYSUS we have followed the microtheory-oriented methodology. While some of the microtheories we use in our systems are developed locally, many others are imported. The nature of the process of adapting a microtheory to the formalism and control conditions of a computational system is illustrated in Nirenburg and Pustejovsky [168] on the example of the microtheory of aspect.

To integrate the various microtheories in a single working system we suggest the use of a version of the blackboard computational architecture, in which a number of processes co-exist and, using a variety of background knowledge modules, collectively produce a desired output. The processors are computational realizations of the various microtheories derived for the corresponding linguistic phenomena. These processors operate using data from the background knowledge repositories, such as grammars and dictionaries, as well as the intermediate results stored on the universally accessible set of blackboards. For a more detailed description of the model and its components see Nirenburg and Raskin [170], Nirenburg [163], and Nirenburg et al. [166].

In this paper we will discuss our theoretical position on the treatment of semantic and pragmatic phenomena in natural language processing environments. We will illustrate two of the components of a theory – the agent's world model and the text meaning representation language.

8.4 REPRESENTATION OF AGENT'S KNOWLEDGE

In formal semantics, one of the most widely accepted methodologies is that of model-theoretic semantics in which syntactically correct utterances in a language are given semantic interpretation in terms of truth values with respect to a certain model (in Montague semantics, a 'possible world') of reality. Such models are in practice never constructed in detail but rather delineated through a typically underspecifying set of constraints and illustrated through typically formal or miniature examples.

In order to build large and useful natural language processing systems one has to go further and actually commit oneself to a detailed version of a 'constructed reality'. In practice, interpreting the meanings of textual units is really feasible only in the presence of a detailed world model whose elements are linked (either directly or indirectly, individually or in combinations) to the various textual units by a *is-a meaning-of* link. World model elements will be densely interconnected through a large set of well-defined ontological links, *properties*, which will enable the world modeller to build descriptions of complex objects and processes in a compositional fashion, using as few basic primitive concepts as possible. Constraints on world model elements and their cooccurrence will serve as heuristics on the cooccurrence of lexical and other meanings in the text, thus facilitating both natural language understanding and generation.

A theoretically sound model of the world, an *ontology*, provides uniform definitions of basic semantic categories (such as objects, event-types, relations, properties, episodes, and many more) that become the building blocks for descriptions of particular domains and the creation of machine-tractable lexicons for comprehensive natural language processing. We believe that an optimum way of organizing this world model is as a multiply interconnected network of ontological units, on which theoretically sound storage, access and update procedures will be developed.

An ontological model must define a large set of generally applicable categories for world description. Among the types of such categories are:

- Perceptual and common sense categories necessary for an intelligent agent to interact with, manipulate and refer to states of the outside world;

- Categories for encoding interagent knowledge which includes one's own as well as other agents' intentions, plans, actions and beliefs;

- Categories that help describe metaknowledge (i.e., knowledge about knowledge and its manipulation, including rules of behaviour and heuristics for constraining search spaces in various processor components);

- Means of encoding categories generated through the application of the above inference knowledge to the contents of an agent's world model (see articles in Brachman and Levesque [18]).

The choice of categories is not a straightforward task, as anyone who has tried realistic-scale world description knows all too well. Examples of the issues encountered in such an undertaking are illustrated in Gates et al. [63].

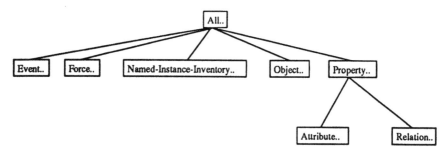

Figure 8.1. A sample ontological subnetwork.

We have used the knowledge acquisition and maintenance system ONTOS (see Nirenburg et al. [167]) to produce several prototype ontological models. Figures 8.1 and 8.2 show several subnetworks from the ontology developed for and used in the KBMT-89 machine translation project (Goodman and Nirenburg [70]). These displays already illustrate answers to some of the above questions. The graphics browser of ONTOS facilitates fast overview and navigation in the ontological model. But this model is, in fact, much more than a set of symbols (frame names) connected through *is-a* and *part-of* links.

Figure 8.3 illustrates the actual content of some of the nodes in this network.

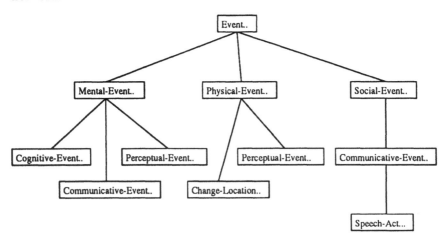

Figure 8.2. An event subnetwork.

The knowledge required in a model of an intelligent agent includes not only an ontological world model, as sketched above, but also records of past experiences, both actually perceived and reported. The *lingua mentalis* equivalent of a text is an *episode*, a unit of knowledge that encapsulates a particular experience of an intelligent agent, and which is typically represented as a temporally and causally ordered network of object and event instances.

The ontology and the episodes are sometimes discussed in terms of the contents of two different types of memory: semantic and episodic (e.g. Tulving [222]). This distinction seems useful in computational modelling as well. In our knowledge base we represent, with a varying degree of specificity, both ontological concepts and remembered instances of events and objects, which comprise the episodic memory.

Episodes are indexed through the type they correspond to and can be interrelated on temporal, causal and other links. The participant roles in the episodes can be either instantiations of object and event types in the semantic memory or references to existing named instances, stored outside semantic memory, but having links to their corresponding types (see figure 8.4). The figure illustrates the typology of structures comprising the world model of an intelligent agent. The basic ontological world model is augmented (for the purposes of specific processing types, such as analogical reasoning) with a repository of the intelligent system's experiential knowledge. Our system must satisfy the knowledge representation needs of such a repository and abundantly cross-index it with the resident ontology. The presence of a systematic representation and indexing method for episodic knowledge is not only necessary for processing natural language but is also an enablement condition for case-based reasoning (Kolodner and Riesbeck [126], Kolodner [125], Schank [202]) and analogical inference (e.g. Carbonell [25]).

A number of actual ontological decisions in the framework of the DIONY-SUS project are described in Carlson and Nirenburg [26].

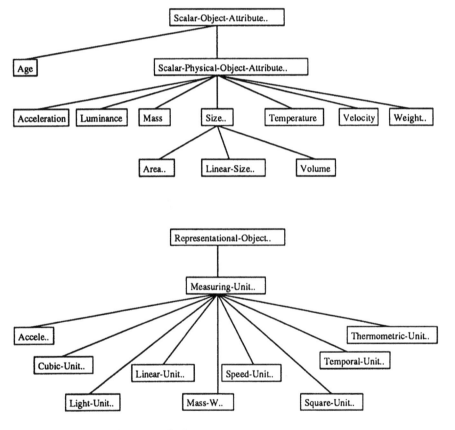

Figure 8.3. Some frames relating to measurement.

8.5 REPRESENTATION OF TEXT MEANING

The knowledge which the producer/consumer manipulates in order to successfully communicate includes the representations of various meanings of language elements, knowledge about the speech situation, including the knowledge about the interlocutor(s), knowledge about analysis and generation of the various language elements and knowledge about the world in general. Knowledge about the world is permanently stored in the ontology. Knowledge about treatment of language elements is stored in the various types of analysis and generation rules (syntactic, semantic, text planning, etc.). When actual processing occurs, structures are instantiated in the working memory of the intelligent agent which capture the knowledge necessary for the agent to 'understand' a text or to produce a text.

We believe that there is a well-defined set of knowledge elements whose existence constitutes a necessary and sufficient condition for a text to be considered 'understood'. In our theory the same elements are required to ensure successful generation of a text. The consumer understands messages communicated by the producer by 1) understanding and symbolically representing the meaning of the natural language text; 2) uncovering rhetorical relations among utterances and their components; 3) detecting the intentions of the producer in generating a discourse (in other words, those of the producer's plans and goals which are relevant to discourse); and 4) detecting the attitudes that the producer holds toward the content of the discourse. The producer, in creating discourse, goes through the following steps: 1) deciding what to say and elaborating a complete propositional meaning of the nascent text; 2) deciding on how to realize this meaning using realization means available in a natural language and paying attention to beliefs about the audience; and 3) taking into account the above and the preceding text (or dialogue), selecting and realizing an appropriate rhetorical structure of the nascent text.

Let us call the collection of knowledge elements sufficient for understanding or production of a text the *text supermeaning*. The supermeaning is a triad:

(8.1)   SM = T, G, S,

where T stands for textual meaning, G represents an agent's active set of goals and plans and S, the setting of the communication situation, including the pragmatic factors, such as forcefulness of expression, and parameters of the speech situation, including the spatiotemporal context and the properties of the participants and their relative social status, etc. In what follows we will discuss each of these elements in turn.

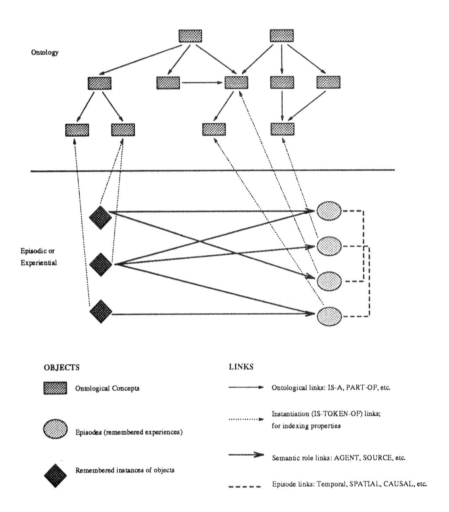

Figure 8.4. Ontology (semantic memory) and experience (episodic memory).

8.5.1 TEXTUAL MEANING

The meaning of a text is a quadruple

$$(8.2) \quad T = \{C, R, A, I\},$$

where $C = \{clause_1, clause_2, \ldots, clause_n\}$ is a set of representations of the meaning of natural language clauses and $R = \{relation_1, relation_2, \ldots, relation_k\}$ is a set of connections among elements of the representation (clause components, clauses, sets of clauses). $A = \{attitude_1, attitude_2, \ldots, attitude_l\}$ is the set of attitudes to the various components of the meaning representation on the part of a text consumer or producer or another intelligent agent (in the case of 'reported attitudes'). $I = \{producer\text{-}intention_1, producer\text{-}intention_2, \ldots, producer\text{-}intention_m\}$ represents the speech act meanings in the text.

The meaning of a clause is a quadruple

$$(8.3) \quad clause_i = \{onto_i, tr_i^j, aspect_i, time_i\},$$

where $onto_i$ is an instance of a concept in the ontology, possibly with additional constraints added to its ontological properties due to contextual influences in the input text. The features of the representation language which we use for representing semantic content of natural language clauses are a modified version of the interlingua knowledge representation language used in the KBMT-89 machine translation system. Basically, we represent the semantic content of natural language utterances by instantiating ontological entities or reasserting remembered instances of such entities that are found (with the help of a lexicon) to be the most closely semantically related to lexical units in the input. The tasks of a) lexical disambiguation of candidate readings of the input lexical items and b) construction of a semantic dependency structure are performed by the semantic analyzer. The creation of the *onto* structures in clause meaning representations and in producer-intention representations is the only process in our theory where the ontology and the text meaning interact. tr_i^j is a pair $\{role\text{-}name_i^j, onto_i^j\}$ where $role\text{-}name_i^j$ is the name of a thematic role (sometimes also called case role or semantic actant – their inventory is listed among the relation-type properties in the ontology) and where $onto_i^j$ is, again, an instance of an ontological concept, possibly with property values modified due to contextual influences. $Aspect_i$ represents the aspectual properties of $clause_i$ through three dimensions – its phase (beginning, continuation, end), duration (momentary or prolonged) and iteration (single or multiple). The $time_i$ component of $clause_i$ is used for representing absolute time references (relative times are represented through relations, see below).

TAMERLAN relations are represented as the triad

(8.4) $relation_i = \{relation\text{-}type_i,\ arguments_i,\ relation\text{-}value_i\}$,

where $relation\text{-}type_i$ is taken from a predefined set of relation types (see section 8.5.4 below); $arguments_i$ can hold either a set of TAMERLAN components or the set $\{first_i,\ second_i,\ third_i\}$. Members of this set refer to a TAMERLAN component, $third_i$ being an optional member (we don't represent relation with more than three arguments); $relation\text{-}value_i$ is an optional member; but when it is present, it refers to a point or a range on a $\{0,1\}$ scale.

The attitudes are represented as a quintuple

(8.5) $attitude_i = \{type_i,\ value_i,\ attributed\text{-}to_i,\ scope_i,\ time_i\}$,

where $type_i$ is the type of the attitude; $value_i$ is the value of the attitude, represented as a point or a region on a $\{0,1\}$ scale; $attributed\text{-}to_i$ points at the intelligent agent this attitude is attributed to; $scope_i$ takes as its value that part of the meaning representation to which the attitude is held; and finally $time_i$ represents the absolute time at which this attitude is held.

A producer-intention is a pair

(8.6) $producer\text{-}intention_i = \{onto_i,\ scope_i\}$,

where $onto_i$ refers to an ontological concept which is a descendent of verbal-action, and $scope_i$ refers to a meaning representation component. This feature is needed because natural language clauses do not always have an illocutionary force. For instance, in the promise 'If you drop by, you'll be able to see my pictures', the first clause (the antecedent to the conditional relation) has no illocutionary force. Rather, the scope of the promise is the whole sentence which, in TAMERLAN, is represented by two clauses. A complete set of producer goals and plans is stored in the G component of the text supermeaning. The producer intention is used to connect those with other meaning components.

8.5.2   THE GOAL AND PLAN COMPONENT

The G component of the text supermeaning is a collection of structures of goal and plan instances which, the text consumer believes, are active in the text producer memory during the production of this text. Since we are interested in language communication, we describe only the goals and plans that a) presuppose the situation with at least two cognitive agents and b) relate to rhetorical realizations of goals. These pointers are not directly realized, but serve as background knowledge during the realization process of other elements of input. Reasoning about goals and plans of the producer during the planning stage of natural language generation is a widely accepted approach (cf. Moore and Paris [155]; Hovy [91]; Allen and Litman [2]). The plans to which these pointers point are realized in the text only when it is decided to produce a direct speech act, in which case the realization usually involves generating a separate target language clause. In the framework of natural language understanding, the representations of producer goals and plans are constructed by the consumer. The success of this process serves as a major halting condition on the process of semantic (and pragmatic) interpretation.

Depending on the context and other parameters, the producer may decide, for instance, to produce 'I will return at 10' or 'I promise to return at 10'. In the latter case the decision is made to realize the speech act overtly. The mechanism for this is as follows: traversing the goal-and-plan hierarchy, the producer gets to the relevant point in the agenda, which is the (primitive) plan *promise* (or *threat*, etc., as the case may be). Since the realization rules for speech acts prescribe their realization as first-person-singular clauses with the lexical realizations of the names of appropriate speech plans (acts), the natural language clause ' I promise X' gets produced, and eventually X is expanded into the subordinate natural language clause 'to return at 10'.

8.5.3 SPEECH SITUATION

The speech situation, S, is represented as the pair

$$(8.7) \quad speech\text{-}situation_i = \{ deictic\text{-}indices_i, \ pragmatic\text{-}factors_i \}.$$

Deictic indices include the time and the place of the utterance of a text and the speaker and the hearer. The pragmatic factors describe stylistic parameters of the speech situation.

The microtheory of pragmatic factors used in our approach is largely inspired by Hovy [91]. The set of pragmatic factors in our model includes *formality, simplicity, colour, force, directness* and *respect*. Values of these factors are represented as points or ranges on the scale from 0 (low) to 1 (high). The default value of pragmatic factors is 0.5.

The various knowledge representation systems in artificial intelligence have traditionally stressed representation of propositional meaning (see, for example, Schank [201], Sowa [213], Creary and Pollard [41], Brachman and Schmolze [19], and many others). In this paper we will describe those components of the text meaning representation which are less frequently included in standard meaning representations – speaker attitudes, pragmatic factors and rhetorical relations.

8.5.4 A MICROTHEORY OF RELATIONS

In our present model we first distinguish text relations, domain relations and relations between intentions and domain-related text components. In what follows we further develop this taxonomy, taking into account semantic and pragmatic phenomena. For some of them we provide an example of lexical realization.[4]

Domain relations

Domain relations connect events, states and objects. We further subdivide domain relations into six main subtypes: causal, conjunction, alternation, coreference, temporal and spatial. Discussion of these groups and their further subdivision follows.

Causal: Causal relations describe a type of *dependence* among events, states and objects. We distinguish the following subtypes:

1.   *Volitional* causal relations hold between a deliberate, intentional action of an intelligent agent and its consequence. ('John turned the ignition key and the engine started.')

2.   *Non-volitional* causal relations hold between a non-intentional action or a state of an intelligent agent and its consequence. ('I fell and broke my leg.')

3.   Relations of *reason* hold between an event or state and a deliberate, intentional action by an agent. Often (but not always) they are lexically realized in English through 'because', 'since' or 'for the reason that'. ('I am prepared to help him because he helped you.')

4.   *Enablement.* An event enables another event or a state when it removes the obstacles that were preventing the latter from occurring. ('Because the weather has improved, we will go on a walk.' 'The plug was leaking, so the water escaped.')

5.   Event A is a *purpose* for event or state B if A describes a goal which an intelligent agent tries to achieve by performing B. ('He will leave early to catch the plane.')

6.   Event or state A is a *condition* for event or state B if A is a cause, reason, enablement or purpose of B and A is an event or a state

---

[4] A full study and description of all the possible realizations of each subtype is needed. At this point we still have only partial results, which will be extended in the future.

which has not actually happened and is, thus, hypothetical. ('If I win in the lottery, I'll travel to Java.')

Conjunction: The relation of conjunction holds among adjacent elements in a text that can be seen as components of a larger textual element. We distinguish the following subgroups:

1. *Addition* is a type of conjunction in which one (or more) of the conjuncts are set apart from others, sometimes for rhetorical purposes. ('Playing this piece involves real musical talent as well as technique.')

2. *Enumeration* is a type of conjunction in which all of the conjuncts have equal status. ('Athos went to Paris, bought a horse, visited his cousin, and strolled along the Seine.')[5]

3. *Adversative* relations connect conjuncts whose differences are stressed in the utterance. ('Playing this piece involves real musical talent, not only technique.')

4. Event or state A stands in a *concessive* relation to event or state B if B is typically not believed to be a result of A. Often introduced in English by '(even) though'. ('Even though the brick hit the window, the glass didn't break.')[6]

5. Entity A stands in the relation of *comparison* to entity B if the speaker believes that A and B are in some sense similar. ('Peter walked around the kitchen table like a hungry wolf.')[7]

Alternation: Relations of alternation are used in situations of choice, parallel to the logical connector *or*.

1. *inclusive or* ('If you are an ex-prisoner of war or handicapped, you are entitled to state benefits.')

2. *exclusive or* ('I'll either go to the seaside or visit Florence.')[8]

---

[5] In Quirk et al. [186], enumeration and addition are subtypes of *and*.

[6] The distinction between adversatives and concessives was found in Rudolph [194].

[7] This relation is adapted from Warner [237]; however, in Warner it is not considered to belong to the conjunction class *in*.

[8] This relation has been adapted from Warner [237].

Coreference: The relation of coreference is established among textual references to an object, an event or a state. Thus, in the following example: '{George Bush} hosted [Gorbachev] at the White House; then {he} invited [him] to Camp David; next day [the Soviet President] left for Minnesota' coreference relations hold among similarly bracketed entities. This relation is similar to *designation* in Quirk et al. [186, page 360].

Temporal: Our current theory of temporal relations is deliberately simplified. In our application work we do not seem to require a finer grain size of description of temporal relations. When such a necessity occurs, we will further develop our microtheory of time.

1.   *at:* two events happen at the same time (the events can be either momentary or prolonged). ('When the war began she was travelling.')

2.   *after:* one event happens after another in time. ('The king abdicated. Later, he was reinstated.')

3.   *during:* one event takes place after the beginning and before the end of another event. ('While the war was raging, they exchanged letters about bird-watching.')

Spatial: We distinguish the following spatial relations: *in-front-of, left-of, above, in, on* and *around.* Just as in the case of temporal relations, we do not, at this point, have a finer-grain microtheory of spatial relations. The development of such a theory is among the directions of future research.

Text relations

The text relations are relations among elements of text – sentences, enumeration items, paragraphs, etc. – rather than among events and/or objects described in the text. We distinguish three types of text relations, as follows:

1.   The *particular* relation connects two textual elements (sentences, paragraphs, etc.) one of which is an example or a special case of the other. ('It is important that young children should see things and not merely read about them. For example, it is a valuable educational experience to take them on a trip to a farm.' (Quirk et al. [186, page 668])).

2.   The two textual elements connected by the relation of *reformulation* have a similar speaker meaning expressed in different ways. ('Peter works too much. That is to say, he neglects his family.')

3.   In the relation of *conclusion*, a text element serves as a marker of end of discourse (including summary) for the other. ('In short, ...')

In an earlier version of this taxonomy (see, e.g. Defrise and Nirenburg [44]), we included additional text 'pointer' relations as well as relations delineating discourse structure boundaries. We believe now that such relations (for instance, meanings like the one which is typically realized in English by 'in the previous chapter') are devices for maintaining text cohesion and readability and that they representationally belong in the **text plan**, the structure which is produced from text meaning representation during the process of natural language generation. In the text planning rules for DIO-GENES, for example, we have used *textual-before* as a relation that connects text plan elements. In general, we would like to use the following taxonomy of these text plan relations.

1.   Text pointers:

   •   *textual-before* ('In the previous chapter, we dealt with the question of anaphora.')

   •   *textual-at* ('We give a further example on page 6.')

2.   Discourse structure boundaries:

   •   *now* ('We will now turn to the next point.')

   •   *pop* ('Anyway, that's why I came back.')

   •   *end* ('And that's the end of the story.')

Intention-domain relations

These relations connect the events described in the text with the intentions of the speaker.

1.   Temporal intention-domain relations connect the time of speech with the time of the action or event expressed by the utterance. There are two subtypes of such relations:

   •   *intention-domain-during* ('It is raining.' 'John is a teacher.')

   •   *intention-domain-after* ('Paul went to Paris.')

2.   Motivation; this relation connects a speech act to a clause expressing an event or an attitude. The content of the clause motivates
the reason to perform the speech act (i.e., the reason to utter the
clause whose illocutionary force corresponds to the speech act).
('Your mother didn't come back last night. Because the mail is
still in the mail-box.' 'Can you meet me at the office before three?
Because I have a meeting at four.') The causal link expressed by
because in the first example above does not express a causal link
between two domain-related facts, namely between a) the mother
not coming back and b) the mail being out. It rather means that
the producer can perform the speech act of *informing* the consumer
of fact a) having made an inference based on fact b). In the second example above, the domain fact 'I have a meeting at 3' is the
reason for the speech act of *request-information*.

8.5.5 ATTITUDES

In this section we will illustrate the types of attitudes we distinguish in our
current microtheory.

The end points on the scale of the **epistemic** attitude correspond to
'speaker doesn't believe that X' and 'speaker believes that X'. A middle
point on this scale corresponds to 'speaker believes that possibly X'. The
following example illustrates lexical realizations of the epistemic attitude
(grouped by *attitude-value*, whose value should be understood as the mid-
point of a fuzzy interval on the scale).

1   Paul left. I know for sure Paul left. I believe without doubt that
Paul left. It is true that Paul left.

0.9   Paul must have left. Most probably, Paul left.

0.8   Paul may have left. I'm prepared to believe that Paul left. Perhaps
Paul left. I'm almost sure Paul left.

0.6   It is possible that Paul left. I would think Paul left. Chances are
Paul left.

0.5   I don't know whether Paul left (or not).

0.3   It is unlikely that Paul left. I doubt whether Paul left.

0   Paul didn't leave. It is impossible for Paul to have left. I don't know
that Paul left. I don't believe (at all) that Paul left. It is not true
that Paul left. I know that Paul didn't leave. I believe (without a
doubt) that Paul didn't leave.

In our representation we do not distinguish what is from what the agent knows, believes or is certain about. 'Objective' reality, thus, doesn't exist in the system. Facts and events belong to the 'projected world' (Jackendoff [95, page 28]), i.e., reality as perceived by an intelligent agent. The fact that something is or is not, happened or did not happen, bears the mark of the agent's perception. Hence the epistemic attitude. Degrees of knowledge are identified with degrees of belief and degrees of certainty. If an agent knows something, he is certain about it and believes it. 'Paul left' = 'I (the text producer) believe that Paul left' = 'I know that Paul left.'

Similarly, we feel that if someone says 'Paul didn't leave', it really means (to the text consumer who interprets it) 'The producer doesn't believe at all that Paul left' = 'The producer doesn't know that Paul left' = 'It is impossible for Paul to have left' = 'The producer doesn't believe that Paul left' = 'It's not true that Paul left'. Negation can be understood as an attitude towards the event 'Paul left'. Hence our decision to collapse the representation of the parity of an utterance with the epistemic attitudes of the agent. Seeing negation as the realization of an agent's attitude has further advantages. Some uses of negation (the 'polemic' use, in denials) as in the following example:

(8.8)   Paul said he came to the party yesterday. But he didn't come.
⟨ I saw him downtown with his girlfriend. At the time of the party, he was ... ⟩.

demand an analysis that takes into account more than parity, contrasting explicitly different agents' attitudes towards the same event (this is similar to Ducrot's [50] 'polyphony'). We can provide a good representation of the above dialogue using the 'attributed-to' slot of an epistemic attitude frame. This representation will include the representation of the meaning of the clause 'Paul came to the party yesterday' in a TAMERLAN clause, say, clause$_1$, and two epistemic attitude frames, as follows:

attitude$_1$

type:	epistemic
value:	1
attributed-to:	Paul
scope:	clause$_1$

attitude$_2$

type:	epistemic
value:	0
attributed-to:	*speaker*
scope:	clause$_1$

In generating spoken text, the fact that the representation contains opposite epistemic attitudes with similar scopes will be realized through marked intonation. In contrast, a text featuring a simple negation (not a denial of a previous assertion, but a simple negative assertion) will not be represented using two opposite-value epistemic attitudes with similar scope.

Furthermore, representing parity as an attitude gives rise to 'formulas' that elegantly translate certain semantic relations between sentences. For instance the synonymy of the natural language sentences 'The book is not interesting' and 'The book is uninteresting' is translated in terms of attitudes as follows:

$attitude_3$

type:	epistemic	
value:	0	
attributed-to:	A	
scope:	$clause_2$	$attitude_4$

$attitude_4$

type:	evaluative
value:	1
attributed-to:	A
scope:	$clause_2$

and

$attitude_5$

type:	epistemic	
value:	1	
attributed-to:	A	
scope:	$clause_2$	$attitude_6$

$attitude_6$

type:	evaluative
value:	0
attributed-to:	A
scope:	$clause_2$

$clause_2$ represents the meaning glossed as 'this book' (because complete sentences only express the attitude toward the book). Therefore,

$$(8.9) \quad \frac{\text{epistemic } 0}{\text{evaluative } 1} = \frac{\text{epistemic } 1}{\text{evaluative } 0}$$

The equality will be valid only if the 'attributed-to' slots of the relevant attitudes have the same fillers. The above means that negation is generally understood as having a 'lowering effect' – something not interesting is *less* than interesting. When the condition about the 'attributed-to' fillers is not fulfilled, negation must be understood as *polemical,* and in this case the meaning of 'the book is not interesting' could, in fact, be as in 'the book is not interesting; it is fascinating'. (Once again, in speech a marked intonation will be used.)

The scale of the **deontic** attitude goes from 'speaker believes that the possessor of the attitude must X' (value 1) to 'speaker believes that the possessor of the attitude does not have to X'. The realization of the deontic attitude can be illustrated as follows:

1	I must go. I have to go
0.8-0.2	I ought to go. I'd better go. I should go. You may go.
0	I needn't go.

The scale of the **volition** attitude goes from 'The possessor of the attitude doesn't desire that X' (attitude value 0) to 'the possessor of the attitude desires that X' (attitude value 1). Some illustrations of the realization of the volition attitude:

1	I wish ... I want to ... I will ... I will gladly ...
0.8-0.2	I hesitate to ... It may be a good idea to ... I'm reluctant to ...
0	I'm unwilling to ... I refuse to ... I don't want ...

The scale of the **expectation** attitude goes from 'The possessor of the attitude doesn't expect that X' through 'the possessor of the attitude somewhat expects that X' to 'the possessor of the attitude expects that X'. Some lexical realizations of the expectation attitude:

1	Not surprisingly ... As expected ... Of course ... Needless to say ...
0.8-0.2	Even (as in 'Even Paul left')
0	Surprisingly ... It couldn't be expected ...

The evaluative and saliency attitudes can have in their scope not only clauses, relations or attitudes like the previous ones, but also objects and properties.[9] It is therefore difficult to give a limited and exhaustive set of examples of realizations.

Evaluative attitudes are held toward events, things, properties and relations among. One can also evaluate another attitude. Evaluation goes from 'the best for the possessor of the attitude' (value 1) to 'the worst for the possessor of the attitude' (value 0). Depending on the value of the scope of this attitude, realizations will greatly vary and may include no lexical realization at all. If the scope is an event, adverbs like *fortunately* and *unfortunately* will be used. If the scope is the physical appearance of a person, the endpoints of the scale of evaluative attitude will be realized as 'attractive' and 'ugly', etc. The meaning representations for the following sentences will centrally feature evaluative attitudes: 'This is the best book I ever read.' 'Blue is my favorite colour.'

The value of the **saliency** attitude varies with the importance that the agent attaches to a text component. High saliency is attached to entities that the agent wants to be stressed. The saliency attitude plays an important role in selecting the syntactic structure of the target sentences and in lexical selection for generation. Thus it will influence the order of elements in a conjunction; it will be realized syntactically through topicalization ('It is Paul who won the contest') and lexically through connective expressions such as 'last but not least' or 'most importantly'.

We allow for the possibility of adding other types of attitudes. We have deliberately limited the number of possible attitude types to only a few, based on the immediate needs of our application work. It is clear however that a more complex and complete microtheory of attitudes will have to be developed. In particular, the *evaluative* attitude is a first-cut simplification of what should become a complex net of categories enabling us to represent the meaning of evaluative verbs, adjectives and adverbs featuring scalar behaviour. When trying to represent the meaning of sentences containing adjectives such as *interesting, important* or *boring,* one realizes that to use a single evaluative scale ranging from *good* to *bad* to represent all three adjectives is vastly inadequate, especially in view of the problem of lexical selection during generation; it only suffices as a first approach to capture argumentative orientations, which, as discussed in Anscombre and Ducrot [3], play an important role in distinguishing, for example, the reasons for using *but* rather than *and* as a connector between two propositions.[10]

---

[9] The evaluative attitude to 'the book' in the example above would, in fact, belong to this latter class. Its scope is a clause only because there is no predication in the sentence other than the attitudinal one. In a sentence like 'John read an interesting book' the attitude is clearly toward an object instance.

[10] The status of attitude markers differs in the contexts of natural language analysis and generation. During analysis the values of attitude are part of the world of the con-

McKeown and Elhadad [146] also treat argumentative scales and attitudinals in a generation environment. They, however, consider these phenomena as part of syntax, thus avoiding the need to add a special pragmatic component to their system. This decision is appropriate from the point of view of minimizing the changes in an existing generator due to the inclusion of attitude information. However, if compatibility were not an issue, introducing a separate component would be a more appropriate choice.

8.5.6 PRAGMATIC FACTORS

Our microtheory of pragmatic factors is a modified version of the set of 'rhetorical goals' from Hovy [91]. In our systems, however, the processing performed with the help of the pragmatic factors is different. Among other differences, treatment of pragmatic factor values becomes in our systems an integral part of the process of natural language *analysis*, not only natural language generation.

Formality

The higher the formality, the closer to a legal or formulaic language one gets. Differences in formality will explain the distinction between 'I hereby inform you that X' and simply 'X', between 'thereby' and 'thus', between 'solicitation' and 'request', between the use of full names and titles and abbreviations, etc. The following strategies were used by Hovy [91, pages 113–114] to make a generation system produce formal text: generate long, complex sentences by subordinating them in relative clauses; use passive voice, use 'more complex' tenses such as the perfect tenses; avoid ellipsis; use long and formal phrases and formal words; nominalize verbs and adverbs, as in 'their flight trajectory circled the tree' instead of 'they flew round the tree'; do not refer directly to the interlocutors; avoid contractions such as 'can't' or slang or colloquial words and expressions.

---

sumer; specifically, they are situated in the consumer's view of the producer. It follows that in this case these attitude values are, in fact, consumer's hypotheses about producer's intentions. The consumer derives these attitude values based on his knowledge about lexical, syntactic and other textual clues, knowledge about the world and a reasoning capability about goals and plans of participants in a discourse situation (which allows him to infer implied attitudes). In the case of generation, the producer's attitudes and agenda are available to him from the outset, so that no conjecture is involved. The task of the producer is to decide whether to generate an explicit attitude marker and, if so, *which* of potentially many realization means to select.

Simplicity

Formality and simplicity are somewhat related, and the values (formality: < 0.5) and (simplicity: > 0.5) will be highly correlated and will often be found together in one representation. Nevertheless, they differ. One can use a complex style (simplicity: < 0.5) and be either formal (formality: > 0.5) or not (formality: < 0.5). (Simplicity: > 0.5) means the text will contain simple and short sentences, easy words, that its structure will be straightforward (the order of sentences will be such as to avoid the use of complex tenses for instance).

Force

'Forceful text is straightforward, direct, and has momentum.' (Hovy [91, page 124]). The strategies that a producer must use to make his text forceful include:

- use of enhancers such as 'not only ... but also' and intensifiers;

- use of direct reference to the interlocutors;

- producing short, simple sentences, by choosing not to link sentences together and by including at most one adverbial clause;

- use of forceful or simple, plain words and phrases;

- no explicit realization of opinions (propositional attitudes) (using 'X' rather than 'I think that X' or 'It seems that X').

Colour

This parameter (a mixture of Hovy's colour and floridity) affects lexical selection in generation. Colourful text contains unusual words, idiomatic expressions, a relatively large number of adjectival modifiers ('a fresh new shop', 'a cruel and pitiless man'), including adjectival clauses ('Mr. X, a cruel and pitiless man, ...').

Directness

This pragmatic factor relates to the amount of direct reference to the interlocutors. Different values of this parameter will influence the decision whether to use second person or impersonal forms of verbs, to express propositional attitudes explicitly or not ('My opinion is that X' vs. 'X'), to use impersonal or personal noun phrases, etc. In addition, a high value on this pragmatic factor will lead to overt representations of speech acts ('I promise that I will finish this assignment by tomorrow').

Respect

The relative status of the participants greatly influences the form of texts. The scale of possible relative social relationships is in reality very complex, and varies greatly from culture to culture. In our model, we simplify matters by keeping only three possible values: high, neutral and low. 'High' means that the producer is socially or hierarchically superior to the consumer; 'neutral' means the producer and the consumer have equal status; 'low' means that the producer is socially or hierarchically inferior to the consumer. This parameter will influence the generation of speech acts such as orders, requests, promises ('Would you be so kind as to X' vs. 'Please, X'; 'Could you tell me the time, please' vs. 'What's the time?') or salutations ('Good morning, Mr. X' vs. 'Hi'). This pragmatic factor will play a very important role in treating languages with well-developed systems of politeness, such as Japanese. In fact, the ability to use this parameter will allow one to parry the criticism directed at meaning-based machine translation[11] to the effect that such 'nuances' are untranslatable and unrepresentable in a general meaning representation framework.

8.5.7 AN ANNOTATED EXAMPLE OF TEXT MEANING REPRESENTATION

The meaning representation we discuss in this paper is used in the natural language analysis system DIANA and the natural language generation system DIOGENES. For details of application-related formalization and actual use of this representation scheme see Nirenburg and Defrise [164]. In this section we would like to illustrate our representation on a small-scale example. Let's take sentence (8.10) as the input text.

(8.10)   The train has, unfortunately, left.

The meaning representation of this sentence in TAMERLAN follows. The goals and plans of the speaker cannot be inferred by the reader of (8.10) outside an actual speech situation and in the absence of a broader textual context.

---

[11]See, for instance, Nagao [160, page 7]: '... [I]n the case of translation through a pivot language, since it is necessary to decide upon expressions in the pivot language which will be appropriate for translations in which *all* of the factors found in *all* of the languages are included – including linguistic expressions dependent upon sex, social status, degree of respect, and so on ... The pivot language must be extremely well constructed if it is to include such subtle factors.'

(8.11) SM_1 $= \{$ $T_1, S_1 \}$

T_1 $= \{$ *clause₁, relation₁, attitude₁,*

attitude₂, producer-intention₁$\}$

clause₁ $= \{$ *head* $=$ *change-location₁,*

theme $=$ *train₁,*

source $=$ S_1.*deictic-indices.place,*

aspect $=$ *aspect₁,*

time $=$ *time₁*$\}$

The head of the clause is an instance of the ontological concept *change-location* with the further constraint to the effect that the *source* thematic role is bound to the place of speech (in the ontology the constraint on the *source* of *change-location* is that it can be bound to any ontological descendant of the concept of *physical-object*). No additional constraints were possible for the *destination* thematic role of *change-location*.

(8.12) *aspect₁* $= \{$ *phase* $=$ *begin,*

duration $=$ *momentary,*

iteration $=$ 1$\}$

Our microtheory of aspect is based on theoretical work of James Pustejovsky and is presented in Nirenburg and Pustejovsky [168]. In this example we treat the aspect of the English *leave* as inchoative and non-iterative. As to duration, we consider this action to be momentary at the grain size of temporal description that we consider adequate for representing the meaning of this word.

(8.13) *attitude₁* $= \{$ *type* $=$ *evaluative,*

value $=$ 0,

scope $=$ *clause₁.head,*

attributed-to $=$ S_1.*deictic-indices.speaker*$\}$

(8.14) *attitude₂* $= \{$ *type* $=$ *epistemic,*

value $=$ 1,

scope $=$ *clause₁.head,*

attributed-to $=$ S_1.*deictic-indices.speaker*$\}$

The speaker's evaluative attitude toward the content of the sentence is very negative. This attitude reflects the meaning of *unfortunately*. The epistemic attitude shows that the speaker is quite sure that the train, in fact, left. Note that if in (8.10) *leave* had been modified by *most assuredly* or a similar intensifier, this meaning would have been realized through a *saliency* attitude, with the value 1, whose scope would include the above epistemic attitude. The times of the attitudes are not informative and therefore are left out of the representation.

(8.15)   *producer-intention*$_1$ = {*onto=assertive-act*$_1$, *scope=clause*$_1$}

assertive-act in our current ontology is a descendant of *illocutionary-act* and a sibling of *commissive-act, directive-act, expressive-act* and *rogative-act*.

(8.16)   *relation*$_1$ = {   *relation-type*   =   *intention-domain-after*
                                      first   =   *time*$_0$
                                      second   =   *time*$_1$
                        relation-value   <   0.3}

The above temporal relation connects the time of speech and the time of the event described in the input. The value of the relation is a measure of the relative temporal distance between the two events. In our example the value in the lower third of the value range means that the event occurred recently.

(8.17) S_1 = {   *deictic-indices*$_1$, *pragmatic-factors*$_1$}
          deictic-indices$_1$ = {   *time*   =   *time*$_0$}
          pragmatic-factors$_1$ = {   *formality*   >   0.5,
                                      force   >   0.5}

The use of *unfortunately* raises the value of formality from the default level of 0.5.

8.6   CONCLUSION

The main points of this paper have been as follows.

- Practical results and systems-oriented research progress in computational linguistics are possible only if semantic analysis is based on a model of an intelligent agent, centrally including a world model, or ontology, a language for representing text meaning and a set of heuristic procedures for assigning meanings to natural language texts. The acquisition and representation of knowledge to support the above type of processing is a central problem of computational linguistics.

- Methodologically, the best approach to building comprehensive natural language processing systems seems to involve: a) producing a microtheory of every linguistic phenomenon that must be treated in a given application; these microtheories can either be developed from scratch or (and this is preferable) be adapted from treatments of various phenomena known from theoretical linguistics; b)

designing a control structure flexible enough to allow integration
of all the procedures necessary for an application and reformulat-
ing the microtheories in terms of the formalism required by the
control structure.

There are many unsolved problems in computational linguistics, and their
complexity is typically very high. It is our belief that the field will be
ill-served by approaches which stress deep and comprehensive treatment
of one single phenomenon or a small group of phenomena. Such type of
work leads to the production of microtheories. The latter are indispensable
for the solution of the more general problems. But their availability alone
does not constitute a sufficient condition for the achievement of practical
computational-linguistic results. Microtheories of syntactic and semantic
processing must be developed (these cannot possibly be derived from theoretical linguistics whose mandate does not include considerations of heuristic text processing). We need both the field work of creating world models
and lexicons and computational environments to test the systems resulting
from integrating microtheories and the software engineering substrate.

ACKNOWLEDGEMENTS

Members of the DIANA and DIOGENES projects have made important contributions to the research reported here. Parts of TAMERLAN have been
suggested and/or improved by Boyan Onyshkevych, Ted Gibson and Ralf
Brown. Thanks are also due to Eric Nyberg, Lynn Carlson and John
Leavitt. Ken Goodman did an excellent job criticizing the theoretical and
methodological components of this paper. The authors are responsible for
any remaining inconsistencies and deficiencies.

Appendix: A formal definition of
the tamerlan language

```
<tamerlan-text> ::= <clause>+ <relation>* <attitude>*
                    <producer-intention>*

<clause>        ::= <head> <aspect> <time>

<head>          ::= <is-token-of> <thematic-role>* <property>*

<is-token-of>   ::= ONTOSUBTREE-OR(all)

                    ;this function returns a DISJUNCTIVE SET
                    ;of all the elements in the ontological
                    ;hierarchy rooted at its argument(s)

<thematic-role> ::= <th-role-name> <value>

<th-role-name>  ::= ONTOSUBTREE-OR(thematic-role)

                    ;this list includes AGENT, DESTINATION,
                    ;THEME, BENEFICIARY, EXPERIENCER, etc.

<value>         ::= <individual> | <collection>

<individual>    ::= ONTOSUBTREE-OR(all) | <concept-instance> |
                    <timed-concept-instance> |
                    <symbolic-set-value> | <numerical-value> |
                    <special-value>

<concept-instance>
                ::= TOKEN(ONTOSUBTREE-OR(all))

                    ;TOKEN is a function that creates a token
                    ;of its argument(s) which must be an
                    ;ontological concept or a set of such

<timed-concept-instance>
                ::= <concept-instance> <instance-time>

                    ;timed-concept-instances are used to refer
                    ;to instances whose properties BUT NOT
```

```
                      ;IDENTITY changed with time (my car before
                      ;I painted it red and my car after I
                      ;painted it red are two timed instances of
                      ;the instance "my car")

<instance-time> ::= since <time> until <time> | since <time> |
                      until <time>

<symbolic-set-value>
                ::= a string from the slot "range" of
                    ONTOSUBTREE-OR(attribute)

<numerical-value>
                ::= <point>* | <semi-interval>* | <interval>*

<semi-interval> ::= > <point> | < <point>

<interval>      ::= <point> <point>

<point>         ::= a number between 0 and 1, inclusive

<special-value> ::= *producer* | *consumer*

<collection>    ::= (UNION <collection><collection>) |
                    (INTERSECTION <collection> <collection>) |
                    (SET-DIFFERENCE <collection> <collection>)
                    | (<element> <collection-type>
                      {<cardinality>})+

<element>       ::= ONTOSUBTREE(all)

<collection-type> ::= disjunctive | conjunctive

<cardinality>   ::= integer

<property>      ::= <property-name> <value>

<property-name> ::= ONTOSUBTREE(property)

<aspect>        ::= phase duration iteration

<phase>         ::= begin | continue | end
```

```
<duration>        ::= momentary | prolonged

<iteration>       ::= integer | multiple

<time>            ::= <absolute-time> | <time-variable>

<absolute-time> ::= ;e.g. 05-12-90-13:45:11.56

<time-variable> ::= time_<integer>

<relation>        ::= <ordered-relation> | <unordered-relation>

<ordered-relation>
                  ::= <relation-type> {<relation-value>}
                      first <relation-argument>
                      second <relation-argument>
                      {third <relation-argument>}


<unordered-relation>
                  ::= <relation-type> {<relation-value>}
                      arguments <relation-argument>
                      <relation-argument>*

<relation-type> ::= <domain-relation> | <textual-relation>

<domain-relation>
                  ::= <causal> | <conjunction> | <alternation> |
                      attribution | coreference | <temporal>

<causal>          ::= volitional | non-volitional | reason |
                      enablement | purpose | result | condition

<conjunction>     ::= <simple-conjunction> | <contrast> |
                      comparison

<simple-conjunction>
                  ::= addition | enumeration

<contrast>        ::= adversative | concessive
```

```
<alternation>    ::= inclusive | exclusive

<temporal>       ::= at | after | during

<textual-relation>
                 ::= particular | reformulation | progression |
                     conclusion

<relation-value>
                 ::= <numerical-value>

<relation-argument>
                 ::= any tamerlan expression or set of such

<attitude>       ::= <attitude-type> <attitude-value> <scope>
                     <attributed-to> <attitude-time>

<attitude-type> ::= epistemic | deontic | volition |
                    expectation | evaluative | saliency

<attitude-value>
                 ::= <numerical-value>

<scope>          ::= any tamerlan expression or set of such

<attributed-to> ::= any instance of the ontological type
                    intelligent-agent

<attitude-time> ::= since <time> until <time> |
                    since <time> | until <time>

<producer-intention>
                 ::= <intention-type> <scope>

<intention-type>
                 ::= ONTOSUBTREE-OR(speech-act)
```

9 Form and content in semantics

Yorick Wilks

9.1 INTRODUCTION

This paper is written from the point of view of one who works in artificial intelligence (AI): the attempt to reproduce interesting and distinctive aspects of human behaviour with a computer, which, in my own case, means an interest in human language use.

There may seem little of immediate relevance to cognition or epistemology in that activity. And yet it hardly needs demonstration that AI, as an aspiration and in practice, has always been of interest to philosophers, even to those who may not accept the view that AI is, essentially, the pursuit of metaphysical goals by non-traditional means.

As to cognition in particular, it is also a commonplace nowadays, and at the basis of cognitive science, that the structures underlying AI programs are a guide to psychologists in their empirical investigations of cognition. That does not mean that AI researchers are in the business of cognition, nor that there is any direct inference from how a machine does a task, say translating a sentence from English to Chinese, to how a human does it. It is, however, suggestive, and may be the best intellectual model we currently have of how the task is done. So far, so well known and much discussed in the various literatures that make up cognitive science.

My first task in this paper concerns epistemology, but in a rather narrow way and does not directly address the large topics I have named above. It is to observe and criticise the fact that one school of AI researchers has, in effect, hijacked the word 'epistemology' and used it to mean something quite unrelated to its traditional meaning: the study of what we know and how we know it. The term has been used within the ongoing dispute in AI about how we represent knowledge (facts, generalizations, performances, etc.) in AI programs so that machines can be said to know things, or rather, how they can be programmed so as to perform as if they know things, such

257

as telling you about the trains to Washington at a station where you type a question to a publicly-available computer.

The AI researchers who use the word 'epistemology' are part of what is frequently called the 'Logic Approach to AI': the claim that the representations required by the task just mentioned are those of first-order predicate logic and its associated model theoretic semantics. My overall task in this paper is to examine that use of 'epistemology' and then move to a criticism of that whole tradition of logic-based-representation in AI. My own view is that we do need representations (as opposed to the current trend of connectionism (e.g. Smolensky [211], Waltz and Pollack [236]) who deny that), but that their form, if interpretable, is largely arbitrary, and we may be confident it has little relationship to logic. I shall restate the view that the key contribution of AI in unravelling how such complex tasks as 'understanding' might be simulated by a machine lies not in representations at all but in particular kinds of procedures (that much at least, my view shares with connectionism). It would be the most extraordinary coincidence, cultural, evolutionary and intellectual, if what was needed for the computational task should turn out to be formal logic, a structure derived for something else entirely. Although, it must be admitted, strange coincidences have been known in the history of science.

The view under criticism here, then, the 'Logic Approach to AI', is not merely being accused of misusing a word ('epistemology'), nor of getting its representations wrong. Its whole larger dream is under attack: that concentrating on the deductive relations of propositions can yield a theory of mind or even machine performance.

There is a well-known tradition, going back to Plato at least, that what we can be said to know includes the deductive consequences of other things we know. But that inquiry alone has never been thought to yield a theory of mind, or an epistemology. If anything in AI were ever to bear on, or contribute to, the study normally indicated by that tired old word, it would surely come when a computer not only behaved as if it knew things (and in a complex, coherent way, not as a recitation of facts) but could also relate them directly to its own physical manipulations, as we can. Moreover, it might (so as to qualify) also have to come to know new things under roughly the conditions we do, and, I suggest, *not* know things that we cannot in principle know, such as aspects of our internal functioning at the level of the brain (see Wilks [245]).

All these possibilities for a serious 'electronic metaphysics' are a long way off. My task here is not to advance such endeavours but is merely domestic, perhaps only housecleaning, by showing that the AI uses of 'epistemology' and the 'Logic Approach to AI' have nothing to do with that task.

9.2 EPISTEMOLOGICAL ADEQUACY AND THE LOGIC-BASED APPROACH TO AI AND NATURAL LANGUAGE PROCESSING

Let us advance scholarship in a video age by hunting our intellectual quarry on videotapes, rather than in journals, though serious scholars will find the distinctions discussed here also in McCarthy [141]. Lifschitz [136], in setting out what he calls the Logic Approach to AI, distinguishes epistemological and heuristic adequacy as follows:

- An *epistemologically adequate* model is one such that a solution to a given problem follows from the model.

- A *heuristically adequate* model is one which provides, in addition, a method for finding that solution.

This he explains best in terms of chess, where the rules of chess give a solution to a board problem, and hence form an epistemologically adequate model; but only additional heuristics give an effective solution, if one is available.

The last phrase is crucial since Lifschitz's illustration ignores a crucial fact about chess: that the game is decidable only from a certain range of positions, usually known as 'saddle points' (Botvinnik [17]), and hence, in no serious sense, are the rules of chess an epistemologically adequate model on Lifschitz's own definition. But let us treat that point as mere carping, even though its flavour will continue to permeate our discussion of those key notions and their impact and significance for the representation of knowledge in AI.

Lifschitz's distinction, under various names and guises, has been central to the 'Logic Approach to AI' since the publication of McCarthy and Hayes [142]. My concern in this paper will be with its impact on the area of processing in AI that I know best, namely natural language processing. But that will not be merely an arbitrary focusing of this paper, within the general area of epistemology and cognition, for two reasons.

First, the areas of natural language representation and processing have been major ones in recent years for developments of formal representations (under influence from the McCarthy and Hayes work in AI, and its successors, and from the work of Montague [219] and its successors in formal linguistic semantics). Secondly, much of the work in the philosophy of language in this century has been to recapitulate, if not absorb, other areas of philosophy, such as the philosophy of mind. So then, to discuss the issue of epistemology from a language-oriented viewpoint is in no way revolutionary.

Lifschitz quotes Bundy approvingly to the effect that AI abounds in formalisms that are plausible but lack a proper semantics. This has been a familiar line in the McCarthy and Hayes tradition in AI: Hayes himself [83] applied this stern medicine to a range of AI formalisms including that of the present author.

That, says Lifschitz, is what happens when you have only a heuristics, but do not have the epistemological part properly worked out. As we shall see, this last means no more or less than having a classic model-theoretic semantics, which has no natural relation to any normal meaning of 'epistemological' or to 'knowledge' at all.

Mere appeal to logic is not enough, he then warns us, since even some users of logic are guilty of insufficient attention to epistemological adequacy, and he cites negation-by-failure in logic programming as an example (one to which we shall return below).

Let us at this point pause and ask again what is this epistemological adequacy? It is still a fair question since, as we saw, the chess example, which was intended to explain the notion, actually raised more doubts than it assuaged. Certainly, the notion has little to do with traditional epistemology: the part of metaphysics that deals with human knowledge, with what we know and how we come to know it and, in the British tradition at least, the intimate relation of those two. Lifschitz's epistemological adequacy (let us call it EA) has nothing to do with that: he never considers or displays any interest in what we know, its degree of certainty, its possible limitations, its contents, or how we come to know anything. If EA has a philosophical antecedent, and its proponents usually assume this without any evidence, it is probably Plato, with his view that we know all consequences of what we know innately. But, again, Plato, unlike our AI colleagues, gave a great deal of thought to what and how we know innately, and it was *that* that made him an epistemologist.

Nor has EA anything to do with cognition, in the sense of the psychology of what we know or how we come to know it: in the chess example, a psychologist would focus almost entirely on what Lifschitz dismisses as the heuristics of the game; the abstract sense in which the rules condition possible moves would probably be of very little interest to a cognitive psychologist. Unlike Chomsky in a similar dilemma over cognition and universal grammar, it will be difficult for Lifschitz to separate himself from these cognitive problems since he clearly does believe that, in some magical way, and independently of any evidence, logic is at the basis of cognition. I suppose this certainly is clearer, even if false, than Chomsky's [35] resort to an inscrutable competence-performance distinction.

So, what is EA about? It is simply another way of putting clothes on the thin skeleton of model theoretic semantics, applied to areas that are not *a prima facie* appropriate for its attentions: common-sense knowledge, natural language, even chess. We need logic, says Lifschitz, because the facts are logically complex. But that is precisely the point at issue: in natural language representation it is not agreed what the facts are, although it is agreed that, whatever they are, they are complex. But why logically complex? What possible evidence is there for that, given that it would be very foolish to deny, at this stage of AI research, that the 'facts of language' can be represented on a (connectionist, non-logical) network of arbitrary complexity (cf. Smolensky [211]). That is a representational claim; as to the corresponding cognitive claim, the disarray is even greater.

But let us stick to man-made domains that might seem to suit Lifschitz's case: chess, above all. EA for chess, as stated by him, establishes the opposite of what he intended, in that it cannot lead to a chess player, artificial or human. That must require heuristics, as practical research has amply shown. And, as I noted, chess does not even support the abstract claim about derivability of positions by formal methods. What can the content of EA then be? I suggest, nothing: it is no more than a disguised statement of faith that a set of logical statements capture a situation and that a semantics will be made available at some point to give computational decidability to any putative consequence of the axioms and rules of inference. To know that some model is EA is to know just that, and yet can we be given some non-trivial domain for which that can be known of a model? If not, then all this may be magnificent, but it is not knowledge representation, let alone AI.

Let us stay, for a moment longer, with another of Lifschitz's chosen domains: the one of negation-by-failure, as implemented in standard Prolog. It is especially revealing for our efforts to find out what the real content of EA is.

Lifschitz maintains that negation as failure (which we shall refer to as NAF) is not EA, which might seem plausible if NAF meant something like an unsound method of reasoning in general, given that it is not always right to take something as true because we cannot prove it false. I cannot prove it false, on the basis of what I know right now, that it is raining in Sydney. But I feel no urge at all to assert that therefore it is raining in Sydney. I simply lack evidence: both the facts and plausible meteorological generalizations and statistics.

But alas, it seems that Lifschitz means nothing so reasonable in his dismissal of NAF. NAF he says has no classical semantics, its semantics are in the form of a procedure, and we all know that procedural semantics is wrong. Let us go slowly here: this point of Lifschitz's, even if true, has nothing whatever to do with epistemology in any standard sense nor, interestingly, has it anything to do with EA as he defined it, as it would if a solution to a problem would not follow in general from the facts of a model and a logical program using NAF, simply because NAF is a perfectly effective procedure within logic programming. It just doesn't (always) fit common-sense intuitions.

The mask is off: the only argument Lifschitz has against NAF is its lack of a classical semantics, and having that feature is all that EA means for him. EA models cover simply and only what can be known by (semantically justified) deduction from assumptions whose knowledge status one is not concerned with, and here we note again that even the very deductively-oriented metaphysicians, like Descartes, did also worry a great deal about the status of the assumptions or first principles.

Lifschitz also concedes that a semantics has in fact been given for NAF (at least for 'stratified' systems, though one can be provided for virtually any effective procedure, given the nature of human ingenuity) so now he has a real problem, in that he wants to reject NAF, presumably on the common-sense grounds given above, but cannot because now it meets the only criterion he has: having a classical semantics. For the moment I rest my case that EA, even if it has content, has nothing to do with epistemology, cognition, problem solving or knowledge representation.

9.3 FORMAL VS. COMMON-SENSE SEMANTICS

Let us now turn from a logic-based approach to AI in general, so as to contrast formal semantics, as a tool for natural language processing in particular, with a different approach: common-sense semantics.

There need be no real dispute here about what is meant, in the broadest terms, by formal semantics (FS) when opposed to common-sense semantics (CSS): commentators on the distinction as different as Israel [94] and Sparck-Jones [214] broadly agree on where the line is to be drawn.

Formal semantics (henceforth FS), at least as it relates to computational language understanding, is in one way rather like connectionism, though without the crucial prop Sejnowski and Rosenberg's work [208] is widely believed to give to the latter: both are old doctrines returned, like the Bourbons, having learned nothing and forgotten nothing. But FS has nothing to show as a showpiece success after all the intellectual groaning and effort. Here I must register a small historical protest at Israel's claim that 'Traditionally (indeed, until Montague, almost undeviatingly) the techniques of pure mathematical semantics were not deployed for formal or artificial languages' [94]. It all depends what you mean by techniques, but Carnap in his *Meaning and Necessity* [27] certainly thought he was applying Tarskian insights to natural language analysis. And the arguments surrounding that work, and others, were very like those we are having now. I need that point if the Bourbon analogy is to stick: FS applied to natural languages is anything but new.

But there have been recent changes in style and presentation in computation as a result of the return: many of those working in the computational semantics of natural language now choose to express their notations in ways more acceptable to FS than they would have bothered to do, say, ten years ago. That may be a gain for perspicuity or may be a waste of time in individual cases, but there are no clear examples, I suggest, of computational systems where an FS theory offers anything integral or fundamental to the success of the program that could not have been achieved by those same processes described at a more common-sense level (what I am calling common-sense semantics, or CSS). I would suggest that recent discussions in AI concerned with inheritance systems, in particular, tend to confirm my hunch on this issue, in that the useful ones at the moment, such as Touretsky's, are CSS systems, and attempts to formalize systems fully has made them intractable. This FS-as-mental-hygiene defence will return later in the paper when discussing McDermott.

I do not at all intend, at this point, to define CSS by any particular type, or level, of notational description; I believe it is best exemplified by the role of semantics in natural language processing within AI, and by a primary commitment to the solution of the major problems of language processing: those problems that have obstructed progress in the field for thirty years. These I take to include: large scale lexical ambiguity in text (i.e., over realistically large ranges of sense ambiguity for lexical items of English), the problems of phrase and other constituent attachment, where those require considerations of meaning to determine, as well as the mass of problems that collect around the notions of expertise, plans, intentions, goals, common knowledge, reference and its relationship to topic, etc.

On these descriptions of FS and CSS, they are not necessarily exclusive: it would be quite conceivable for an FS system to aid with the solution of a problem important to CSS. And it will always be possible for a successful CSS theory to be subsequently axiomatized. But that does not equate CSS and FS any more than axiomatizing physics does away with experiments: theories come first, axiomatizations follow. In fact that axiomatization has not been done for natural language processing and there is no reason to believe it will, because the origins and ultimate preoccupations of FS are always elsewhere. The examples Israel chooses to discuss in detail (Henkin and Kripke) make my point exactly. He notes that he could have taken others when defending FS and that 'the nature of the languages studied makes no essential difference' [94]. But, as he seems to concede elsewhere in the paper, those are the very areas where the techniques can be shown to work and that is why they are always chosen ('the choice of tools ...should be grounded somehow in the nature of the phenomena to be analysed'). My case, to be set out in a little more detail below, is that the kind of language chosen for analysis (natural versus artificial) makes as much difference as any choice could make, and that in the last quotation Israel is dead right, though not in the way he intended.

A small concrete example may help: the choice between generating 'a' and 'the' is notoriously difficult in English, one that non-native speakers continually get wrong. Examples are sometimes hard to grasp in one's own language, and the choice between 'des' and 'les' in French is similarly crucial and notorious, though it is not the same distinction as the English one, yet it rests on the same kind of semantic criteria. It is not a problem with an arbitrary solution: French grammar books claim to offer principles that underlie the choice.

It also seems, on the surface, to be a problem that FS, or any logical approach to language structure, ought to help with: it is certainly some form of idiosyncratic quantification. Those particles are exactly the kind that Montague grammar, say, offers large, complex structures for; just as, as Sparck-Jones notes [214], such systems offer such minimal, vacuous, codings for content words. This is probably the clearest quantitative distinction between FS and CSS. As far as I am aware no FS solutions have ever been offered for these problems, nor would seem remotely plausible if they were; at best they would simply be a recoding in an alternative language of criteria satisfactorily expressed in other ways. Yet this is exactly the sort of place where FS should offer help with a concrete problem if it is to be of assistance to the NLP task at all, for it is to such items that its representational ingenuity has been devoted.

The historical and intellectual sources of FS lie in an alternative approach to what constitutes a proof: to meta-logical methods for the establishment of properties of whole systems, such as complete, consistent, etc., and the employment of properties such as decidability to establish the validity of theorems independently of normal proof-theoretic methods, i.e., by 'semantic' methods, in that special sense. The applicability of this methodology has been perfectly clear in the case of programming languages and proofs of correctness of programs (even if the scope of the applications is still depressingly small), but in the application to natural language understanding its original aims have simply got lost.

From time to time, an application within the original methodology surfaces, such as Heidrich's [84] proof of the equivalence of the methods of generative semantics and Montague grammar, but the result proved is then seen to be vacuous, in the terms of CSS at least, in that nothing was established whose absence had constituted any pre-existing problem. The usefulness or (in)adequacy of generative semantics was not anything that could be established or questioned by the sort of guaranteed equivalences that the proof offered. The problems with generative semantics, whatever they were, lay elsewhere and were not alleviated by any such proof.

The heart of the issue is good old decidability, or whether or not the sentences of a language form a recursive set in any interesting sense. It is clear to me that they do not, although I contrasted various senses in which they might back in 1971 [240]. Contributions like Israel's only make sense on the assumption that sentences do form some such set, unless he is adopting only a 'descriptive logical language position' (see below position #1), and his whole position paper suggests he is doing far more than that.

The alternative position is that natural language is not a phenomenon of the sort required and assumed by the various systems of logic under discussion; and that the interpretation of a sentence in a context is an approximative matter (including whether or not it has a plausible interpretation at all, and hence whether or not it is a sentence at all), one computed by taking a best-fit interpretation from among a number of competing candidates. That is not a process reducible to a decidable one in any non-trivial manner. Indeed, I recall going further [240] and arguing that the process of assigning an interpretation to a string, from among competing candidates, could be taken as a criterion of having a meaning: namely, having one from among a set of possible meanings. I mention this point for purely self-serving reasons: I do not want Israel to get away with identifying CSS with Schank [201] and Chomsky as he does in his paper. I do not object to him joining them as bedfellows: that has been done before, and all serious opponents are said to share premises. In the case of those two, the similarities become clearer as time goes on, and include a certain commitment to genetic claims, but above all a commitment to representations rather than procedures. My self-servingness is to point out that my own approach, preference semantics, was not about commitment to representations of a particular kind at all, but only to certain procedures (based on coherence and connectedness of representations) as the right way to select interpretations from among competitors, for competitors there will always be. CSS can be about procedures as much as representations. In his own commitment to representations and dismissal of procedures ('semantics, even construed as a theory of language use, is not directly a theory of processing') Israel is actually in the same bed with that distinguished company. But not to worry, it is a big bed.

Preference semantics was, in a clear sense, procedural and had the advantage of declaring strings that did not admit the assignment of a single interpretation (i.e., remained ambiguous with respect to interpretation) as meaningless. Meaninglessness on that view was not having no meaning but having too many. I found, and still find, that a satisfying position, one true to the process of language interpretation. Moreover, it also offers an opportunity, for computation, processing, artificial intelligence, or what you will, to have something to say about fundamental questions like meaning. It is clearly an assumption of Israel, and all who think like him, that that cannot be: 'real semantics', as he puts it, is being done elsewhere.

It is one of the advantages of connectionist fun and games, from my point of view, that it has, against FS, brought implementation back to centre stage from the wings; thus the new movement can be of enormous political interest and importance, whether or not one is a believer in it.

Let me try to separate levels (or perhaps just a continuum of positions, or aspects) that the claims of FS make about natural language processing:

1. There must be a certain style of formal description as the basis of any system of natural language description or processing. That this claim can be pretty weak can be seen clearly if we remember McCarthy's insistence on first order forms of expression combined with his advocacy of heuristics and, indeed, his claim that heuristics constitute the essence of AI. One can accede to this demand without giving any support to the central part of the FS claim about decidability.

2. The assumption of compositionality has been central to FS since Frege. From a computational point of view that doctrine is almost certainly either trivial or false. I am sure this has been said many times; but I discovered it in 1984 [246], and it has been argued strongly by Schiffer [205].

3. FS puts an emphasis on the particular role of quantifiers and the need for a field of distinguishable entities to quantify over (this is quite independent of #1, and more central to FS). The set of distinguishable entities is easily provided with labels like Lisp 'gensyms' and doing that in no way concedes the FS claim. It must be admitted that it was a notable weakness in some early CSS systems (e.g., Conceptual dependency or Preference Semantics) that they did not offer a clear identification of individual entities, independent of intensional codings of concepts. But that lack was easily remedied. The first demand can always be met by special quantifier procedures (e.g., Woods in his papers on procedural semantics [251]). Nothing more is needed and demonstrations like Montague's stock example of radical quantifier ambiguity ('Every nice girl likes a sailor') are effectively quantificational garden paths and no plausible natural language processing system is under any

obligation to treat them. How could any system for the representation of natural language depend upon such cases, for they have no relation at all to crucial experiments in the sciences?

4. The relation of reference to the world: the claim that FS captures this relation is its weakest one, yet practitioners return to it repeatedly. If you do not adopt our methods, the claim is, you are trading in mere symbols, unrelated to the real world we, as plain men, know we share. I never cease to be amazed at the barefacedness of this. The classic statement of the position is David Lewis' [135] attack on Fodor and Katz as peddlers of markerese. But what else did he, or anyone else in FS, offer but symbol-to-symbol transformations? What else could they, in principle, ever offer by any conceivable formal methods? For symbols, and only symbols, are as much the trade and language of the denotational semanticist as of any computer modeller. Whatever the mysterious nature of the relation of symbols to things, it is not one on which FS could possibly throw light. Their solipsism is CSS's solipsism, and their position is metaphysically identical to ours.

Of course, arbitrarily named nodes identifying individuals are a handy, not to say essential, device, but no monopoly of FS. Worse yet, the proof procedures of FS demand such sets of entities to quantify over, but there is no formal way of guaranteeing that the entities established (so as to provide the guarantees that the proved theorems are true within the model that such entities form) are appropriate, in the sense of corresponding to any plausible real entities in the world. Any model set whatever that allows proved theorems to be true would suffice for the purposes of FS, a point that Potts [183] among others has pointed out repeatedly. Proofs of program correctness have faced this problem, but FS applied to natural languages and common sense reasoning has not and cannot. Any claims to give access by such means to a plausible and appropriate world are not only false but utterly misleading as to the nature of FS.

What we reach by any formal or computational methods is always other symbols, and a 'theory of meaning' for computational processes over natural language should recognise this fact. A suggestion along these lines was made in Wilks [242] under a potentially misleading slogan 'meaning is always, in fact, other words', but sophisticated forms of that view are to be found in the work of Wittgenstein and Quine as well as, on a different cultural planet, Habermas. It was work of the last author that led Winograd to a version of this view (e.g. Winograd [249]).

An important additional claim of FS, certainly made in Israel's paper, is that semantics, whatever it is, must be separated off from knowledge of the world: 'Lexical semantics does not yield an encyclopedia' and 'Any plausible semantic account, then, will have to distinguish between analytic truths and world-knowledge'. It is interesting to see that baldly and forthrightly stated without qualification, as if Quine were not still alive and well, but had never been. Practical experience with natural language processing always suggests the opposite: Sparck-Jones [214] shows in her paper how this borderline has to be fudged by peculiar means in certain FS approaches to practical problems. Real lexicons are such that information about meanings and the world are inextricably mixed, or are simply alternative formulations (at least Carnap [27], in opposing his 'formal' and 'material' modes of expression, got that right).

We should notice the repeated offer, to our sloppy and heuristic discipline, of a Real Serious Theory for the field (remember Chomsky's similar offer [34] to machine translation and language well-formedness; and, more recently, FS's for the semantics of selected AI systems). The chances always are that this prescription is unrelated to the disease; has Chomsky really helped computer language processing? We do indeed need a good theory but these are quack cures trading chiefly on the fears and inadequacies of practitioners and patients in the field.

One other consistent position is possible (I suspect it may be Dijkstra's [47]): one can point out frequently, as he likes to do, the gap between the interpretations normally given to logical entities (e.g., propositional implication or conjunction) and the interpretations given to apparently corresponding language items. One can also, at the same time, advocate the most stringent formal methods in computational applications to areas whose underlying structure or properties will support such methods. By such standards, natural language is not such an area and therefore one should not attempt this form of computational activity. That is a consistent position, but not one that those committed to the computer understanding of natural language can take. It poses no problem for CSSers, but does, I believe, put a serious choice before FSers who want to remain in some way relevant to language processing.

9.4   An interesting intermediate case: McDermott

Let us turn now to examine McDermott's various positions on the logic approach to AI. My aim will be to show that maintaining proposition p (that formal semantics is the proper basis of AI) at one time and *Not-p* at another is not, in itself, a guarantee of being right at least once.

All well-brought up children know that there is more joy in heaven over one sinner that repenteth, etc ... but this is not heaven so I shall push ahead, uncharitable though it may be to do so. The plan will be as follows: first a discussion of McDermott [143] which has been reprinted many times and contains the germ of his logicism. Secondly, we examine McDermott [144] where the espousal of Tarskian semantics became explicit and, finally, McDermott [145] where his recantation was announced.

9.4.1 AI MEETS NATURAL STUPIDITY (1976)

Any writer in this field who has ever used the phrase 'natural language' in a paper must have felt acute pain while reading McDermott's inspired Artificial Intelligence meets Natural Stupidity (AINS for short); the quick and easy use of 'epistemology' was also savaged, as was a whole mass of pretentious usage in AI and linguistics: particularly wish-fulfillment programming, the naming of flow-chart modules with terms like UNDERSTAND. However, we should, in honesty, concede that that is very much the same point that Dreyfus made about AI for years, in particular about Bobrow's use of 'understand' [49, page 46].

But McDermott overstated his case at one point: when he attempts to determine what he calls the 'intrinsic description' of a link in a semantic net, and thereby commits what I shall call the Gensym Fallacy. McDermott takes the IS-A link between FIDO and DOG, in a semantic network of the sort that is standard in AI, and says that its intrinsic description is 'indicator value pair inheritance link' (AINS, p. 5). His argument is that it is begging the question to call it IS-A because one sense of 'is a' is what it is supposed to explicate. In the same vein he asks those who would use a node labelled STATE-OF-MIND to rename it Gl073 and see if they still admire their system as much.

McDermott is clearly right that such systems have never, as yet, done much in practice, and the inflated naming of nodes gives a spurious satisfaction to the researcher involved. But the essence of the error is the failure to deliver, and the ability to fool oneself that one has delivered; it is certainly not node naming as such. If the system is bad then naming the node Gl073 doesn't make it better, but is irrelevant. McDermott is slipping into the Gensym Fallacy: that everything is logically all right if names are all (arbitrary) number names. Shakespeare might not have been so pleased with one of his sonnets if the words had been named, in order, Gl to Gl40, but that proves nothing, and nor does the disillusion of the researcher who is forced to write Gl073 instead of the more fulsome STATE-OF-MIND. He could still produce just as silly a program and make just as silly claims.

I think McDermott's error is to believe that there really are 'intrinsic descriptions' and that we could use these innocently, in a way that wishful descriptions are not innocent. This is an error because our high level program items are not, and cannot be, purpose-free if we are to understand and communicate what we are doing. Suppose someone said that to call the truth table mapping that we could write by the vector (1 0 1 1) 'material implication' was begging the question, and it should always be called 'truth table mapping type 4' until shown to explicate implication. Sorry, 'truth' begs the question too, so let's be even purer and say it should be called 'TF table mapping type 4'. Communication would be impeded, would it not, and no one would have any idea of what the purpose of such descriptions, and the papers containing them, was? One could make just such a remark about material implication itself: Schapiro [204, page 5] quotes the great phrase of Anderson and Belnap where they write that '(material implication) is no more a kind of implication than a blunderbuss is a kind of bus'.

McDermott has not followed through the logic of his own arguments and, were he to do so, he would, in my view, be forced to choose one of the following more radical positions (in AINS his own general position is never explicitly stated, for the soft target shooting is much more fun):

1.   There should be no perspicuous representation (meaning: easily interpretable with respect to some natural language, such as English) in AI natural language processing.

      That is consistent with his view that

            It seems much smarter to put knowledge about translation from natural language to internal representation in the natural language processor and not in the internal representation. [143, page 6]

      On that view, the representation could be largely or wholly arbitrary. If he means largely, I agree with him for the reasons stated earlier; but if he means wholly arbitrary (and his use of Gensyms suggests that) then either he commits the Gensym Fallacy, or he is a closet connectionist, where implementation procedures are everything, and representations are totally unperspicuous, as their critics have claimed (Charniak [29]). My intuition is that McDermott is no connectionist and that he believes symbolic but arbitrary representation can still be defended.

2.   The interpretation of a representation, however arbitrary its symbols, can be provided by scientific procedures in some direct relation to the arbitrary items. No natural language need creep into this process.

I am sure that McDermott would be strongly tempted by that possibility, and it is, of course, no more or less than the grand design of the Vienna Circle: the Unified Science grounded in Protokolsaetze (Neurath [162]). That project, incorporating Carnap's Logical Syntax of Language, was a clear precursor of both AI and Chomskyan linguistics.

But alas, it was all a magnificent mistake: there are no protocol, or basic, sentences and no scientist now believes such things, any more than he or anyone else should believe McDermott when he writes that 'Eventually, though, we all trick ourselves into thinking that the statement of a problem in natural language is natural'. Yes, we do and it is not a trick, and the collapse of Unified Science showed just that.

3.   There is a representation with some degree of (non-arbitrary) interpretation and that can be provided by logic, properly conceived.

McDermott never states this view explicitly, but it is the ground of his later views and implicit in 'Clearly, there must be some other notation, different in principle from natural language'. This is an essential plank in the logicist case, and one for which there is no evidence. There is of course mathematics, but we are here discussing commonsense subject matter (love, life, chairs, tables, smart weapons, cars and intentions) and not the domains of which mathematics treats.

My argument is that this choice is not really available, at least if that means an interpretation wholly unconnected to, and independent of, natural languages. A language of Gensyms without interpretation is as vacuous as any other calculus, logical or otherwise, without interpretation. Nor can 'Unified Science' provide interpretations, and so bypass natural language considerations. Weighted networks may do so, but no one is very clear about that issue yet.

I am sure that (3) would have been McDermott's choice at the time he wrote AINS. He was led into confusion by his own assertion that 'Many researchers tend to talk as if an internal knowledge representation ought to be closely tied to the structure of native language.' He gave no references at that point to AI researchers, and it would be hard to do so. To the best of my knowledge I am the only person who has argued thus within AI and then only very surreptitiously, because it is so unacceptable (even if true).

McDermott probably believed when he wrote those words that Schank and the Yale School did believe that proposition, but he was simply confusing two things if he did. Schank always strongly denied that his representations were related, in their representational structure and primitive alphabet, to natural language, specifically to English. Unkind critics like myself repeatedly pointed out (e.g., Wilks in Charniak and Wilks [30]) that Yale representations did in fact have many residues of surface English, both in form and content.

But none of that is what McDermott claimed: that the researchers wanted that similarity. This is not mere nit-picking, but evidence of radical confusion in McDermott. He fails to distinguish:

i.   claiming one's representation is based on natural language,

from

ii.   having one's representation interpretable only in terms of natural language.

If I am right, this last charge (ii) tells as much against McDermott as anyone, because there are no viable alternatives: a language of uninterpreted Gensyms or any logic of uninterpreted predicates is just gibberish, unless and until connectionism saves the day for us all. McDermott is as guilty as those he criticises: if there is a 'natural language fallacy', he too must be committing it, unless he shows us a clear way out, and AINS certainly does not.

9.4.2   MCDERMOTT ON TARSKIAN SEMANTICS (1978)

In a later paper [144, abbreviated as NSWD: No Semantics Without Denotation] McDermott more forcefully brings out the assumptions of the earlier AINS and ties them to the denotational semantic theories associated with Tarski. And yet the doubts that overcome him later are already present, as when he writes: 'the application of SD (systematic denotational semantics) in an informal way can still be valuable' [144, page 278], a remark that only has sense on the assumption that the full rigorous application of the method will not be possible, as is indeed the case in AI and programming in general.

The bulk of NSWD is an informal examination of a small number of well-known AI systems such as Schank's, and the observation that some of the rules proposed for it are not generally true. Two most important points must be made here, one polemical and one substantial. First, even if it is of value to show that a rule in an AI system is not generally true, or is inconsistent with other rules, then that can always be seen simply by argument and careful observation, and with no call for the tools McDermott uses in NSWD. There is no sense in which the application of denotational semantics, formally or informally, helps one to see that: indeed, in the end it is known that there can be no such proof of inconsistency of any system of interesting richness, so the defect is more than practical. There is no clear relation between the disease (false rules, if that be a disease) and the remedy proposed.

Although NSWD is intended as a robust defence of denotational semantics in Artificial Intelligence it does contain an argument against its use:

> It would perhaps be surprising for an outsider to learn that computer scientists, in spite of the fact that they study purely formal objects like programs and data structures, have a pronounced 'anti-formalist' streak. This arose initially from the painful discovery that even the most formal objects have to be debugged. [144, page 8]

He is right about many of his colleagues, but, as ever, the reason given is the wrong one. The anti-formal 'streak', insofar as there is one, is not about formalisms as such at all: programs must be totally formal or they do not run. The opposition, from papers like the present one, is to the application of a particular methodology – model theoretic semantics – and not at all on any ground to do with debugging, which is a pure red herring. It has to do with the application of computational methods to areas of AI like natural language processing where the formal structure of the area to be explicated does not support such methods.

This fact was touched on earlier, and this argument appeared in fuller form in Wilks [240], but it can be set out again here in simple form. The argument is that the meaningful sentences of a natural language like English do not form a recursive or decidable set, and that fact makes any strong application of model theoretic semantics to, say, a natural language understanding system inappropriate.

The argument that natural language sentences are not such a set goes as follows: given any string of English words it can be rendered meaningful, and given an established use, by successive explanations in the way Wittgenstein [250] constantly illustrated. It is merely a question of ingenuity and determination.

If that is the case, then there is no prior survey of the 'theorems of English' in the way that there is for, say, the Propositional Calculus. In that formalism we knew, in advance of the production of a decision procedure (the truth tables in 1919), what was and was not a theorem of the Propositional Calculus. There were firm intuitions as to the truth of certain well-formed formulas, and well-established deduction procedures to establish others. The semantics associated with the calculus – the truth tables – then underpinned that 'syntactically based' deduction with a decision procedure.

None of that is available for a natural language, and it is an essential feature of it that it is not. If it were, we would not be dealing with a natural language. Any fragment of, say, English that could be so axiomatized, would not then be a natural language precisely because the freedom to extend it, as we all do every day, would be gone.

What does it mean to claim that the prior survey of English sentences is not available? It is simply that we cannot construct lists of definite sentences and definite non-sentences in the way that we can for formal languages, and which we must be able to do if the Tarskian techniques devised to underpin theoremhood and deduction are to grip. Tarski himself, as we all know, did not believe natural languages were susceptible to these techniques, though that fact is in no way decisive.

What this claim does not mean is anything in particular about the intuition of what a meaningful sentence in English is, or how that is related to the meanings of its parts. There is nothing compositional about the point I am making. It does follow from this claim that an axiomatization of English, if it were conceivable, could not be a good way to enumerate English sentences, for there would always be a denumerable infinity of English sentences it could not produce.

The position above, if true, has consequences for the semantics of internal representations, too, in spite of McDermott when he writes:

> The objection has been made that denotational semantics cannot be the semantics of natural language in all its glory. This may or may not be true ... but has nothing to do with its use as a semantics of internal knowledge structures. [144, page 281]

But that is simply not so, and the consequence is fatal to McDermott's whole case, given the non-recursive property of sets of sentences of a natural language, for that property will also be true of the formulas of the internal representation if there is any kind of straightforward mapping between them. Human beings provide that mapping (on any kind of 'internal representation' theory of a mental processing) as do parsers between computer representations and sentences. So McDermott's point fails unless the natural language and the internal knowledge structure are independent. They are not and McDermott has never suggested for a moment that they are.

This point can even be strengthened in the following way: let us make the fairly sensible assumption (to all except adherents to 'fuzzy logic') that quantification is a discrete phenomenon, as regards any semantics to be given for its appearance in a natural language or in an internal representation language. Now, if the semantics given for quantified formulas of an internal representation language is a Scott-Strachey semantics for programs (and in AI that might seem a natural additional assumption), then that semantics requires phenomena to be continuous overall [207]. This fact can be interpreted in a number of ways with respect to the discussion so far, but the most rational is to take it as evidence that a program semantics cannot be given for internal representations of at least one basic aspect of natural language.

That conclusion may be too facile, however, given the possible interactions of the assumptions required to reach it. But on any manipulations of those, the conclusion tends to tell against McDermott's assertion in the last quoted passage, namely, that we might reasonably expect a more rigorous semantics for an internal representation than for a 'decoupled' and less rigorous natural language, one that corresponded to internal expressions in some one-to-one or many-to-one manner (over sets of sentences or formulas).

9.4.3   THE CRITIQUE OF PURE REASON (1987)

In his most recent work [145, abbreviated CPR] McDermott has seized on a Kantian title to withdraw much of the content of AINS and NSWD, although he does it not by withdrawing earlier arguments, but by attacking other logicist positions and drawing new conclusions inconsistent with those of the two earlier papers. The burden of the paper is that

i.   in understanding, including the understanding of natural language, many or most inferences are non-deductive.

ii.   deductive techniques (and hence the formal semantics machinery that underlie them) have no role in assessing confirmation of belief, which is a quantitative matter.

As the author of a paper [241] called 'Understanding without proofs' (one which drew attention to Hume's point that the proofs of non-mathematical conclusions are short and non-deductive, a claim McDermott attributes to Pat Hayes!) I can only welcome such conversion, while trying to keep at bay the slightly sour response of the lifelong tee-totaller welcoming recently reformed drunks.

The second point carries a strong flavour of discussions of connectionist computation, prevalent everywhere in artificial intelligence at the moment, and might yet lead to a further radical shift in McDermott's position, one hinted at also in:

> What we now conclude is that content theories are of limited usefulness in the case where the contemplated inferences are non-deductive. [145, page 14]

Connectionism is, of course, almost by definition, a non-content theory, as all its critics have pointed out in their different ways. What McDermott means, in this last quotation, is to be understood in opposition to a clear case of a content theory: logic programming, and the belief associated with it that the content of our knowledge would be simply written down in an appropriate formalism, a position of McDermott himself at one time, and close to what we earlier called the classic logicist position of McCarthy and Hayes.

There is a small but crucial difference here between the content theory (in the sense of procedure-free logic programming) on the one hand, and the older logicist programme in AI, on the other. The logicists, like McCarthy and Hayes, never thought that what they were advocating was procedure free: it naturally required some set of trusty machine logic procedures. So, too, of course, does logic programming, even though they are hidden tidily away in the Prolog interpreter.

McDermott himself draws on this very distinction between logic and logic programming for a different purpose, but fails to see that it undermines his discovery (appearing just before the last quotation) that 'there is no way to develop a "content theory" without a "process model" ' [145, page 14].

But that is as true of classical machine logic as of any other part of AI, and the logicists knew it. In itself, it constitutes no reason at all to flirt with procedural (as opposed to denotational) semantics for knowledge representations. I write that as one who does firmly believe (Wilks [244]) in a procedural semantics, whatever it may turn out to be. My point here is that McDermott's reasons are bad ones for shifting from a wrong view to a right one.

That is equally true of his discovery of (i) above, construed as a claim about human psychology. It may be true, as Russell once said, that no one has ever performed a useful or practical deduction on any serious topic, but he did not allow that to interfere with his technical work. Even if true, it says nothing about how research in machine logic should proceed, nor about whether formal deductions can be produced to cover the inferences humans make. It has always been an assumption in traditional logic that any enthymeme (inference or truncated deduction) can be made deductive by the addition of suitable additional premises, and logicians could always provide these by, as it were, inspection. It is an open question whether a machine logic can locate such assumptions, in general, so as to produce a consequence that is deductive. The logicists continue with their programme in the belief that it can be done but, whatever is the case there, McDermott's observations like the following do nothing to throw doubt on that programme:

> But many inferences are not deductive. If I come upon an empty cup of soda pop that was full a while ago, I may infer that my wife drank it, and that's not a deduction …but an inference to the best explanation. (The only way to mistake this for a deduction is to mistake logic programming for logic …) [145, page 8]

But logicists know all this, and that the inferences can be made deductive. Nothing follows from these observations that the logicists are not already fully aware of, and it cannot of itself throw any general doubt on the logicist programme for AI (as opposed to, say, one for psychology).

The bulk of McDermott's CPR consists of technical criticisms of devices in recent AI logic (non-monotonic, circumscription, etc.) that have been produced to support, and develop, the logicist case. The criticisms are admirable in themselves, interesting largely because of the past views of the author, and I have no wish here to dispute either their detail or general thrust. They are in fact unimportant for the purpose of this paper—other than their intense biographical interest, of course—since the criticisms do not bear directly on the general issues of principle raised in the paper. As I just noted above, any logicist can say of these criticisms that they are merely technical details being fixed, just as he can say that diagnosing most human inferences as enthymemes, or incomplete deductions, in no way bears on the logicist programme or on the general viability of machine deduction.

There are, I believe, two casual remarks in CPR where McDermott moves close to the real problems for the logicist programme – of principle not detail. They are:

a.   when he notes (page 2): 'The notation we use must be understandable to those using it and reading it.'

b.   when writing of non-monotonic logic (page 6): 'Either theories like this don't have theorems, in which case they can't serve as the idealized inference engines we are seeking; or we are stuck with a weak notion of theorem, …'

The first remark is interesting in that, although implicit, it is one of the few direct withdrawals of a claim in one of the earlier papers: it is clearly a withdrawal of the whole line of argument in AINS that terms in the knowledge representation should be replaced by (inscrutable) Gensyms, so as to give moral health to a program description by removing the overtones imported from natural language.

It is obvious to anyone with experience in writing programs in high-level languages that this cannot be done or, if it can, it removes the point of using such languages in the first place. McDermott does not note the significance of such a retraction but, in the light of the previous discussion in this paper, it should be clear that insofar as such notations for knowledge representation are understandable, they are to that degree dependent on some natural language, and hence cannot have a semantics independent of it. From that point, ignored by McDermott, most of the arguments of this paper follow.

Point (b) simply notes a possibility and is passed over immediately, but it is of course a possibility that is argued in this paper as a fact concerning the status of natural languages for axiomatization (as regards their meaningfulness, at least), and is the issue of principle on which, in my view, the logicist enterprise hangs.

In view of the nature of the arguments in CPR, and the virtual ignoring of issues of principle, while concentrating on ones that give the logicist no more than passing problems, it will not be surprising that I conclude that, although McDermott has apparently reversed his position, he remains wrong on the core issues. There need be no formal problem in saying that: one can perfectly well maintain p and *Not-p* at different moments, while retaining some false q throughout, where q is in the chain of inference to both p and *Not-p*. It is such q's that I have sought to isolate here, particularly as regards the non-independence of the representation language and natural language(s), and the status of statements of meaningfulness for natural languages as constituting a formal language whose meta-logical properties are to be investigated.

9.5   CONCLUSION: ARE THERE EMPIRICAL DIFFERENCES BETWEEN THESE RESEARCH PROGRAMMES?

If we stand back now from McDermott's intellectual struggles and return to the general fray, the obvious general question to ask is whether there are, or will be, genuine testable differences between the logicist programme for AI and any discernible alternatives such as CSS. That is to say, will there be programs inspired by one of these classes of formalism capable of performing some indisputably AI task, where the other cannot? All parties should agree to such a test and probably would. But does this fact allow us to sit back comfortably, taking an optimistic view of scientific progress, and await outcomes? I fear the matter is not so simple.

Let us consider an empirical task in natural language processing, one often tackled by AI techniques and occasionally by those of formal semantics: machine translation (MT) from one natural language to another. This is not at all a task chosen at random; it is the original, founding, task of computational linguistics, a task rather like that of playing the piano sonatas of Mozart according to Rubenstein: too easy for the amateur, too hard for the master.

There is no doubt that MT is now possible with some degree of success, but that the very hard problems required for a proper solution (like the 'des'/'les' problem mentioned earlier) are nowhere near solution. Much of the recent success of MT, it must be said, gives no comfort to either kind of semantics discussed in this paper: it has often been a matter of the very crudest theories, whose performance has been improved, over anything thought possible twenty tears ago, simply by the use of software engineering techniques. One might risk the following principle:

> *There is no theory of language structure so ill-founded that it cannot be the basis for some successful MT.*

Those who doubt this should study the history of the SYSTRAN system (Hutchins [92]). The point of the principle, if true, is that it makes any prospect of an empirical test, or decision, as between formal semantics and any other type, applied to a concrete empirical task like MT, very improbable indeed, and that is exacerbated by another principle that lurks behind much of the discussion of this paper:

> *AI programs in general (including MT programs) do not always work by means of the formalisms that decorate them.*

This is an important issue, and one which serves to separate the issue under discussion (that of finding some empirical programming task to settle the issue between types of AI representations and their associated semantics) from what might be an illuminating historical parallel, that of rival theoretical descriptions of physical phenomena, between which a crucial experiment was sought: ether waves versus relativity, say, or particle versus wave accounts of sub-atomic phenomena.

Programming, alas, is not like that in the following sense: it is perfectly possible to write a program to perform some task (MT will still serve) using a descriptive theory or language, even though, in fact, and sometimes hardly perceived by the programmer, the results are achieved by part of a program that functions in such a way that it cannot be appropriately described by the upper-level theory at all, but requires some quite different form of description. Sometimes this happens for totally banausic reasons, ones which involve an element of deceit or flattery: a student programs a system for his supervisor, describing what he is doing in terms consistent with the cherished theory of that supervisor, who does not himself write programs. In order to make the system function, the student is forced to reconceive the task at another level, and it is there that he develops the 'real' theory, one which never emerges in any published description.

Cases like this are not as unusual as one might hope; but a more common situation is what happened to the SYSTRAN Russian-to-English MT itself. It had and has a very elementary system of linguistic description in terms of grammar rules. After nearly thirty years of operation a very large number of lexical 'patches' have been added to the system (of the order of half a million (see Wilks [243]) which deal with particular input strings in Russian, rather as if one had a special dictionary of syntagms, such that the grammar was only accessed where the syntagms failed to 'match' the input.

Now, consider the situation where, as I believe to be the case, SYSTRAN is described by its simple grammatical theory, although in fact the system's success is largely attributable to the dictionary of 'semi-sentences' that does not appear in the top-level description. It should be clear that, whatever the details of this particular system, the situation is not at all one of rival theoretical descriptions of phenomena, as in physics, but of determining what are the real, operational, principles by which a program works, as opposed to its apparent, sometimes decorative, ones.

This problem is well known in the field, but has no obvious solutions: in one sense it is precisely the problem of finding a proper semantics for programs, in the Scott and Strachey sense [207], one that is close in methodology to formal semantics in the sense in which we have discussed it here. Unfortunately, and whatever the claims of its devotees, the semantics of programs cannot provide this service, even in principle, since that technique requires only the specification of objects and relations so that input is reliably transformed to output, as in a deduction. There is no requirement whatever that the objects chosen have any relationship to the 'natural' objects of the theory with which the program works: they could be as remote as were the loyal student's principles from those of his advisor. They can be simply incommensurable in just the way that the semantics of a program at different levels of internal programming language translation are incommensurable (Scott and Strachey [207]).

This conclusion may seem pessimistic but, even in a situation of no reliable test or outcome, the social and psychological forces at work in an empirical and formal discipline like AI continue to function nonetheless. Machine understanders and translators will continue to appear and we shall be able to judge to some degree whether they benefit from formal semantics techniques or not. For those cases where there are reasonable doubts about that, there is coming into being a battery of techniques of reimplementing systems with somewhat changed and controlled principles and structures (see Ritchie and Hanna [190]) and that can do much to help us decide what are and are not the formal principles underlying AI programs. So, as Leibniz would write at this point in an argument: come let us compute together!

10 Epilogue: on the relation between computational linguistics and formal semantics

Margaret King

10.1 RELATING THE DISCIPLINES

My role in the original workshop which gave rise to this book was to sum up what had been said during the week, trying to relate the different contributions one to another. In preparing for what threatened to be an arduous task, it occurred to me that a fundamental assumption underlying the organization of such a workshop needed to be taken out and examined overtly: calling a workshop 'Computational Linguistics and Formal Semantics' assumes that these two areas of academic endeavour have something to say to each other; may, even, be inextricably related.

Superficially, of course, this seems likely to be true: an investigation of language and its use could be seen as the core interest of both disciplines. But, on looking a little more closely, the intimate connection tends to evaporate. For most computational linguists, the task is to define and implement an adequate treatment of (some subset of) some natural language within the framework of a computer application. Even when they are primarily interested in demonstrating that a particular linguistic theory or a particular paradigm of computation is superior to its rivals, the argument will frequently be couched in application-oriented terms: such and such a theory is superior because it leads to clearer linguistic descriptions which are easier to modify and to debug, for example, or such and such a computational paradigm is superior because it allows linguistic programmers to compartmentalize their knowledge of a language, describing sub-parts independently without having to worry about all the possible intricate complexities of interactions between them. Despite some recent pleas of Martin

Kay's [115], there are very few computational psycholinguists – computational linguists who base the justification for their technical choices on an attempt to mirror human language behaviour. Even those who do – and they would often prefer to describe themselves as workers in artificial intelligence rather than as computational linguists – finish up quite quickly arguing in terms of correct functioning of the computer system. It is rather hard to imagine someone saying 'My question answering system fails to answer any questions, but is based on sound experimental evidence on how human beings understand language. It must nonetheless therefore be taken seriously'.

To say this rather differently, the real world for computational linguists is the world of their computer application. The external reality in which we live may provide a source of inspiration, may guide their ambitions or inform their frustrations, but the ultimate test is always going to be whether the computer system produces the appropriate output for any given piece of input, and whether it does so will be determined by their mastery of the semantics imposed by the hardware and software they use.

The formal semanticists' concerns are traditionally rather different. Their primary concern is likely to be with the notation they are using or developing. Thus, classically, they are concerned with how the truth conditions of a complex expression relate to the truth conditions of its constituent parts. The resemblance between this work and that of the computational linguist comes from the fact that the stimulus towards developing the notation and investigating its characteristics comes from a consideration of language and the mechanisms of argument, so that the connectors linking simple expressions can be glossed (misleadingly) by ordinary words like 'and', 'or', 'if' and the constants and variables constituting the individual objects of the notation can be taken, under suitable circumstances, to stand for entities in an external world, so that, in the end, it is tempting to think of the formal expressions which are being manipulated as more precise formulations of natural language sentences.

Taken to its obvious conclusion, this move will lead to direct application of formal methods to the analysis of natural language inputs. If the analysis takes the form of a computer program, there is a clear sense in which the formal semanticist has become a computational linguist. But here, the notion of an application becomes critical again. It would, of course, be a perfectly legitimate exercise for someone to construct a program with no other purpose than that of checking more exhaustively than he could by hand that his theory functioned as he expected it to. But if an application to one of the traditional computational linguistics tasks is envisaged, a preoccupation with truth and truth conditions may well turn out to be more of a limitation than a virtue. Whilst some applications working in a closed semantic world (data base systems, for example) may lend themselves fairly easily to the design and use of a formal model, it is rather harder to imagine a machine translation system, say, working in terms of a truth conditional semantics.

Lest anyone should think that the formal semanticists are being unfairly accused of a narcissistic obsession with a notation detached from real language on the one hand and from the real world on the other, we should point out that some recent work in formal semantics seems to be concerned with escaping the limitations sketched above through an attempt to motivate the formal apparatus through its relation to the external reality. Thus, Barwise and Perry [15] begin their exposition of the basic ideas of situation semantics as follows:

> Reality consists of situations – individuals having properties and standing in relations at various spatio-temporal locations. We are always in situations; we see them, cause them to come about, and have attitudes towards them. The Theory of Situations is an abstract theory for talking about situations. We begin by pulling out of real situations the basic building blocks of the theory: individuals, properties and relations, and locations [....]. We then put these pieces back together, using the tools of set theory, as abstract situations. Some of these abstract situations, the actual situations, correspond to the real ones; others do not. [...]
>
> All of these entities are abstract set-theoretic objects, built up from the individuals, properties, relations and locations abstracted from real situations. They play no role in the causal order. People don't grasp them, see them, move them, or even know or believe them. But as semanticists we can use them to classify real situations. Then, by assigning our classifiers of real situations to expressions and to mental states, we study their property of meaningfulness. [op. cit., pages 6–7].

See Rupp et al. [198] and Fenstad et al. [57] for related work applied in a computational linguistics framework.

Note, though, that the earlier point about finding suitable applications still holds. If an attempt is made to construct a theory of situations able to encompass reality as a whole, the theory runs into severe metaphysical and ontological difficulties. (See Cooper [40] for initial discussion of some of them). If it is taken simply as a more flexible tool to be used within a limited domain, then, once again, it may well turn out to be the case that the choice of application is critical.

At the end of the workshop in Lugano, I arrived at what one might call a 'faute de mieux' conclusion: on the grounds that potential suitability for some applications was, if nothing else, a starting point, I concluded that computational linguists should at least follow work being done in formal semantics. This conclusion I thought reinforced by the observation that the informality of other kinds of semantics frequently found in computational linguistics applications led almost inevitably to problems of consistency and coherency once any large-scale application was attempted, so that even if no formal theory ever proved to be directly applicable, the dialogue was worth pursuing if only to refine the computational linguist's understanding of what can count as a rigorous definition.

The advantage to the formal semanticist would be, I thought, to be continually reminded of the complexities of real language, and thereby encouraged to resist the temptation to believe that language consists primarily of simple assertive sentences with a few tricky features like quantification sometimes thrown in to jolt us out of premature complacency.

Put like this, this conclusion sounds rather defeatist, rather similar to a Bernois saying that if the Genevois and the Appenzeller just keep talking long enough some thread of mutual agreement must eventually emerge, if only because in broader terms they inhabit the same geo-political territory. On further reflection, the defeatist tone seems to me inappropriate, and to reflect a mistaken notion that if some theory, method or technique is not good for absolutely everything, it is no good for anything. That such an idea is positively dangerous as well as mistaken has been amply demonstrated within the history of computational linguistics itself. In the early days of machine translation, it was simply taken for granted that the only acceptable system was one which would translate any kind of text and produce results needing no substantial amount of revision. The direct consequence of failing to live up to this ambition was a loss of credibility (and funding), which has still not totally been redressed even after the construction of systems tailored to particular contexts and providing their users with much satisfaction. It may be that one of the more important insights gained in Computational Linguistics over the last few years has been that there is no shame in finding ingenious uses of the technology available, and that, by doing so, the fundamental research work required to push the technology further gains in both perceived utility and in stimulus.

This shift towards a more positive view of the potential interaction between Computational Linguistics and Formal Semantics was in part brought about by re-reading the other papers included in this volume. Perhaps this is the place also to acknowledge the influence of a much earlier paper, Woods' [252] classic paper on the semantics of semantic networks, which I re-read at the same time, in an attempt to discover how it could be the case that I could simultaneously largely agree with papers which seemed to take the utility of formal methods for granted and with papers that explicitly attacked them. Whilst contemplating how this could be so, it began to seem to me that a certain amount of conceptual confusion was getting in the way of fruitful discussion. In the rest of this chapter, therefore, I want to try to make a modest contribution to the debate by picking out some of these areas and discussing where the confusion may lie. The exercise is primarily terminological, and I can only ask the indulgence of those readers to whom all I have to say seems self-evident.

10.2   WHAT COUNTS AS BEING FORMAL

The terms 'Formal Semantics' and 'Computational Linguistics' may themselves turn out to be a source of confusion if we automatically assume them to relate to some single clear paradigm. Looking at the chapters of this book is enough to show us that, in practice, rather a wide range of different viewpoints is covered by the two terms. I want to start my terminological exercise by examining that range, not in the hope of convincing anyone that there is some correct use of the terms and that only this correct use should be adhered to, but rather in an attempt at consciousness raising: if we know that the same term may mean different things to different people, we can at least check what is to be understood by it on any specific occasion.

Barbara Partee offers the following indirect definition of what counts as formal:

> But Montague was convinced, as the title of his paper 'English as a formal language' shows, that natural languages can be described with just as systematic and rigorous a correspondence between form and structure as the logician's formal languages, and in practice he stayed remarkably close to surface structure in doing so. [175, page 101]

This is perhaps the strongest definition of what it is to be formal about semantics. The task is to describe, in precise and rigorous terms, a relation between the sentences of a natural language and a semantic representation, where the semantic representation will in its turn provide a link between the sentence and a set of possible worlds in truth conditional terms, so that sentences are seen as truth value denoting entities, and a possible world is a model of the theory captured by the formal description of the relation between sentences and semantic representation if and only if all the sentences which evaluate to true in the theory correspond to true states of affairs in the world. The job of the semanticist is then to ensure that the set of sentences for which the relation can be described corresponds as closely as possible to the sentences of a natural language, and it is this which distinguishes him from a pure logician.

> ...in the old days when many logicians were inclined to dismiss natural language surface structure as not being anything to take very seriously, the fact that *John* and *every man* both showed up as noun phrases was just one more piece of evidence about how illogical ordinary language is. [175, page 101]

A natural consequence of the view that surface structure and semantic content are intimately related is a commitment to compositionality, the idea that the meaning of a sentence is a function of the meaning of its parts and of how the meanings of the parts are combined. In its strongest form, compositionality implies that for every syntactic rule there is a corresponding semantic rule, which states how the semantic representation of the larger syntactic structure can be composed from the semantic representations of its constituents.

The intuitive appeal of this notion, first articulated by Frege [58], is so strong that for some it has become the distinguishing mark of the formalist, whether or not it is accompanied by a commitment to a model theoretic semantics of the sort sketched above.

Indeed, it is possible to find, although mainly in the computational linguistics world rather than in the logic-related formal world, those who hold to some version of the compositionality principle whilst being content to let the rest of their semantics remain rather informal and intuitive. (One example would be work in the Eurotra project, at least in some phases of its evolution (Arnold and des Tombe [4]).) Those making this move would not, however, normally call themselves formal semanticists.

Conversely, there are those who believe strongly that the compositionality principle is mistaken, and argue that its importance in the strong version of formal semantics outlined above invalidates the whole enterprise of formal semantics. Thus, Wilks,

> The assumption of compositionality has been central to formal semantics since Frege. From a computational point of view that doctrine is almost certainly either trivial or false. [247, page 266]

also gives Schiffer [205] as support for this claim.

Not surprisingly, adopting this strong version of what it means to do formal semantics also tends to go hand in hand with using some form of logic as the medium in which the rules governing the correspondence between linguistic structure and semantic representation are expressed. This is not, I think, to be confused with the 'logicalist approach' in Artificial Intelligence, as set out, for example, in McCarthy and Hayes [142] and as attacked by Wilks in this volume. There, the primary concern is with finding a good notation for knowledge representation, and, as we shall see below, the representation in question is quite different in status from the semantic representations associated with syntactic rules in the sort of approach we have been talking about. In particular, in the knowledge representation case, there is an explicit link between the logic used as an expressive tool and the real world being described through the logic, so that it makes sense, for example, to worry about whether the logical connectives (e.g. material implication) correctly reflect the kind of reasoning used by human agents in the real world. This kind of concern is quite different from that of the formal semanticist interested in defining a correspondence between linguistic inputs and expressions in a formal symbolic system, except insofar as the linguistic input directly reflects 'real world' reasoning.

To see what I mean here, consider McDermott's cup of soda pop example:

> But many inferences are not deductive. If I come upon an empty cup of soda pop that was full a while ago, I may infer that my wife drank it, and that's not a deduction [...] but an inference to the best explanation. (McDermott [145], also quoted by Wilks).

McDermott's concern here is that his computer system should be able to make the same kind of inference as he does, and that, therefore, whatever notation he is using for his knowledge representation should be able to support this kind of inference. The formal semanticist would be concerned with finding an appropriate representation for the linguistic expression of what is going on, i.e. for sentences in a natural language like, say, 'That cup is empty. My wife has drunk the soda pop', and his use of logic intervenes in defining the mapping between the sentences and the representation. Since there is no overt linguistic sign of the inference made by the speaker, the logic needs no expressive tool to deal with it. (At least, not at this point of the game. Whether or not something does have eventually to reflect the inference will depend on what, if anything, happens to the semantic representation after it has been constructed.)

The formality of the classic formal semanticist, in summary, lies within the system itself. He is attempting to construct a formal system through which a rigorous definition can be given of the correspondence between the structure of the sentences of a language and a semantic (usually truth conditional) representation of their content. And it is perhaps worth pointing out that just as the formal semanticist automatically becomes a computational linguist as soon as he automates the process of computing a representation from an input, so the computational linguist can hardly avoid being a formal semanticist, perhaps without even being aware of it, since computer programs are formal objects and he too is in the business (usually, at any rate) of computing a representation from a linguistic input. The nature of the representation is not really relevant here: it may have no aspirations to being semantic at all in any conventional sense. Indeed, even if one imagined a caricature system which assigned as representation of a sentence an integer representing the number of words in the sentence, the point would still hold. The program calculating the integer is still a formal system assigning a representation to an input string.

There is another sense, though, in which a computational linguist – or, perhaps more probably, a worker in artificial intelligence – may perceive himself as being a formalist. This is when his computer system makes use of primitive objects or relations for which he attempts to give a formal definition not intended for direct use within the system itself, but for system external justification or explanation.

The clearest example of this comes with the quite widespread use of named semantic categories assigned to lexical items or forming part of an internal representation: the most familiar are categories like 'animate object', 'physical object', 'concrete', 'abstract' etc., often written in capital letters to distinguish them from the ordinary language use of the words used for the names of the categories (and, one might sometimes uncharitably suppose, to make them look more formal).

When a system is larger than the tiny one-person prototypes so depressingly familiar to us, it is notoriously difficult to ensure consistent use of such semantic categories. Even the same person, over a lapse of time, may decide on one occasion to assign one category to a particular lexical item, and a different category on a later occasion. Numerous proposals aimed at alleviating the problem can be found in the literature. Some, especially of the more recent ones (see, for example, Guthrie et al. [74]), explicitly or implicitly reject the distinction between the name of a semantic category as a formal object and the use of ordinary language terms to classify other ordinary language terms or to explain their use, by basing the assignment on automatic extraction of the relevant information from conventional dictionaries. But other proposals keep the distinction and propose some sort of decision procedure to be followed by the human dictionary coder when deciding on an assignment (see, for example, Steiner et al. [217]).

The authors of these proposals would certainly see themselves as formalists, in the sense that the decision procedure is intended to be formal. Whether it succeeds in being so or not must surely depend entirely on the results: if, in practice, consistent and replicable assignments are produced, then the decision procedure is formal. Such evidence as I have seen does not lead to great optimism in this respect.

Amongst those working with semantic categories and perceiving themselves as formalists, an extreme position is adopted by those who believe their categories to be grounded in universality, whether the universality is claimed as universality across languages ('All languages have this concept' (e.g. Nirenburg et al. [171])) or as being cognitive ('The human brain is such that all humans will make use of this category' (e.g. Jackendoff [95])). On this view, no decision procedure is needed to ensure consistent assignment. Rather, the question is one of discovering what the universal categories are; once discovered, their communication is a matter of revelation rather than of explanation.

I have argued elsewhere against the plausibility of this view (King [123]) and do not intend to go into the arguments again here. Let it suffice to say here that the position cannot be formal in any sense interesting for the present discussion, precisely because it does depend on revelation.

As a summary of this section, let us now try to answer the question which serves as a title for it: a system counts as a formal system if and only if it allows the rigorous specification of a correspondence between an input and an output in computational, human or machine, terms; the results of such a procedure must be replicable – the specification of the correspondence is not rigorous if the same input gives rise to different outputs on different occasions.

10.3 WHERE DOES THE FORMALITY COME IN?

In this section, I want to pursue further a question which has already surfaced to some extent in the preceding section, that of where the use of formal methods might intervene in a computational linguistics application. It takes very little reflection to see that the answer is not totally straightforward, especially if we take into account work in the natural language processing tradition of artificial intelligence, as well as more conventional computational linguistics work.

Let us, for the moment at least, limit ourselves to talking about the analysis of a natural language input, and assume that the analysis aims at producing a representation of some kind. (There are systems which do not in fact produce a representation; we shall return to this later.) All we shall assume about the representation is that it is not ambiguous, unlike the natural language input, which may well be so. If the analysis makes use of any kind of world knowledge in order to disambiguate the input, there may be a second representation involved which we shall call the knowledge base in order to distinguish it from the first, linguistic representation. Just as there are systems which make no use of a knowledge base, there are systems which produce no independent linguistic representation. In this case, analysis may result in modification or extension of the knowledge base. But for our present purposes, it is useful to keep the two representations conceptually distinct, and to note that there is no necessary reason for them to be formally the same kind of object, so that the linguistic representation may be, for example, nothing more than a hierarchically organized trace of a derivation in a grammar and the knowledge base a collection of independent if-then rules.

The point is not, of course, that all systems have these three components – they don't – but that any single one may be the object of formal specification, without that affecting the others.

Thus, the analysis process itself might take the form of a set of axioms in a logic formalism of some kind and analysis be performed by determining whether the input sentence can be deduced from those axioms. One could argue then, as Wilks does, that such a grammar could never fully cover a natural language, on the grounds that since the sentences of a given language do not form a recursive or decidable set, there is no way to provide what he calls a 'prior survey of the axioms of English'. Or one could argue that the formal system itself was not adequate to the task and needed to be replaced or modified, as Martin Kay does in his discussion of phrase structure grammar. But it is important to notice that the argument is about the nature of the analysis component, and says nothing about either the linguistic representation achieved or about the knowledge base. (Although one could of course imagine it being argued against a particular formalism that use of it precluded the construction of some desirable representation.)

Conversely, Woods' argument in [4] is a plea that a system designer should aspire to formality in defining his representations, as opposed to basing a representation on intuitive interpretation of items optimistically named with something resembling ordinary language words and hoping that everyone will interpret them in the same way. The sort of arguments one gets into here are quite different: they have to do with the ontological status of the primitive objects in the representation, problems of reference and denotation, of truth and of negation.

It is important to recall here that the formal definition may be intended for human consumption as much as for machine consumption. This is clearest when applied to a linguistic representation. Many such are based on the use of deep case structures and semantic categories which are considered in some sense primitive. As we have already noticed, ensuring consistency across a number of people constructing, say, the dictionary entries which will furnish the raw material from which the final representation is built is a notorious problem, and one which would clearly benefit from the introduction of some kind of definition which did not rely on the coder's intuitions.

That the formal definition is relevant also to machine behaviour becomes clear when we think of the knowledge base and imagine that there may be inference procedures associated with it. As both Woods and Wilks point out, what the computer system actually does, what inferences it actually makes, defines an operational semantics for the representation and its associated inference engine. (Woods, rather confusingly in the light of later discussion, calls this a 'procedural' semantics.) But it would clearly be convenient if the machine's behaviour matched the system constructor's expectations, and this could most easily be achieved via a formal definition of the semantics of the representation, which was then encapsulated in the form of a program.

If we think specifically of formal semantics, instead of thinking of formal methods in general, there is yet a third way in which formality may enter into analysis of a linguistic input. This way is typified by those systems which carry out a semantic interpretation in terms of some model during the process of analysis, rather than construct a linguistic representation which is subsequently interpreted. We shall come back to the relation between representations and interpretations in the next section; it is sufficient to note here that it is just about possible to imagine a system where syntactic analysis was completely ad-hoc, and only formal in the very weak sense that someone had once programmed it, but where there was a systematic attempt at semantic interpretation in the style, say, of Montague grammars (Dowty et al. [48]).

In this case, the kind of discussion one got into would be different again, at least to the extent that the actual mechanisms whereby the interpretation was produced would be of critical importance, so that one would be very close to traditional logic's concern with the formulation of appropriate truth conditions for complex propositions.

10.4 WHAT CAN BE INTERPRETED?

Most of the authors in this book talk at some point about interpretation, but the range of entities serving as source and target for interpretation varies quite considerably. In this section I want to try to make the variety explicit.

To start with the most succinct, Turner, constructing a formal language, says:

> This language needs to be given some interpretation; we need
> to spell out the truth conditions for the logical connectives and
> quantifiers. [225, page 165]

The meaning of interpretation here is quite clear, and needs no supplementary comment. It is, however, rather different from the proposal of Fenstad et al. to interpret a representation in terms of situation schemata into formulae in a logic, where one formal language is interpreted into another formal language, but the first is intended to reflect the linguistic structure of the input, whilst the second relates directly to the model:

> Another important trend in 'applied logic' has been the use
> of model theory in the study of knowledge representation. ...
> Computing a representation in higher order intensional logic
> may throw some light on specific linguistic phenomena. But it
> is not the case that *any* computable representation may be a
> fruitful starting point for further processing, and this for several reasons. The representation may not be computationally
> tractable, which is the case if it is a formula in higher order
> logic, thus belonging to a system without a complete proof procedure. Also, we must also pay equal attention to the representational forms developed in knowledge representation theory
> and choose our representation of linguistic information accordingly. [57, page 32]

For Fenstad, then, there is a clear sequence in analysis: first a representation is constructed, then that representation is interpreted in terms of a model. The shape the representation takes is influenced both by the structure of the input and by the structure of the knowledge base. (The practical application which serves as an experimental test bed is a question answering system. Questions are transformed into logical expressions and answered via a theorem prover working over the knowledge base.)

Rupp et al. seem to have much the same picture, except that for them the representation seems to be relatively independent of the final application domain or of any specific knowledge base. Consequently, the representation achieved as a first result of analysis increases in relative importance as the interpretation diminishes:

> There may well be theoretical arguments for some level of semantic representation, such as psychological plausibility or the
> need to provide discourse referents, but the most common motivations for maintaining a level of semantic representation are

more technical and practical. Whatever form of semantic interpretation is assumed, and here differences may arise out of philosophical preference, it will be useful to have a *syntactically precise metalanguage* for talking about those interpretations, independently of the original linguistic forms, and if possible, of the nature of the intended interpretation, e.g. whether the objects referred to are in the world or in the mind. [198, page 192]

So far, the source to be interpreted has been some sort of artificial construct: an expression in a formal language, or a linguistic representation. An alternative use of interpretation starts with the linguistic input as source. Thus, workers in the tradition of Montague-style semantics often talk of the semantic composition rules as carrying out an interpretation into a truth conditional semantic representation, as van Benthem here:

Categorial derivation with its associated semantic interpretation as presented here may be viewed as a general mechanism for 'pooling' of denotational constraints contributed by the various components of an expression into the eventual semantic behaviour of the whole. [233, page 139]

Halvorsen also takes the linguistic string as input and avoids the construction of an intermediate representation, although the result of the interpretation is not constrained to be truth conditional expressions:

The proposed interpretation mechanism allows functional structures and semantic structures to be constructed in parallel. This proposal differs from previous ones in that it does not take functional structures to be the input to semantic interpretation, and consequently all semantically relevant information does not have to be funnelled through the f-structure. Yet, it permits the dependencies between functional and semantic information to be captured through the association of functional and semantic annotations on nodes. The projection mechanism itself does not impose a pivotal role on the f-structure any more than on the semantic structure. In fact, the f-structure could be viewed as a projection from the semantic structure, or as a combined projection from c-structure and semantic structure. The projections are functions from structural level to structural level and can be composed and inverted to model these complex dependencies. [78, page 182]

In contrast to all of the above, Wilks, I think, sees 'interpretation' as a noun rather than a verb; it is the result of a successful analysis, however obtained:

> ... the interpretation of a sentence is an approximative matter (including whether or not it has a plausible interpretation at all, and hence whether or not it is a sentence at all), one computed by taking a best-fit interpretation from among a number of competing candidates. ... my own approach, preference semantics, was not about commitment to representations of a particular kind at all, but only to certain procedures (based on coherence and connectedness of representation) as the right way to select interpretations from among competitors, for competitors there will always be. [247, page 265]

But it is perhaps worth noticing that this is not the same sense of interpretation, I think, as when Wilks uses the same word in discussing what he calls the 'Gensym fallacy' in McDermott's work. Here, the interpretation in question is most plausibly by human agents constructing and understanding a knowledge representation, rather than by a machine procedure trying to arrive at an analysis of a sentence. That this is so is suggested to me by Wilks' claim that McDermott

> fails to distinguish:
> i) claiming one's representation is based on natural language from
> ii) having one's representation interpretable only in terms of natural language.
> If I am right, this last charge (ii) tells as much against McDermott as against anyone, because there are no viable alternatives: a language of uninterpreted Gensyms or any logic of uninterpreted predicates is just gibberish, unless and until connectionism saves the day for us all. [247, page 272]

All that this comes down to saying is that there must be an understandable connection between the formal language of the representation and the world the language is used to describe, and that, ultimately, only natural language can serve the purpose of elucidating this connection. In this Wilks must surely be right, but the sense of 'interpretation' is quite other than its earlier sense.

Before leaving this topic, we should perhaps notice that just as some of our authors have suggested interpretation without intervening representation, it is possible to imagine a system in which there is no interpretation at all in any strong sense, and in which a representation carries all the load which in other systems is split between representation and interpretation or is carried by interpretation alone. It is perhaps this kind of system which Partee has in mind:

> ... explanations that rest on the structures of the domains that we use our language to talk about – the further structure that Link hypothesizes on the domain of entities, for instance – are interestingly different from explanations which are or can be cast in terms of properties of (language-like) representations.

> The kinds of phenomena which seem most likely to get a nice account in terms of the structure of the domains that the language is talking about, such as the similarities and differences in the behaviour of mass nouns and plurals, pose interesting challenges to typical kinds of computational models. These work almost exclusively on a representational level and try to capture both entailment relations, and similarities and differences in truth conditions, in terms of syntactic operations or manipulations on representations. [175, page 98]

10.5   PROCEDURALITY

The astute reader may have noticed that the only author who was not quoted at all in the last section was Martin Kay, simply because, by talking consistently in terms of descriptions, he avoids entering the minefield of interpretation and representation. In compensation, I want briefly in this final section to pick up one of the points he raises, where again I think there is some inconsistency in use of the same term by different authors. Let me open the issue by quoting Kay:

> One of the effects of observing the restriction that makes logical variables of program variables is to shift the emphasis in the design of a system from *process* and *temporal sequence* to *relations* and *constraints*. It is extremely striking that computational linguists, like computer scientists, whose subject matter *par excellence* is abstract processes and changes of state through time, seek to eliminate time dependencies wherever they are inessential. As the jargon has it, they seek *declarative* rather than *procedural* formulations of problems.

> Theoretical linguists have tended to prefer procedural formalisms to declarative ones and, indeed, much of the discussion

among linguists has concerned the fine adjustment of temporal sequences. In transformational grammar, for example, that
we referred to earlier, the particular order in which transformational rules are applied has an important effect on the outcome
and much has been made of this. As a consequence, however,
transformational grammar is a system that has no known algorithm for analyzing sentences. [116, page 20]

Procedurality here is intimately associated with having to worry about the
order in which things are done. This is in counter distinction to Woods'
use of procedural semantics which we noticed earlier; there he argues that
specification of truth conditions can be made by means of a procedure or
function assigning truth values to propositions in particular possible worlds:
if the procedure is a programmed procedure, the behaviour of the program
will then provide a *de facto* semantic interpretation.

But it is also different from the use of procedural semantics by Wilks,
who explicitly contrasts an interest in defining representations with procedurality:

I shall restate the view that the key contribution of AI in unravelling how such complex tasks as 'understanding' might be
simulated by a machine lies not in representations at all but in
particular kinds of procedures ...

Later, however, Wilks himself makes the point that there can be no
procedure-free computation; even declarative logic programming languages
are interpreted. The contrast then becomes a contrast between a procedural semantics as opposed to a denotational semantics for knowledge representations. But even here I suspect that the opposition may be a false
opposition: could it not be possible for a representation to have a denotational semantics which applied to its definition and a procedural semantics
which applied to its use within a computer application? The denotational
semantics would then be primarily intended for use by the human defining
and interpreting the representation, the procedural semantics a procedural
semantics in exactly the sense of Woods. The denotational semantics and
the procedural semantics would, of course, be consistent, but neither would
replace the other.

10.6   OMISSIONS

Mention of a denotational semantics highlights one issue which is central
to both computational linguistics and formal semantics and where there is

much disagreement and much terminological confusion but which has been neglected here: the issue of how, in constructing any kind of representation or formal system, one tries to determine what the appropriate individuals which will serve as primitive objects in the representation will be, and how these primitive objects relate to their counterparts in some external reality. This omission is deliberate. The metaphysical and ontological questions are difficult and complex, but what answer one gives seems to me to make very little difference to the way one behaves when constructing the system. To quote Sag and Pollard:

> Meanings are meaningful only to those organisms who are attuned to the constraints that give rise to them; in the case of conventional constraints (including linguistic ones), this attunement consists of knowledge that is socially shared, culturally transmitted and mentally encoded. It seems to us pointless to prolong the debate about whether the language is the system of situation types that conform to the conventions, or the system of shared knowledge by virtue of which the conventions can be used and transmitted. Given that the organisms and their minds are themselves constituents of the language use situations in any case, the difference between the two may well be far less significant than recent debates have suggested. Much as one can do quantum mechanics without ever developing commitments about (or even caring about) the ontological status of the theoretical constructs, a science of signs is imaginable in the absence of certainty about whether they are in the mind, out of the mind, or somewhere in between. [200].

Bibliography

[1] P. Aczel. Frege structures and the notions of proposition, truth and set. In J. Barwise, Keisler and E. Keenan, editors, *The Kleene symposium*, Studies in Logic, pages 31–39. North-Holland, Amsterdam, 1980.

[2] J. Allen and D. Litman. Discourse processing and commonsense plans. In P. R. Cohen, M. Pollack and J. Morgan, editors, *Intentions and Plans in Discourse*. MIT Press, Cambridge, MA, 1987.

[3] J.-C. Anscombre and O. Ducrot. *L'argumentation dans la langue*. Mardaga, Brussels, 1983.

[4] D. Arnold and L. des Tombe. Basic theory and methodology in Eurotra. In S. Nirenburg, editor, *Machine Translation: Theoretical and Methodological Issues*, pages 114–135. Cambridge University Press, Cambridge, 1987.

[5] A. Avron. The semantics and proof theory of linear logic. *Theoretical Computer Science*, 57:161–184, 1988.

[6] E. Bach. Natural language metaphysics. In R. Barcan Marcus, G. Dorn and P. Weingartner, editors, *Logic, Methodology and the Philosophy of Science VII*. North-Holland, Amsterdam, 1986.

[7] E. Bach. Control in Montague grammar. *Linguistic Inquiry*, 10:515–531, 1979.

[8] E. Bach and B. H. Partee. Anaphora and semantic structure. In J. Kreiman and A. Ojeda, editors, *Papers from the Parasession on Pronouns and Anaphora*, pages 1–28. Chicago Linguistics Society, Chicago, 1980.

[9] T. Ballmer. Is Keen an' faltz keen or false. *Theoretical Linguistics*, 7:155–170, 1980.

[10] H. Barendregt. *The Lambda Calculus. Its Syntax and Semantics.* Studies in Logic. North-Holland, Amsterdam, 1981.

[11] J. Barwise. Noun phrases, generalized quantifiers and anaphora. CSLI report CSLI-86-52, CSLI, Stanford, 1986. Reprinted in P. Gärdenfors [62], pages 1–29.

[12] J. Barwise. *The Situation in Logic.* Number 17 in CSLI Lecture Notes. CSLI, Stanford, 1989.

[13] J. Barwise and J. Etchemendy. *The Liar.* Oxford University Press, Oxford, 1987.

[14] J. Barwise. The situation in Logic-II. In E. Traugott, C. Ferguson and J. Reilly, editors, *On Conditionals*, pages 21–54. Cambridge University Press, Cambridge, 1986.

[15] J. Barwise and J. Perry. *Situations and Attitudes.* MIT Press, Cambridge, MA, 1983.

[16] M. Bennett. *Some Extensions of a Montague Fragment of English.* PhD thesis, UCLA, 1974.

[17] M. Botvinnik. *Computers, Chess and long-range planning.* Longman, London, 1971.

[18] R. Brachman and H. Levesque, editors. *Readings in Knowledge Representation.* Morgan Kaufmann, San Mateo, CA, 1985.

[19] R. Brachman and J. Schmolze. An overview of the KL-ONE knowledge representation language. *Cognitive Science*, 9:171–216, 1985.

[20] J. Bresnan. *The Mental Representation of Grammatical Relations.* MIT Press, Cambridge, MA, 1982.

[21] R. Brown and S. Nirenburg. Human-computer interaction for semantic disambiguation. In *Proceedings of the 13th International Conference on Computational Linguistics, COLING 90*. Helsinki, August 1990.

[22] R. Burton. Semantic grammar: An engineering technique for constructing natural language understanding systems. Technical Report 3453, Bolt, Beranek and Newman Co., Cambridge, MA, 1976.

[23] W. Buszkowski. *Lambek's Categorial Grammars.* PhD thesis, Mathematical Institute, Adam Mickiewicz University, Poznan, 1982.

[24] W. Buszkowski, W. Marciszewski and J. van Benthem, editors. *Categorial Grammar*. John Benjamin, Amsterdam, 1988.

[25] J. Carbonell. Derivational analogy and its role in problem solving. In *Proceedings of the 1983 National Conference on Artificial Intelligence*, pages 64–69. 1983.

[26] L. Carlson and S. Nirenburg. World modeling in nlp. CMT Technical Report 90-118, CMU, 1990.

[27] R. Carnap. *Meaning and Necessity*. Phoenix Books, Chicago, 1947.

[28] E. Charniak. Parsing, how to. In K. S. Jones and Y. Wilks, editors, *Automatic Natural Language Parsing*, pages 156–163. Ellis Horwood, Chichester, 1983.

[29] E. Charniak. Connectionism and explanation. In Y. Wilks, editor, *Theoretical Issues in Natural Language Processing*, pages 73–77. Erlbaum, Hillsdale, NJ, 1991.

[30] E. Charniak and Y. Wilks, editors. *Computational Semantics*. North-Holland, Amsterdam, 1976.

[31] G. Chierchia. Nominalization and Montague grammar. *Linguistics and Philosophy*, 5:303–354, 1982.

[32] G. Chierchia. *Topics in the Syntax and Semantics of Infinitives and Gerunds*. PhD thesis, University of Massachusetts, Amherst, 1984.

[33] G. Chierchia and R. Turner. Semantics and property theory. *Linguistics and Philosophy*, 11(3):261–302, 1988.

[34] N. Chomsky. *Syntactic Structures*. Mouton, The Hague, 1957.

[35] N. Chomsky. *Aspects of the Theory of Syntax*. MIT Press, Cambridge, MA, 1965.

[36] A. Cohn. A more expressive formulation of many sorted logic. *Journal of Automated Reasoning*, 3:113–200, 1987.

[37] E. Colban. Prepositional phrases in situation schemata. In J. E. Fenstad, P.-K. Halvorsen, T. Langholm and J. van Benthem, editors, *Situations, Language and Logic*, pages 133–156. Reidel, Dordrecht, 1987.

[38] R. Cooper. Verb second – predication or unification. Delivered at the Workshop on Comparative Germanic Syntax, Reykjavik, June 1986.

[39] R. Cooper. *Montague's Semantic Theory and Transformational Syntax*. PhD thesis, University of Massachusetts, 1976.

[40] R. Cooper. Meaning representation in Montague grammar and situation semantics. In *Proceedings from the Workshop on Theoretical Issues in Natural Language Processing*, pages 28–30. Halifax, Nova Scotia, May 1985.

[41] L. Creary and C. Pollard. A computational semantics for natural language. In *Proceedings of the 23rd Annual Meeting of the Association for Computational Linguistics*, pages 172–179. 1985.

[42] R. Cullingford. SAM and Micro-SAM. In R. Schank and C. Riesbeck, editors, *Inside Computer Understanding*, pages 77–135. Erlbaum, Hillsdale, NJ, 1981.

[43] M. Dalrymple. *Syntactic Constraints on Anaphoric Binding*. PhD thesis, Stanford University, 1990.

[44] C. Defrise and S. Nirenburg. Aspects of text meaning: Using discourse connectives and attitudinals in natural language generation. CMT memo, CMU, 1989.

[45] K. Devlin. Infons and types in an information-based logic. In R. Cooper, K. Mukai and J. Perry, editors, *Situation Theory and Its Applications*, volume 1, pages 79–95. CSLI, Stanford, 1990.

[46] K. Devlin. *Logic and Information*. Cambridge University Press, Cambridge, 1991.

[47] E. Dijkstra, Public lecture. New Mexico State University, 1986.

[48] D. R. Dowty, R. E. Wall and S. Peters. *Introduction to Montague Semantics*. Reidel, Dordrecht, 1981.

[49] H. Dreyfus. *What Computers Can't Do*. Harper and Row, New York, second edition, 1979.

[50] O. Ducrot. Puisque, essai de description polyphonique. *Revue Romane*, nr. spécial 24:166–185, 1983.

[51] H. Dyvik. Sentence synthesis from situation schemata: A unification-based algorithm. *Nordic Journal of Linguistics*, 11(1–2):17–32, 1988.

[52] E. Engdahl. *Constituent Questions*. Reidel, Dordrecht, 1986.

[53] S. Feferman. Towards useful type-free theories 1. *Journal of Symbolic Logic*, 49:75–111, 1984.

[54] J. E. Fenstad. Natural language systems. In R. T. Nossum, editor, *Advanced Topics in Artificial Intelligence*, pages 189–233. Springer-Verlag, Berlin, 1988.

[55] J. E. Fenstad, P.-K. Halvorsen, T. Langholm and J. van Benthem. Equations, schemata and situations: A framework for linguistic semantics. CSLI report CSLI-85-29, CSLI, Stanford, 1985.

[56] J. E. Fenstad, P.-K. Halvorsen, T. Langholm and J. van Benthem. *Situations, Language, and Logic*, volume 34 of *Studies in Linguistics and Philosophy*. Reidel, Dordrecht, 1987.

[57] J. E. Fenstad, T. Langholm and E. Vestre. Representations and interpretations. In M. Rosner and R. Johnson, editors, *Computational Linguistics and Formal Semantics*. Cambridge University Press, Cambridge, 1992.

[58] G. Frege. On sense and reference. In P. G. M. Black, editor, *Translations from the Philosophical Works of Gottlob Frege*, pages 56–78. Basil Blackwell, Oxford, 1960.

[59] W. Frey and U. Reyle. A Prolog implementation of Lexical Functional Grammar. In *Proceedings of the Eighth International Joint Conference on Artificial Intelligence*, volume II, pages 693–695. IJCAI, Karlsruhe, 1983.

[60] D. Gabbay and F. Guenthner, editors. *Handbook of Philosophical Logic*, volume II (Extensions of Classical Logic). Reidel, Dordrecht, 1984.

[61] D. Gallin. *Intensional and Higher-Order Modal Logic*. North-Holland, Amsterdam, 1975.

[62] P. Gärdenfors, editor. *Generalized Quantifiers. Linguistic and Logical Approaches*. Reidel, Dordrecht, 1987.

[63] D. Gates, D. Haberlach, T. Kaufmann, M. Kee, R. McCardell, T. Mitamura, I. Monarch, S. Morrisson, E. Nyberg, K. Takeda and M. Zabludowski. Lexicons. *Machine Translation*, 4:67–112, 1989.

[64] J. M. Gawron. Types, contents and semantic objects. *Linguistics and Philosophy*, 9(4):427–476, 1986.

[65] J. M. Gawron, J. Mark, J. King, J. Lamping, E. Loebner, A. Paulson, G. Pullum, I. A. Sag and T. Wasow. Processing English with a generalized phrase structure grammar. Technical report, Hewlett-Packard Computer Science Laboratory, Palo Alto, CA, 1982.

[66] J. M. Gawron and S. Peters. *Anaphora and Quantification in Situation Semantics*. Number 19 in CSLI Lecture Notes. CSLI, Stanford, 1990.

[67] G. Gazdar. A cross-categorial semantics for coordination. *Linguistics and Philosophy*, 3:407–409, 1980.

[68] J.-Y. Girard. Linear logic. *Theoretical Computer Science*, 50:1–102, 1987.

[69] J. Goguen and J. Meseguer. Equality, types, modules and generics for logic programming. CSLI report CSLI-84-5, CSLI, Stanford, 1984.

[70] K. W. Goodman and S. Nirenburg. KBMT-89. CMT research report, CMU, 1989.

[71] J. Groenendijk and M. Stokhof. Dynamic predicate logic: Towards a compositional and non-representational discourse theory. Technical report, University of Amsterdam, 1987.

[72] J. Groenendijk and M. Stokhof. Dynamic predicate logic. *Linguistics and Philosophy*, 14:39–100, 1991.

[73] Y. Gurevich. Logic and the challenge of computer science. In E. Börger, editor, *Current Trends in Theoretical Computer Science*. Computer Science Press, 1987.

[74] L. Guthrie, B. M. Slator, Y. Wilks and R. Bruce. Is there content in empty heads? In *Proceedings of the 13th International Conference on Computational Linguistics, COLING 90*, pages 138–143. 1990.

[75] P.-K. Halvorsen. Order-free semantic composition and lexical-functional grammar. In J. Horecký, editor, *Proceedings of the 9th International Conference on Computational Linguistics, COLING 82*, pages 115–120. North-Holland, Amsterdam, 1982.

[76] P.-K. Halvorsen. Semantics for lexical-functional grammars. *Linguistic Inquiry*, 14(3):567–615, 1983.

[77] P.-K. Halvorsen. Situation semantics and semantic interpretation in constraint-based grammars. CSLI Report CSLI-87-101, CSLI, Stanford, 1987.

[78] P.-K. Halvorsen. Algorithms for semantic interpretation. In M. Rosner and R. Johnson, editors, *Computational Linguistics and Formal Semantics*. Cambridge University Press, Cambridge, 1992.

[79] P.-K. Halvorsen and R. M. Kaplan. Projections and semantic description in lexical-functional grammar. In *Proceedings from the International Conference on Fifth Generation Computer Systems, FGCS-88*, pages 1116–1122. Institute for New Generation Computer Technology. Tokyo, 1988.

[80] C. L. Hamblin. Questions in Montague English. *Foundations of Language*, 10:41–53, 1973.

[81] D. Harel. Dynamic logic. In D. Gabbay and F. Guenthner, editors, *Handbook of Philosophical Logic*, volume II (Extensions of Classical Logic), pages 497–604. Reidel, Dordrecht, 1984.

[82] J. Haugeland, editor. *Mind Design*. MIT Press, Cambridge, MA, 1976.

[83] P. Hayes. Some problems and non-problems in representation theory. In R. Brachman and H. Levesque, editors, *Readings in Knowledge Representation*, pages 3–22. Morgan Kaufmann, Los Altos, CA, 1985.

[84] C. M. Heidrich. Should generative semantics be related to intensional logic? In E. Keenan, editor, *The Formal Semantics of Natural Language*. Cambridge University Press, Cambridge, 1975.

[85] I. Heim. *The Semantics of Definite and Indefinite Noun Phrases*. PhD thesis, University of Massachusetts, Amherst, MA, 1982.

[86] I. Heim. File change semantics and the familiarity theory of definiteness. In R. Bäuerle, C. Schwarze and A. von Stechow, editors, *Meaning, Use, and Interpretation of Language*, pages 164–189. Walter de Gruyter, Berlin, 1983.

[87] H. Hendriks. *Generalized Generalized Quantifiers and Natural Natural Language*. Institute for Language, Logic and Information, University of Amsterdam, 1988.

[88] J. Hintikka. Individuals, possible worlds, and epistemic logic. *Noûs*, 1:33–62, 1967.

[89] J. Hobbs and S. Rosenschein. Making computational sense of Montague's intensional logic. *Artificial Intelligence*, 9:287–306, 1978.

[90] J. Hopcroft and J. Ullman. *Introduction to Automata Theory, Languages, and Computation.* Addison-Wesley, Reading, MA, 1979.

[91] E. H. Hovy. *Generating Natural Language Under Pragmatic Constraints.* PhD thesis, Yale University, 1988.

[92] J. Hutchins. Linguistic models in machine translation. In *UEA papers in linguistics.* Norwich, England, 1979.

[93] N. Immerman. Upper and lower bounds for first-order expressibility. *Journal of Computer and Systems Sciences*, 25(1):76–98, 1982.

[94] D. Israel. On formal versus commonsense semantics. In Y. Wilks, editor, *Theoretical Issues in Natural Language Processing*, pages 123–129. Erlbaum, Hillsdale, NJ, 1991.

[95] R. Jackendoff. *Semantics and Cognition.* MIT Press, Cambridge, MA, 1983.

[96] R. Jakobson, G. Fant and M. Halle. *Preliminaries to Speech Analysis: The Distinctive Features and their Correlates.* MIT Press, Cambridge, MA, 1952. Second printing.

[97] M. Johnson and E. Klein. Discourse, anaphora and parsing. In *Proceedings of the 11th International Conference on Computational Linguistics, COLING 86*, pages 669–675. Bonn, 1986.

[98] M. Johnson. *Attribute-Value Logic and the Theory of Grammar.* Number 16 in CSLI Lecture Notes. CSLI, Stanford, 1988.

[99] R. Johnson and M. Rosner. Machine translation & software tools. In M. King, editor, *Machine Translation*, pages 154–167. Edinburgh University Press, Edinburgh, 1986.

[100] R. Johnson and M. Rosner. A rich environment for experimentation with unification grammars. In *Proceedings of the Fourth Conference of the European Chapter of the Association for Computational Linguistics*, pages 182–189. Manchester, 1989.

[101] A. K. Joshi. An introduction to tree adjoining grammars. In A. Manaster-Ramer, editor, *Mathematics of Language*, pages 87–114. John Benjamins, Amsterdam, 1987.

[102] F. Kamareddine. *Semantics in a Frege Structure.* PhD thesis, University of Edinburgh, 1988.

[103] H. Kamp. A theory of truth and semantic representation. In J. Groenendijk, T. Janssen and M. Stokhof, editors, *Formal Methods in the Study of Language*, volume 136 of *Mathematical Centre Tracts*, pages 277–322. Mathematical Centre Tracts, Amsterdam, 1981.

[104] R. M. Kaplan. Three seductions of computational psycholinguistics. In P. Whitelock, M. M. Wood, H. L. Somers, R. Johnson and P. Bennett, editors, *Linguistic Theory and Computer Applications*, pages 149–188. Academic Press, London, 1987.

[105] R. M. Kaplan and J. Bresnan. Lexical-functional grammar: A formal system for grammatical representation. In J. Bresnan, editor, *The Mental Representation of Grammatical Relations*, pages 173–281. MIT Press, Cambridge, MA, 1982.

[106] R. M. Kaplan and C. Kiparsky. The LFG grammar writer's workbench. Technical report, Xerox Palo Alto Research Center, 1984.

[107] R. M. Kaplan and J. Maxwell. An algorithm for functional uncertainty. In D. Vargha, editor, *Proceedings of the 12th International Conference on Computational Linguistics, COLING 88*, pages 203–206. John von Neumann Society for Computing Sciences. Budapest, 1988.

[108] R. M. Kaplan and J. Maxwell. Constituent coordination in lexical-functional grammar. In D. Vargha, editor, *Proceedings of the 12th International Conference on Computational Linguistics, COLING 88*, pages 303–305. John von Neumann Society for Computing Sciences. Budapest, 1988.

[109] R. M. Kaplan and A. Zaenen. Long-distance dependencies, constituent structure, and functional uncertainty. In M. Baltin and A. Kroch, editors, *Alternative Conceptions of Phrase Structure*, pages 17–42. Chicago University Press, 1988.

[110] L. Karttunen. The syntax and semantics of questions. *Linguistics and Philosophy*, 1:3–44, 1977.

[111] L. Karttunen. Features and values. In *Proceedings of the 10th International Conference on Computational Linguistics, COLING 84*, pages 28–33. Stanford, CA, 1984.

[112] L. Karttunen. Radical lexicalism. CSLI Report CSLI-86-68, CSLI, Stanford, 1986.

[113] R. Kasper. *Feature Structures: A Logical Theory With Application to Language Analysis.* PhD thesis, University of Michigan, 1987.

[114] M. Kay. Functional unification grammar: A formalism for machine translation. In *Proceedings of the 10th International Conference on Computational Linguistics, COLING 84*, pages 75–78. Stanford, 1984.

[115] M. Kay. Key-Note Address: Constitutive Assembly, SGAICO, NLP Special Interest Group. Lugano, 1990.

[116] M. Kay. Unification. In M. Rosner and R. Johnson, editors, *Computational Linguistics and Formal Semantics*. Cambridge University Press, Cambridge, 1992.

[117] M. Kay. Functional grammar. In *Proceedings of the Fifth Annual Meeting of the Berkeley Linguistics Society, University of California*, pages 142–158. Berkeley, 1979.

[118] E. Keenan. Semantic case theory. In R. Bartsch, J. van Benthem and P. van Emde Boas, editors, *Semantics and Contextual Expression*, pages 33–56. Foris, Dordrecht, 1990.

[119] E. Keenan and L. Faltz. Logical types for natural language. UCLA Occasional Papers in Linguistics 3, UCLA, Department of Linguistics, 1978.

[120] E. Keenan and L. Faltz. *Boolean Semantics for Natural Language.* Reidel, Dordrecht, 1985.

[121] E. Keenan and Y. Stavi. A semantic characterization of natural language determiners. *Linguistics and Philosophy*, 9:253–326, 1986.

[122] J. Ketting. *Fuzzy Determinatoren en Kwantifikatie over Fuzzy Deelverzamelingen.* Master's thesis, University of Amsterdam, 1988.

[123] M. King. On the proper place of semantics in machine translation. In M. Nagao, editor, *Language and Artificial Intelligence*, pages 283–304. North-Holland, Amsterdam, 1987.

[124] E. Klein and I. A. Sag. Type-driven translation. *Linguistics and Philosophy*, 8:163–201, 1985.

[125] J. Kolodner. *Retrieval and Organizational Strategies in Conceptual Memory: A Computer model.* Erlbaum, Hillsdale, NJ, 1984.

[126] J. Kolodner and C. Riesbeck, editors. *Experience, Memory and Reasoning*. Erlbaum, Hillsdale, NJ, 1986.

[127] S. Kripke. Semantical considerations on modal logic. *Acta Philosophica Fennica*, 16:83–89, 1963.

[128] J. Lambek. The mathematics of sentence structure. *American Mathematical Monthly*, 65:154–169, 1958.

[129] J. Lambek and P. Scott. *Introduction to Higher-Order Categorial Logic*. Cambridge University Press, Cambridge, 1986.

[130] J. Landsbergen. Machine translation based on logically isomorphic Montague grammars. In *Proceedings of the 9th International Conference on Computational Linguistics, COLING 82*, pages 175–181. Prague, 1982.

[131] J. Landsbergen. Isomorphic grammars and their use in the Rosetta translation system. In M. King, editor, *Machine Translation Today: the State of the Art*, pages 351–372. Edinburgh University Press, Edinburgh, 1987.

[132] T. Langholm. *Partiality, Truth and Persistence*. Number 15 in CSLI Lecture Notes. CSLI, Stanford, 1988.

[133] T. Langholm. Describing sets with sets. COSMOS report, Mathematics Institute, University of Oslo, 1989.

[134] T. Langholm. How to say no with feature structures. COSMOS report, Mathematics Institute, University of Oslo, 1989.

[135] D. Lewis. General semantics. In D. Davidson and G. Harman, editors, *Semantics of Natural Language*, pages 169–218. Reidel, Dordrecht, 1972.

[136] V. Lifschitz. The logic approach to AI. *Stanford Computer Science Video Journal*, 1987.

[137] G. Link. The logical analysis of plurals and mass terms: A lattice-theoretical approach. In R. Bäuerle, C. Schwarze and A. von Stechow, editors, *Meaning Use, and Interpretation of Language*, pages 302–323. Walter de Gruyter, Berlin, 1983.

[138] G. Link. Generalized quantifiers and plurals. In P. Gärdenfors, editor, *Generalized Quantifiers: Linguistic and Logical Approaches*, pages 151–180. Reidel, Dordrecht, 1987.

[139] J. T. Lønning. Mass terms and quantification. *Linguistics and Philosophy*, 10:1–52, 1987.

[140] J. T. Lønning. Some aspects of the logic of plural noun phrases. COSMOS Report 11, Mathematics Department, University of Oslo, 1989.

[141] J. McCarthy. Epistemological problems of artificial intelligence. In *Proceedings of the 5th International Joint Conference on Artificial Intelligence*, pages 1038–1044. 1977.

[142] J. McCarthy and P. Hayes. Some philosophical problems from the standpoint of artificial intelligence. In B. Meltzer and D. Mitchie, editors, *Machine Intelligence*, volume 4, pages 463–502. Edinburgh University Press, Edinburgh, 1969.

[143] D. McDermott. Artificial intelligence meets natural stupidity. *SIGART Newsletter*, 57:4–9, 1976. Reprinted in J. Haugeland [82], pages 143-160.

[144] D. McDermott. Tarskian semantics, or no notation without denotation. *Cognitive Science*, 2:277–282, 1978.

[145] D. McDermott. A critique of pure reason. *Computational Intelligence*, 3:1–24, 1987.

[146] K. McKeown and M. Elhadad. A comparison of surface language generators: A case study in choice of connectives. Manuscript. Columbia University, 1989.

[147] J. A. Makowsky. Model theoretic issues in theoretical computer science, part I: Relational data bases and abstract data types. In G. Lolli, G. Longo and A. Marcja, editors, *Logic Colloquium '82*. North-Holland, Amsterdam, 1984.

[148] R. May. *The Grammar of Quantification*. PhD thesis, MIT, 1977.

[149] J. Meier, D. Metzing, T. Polzin, P. Ruhrberg, H. Rutz and M. Vollmer. Generierung von Wegbeschreibungen. KOLIBRI Arbeitsbericht, DFG-Forschergruppe Kohärenz, Fakultät für Linguistik und Literaturwissenschaft der Universität Bielefeld, 1988.

[150] I. Meyer, B. Onyshkevich and L. Carlson. Lexicographic support for knowledge-based machine translation. CMT Technical Report 90-118, CMU, 1990.

[151] I. Monarch and S. Nirenburg. Ontology-based lexicon acquisition for a machine translation system. In *Proceedings of the Fourth Workshop on Knowledge Acquisition for Knowledge-Based Systems*. Banff, Canada, November 1989.

[152] R. Montague. Universal grammar. *Theoria*, 36:373–398, 1970. Reprinted in R. H. Thomason [219], pages 222–246.

[153] R. Montague. English as a formal language. In B. Visentini et al., editors, *Linguaggi nella Società e nella Tecnica*, pages 189–224. Edizioni di Comunità, Milan, 1970. Reprinted in R. H. Thomason [219], pages 108–221.

[154] R. Montague. The proper treatment of quantification in ordinary English. In J. Hintikka, J. Moravcsik and P. Suppes, editors, *Approaches to Natural Language*, pages 373–398. Reidel, Dordrecht, 1973. Reprinted in R. H. Thomason [219], pages 247–270.

[155] J. D. Moore and C. L. Paris. Planning text for advisory dialogues. In *Proceedings of the 27th Annual Meeting of the Association for Computational Linguistics*, pages 203–211. Vancouver, British Columbia, 1989.

[156] M. Moortgat. *Categorial Investigations: Logical and Linguistic Aspects of the Lambek Calculus*. Foris, Dordrecht, 1988.

[157] G. Morrill. Grammar and logical types. In G. Barry and G. Morrill, editors, *Studies in Categorial Grammar*, volume 5 of *Edinburgh Working Papers in Cognitive Science*, pages 127–148. Centre for Cognitive Science, University of Edinburgh, 1990.

[158] M. D. Moshier and W. C. Rounds. A logic for partially specified data structures. In *Proceedings of the 14th ACM symposium on Principles of Programming Languages*, pages 155–167. Munich, 1987.

[159] R. Muskens. *Meaning and Partiality*. PhD thesis, University of Amsterdam, 1988. To appear with Foris, Dordrecht.

[160] M. Nagao. *Machine Translation*. Oxford University Press, Oxford, 1989.

[161] H. Nakashima, S. Hiroyuki, P.-K. Halvorsen and S. Peters. Towards a computational interpretation of situation theory. In *Proceedings of the International Conference on Fifth Generation Computer Systems, FGCS-88*, pages 489–498. ICOT, 1988.

[162] O. Neurath. Protocol sentences. *Erkenntnis*, 3, 1932.

[163] S. Nirenburg. A system for natural language generation that emphasizes lexical selection. In *Proceedings of the Workshop on Planning Natural Language Technologies*. Blue Mountain Lake, NY, September 1987.

[164] S. Nirenburg and C. Defrise. Lexical and conceptual structure for knowledge-based machine translation. In J. Pustejovsky, editor, *Semantics and the Lexicon*. Kluwer, Dordrecht, forthcoming.

[165] S. Nirenburg and V. Lesser. Providing intelligent assistance in distributed office environments. In *Proceedings of the Third International ACM Conference on Office Automation Systems*, pages 104–112. Providence RI, October 1986.

[166] S. Nirenburg, V. Lesser and E. Nyberg. Controlling a language generation planner. In *Proceedings of the Eleventh International Joint Conference on Artificial Intelligence*, pages 1524–1530. Detroit, 1989.

[167] S. Nirenburg, I. Monarch, T. Kauffmann, I. Nirenburg and J. Carbonell. Acquisition and maintenance of very large knowledge bases. CMT research report, CMU, 1988.

[168] S. Nirenburg and J. Pustejovsky. Processing aspectual semantics. In *Proceedings of the Tenth Annual Meeting of the Cognitive Science Society*. Montreal, August 1988.

[169] S. Nirenburg and V. Raskin. A metric for computational analysis of meaning: Toward an applied theory of linguistic semantics. In *Proceedings of the 11th International Conference on Computational Linguistics, COLING 86*, pages 338–340. 1986.

[170] S. Nirenburg and V. Raskin. The subworld concept lexicon and the lexicon management system. *Computational Linguistics*, 13(3-4):276–289, 1987.

[171] S. Nirenburg, V. Raskin and A. B. Tucker. Interlingua design in TRANSLATOR. In S. Nirenburg, editor, *Machine Translation: Theoretical and Methodological Issues*, pages 90–113. Cambridge University Press, Cambridge, 1987.

[172] S. Nirenburg, J. Reynolds and I. Nirenburg. Studying the cognitive agent: A theory and two experiments. CMT research report, CMU, 1986.

[173] R. Oehrle, E. Bach and D. Wheeler, editors. *Categorial Grammars and Natural Language Structures*. Reidel, Dordrecht, 1988.

[174] B. Partee. Noun phrase interpretation and type-shifting principles. In J. Groenendijk, D. de Jongh and M. Stokhof, editors, *Studies in Discourse Representation Theory and the Theory of Generalized Quantifiers*, pages 115–143. Foris, Dordrecht, 1987.

[175] B. Partee. Syntactic categories and semantic type. In M. Rosner and R. Johnson, editors, *Computational Linguistics and Formal Semantics*. Cambridge University Press, Cambridge, 1992.

[176] B. Partee. Montague grammar and transformational grammar. *Linguistic Inquiry*, 6:203–300, 1975.

[177] B. Partee and M. Rooth. Generalized conjunction and type ambiguity. In R. Bäuerle, C. Schwarze and A. von Stechow, editors, *Meaning, Use, and Interpretation of Language*, pages 361–383. Walter de Gruyter, Berlin, 1983.

[178] F. Pelletier. Non-singular references. In F. Pelletier, editor, *Mass Terms: Some Philosophical Problems*, pages 1–40. Reidel, Dordrecht, 1975.

[179] F. Pereira and S. Shieber. The semantics of grammar formalisms seen as computer languages. In *Proceedings of the 10th International Conference on Computational Linguistics, COLING 84*, pages 123–129. Stanford University, 1984.

[180] F. Pereira and D. Warren. Definite clause grammars for language analysis – a survey of the formalism and a comparison with augmented transition networks. *Artificial Intelligence*, 13:231–278, 1980.

[181] S. R. Petrick. *A recognition procedure for transformational grammars*. PhD thesis, MIT, Cambridge, MA, 1965.

[182] C. Pollard and I. A. Sag. *Information-Based Syntax and Semantics: Volume 1 Fundamentals*. Number 13 in CSLI Lecture Notes. CSLI, Stanford, 1987.

[183] T. Potts. Montague's semiotic: A syllabus of errors. *Theoretical Linguistics*, 3, 1976.

[184] W. Quine. On what there is. In *From a Logical Point of View*. Harper and Row, New York, 1963.

[185] W. Quine. Variables explained away. In *Selected Logic Papers*. Random House, New York, 1966.

[186] R. Quirk, S. Greenbaum, G. Leech and J. Svartvick. *Comprehensive Grammar of the English Language*. Longman, London, 1985.

[187] V. Raskin. What is there in linguistic semantics for natural language processing? In *Proceedings of the Natural Language Planning Workshop*. Northeast Artificial Intelligence Consortium. Blue Mountain Lake, New York, September 1987.

[188] H. Reichenbach. *Elements of Symbolic Logic*. University of California Press, Berkeley, 1947.

[189] U. Reyle. Compositional semantics for LFG. In U. Reyle and C. Rohrer, editors, *Natural Language Parsing and Linguistic Theories*, pages 448–479. Reidel, Dordrecht, 1988.

[190] G. Ritchie and K. Hanna. AM: A case study in AI methodology. In D. Partridge and Y. Wilks, editors, *The Foundations of Artificial Intelligence*, pages 247–265. Cambridge University Press, Cambridge, 1990.

[191] R. Rodman. Scope phenomena, "movement transformations", and relative clauses. In B. H. Partee, editor, *Montague Grammar*, pages 165–176. Academic Press, New York, 1976.

[192] M. Rooth. Noun phrase interpretation in Montague grammar, file change semantics, and situation semantics. CSLI Report CSLI-86-51, CSLI, Stanford, 1986. Reprinted in P. Gärdenfors [62].

[193] W. C. Rounds and R. Kasper. A complete logical calculus for record structures representing linguistic information. In *Proceedings of the First IEEE Symposium on Logic in Computer Science*, pages 38–43. Boston, 1986.

[194] E. Rudolph. Connective relations – connective expressions – connective structures. In J. S. Petöfi, editor, *Text and Discourse Constitution*. Walter de Gruyter, New York, 1988.

[195] C. J. Rupp. Situation semantics and machine translation. In *Proceedings of the Fourth Conference of the European Chapter of the Association for Computational Linguistics*, pages 308–318. Manchester, 1989.

[196] C. J. Rupp. *Semantic Representation in a Unification Environment.* PhD thesis, University of Manchester, 1990.

[197] C. J. Rupp. Abstraction mechanisms in constraint-based linguistic formalisms. Working Paper 6, IDSIA, 1992.

[198] C. J. Rupp, R. Johnson and M. Rosner. Situation schemata and linguistic representation. In M. Rosner and R. Johnson, editors, *Computational Linguistics and Formal Semantics.* Cambridge University Press, Cambridge, 1992.

[199] G. Russell. Compound verbs and constituent order in German. Technical report, University of Sussex, 1983.

[200] I. A. Sag and C. Pollard. Head-driven phrase structure grammar: An informal synopsis. CSLI Report CSLI-87-79, Stanford University, 1987.

[201] R. Schank. *Conceptual Information Processing.* North-Holland, Amsterdam, 1975.

[202] R. Schank. *Dynamic Memory.* Erlbaum, Hillsdale, NJ, 1982.

[203] R. Schank and R. Abelson. *Scripts, Plans, Goals and Understanding.* Erlbaum, Hillsdale, NJ, 1977.

[204] S. Schapiro. The relevance of relevance. Technical report, Indiana University Computer Science Department, March 1976.

[205] S. Schiffer. *Remnants of Meaning.* MIT Press, Cambridge, MA, 1987.

[206] L. Schubert and J. Pelletier. From English to logic: Context-free computation of "conventional" logical translation. *American Journal of Computational Linguistics*, 8:27–44, 1982.

[207] D. Scott and C. Strachey. Toward a mathematical semantics for computer languages. In *Proceedings of the Symposium on Computers and Automata*, pages 19–46. Polytechnic Institute of Brooklyn, 1971.

[208] T. Sejnowski and C. Rosenberg. NETtalk: A parallel network that learns to read aloud. Technical Report JHU/EECS-86/01, Johns Hopkins University, EE and CS Department, 1986.

[209] P. Sells. *Lectures on Contemporary Syntactic Theories.* Number 3 in CSLI Lecture Notes. CSLI, Stanford, 1985.

[210] S. M. Shieber. *An Introduction to Unification-Based Approaches to Grammar.* Number 4 in CSLI Lecture Notes. CSLI, Stanford, 1986.

[211] P. Smolensky. On the proper treatment of connectionism. *Behavioral and Brain Sciences*, 11, 1988.

[212] G. Smolka. A feature logic with subsorts. LILOG Report 33, IBM Deutschland, Stuttgart, 1988.

[213] J. Sowa. *Conceptual Structures: Information Processing in Mind and Machine.* Addison-Wesley, Reading, MA, 1984.

[214] K. Sparck-Jones. They say it's a new engine but it's still the same SUMP. In Y. Wilks, editor, *Theoretical Issues in Natural Language Processing*, pages 136–140. Erlbaum, Hillsdale, NJ, 1991.

[215] R. Statman. On the existence of closed terms in the typed lambda calculus (I). In J. Seldin and J. Hindley, editors, *To H. B. Curry: Essays on Combinatory Logic, Lambda Calculus and Formalism*, pages 511–534. Academic Press, New York, 1980.

[216] R. Statman. Completeness, invariance, and λ-definability. *Journal of Symbolic Logic*, 47:17–26, 1982.

[217] E. Steiner, P. Schmidt and C. Zelinsky-Wibbelt, editors. *From Syntax to Semantics: Insights from Machine Translation.* Pinter Publishers, London, 1988.

[218] M. E. Szabo. *The Collected Papers of Gerhard Gentzen.* North-Holland, Amsterdam, 1969.

[219] R. H. Thomason, editor. *Formal Philosophy: Selected Papers of Richard Montague.* Yale University Press, New Haven, CT, 1974.

[220] R. H. Thomason. A model theory for the propositional attitudes. *Linguistics and Philosophy*, 4:47–70, 1980.

[221] F. B. Thompson. The semantic interface in man-machine communication. Technical Report RM 63TMP-35, General Electric Co., Santa Barbara, CA, 1963.

[222] E. Tulving. How many memory systems are there? *American Psychologist*, 40:385–398, 1985.

[223] R. Turner. A theory of properties. *Journal of Symbolic Logic*, 52(2):445–472, 1987.

[224] R. Turner. Lectures on property theory. *European Conference on Artificial Intelligence*, 1988.

[225] R. Turner. Properties, propositions and semantic theory. In M. Rosner and R. Johnson, editors, *Computational Linguistics and Formal Semantics*. Cambridge University Press, Cambridge, 1992.

[226] H. Uszkoreit. *Word Order and Constituent Structure in German*. Number 8 in CSLI Lecture Notes. CSLI, Stanford, 1987.

[227] J. van Benthem. *Essays in Logical Semantics*. Reidel, Dordrecht, 1986.

[228] J. van Benthem. Towards a computational semantics. In P. Gärdenfors, editor, *Generalized Quantifiers. Linguistic and Logical Approaches*, pages 31–71. Reidel, Dordrecht, 1987.

[229] J. van Benthem. *A Manual of Intensional Logic*. Chicago University Press, second revised edition, 1988.

[230] J. van Benthem. The fine-structure of categorial semantics. Technical Report LP-89-01, Institute for Language, Logic and Information, University of Amsterdam, 1989.

[231] J. van Benthem. Polyadic quantifiers. *Linguistics and Philosophy*, 12(4):437–464, 1989.

[232] J. van Benthem. *Language in Action: Categories, Lambdas and Dynamic Logic*. North-Holland, Amsterdam, 1991.

[233] J. van Benthem. Fine-structure in categorial semantics. In M. Rosner and R. Johnson, editors, *Computational Linguistics and Formal Semantics*. Cambridge University Press, Cambridge, 1992.

[234] J. van der Does. *Plurals in Progress*. PhD thesis, Institute for Language, Logic and Information, University of Amsterdam, 1991.

[235] E. Vestre. *Representasjon av Direkte Spørsmål*. Master's thesis, University of Oslo, 1987.

[236] D. Waltz and J. Pollack. Massively parallel parsing: A strongly interactive model of natural language interpretation. *Cognitive Science*, 9, 1985.

[237] R. G. Warner. *Discourse Connectives in English*. PhD thesis, Ohio State University, 1979. Garland, New York, 1985.

[238] P. Whitelock. Shake-and-bake translation. In M. Rosner, C. J. Rupp and R. Johnson, editors, *Constraint Propagation, Linguistic Description, and Computation – Draft Proceedings of a Workshop held 18th–20th September 1991. IDSIA Working Paper No. 5*, pages 215–239. 1991.

[239] R. Wilensky. *Planning and Understanding*. Addison-Wesley, Reading, MA, 1983.

[240] Y. Wilks. Decidability and natural language. *Mind*, 70, 1971.

[241] Y. Wilks. Understanding without proofs. In *Proceedings of the Third International Joint Conference on AI*, pages 270–277. Stanford, CA, 1973.

[242] Y. Wilks. One small head: Models and theories in linguistics. *Foundations of Language*, 1974.

[243] Y. Wilks. Comparative translation quality analysis. Technical Report F33657-77-C-0695, AFOSR, 1979.

[244] Y. Wilks. Some thoughts on procedural semantics. In M. Ringle and W. Lehnert, editors, *Strategies for Natural Language Processing*, pages 495–516. Erlbaum, Hillsdale, NJ, 1981.

[245] Y. Wilks. Consciousness and machines. In C. Hookway, editor, *Minds, Machines, and Evolution*, pages 105–128. Cambridge University Press, Cambridge, 1984.

[246] Y. Wilks. Is Frege's principle trivial or false? In *Proceedings of the Annual Conference of the Linguistic Association of Great Britain*. 1984.

[247] Y. Wilks. Form and content in semantics. In M. Rosner and R. Johnson, editors, *Computational Linguistics and Formal Semantics*. Cambridge University Press, Cambridge, 1992.

[248] E. Williams. Semantic vs. syntactic categories. *Linguistics and Philosophy*, 6:423–446, 1983.

[249] T. Winograd. Moving the semantic fulcrum. *Linguistics and Philosophy*, 8(1):91–104, 1985.

[250] L. Wittgenstein. *Philosophical Investigations*. Blackwells, Oxford, 1953.

[251] W. A. Woods. Procedural semantics for a question-answering machine. In *Proceedings, 1968 Fall Joint Computer Conference*, pages 457–471. 1968.

[252] W. A. Woods. What's in a link: Foundations for semantic networks. In D. G. Bobrow and A. M. Collins, editors, *Representation and Understanding: Studies in Cognitive Science*, pages 35–82. Academic Press, New York, 1975.

[253] W. A. Woods. Cascaded ATN grammars. *American Journal of Computational Linguistics*, 6:1–12, 1980.

[254] H. Zeevat, E. Klein and J. Calder. Unification categorial grammar. In *Working Papers in Cognitive Science, Volume 1: Categorial Grammar, Unification Grammar and Parsing*, pages 195–222. University of Edinburgh: Centre for Cognitive Science, Edinburgh, 1987.

[255] A. Zwicky, J. Friedman, B. C. Hall and D. E. Walker. The MITRE syntactic analysis procedure for transformational grammars. In *Proceedings, 1965 Fall Joint Computer Conference*. Thompson Books, Washington, 1965.

9 780521 419598